Portrait in Light and Shadow

MARIA TIPPETT

PORTRAIT IN LIGHT AND SHADOW

THE LIFE OF YOUSUF KARSH

ANANSI

Published in 2007 by
House of Anansi Press Inc.
110 Spadina Avenue, Suite 801
Toronto, ON, M5V 2K4
Tel. 416-363-4343
Fax 416-363-1017
www.anansi.ca

Distributed in Canada by
HarperCollins Canada Ltd.
1995 Markham Road
Scarborough, ON, M1B 5M8
Toll free tel. 1-800-387-0117

Permission is gratefully acknowledged to reproduce photographs from the following: pages 7 (MP-
1982.133.247), 11 (MP-1982.133.12), 23 (MP-1982.133.129), 33 (MP-1982.133.124), McCord Museum of
Canadian History, Montreal; pages 19, 57, 75, 83, 121, 143, 181, 255, 325, National Archives of Canada;
pages 109, 225, 337, courtesy of Barbara Karsh; pages 117, 247, courtesy of Salim Karsh; page 297,
courtesy of Hella Graber; all other photographs reproduced courtesy of Jerry Fielder, Karsh Curator.

11 10 09 08 07   1 2 3 4 5

LIBRARY AND ARCHIVES CANADA CATALOGUING IN PUBLICATION DATA

Tippett, Maria, 1944–
Portrait in light and shadow : the life of Yousuf Karsh / Maria Tippett.

Includes bibliographical references and index.
ISBN-13: 978-0-88784-198-9 · ISBN-10: 0-88784-198-8

1. Karsh, Yousuf, 1908–2002. 2. Portrait photographers—Canada—Biography.
3. Photographers—Canada—Biography. I. Title.

BIOGRAPH

TR140.K3T56 2007   779'.2092   C2007-902344-4

Jacket and text design: Ingrid Paulson
Jacket photographs: Yousuf Karsh: front cover—Humphrey Bogart, John F. and Jacqueline
Kennedy, Winston Churchill, Princess Elizabeth, Albert Einstein, Ernest Hemingway;
spine—self-portrait; back cover—Eleanor Roosevelt, Grey Owl, Marion Anderson,
Tom Wolfe, Nikita Khrushchev, Elizabeth Taylor
Author photograph: David Thomas

Canada Council   Conseil des Arts
for the Arts   du Canada

ONTARIO ARTS COUNCIL
CONSEIL DES ARTS DE L'ONTARIO

*We acknowledge for their financial support of our publishing program
the Canada Council for the Arts, the Ontario Arts Council, and the Government of
Canada through the Book Publishing Industry Development Program (BPIDP).*

Printed and bound in China

To Fay Bendall and Vivian and Diane Nelles

Be not afraid of greatness: some are born great,
some achieve greatness, and some have greatness thrust upon them.
— *Twelfth Night*, William Shakespeare

Contents

Illustrations

Note: Unless otherwise indicated, photographs are by Yousuf Karsh.

Preface

During his lifetime Yousuf Karsh was not only one of North America's most prominent public figures but also that most dearly beloved archetype, the striving immigrant who makes good in the limitless opportunity of the New World. Karsh rose to become court photographer to the powerful and famous. He lived in the spotlight. Countless newspaper articles and magazine profiles told his story over and over again, and Karsh presented himself for posterity in his own autobiographical writings. But, even at the height of his fame, few really knew Karsh or fully understood his achievements.

In an age that still loves heroes but not as much as it enjoys knocking them off their pedestals, a photographic portrait by Yousuf Karsh might strike us at first glance as rather dated today. So might other things about him: the bit of string that he used to determine the distance between his subject and the lens of his camera; his cocky Borsalino hat; his long coat elegantly draped over his broad shoulders; the gold cufflinks that he used to fasten the shirts created for him by an Ottawa tailor who boasted King Farouk as a client (hardly a name to conjure with today). Above all, Karsh's old-world and old-fashioned manners, which turned hard-boiled businessmen, time-constrained heads of state, and celebrities into putty before his camera, belong to another era.

The fact remains that, whether we realize it or not, our visual images of Churchill, Shaw, Einstein, Hemingway, Bogart, Castro, Trudeau, Elizabeth Taylor, Martin Luther King, Jr., Leonard Bernstein, Indira Gandhi, Andy Warhol, Robert Frost, Mikhail Gorbachev, every American president from Herbert Hoover to Bill Clinton, and scores of other twentieth-century icons have been shaped by the portraits that Yousuf Karsh took of them during his sixty-year-long career. So extensive was his coverage of notable personalities that when, in 2001, the *International Who's Who* compiled a list of the most influential hundred people of the twentieth century, Karsh's name was on it. Moreover, Karsh was the only Canadian—and the only photographer—on the list.

So why don't more people, especially young people, know more about Karsh today? Surely it can't be for lack of exposure to his work—his portraits continue to appear in newspapers, magazines, and books around the world. Nor can it be due to the absence of exhibitions. Over the last decade alone, galleries in Berlin, London, Boston, and Nice have featured his work. And, during the centennial of his birth in 2008, numerous galleries in the United States are poised to celebrate the life and work of Karsh. Could it be that Karsh's reputation is greater outside Canada than at home? And, if this is true, is it because Canadians, unlike Americans and Britons, are often ambivalent about and sometimes even hostile to power—embarrassed by success and ambition, and inclined to forget their history?

The fact is that little is known about how this refugee from southeastern Turkey became the world's leading portrait photographer. Was Karsh's singular success due to his training with his uncle, George Nakash, and later with the American photographer John Garo? Did he owe a special debt, in the early 1930s, to the Ottawa Little Theatre? How crucial was the emergence of large-format magazines and better printing processes in making Karsh as well known as the people he photographed? Was there something special about his living in Canada? Was there something unique about Karsh himself, something that lay beyond his technical know-how, beyond hard work? Or was Karsh's extraordinary success due to a mixture of luck and self-promotion? I knew that it could hardly be true that his international reputation was really due to just one act, when he famously removed a cigar from the lips of Winston Churchill before clicking the shutter.

I wrote to Yousuf Karsh in 1998. I had just finished my biography of Group of Seven artist F. H. Varley and was looking for a new project. Karsh was a tempting choice. I had long admired his stunning portraits and was curious to know how he came to make them. There were good sources: the National Archives of Canada had recently acquired Karsh's massive textual and visual archive. No biographer, to my knowledge, had consulted Karsh's manuscripts or viewed the thousands of visual images that were preserved in acid-free Solander boxes. There were, finally, many friends, acquaintances, and colleagues of Karsh who could be interviewed.

A response to my initial letter came through Karsh's trusted assistant, Jerry Fielder: Mr. Karsh was not interested in having me or anyone else write his biography. As he graciously pointed out, he had written his own autobiography. The Karsh story had thus already been told — by Karsh. There was nothing further in his view to say.

Or was there?

Karsh had indeed published an autobiography, *In Search of Greatness*, midway through his career. He had also written numerous anecdotal essays to accompany the portraits that appeared in his many large-format books. Composed from fragmented notes, and often written by other hands, the so-called autobiographical writings mixed up dates, failed to consider important events, and were seldom reflective. Though there is mention of Karsh's marriages — first to Solange Gauthier and, after her death, to Estrellita Nachbar — the influence of these women is hardly given its due. Indeed, most of what Karsh published was significant for what is not there. As with his black-and-white portraits, Karsh left some parts of his life in light and other parts in shadow. The result was a heroic portrait that froze the image of his own life. Karsh thus "Karshed" himself.

As a biographer it would be my challenge to get behind this image, to explore not only the light and shadow of his life but also the grey areas in between. Karsh left no diaries that would help me do this. His vast written archive — there are over four hundred boxes of papers—consists largely of financial records, newspaper clippings, and business correspondence. There are, sadly, few letters written by Karsh himself. When he chose to communicate with a client, he let his secretary, or Solange or Estrellita, transpose his reply into "good" English. Nor do his interviews with the press add much to the published record. During interviews, Karsh told stories of his sittings with his famous subjects as a means to avoid talking about himself. As one frustrated journalist put it, Karsh would remain largely an unknown quantity even if he gave him two interviews twice daily.[1]

YOUSUF KARSH DIED IN 2002, four years after our correspondence. I had just completed another book, my biography of Bill Reid, and was still hopeful of writing Karsh's life story, so I approached the executors of his estate. This time my letter met with a positive response. Estrellita Karsh and Jerry Fielder (now Karsh's archivist) gave my project their blessings and agreed to help. So did Karsh's friends, his relatives—particularly his brother Salim—and his staff.

During the course of my research I've often been humbled by the accomplishments of the many people I encountered: Salim for his humanitarian work; Estrellita for her knowledge of medical history and her compassion towards Yousuf during the last decade of his life; Joyce Large for running Karsh's various companies for almost three decades; and finally, Jerry Fielder for the way in which he has helped to keep Karsh's reputation alive. Many of the people who touched Karsh's life deserve biographies of their own. Most put their own egos aside and talked about Karsh. This book is the result of the work that these and many other people facilitated—but never sought to control—during my writing and research over the last three and a half years.

I have physically or metaphorically followed Karsh from Mardin in Turkey and Aleppo in Syria to Sherbrooke, Quebec; thence to Ottawa, to Boston, and to the many other places in North America, Africa, Europe, and Japan where he lived and worked. I have spent long days and late nights poring over Karsh's manuscripts and photographs at the National Archives of Canada. During my trek through Karsh's life, I was prompted to consider many factors that helped shape his career. Among them are Karsh's initial training with his uncle, George Nakash, and his mentor, John Garo, along with his introduction to the Ottawa Little Theatre, to film noir, and to the fast-paced advertising world in New York. I've put Karsh's life into the political context of the Second World War and the Cold War that ensued. I've considered his work in relation to other photographers. I've stressed the significance that Karsh's collaboration with his subject played in the outcome of a portrait. I've described how, during the 1950s, Karsh was not only a portraitist but a commercial photographer and a recorder of Canadian cities, of factories, and of the lives of ordinary Canadian people. I've demonstrated the extent to which his assistants — whether in the camera room, the office, or the developing room — contributed to the making of his portraits and to the success of his business. Finally, I've shown how his marriages helped shape the work of the Karsh Studio while cultivating and broadening Yousuf Karsh himself.

It is too little known that Karsh's talents lay outside the camera room as well as in it. He was not exaggerating when he told a reporter in 1978: "I am probably one of the most qualified goodwill ambassadors Canada has had."[2] For behind his gracious facade, elegant clothing, and smokescreen of stories that enabled him to ingratiate himself with those he met was a fun-loving man who was devoted to his staff, to his family, and to his friends.

Nor do many people know that he was a man who loved teaching and performing. Here was a man who gained satisfaction from revealing what he felt to be "the inward power" of his subjects, be they Hollywood film actors, prime ministers, humanitarians, hockey players, rock stars, or business executives.[3] It is also little known that Karsh championed young photographers whose style was very different from his own. Moreover, even after he had achieved critical acclaim and financial success, he was subjected to ethnic prejudice.

It is hardly too much to claim that, like many of the famous people he photographed, Karsh was heroic too. Here was a man who travelled to Cuba at a time when it was radical to do so in order to capture an image of Fidel Castro, and to the Soviet Union to give the world a different take on the shoe-banging Nikita Khrushchev. A man who photographed Paul Robeson and Marion Anderson when African-Americans were barred from white hotels and restaurants. A man who gave a touch of celebrity not only to company directors and factory workers but also to children suffering from muscular dystrophy. A man who put Canada on the cultural map during the darkest years of the Second World War, and who later fought for the rights of New Canadians when it was not yet fashionable to do so.

Any one of the things that Karsh had achieved by the end of his long life would have been significant in itself. But Karsh did them all. The thousands of portraits that form his legacy are there for all to see. It is time to tell the full story behind them.

PART ONE

THE
MAKING
OF THE
MAN

CHAPTER ONE

Beginnings in Armenia

The story of Yousuf Abdul Karsh has to begin in Turkish Armenia. Though he became one of the most famous Canadians of his day, his identification as an Armenian is so well known that it merits immediate mention. But it also requires some further explanation.

Yousuf Karsh was born in Mardin, in the southeastern corner of present-day Turkey, in 1908 — the year that the Young Turks came to power in Istanbul. Modern Turkey is essentially their creation; they set out to make a nation-state from the remnants of the ancient Ottoman Empire, with its image of decadence consorting with a long and lazy tradition of religious tolerance throughout its vast and sprawling territories. Nowhere was this better illustrated than in Mardin as it developed until the late nineteenth century.

Built on the southern slope of a flat-topped mountain, the town was home to 25,000 Syrian, Greek, and Armenian Christians, to Jews, and to Muslims. This is why the town's tiered layers of handsome, single-storey, Arab-style stone houses were broken by towers, domes, cupolas, and minarets. Why the call of the muezzin competed with the peals of church bells. And why the voices of traders from all over the Levant could be heard in the narrow, cool, dimly lit, high-vaulted passages of Mardin's Kayseriye Bazaar.

Today the majority of Mardin's churches and synagogues have been converted into mosques. The ruins of the ancient citadel, which once dominated the town, are overlooked by a maze of military radar installations and antennae. Mardin's non-Muslim population is now a fraction of what it used to be and is scattered throughout the city. And the Armenian survivors and their descendants have been scattered across the world in a diaspora of which the Karsh family was part.

Like every other village and town in the Ottoman Empire, Mardin's inhabitants were segregated, according to their religious affiliation, into self-governing millets. The Karshes lived in the Armenian millet. Though political power within the Ottoman Empire rested with the sultan in Istanbul, the inhabitants of the millet followed the rules, the customs, and the religious practices of the Armenian patriarch. By giving legal status to the multi-religious composition of the Ottoman Empire, the government in Istanbul had ensured that everyone was defined according to his or her religious belief.

The former nation of Armenia, which comprises some 30,000 square kilometres in present-day Anatolia in southeastern Turkey, has a long and contentious history. There are many myths, both ancient and modern, about the region. It is claimed that the area was converted to Christianity by King Tiridates III around 301, making Armenia the first Christian nation in the world and lending some credence to the belief that one of its principal cities, Mardin, was the site of the Garden of Eden.

Armenia functioned as a united kingdom only during two periods of its long history: first, from the second century B.C. to the fifth century A.D.; and, secondly, from the ninth century to the thirteenth century. That was the last time that Armenia would exist as a country. In 1236 Armenia was overrun by the Mongols, and then, three hundred years later, by the Turks, who still govern Turkish Armenia today.

Living throughout much of its history under repressive regimes reinforced the social cohesiveness of the Armenian community. It also made the Armenians, like their Jewish counterparts in western Europe, adept at integrating their skills into the dominant society. Under the rule of sultans in the Ottoman Empire, the Armenians were renowned as bankers and merchants. They held positions in the government and in the diplomatic service. They made a significant contribution to Turkish culture as playwrights, musicians, and writers. Above all, their skills in the applied arts, particularly silver- and goldsmithing as well as illumination and weaving, were celebrated throughout the Levant.

The Armenian people contributed to the predominantly Muslim Ottoman Empire and existed relatively peacefully within it for a millennium and a half. Then things began to change for the worse. In 1878 the Armenians became unpopular with the Istanbul government when they openly supported the Christian Russians during the Turco-Russian war. A few years later, their insistence that the geographical area of former Armenia be reunited—it had been divided between Turkey and Russia since 1828—met with further official disapproval. In 1895 Sultan Abdul Hamid II countered the call for Armenian reunification and eventual independence. He encouraged Muslim Kurds to alter the demographic makeup of Anatolia by occupying the southeastern corner of the country. Even more distressing, the sultan patently sanctioned the annihilation of Turkey's Armenian population. The rape, the looting, and the killing—some 20,000 to 30,000 people were murdered—that followed was responsible for the first wave of Armenian immigration to North America.

The political uncertainty of every Armenian and other non-Muslim reached a crisis again in 1908. Once in power, the Young Turks were determined to build an all-Muslim nation. Convinced that non-Muslims were unassimilable, they unleashed repressive measures that threatened the autonomy of every non-Muslim millet. Not surprisingly, this instigated a second wave of Armenian immigration to the New World.

Karsh family lore is ambiguous about exactly when its first members came to Canada. One story, which is supported by some circumstantial evidence, has it that Aziz Setlakwe, the brother of Yousuf Karsh's grandmother, was among the 563 Armenians who immigrated to Canada in 1908 following the second wave of atrocities. Another, equally plausible story, suggests that Aziz came as early as 1904. What is beyond doubt is that, along with his second wife, Marie Barakett, and two of his brothers, Aziz left Damascus, where they were living, and settled in the asbestos capital of Canada, Thetford Mines, in the Eastern Townships of Quebec.[1] Aziz and his family did not enter Canada as refugees, if only because the Canadian government had no policy for admitting refugees at that time. Even so, Aziz's status when he arrived in Canada at the age of twenty-nine was as a second-class citizen.

At the turn of the twentieth century, few Canadians disagreed with the notion that their country needed to expand its population. Armenians, however, along with newcomers from central, southern, and eastern Europe as well as from Asia, were, as Canadian immigration officials put it, "non-preferred." Some people went so far as to label those immigrants as "undesirable" or "less desirable." This sort of thinking arose from the popular belief that "non-preferred" immigrants would challenge Anglo-Saxon traditions of self-government, would never become true Canadians, and would, above all, be a burden on the economy. In *Strangers Within Our Gates* Rev. James S. Woodsworth echoed the views of most Canadians when he noted that the Armenians and Syrians constituted "one of the least desirable classes of our immigrants" because they possessed low intelligence and brought contagious diseases into the country. According to Woodsworth, this meant that any "undesirable" like Aziz Setlakwe could never be assimilated.[2]

Aziz Setlakwe, by George Nakash, 1928

Aziz Setlakwe, almost six feet tall and with a swarthy complexion, was unable to speak either of Canada's two founding languages. He looked, acted, and sounded different from the Anglo-French majority. Nonetheless Aziz did not settle in the large Armenian community in Toronto or Montreal in order to take refuge from the suspicion, hostility, discrimination, and other negative stereotyping that he and other non-preferred immigrants encountered when they came to Canada. Rather, he and his family chose to join the small group of Christian Syrians and Armenians who were scattered throughout the Appalachian Mountains in the Eastern Townships. Among people from the Levant, Aziz was able to speak his own language, Arabic. He could enjoy Middle Eastern foods such as pickled turnips, yogurt, and salted cheese. And, finally, he had like-minded people with whom he could share news from back "home."

In keeping with Woodsworth's insidious prediction that "undesirables" would most often become itinerant merchants, Aziz became just that. Loaded with a heavy box of dry goods on his back, Aziz carried his products to the

farming and mining communities surrounding Thetford Mines. Highly skilled in marketing his wares, Aziz accumulated enough capital to establish a dry-goods store. Complete with its distinctive banner—similar to those carried at the head of an Arabian caravan—this was the first of what was to become a chain of department stores throughout the region.

Aziz was part of the mass immigration that, between 1900 and 1914, helped to increase Canada's population by 40 percent and to double its gross national product. Nineteen twelve and 1913 were record years for the admission of new-comers, who opened up the Prairies, worked in the factories and the mines, and established small-scale businesses. Aziz not only enhanced the economic welfare of the Eastern Townships; by 1913 he was in a financial position to contribute to the growth of the population by helping many of his family and friends from Mardin immigrate to Canada. As the instigator of this Armenian chain of migration, Aziz earned a reputation for being the judge, the counsellor, the decider, and, as his great-nephew Salim Karsh put it, "the helper of everybody."[3]

One of the first people to reap the benefit of Aziz Setlakwe's hard-earned prosperity was his sister's son, Aziz George Nakash. George—as he was usually known once he arrived in North America, although his relatives still called him by his first name—was the son of an engraver, as the name Nakash indicates in Arabic. Although his father was born a Jew in Baghdad, Nakash was born in Mardin and raised as a Methodist. It was the church of his Armenian mother that his father had also joined on converting to Christianity.

Young George was better prepared for life in the New World than Aziz Setlakwe. Unlike his uncle, George had attended the American Mission School in Mardin. There he added English to his knowledge of Turkish and Arabic. He also reinforced his Protestant faith and he was introduced to Western ideas and to Western technology. Thus when he arrived in New York in 1913 and gave his profession as a photographer, he had what prejudiced immigration officials deemed to be a reputable profession.

The career of George Nakash deserves attention, not least because it foreshadows that of his famous nephew, Yousuf Karsh, on whom he was to have a very direct influence. Nakash had been introduced to photography at the age of ten in Mardin by a friend of his father's who was visiting the family from New York. And yet it was not until 1910, a year after Nakash had moved to Beirut, that the eighteen-year-old took his first photograph.

A distant relative of the Nakash family owned Serafian's Department Store in Beirut. George began working there as a salesman and then, intrigued by photography, he became an apprentice in the store's portrait studio. It was here that he made his first portrait. The subject, who happened to be the French consul general and one of the most important men in town, was pleased with the results and placed a large order. Although taking this photograph launched George Nakash in his career, he saw no future as a photographer in the Middle East. Like many others who were attracted to the New World by the promise of social, economic, and political stability, he gladly accepted a relative's offer to help him leave the Middle East.

When George Nakash arrived in New York in 1913, he landed a job at the Fifth Avenue photography studio of Aimé Dupont. But the economy was depressed and, since immigrants were the last to be hired and the first to be fired, he was soon laid off. Unsuccessful at finding another job as a photographer, Nakash was reduced to washing dishes. Then he fell ill. Unable to care for himself, he was forced to accept help from his supportive uncle, Aziz Setlakwe.

For a time after moving from New York to Thetford Mines, Nakash worked as a salesman in his uncle's store. When he had saved enough money to open a photography studio, he moved to the nearby town of Saint-Méthode and then to Beauceville. Like the itinerant silhouette artists of an earlier generation, George Nakash plied his trade and exerted his considerable charm among the inhabitants of the farming and industrial communities in the Eastern Townships. By 1915, however, small-town life had lost its charm. There was no opportunity for Nakash to learn more about photography. When he had accumulated $200, he moved back to the United States.

There is little known about the three or so years that George Nakash spent on his return to New York. But as his 1925 portrait of Aziz Setlakwe's mother-in-law, Malaky Karwashian, clearly reveals, the young photographer must have come under the influence of those American photographers who called themselves Pictorialists.

Like France's Barbizon school of artists, who softened their brushwork to achieve atmospheric effects, the Pictorialists avoided abrasive lines, harsh details, and sharp contrasts in tonal values. Instead, they created what they called a "pictorial effect" in various ways. They nudged the camera so that the resulting print would be slightly out of focus. They used a soft-focus lens with a long focal length. And, during the printing process, they manipulated the negative. The methods were various but the results were the same. By altering the tonal qualities of the finished print and by paying close attention to the arrangement of the lines, curves, and textures, the Pictorialists were able to create a personal vision of their subject.

Though consciously emulating the effects achieved by the painter's brush and by the etcher's burin, the Pictorialists demonstrated that photography was neither reportage nor documentary nor a second cousin to painting. Rather, in their view it was a distinctive medium of expression that was capable of grasping the essential qualities of the mood, the form, and the composition of whatever subject they photographed. The Pictorialists also believed that, just like paintings, photographs possessed a timeless quality.

Malaky Karwashian, by George Nakash, circa 1925

There was never any doubt in George Nakash's mind as to whether photography was a science or an art. Or whether the photographer had a right to intervene during the process of taking and printing a photograph. Or whether the photograph was a product of the photographer's skill and imagination or simply the result of a mechanical device. After his sojourn in New York, Nakash was convinced that a portrait could be infused with the emotions and the skill of the person behind the camera. And, most important of all, that the photographer was an artist.

THE YEAR THAT NAKASH was introduced to the Pictorialists in New York saw a new wave of violence against the Armenian peoples living in Turkish Armenia. The hostilities began in mid-February 1915 when every Armenian official and employee in the Turkish government was dismissed. In March, large numbers of Armenians were jailed, murdered, or deported. By early April, the jihad,

which was being carried out by Turkish soldiers with the help of Kurdish and Circassian Muslim tribesmen, had formed a frightening pattern. First, all the Armenian men in the villages and towns were rounded up and shot. Then the women, children, and elderly, who had escaped murder, were force-marched through the burning desert of southern Turkey to northern Syria. Lacking sufficient food, water, and clothing, and tormented by the Turkish soldiers who accompanied them to the Syrian border, many died. Those who were lucky enough to reach the makeshift refugee camps in Syria faced disease and poverty.

So efficient was this ethnic cleansing that by 1916 the Turks had managed to eradicate most of the Armenians living in Anatolia through death—the estimates range between 550,000 and one million—or deportation. Little wonder that the operation has increasingly been recognized as the first full-scale genocide of the twentieth century.

George Nakash could never mention the massacres without weeping. Two of his uncles were murdered in front of their mother. Two of his brothers were jailed, only to die later in prison. One sister, Lucia, hid in a ditch, feigned death, and thereby escaped rape or murder. Another sister, Nazlia, was thrown down a well. One story has it that she was rescued by Presbyterian missionaries. Another suggests that Nazlia would certainly have died if her brother-in-law Massih had not bribed a Turkish soldier to let him to pull her out of the well to safety. Family legend held that Massih could talk his way out of anything.

Abdel al-Massih Karsh—also given as Abdel-Ahad Karsh—had been born in 1872 and was later to become known as Amsih after immigrating to Canada. This much is clear, though his exact origins are as complex as his various names. He was born in Mardin, although his family came from Iran, with a possible Syriac or Jewish ancestry. In 1902 Massih married George Nakash's favourite sister, nineteen-year-old Bahiyah Jurjos Nakash. Bahiyah—also spelled Bahiyya or Bahia—had been born in Mardin in 1883. While not wealthy, the hardworking, quickstepping Massih was a successful merchant who imported indigo, spices, fine silks, and cloths by caravan, or Kafilas, from Basra in the Persian Gulf to Mardin. When he wasn't travelling by donkey and camel down the Tigris River to Baghdad, he worked at his loom, where he wove red scarves and socks for the Turkish army.

When Massih himself was arrested by Turkish soldiers, he put his uncanny abilities to work in contriving to win his freedom. He had been forced to build a road with the expectation that once it was finished he would be shot. Recognized by the commander of the camp as a family acquaintance, Massih reminded him that he had shared salt and broken bread with the commander's uncle, thus making them, according to Muslim custom, "brothers." Massih, who had been in hiding before his detention, was released, but at a price: he was forced to evaluate the jewellery and other precious objects that the Turkish army had taken from his fellow Armenians. Though Massih found this job understandably repellent, agreeing to do it probably saved his life. Finally, in 1921, in almost biblical fashion, the Turkish army gave Massih Karsh a donkey and told him that he and his wife, Bahiyah, together with their three young children, could make the perilous journey to find salvation in a promised land.⁴ Initially this meant neighbouring Syria; ultimately it meant Canada.

THIS WAS HOW Abdul Yousuf Karsh came to leave his native Armenia. Aged twelve in 1921, he was the eldest of Massih and Bahiyah's three sons. His brother Malak was six at the time and Jamil only an infant.

Carrying only what their donkey could bear on its back, the Karsh family joined a caravan composed of two other Christian families, some merchants, and a number of Turkish and Kurdish soldiers. Then they walked for seventeen days across the desert to the Syrian border.

Massih Karsh's earlier experience as a caravan merchant helped his family settle fees and bribes, survive the harsh desert conditions, and cope with the lack of food, for during his travels it had been customary for members of a caravan to eat only one meal a day. But it was the height of summer when the Karsh family left Mardin. During their long, terrifying trek there was not enough food to feed the whole family. (It was always black, never white, bread that the family ate.) There was little fresh water since the rivers and brooks had been contaminated from the corpses of those who had not made it to Syria. There was the unforgiving desert landscape, which was strewn with gravel or covered in sand or caked with dried, white mud. Then there were the sheiks who depleted the Karshes' savings by extracting fees when the family passed through their villages. If all of this wasn't hard enough on the Karsh family, there was the innocent but potentially deadly action of eleven-year-old Yousuf, who put his family at risk when he made a sketch of sun-bleached bones—the remnants of the earlier forced marches—that were protruding from a mud wall. "When the Turks saw that I was scribbling something," Karsh recalled years later, "they set up a cry that I was a spy."⁵ The family's last piece of silver, along with some persuasive talking by Massih, saved the family from death.

The Karsh family's destination was the northern Syrian town of Deir-ez-Zor. Lying on the southern banks of the Euphrates River, the town was surrounded by silver-grey olive groves and dominated by melon-ribbed cupolas. Recently under the jurisdiction of the French mandate like the rest of Syria, the town was a haven from the deprivation and terror that the Armenian families had experienced in Turkish Armenia. Deir-ez-Zor would have seemed like an oasis to the Karsh family after the barren Syrian desert if the town had not been teeming with refugees and diseases—mainly trachoma and scabies. And if it had not been haunted by horrific memories. It was here, just a few years earlier, that the Turks had locked 2,000 children into several houses and then left them to die.

BY 1916 THE MAJORITY of Armenians had been killed or deported or, less frequently, had agreed to convert to Islam in order to save their lives. Massih's putative Syriac origins might explain why the Karsh family had remained in Mardin after it would have been prudent—or even possible—for them to do so; and why, as Karsh wrote in a draft of his memoir, "Father was drafted into the Turkish army in 1914–1915."⁶ It would certainly explain why they left for Syria only four years later, when the jihad against the Armenians had spread to other Christian "infidels"—Greek Orthodox, Jews, *and* Arab Christians—in an effort to establish an all-Muslim state. Moreover, it would explain why the Karsh family were, with two other families, the first Christians, as Yousuf later claimed in an interview, to be given official passports.⁷ Furthermore, it would explain why, when Yousuf Karsh arrived in Canada on the last day of 1923, he gave both his citizenship and his "race of people" as Syrian.⁸

When Malak Karsh applied for entrance to Canada from his Syrian base fourteen years later, he told Yousuf, "Of course I am not an Armenian." But Malak now received a stern reply from his brother: "I am quite sure that you, like myself were born in Mardin, which as you know, was before the war and still is in Turkish Armenia. I know," Yousuf continued, "that Mardin is geographically in one of the old Armenian milliyet. After all, it is the country of your birth and not that of your present residence nor the religion to which you belong which constitutes your nationality." But there was a catch. "Then frankly," he added, "there is something which you have no knowledge of and it is that in this country the type of Syrian...one meets is not very well thought of and generally I keep rather apart. Of course, I am not going to tell you that being an Armenian may or may not be considered much better but the fact is that there are very few Armenians and, therefore, they are not considered in the same class as Syrians. So it is a case 'of the two evils, choose the less'—and that is Armenian."[9]

Yousuf was right. There were fewer Armenian than Syrian immigrants and the latter, who lived primarily in the towns and cities, did not, according to one popular belief, make good citizens because they did not remain in Canada but returned home.

All of this suggests that the history of the Karsh family is more complex than Yousuf ever suggested—or even knew. Perhaps the family's late arrival in Syria had something to do with Massih Karsh's forced collusion with the Turkish authorities after he was released from detention. Or perhaps it had something to do with his ethnicity.

According to Massih's cousin, Faud Karsh, who lives in the Syrian-Turkish border town of Hasaka and Issa Touma and is a photographer in Aleppo, Abdel al-Massih Karsh was not an Armenian but a Syriac Catholic.[10] On the other hand, every member of the Karsh and Setlakwe families living in Canada denies this line of thinking. Indeed, according to Salim Karsh, his father's uncle was an Armenian bishop.

Though culturally an Arab, Massih might very well have belonged to one of the oldest Christian communities in the Levant. After all, he spoke Syriac, the language of Christ. Massih's children had Arabic names. He identified with the

Arabic culture, of which Arabic music, food, customs, myths, and folklore were components. Nor was it unusual for a Syriac Catholic to marry an Armenian woman like Bahiyah Jurjos Nakash. Until the middle of the nineteenth century, the Syriacs lived in the Armenian millet. And even when Syriac Christians got their own millet, it was located adjacent to the Armenian one.

Moreover, Bahiyah herself was an atypical Armenian. She did not speak the demotic Armenian language. She did not read Grabar, the classical Armenian language used by scholars and priests. And whereas most Armenian names end in -ian, -ants, -ints, -unts, or -ents, her maiden name, Nakash, was not recognizably Armenian and may very well have been changed. Bahiyah was not a Catholic like most Armenians, but a Protestant. She had not been educated in the Armenian school in Mardin. Like her brother Nakash, Bahiyah had attended the American Mission School, which had been established in the Levant by the Presbyterian Board of Foreign Missions in 1870. This is why she could read and write. And this is why she was a devout parishioner of the Methodist Church.

Ethnic identity was not clearcut for the Karsh children. How did they identify themselves? As those Armenians, forming a small group in southeastern Anatolia who gave their children Arab names and did not speak Armenian? As Jews, who were everywhere in the Middle East? Or, as some suggest, as Syrians?

Although the first three Karsh children were born in Turkey, they were certainly not Turkish. Although their parents were most likely of Armenian-Jewish-Syriac origin, they identified with Arabic rather than with Armenian culture. And while they lived in a country, Turkey, where people took their identity from their religion, this presented problems for the Karsh children. Yousuf attended Mardin's Franciscan Catholic School and accompanied his father to the Catholic cathedral. Once the family reached Syria, Malak and Jamil, and later Salim too, attended the American Mission School.

The Karsh children had not been immune from the suffering experienced by members of the Armenian community during the atrocities. Young Yousuf had seen a slain Armenian infant hanging from a meat hook. He had been taunted by young Muslim boys on his way to and from school. (He later often told how he carried stones in his pocket but, on his mother's advice, purposely missed hitting the boys when he threw them.) Yousuf had taken food to his mother's two brothers when they were jailed in 1915. And the Karsh family took into their home a young Armenian girl, Mary, who had been blinded by her captors. "Although we had neither room or food to spare," Yousuf wrote later, "my mother took her in."[11] Then the children experienced the disappearance of their father and the necessity of keeping his hiding place a secret before his arrest.

Even before the atrocities began in 1915, the Karsh family had, like so many other families in the Levant, already suffered many hardships. According to Salim, shortly after Bahiyah's marriage to Massih, she gave birth to her first child, Josephine, who died of starvation. This was followed by the birth of two more children, Jamil and Malak, who died from typhoid aged four and six. The names were to be reused (or adapted) when subsequent babies were born. Yousuf, born in 1908, was the Karsh's first child to survive into adulthood. Three further children, Malak, Jamil, and Salim, were born in 1915, 1920, and 1925, respectively.

Not only were there deaths and disease to overcome, Massih Karsh had to provide for his growing family by following a profession as a merchant that was precarious at the best of times. During the three-month-long journey by caravan from Mardin via Baghdad to Mosul, the Bedouin extracted payments from the merchants in exchange for immunity while the riverain Arabs had a reputation for thieving and murder. Then there was the constant fear that the small desert harbours, the oases, would be dry or occupied by robbers once the caravan reached them. Even so, Massih Karsh was successful enough to see to it that his family had the best quality of clothing. "And," his son Salim remembered, "Father and Mother squeezed everything to have us educated."

Like most Armenian women, Bahiyah did not go out to work. Left on her own for several months each year, she had to devote her full time to raising the children. Consequently, it was Namie, as the children called her, who took charge of the children's religious instruction. According to her youngest son, Salim, she read the Bible to them for fifteen minutes every day. Namie, which means slave of God, was not only a devout woman. Like many Arab Christian and Armenian women whose object in life was to make themselves useful to others, Bahiyah was a "counsellor." She not only helped her fellow Armenians, she also assisted the poor with food and money. "She didn't have any difference between people," Salim recalled. This was true. Bahiyah's letters to her sons show that she had a wide range of friends and acquaintances among whom were Syrians, Armenians, and Muslims.

While Bahiyah was the dominant force in the family, Massih—or, as the children variously called their father, Abu or Baba (father), or occasionally Jido (grandfather)—was a quiet man. Though, according to Salim, he was "a small talker." Massih Karsh "would hear everything." And despite, or more likely because of, the fact that he could neither read nor write, he possessed a phenomenal memory. Once the Karsh children were literate, Massih elicited their help in his business. This is when the children discovered the extent to which their father had an amazing ability to retain every aspect of his complicated commercial transactions in his head. Indeed, his computer-like mind often put the other, literate members of his family to shame.

It is not known how long the Karsh family remained in Deir-ez-Zor after their exodus from Armenia and before moving south to the larger town of Aleppo near the Mediterranean coast. A rival to Venice in the eighteenth century, Aleppo shared many similarities with Mardin. The inhabitants of both cities experienced bitterly cold winters and scorching summers. Both towns were walled and beyond their fortifications lay fertile plains. Aleppo, like Mardin, possessed a large merchant community and an enormous souk. And, just like pre-1915 Mardin, the city counted Muslims and Jews, Arab and Greek Orthodox Christians, as well as Armenians among its population. But there was one difference between the two cities during the early 1920s. In Aleppo, Christians and Muslims lived side by side in relative harmony. Indeed, the dominant Muslim population went out of its way to welcome the Christian and Jewish refugees in its midst. This meant that once the Karsh family arrived in Aleppo they had, as Salim recalled, "no big problems." As long as they did not criticize the Muslims or engage in political debate, things went well.

Certainly by the mid 1920s, the Karsh family had settled in the Jdayah quarter of Aleppo. Lying just beyond the medieval walls of the city, the area had been

home to Syriac Catholics, Marinotes, and Armenians who, just like Massih, had worked as merchants and traders since the seventeenth century. The Karshes' Italianate-style house in the Rue Ichtara stood at the end of a cul-de-sac in the Shtamma district of Jdayah. The house had neither electricity nor running water. Consequently, Bahiyah, who was in her forties when they arrived, had to carry the water from the well up twenty-five stone steps. However, her sons, particularly the youngest, Salim, helped with the chores.

Things should have been better for a dry-goods merchant like Massih. After all, the French regime that took power through the Mandate in 1920 had established bonded warehouses and special transit provisions to enhance trade. But it took Massih a long time to get his business on its feet. Initially he worked in Deir-ez-Zor. Then he became the manager of a dry-goods store in the small market centre of Hasaka, located on the Syrian-Turkish border. It was only when the family moved to Aleppo that Massih was able to work as a dry-goods commissioner. And even then, the family never reached the level of prosperity they had enjoyed in pre-1915 Mardin.

GIVEN ALL OF THE difficulties that Massih and Bahiyah experienced after leaving Mardin in 1921, it is not surprising that when George Nakash asked his favourite sister, Bahiyah, if she would like to send one of her sons to Canada to assist him in his photography business, she agreed. Canada was a Christian nation. It was free, and politically stable too. The government had recently made it easier for immigration applicants by dropping the $250 entry fee. And, as the Karshes learned through Nakash's letters, Canada was prosperous. With one son earning his own living abroad, there would be one less mouth to feed in the Karsh family. But above all, George Nakash was offering the entire family a future because if their son made good he would, as was expected of the eldest son in any Armenian family, send for them too. For all these reasons, Massih and Bahiyah agreed to send their eldest son, Yousuf, to Canada in the autumn of 1923.

CHAPTER TWO

Welcome to Canada

By the time George Nakash wrote to Bahiyah Karsh offering to sponsor her son's travel to Canada, Nakash was an established photographer in Sherbrooke, Quebec. Also known to locals as "The Queen of the Eastern Townships" or, less poetically, as "The City of Electricity," Sherbrooke was situated in a deep valley on the confluence of the Magog and St. Francis rivers. Once the site of hunting and fishing grounds to the Abenaki tribes of the Algonquin Nation, Sherbrooke was settled in the late eighteenth century by the United Empire Loyalists, who had fled the American colonies as a result of the war of American Independence. In the mid-nineteenth century the town also became home to a large number of French Canadians, who supplied the labour for the town's woollen and saw mills and foundry.

When Nakash arrived there in the early 1920s, Sherbrooke's population had reached 27,000—the same size as his native Mardin. Sherbrooke had just recovered from the effects of the 1918–19 Spanish flu pandemic. Its textile, mining, and timber industries, which had been converted during the Great War to military production, were back on a peace-time footing. And most of the victims of Sherbrooke's post-war depression were no longer unemployed. Sherbrooke's diverse economy, its plentiful supply of hydro-electricity, and its access by rail to Maine, New Hampshire, the Maritimes, and Montreal, enhanced its recovery from the post-war slump exponentially. Indeed, by 1923 Sherbrooke's businessmen were poised to break all previous records in industrial investment.

Nakash was an outgoing man who liked people. He was dapper. He always wore a suit, even when developing negatives in the darkroom. Yet he possessed no inherited status that would have allowed him to enter the higher echelons of Sherbrooke's political life, business, education, or civil service. Nor could he have hoped to become a board member of the town's leading cultural institution devoted to the arts and science: the Sherbrooke Library and Art Association. Even so, Nakash had a profession and possessed the kind of personality that enabled him to capitalize on the town's growing prosperity. He joined the Rotary Club, where he met and made friends with many of the city's most prominent citizens. And he became a close friend of the Congregational minister, Dr. G. Ellery Read. Family tradition has it that when Nakash arrived in Sherbrooke, he was accepted immediately. As his daughter Vivian recalled, for the Nakash family "there was no such thing as being an immigrant."[1]

Self-Portrait, by George Nakash

In the mid-nineteenth century a formal portrait helped to establish a person's social status, display their civic virtue, and confirm their respectability. By the 1920s, the citizens of Sherbrooke demanded no less of their local photographer than had their nineteenth-century forebears. The Nakash Portrait Studio, which doubled as George's residence, attracted the local merchants and civic officials who inhabited the nearby handsome brick office buildings. It was here at 25a Wellington Street, above a shoemaker's store, that students from Sherbrooke High School and Bishop's College sat for their graduation photographs. It was here, too, that people from the surrounding towns and villages came to confirm their worthiness to be represented by having George Nakash take their portrait. This was how he became acquainted with the men and women in the upper and middle echelons of the community to whom most "non-preferred" New Canadians, like his uncle Aziz Setlakwe, were denied access.

George Nakash, it should be stressed, had no lack of talent. He possessed a courtly manner that made his clients relax. He was quick — when he moved

his studio to T. Eaton Company in Montreal in the early 1930s, he had up to twenty-five sittings a day. And he was modern in his approach. Following a trend that had begun in the 1880s, Nakash eschewed taking his pictures by daylight. For him artificial lighting had three advantages. His clientele could come to him at any time of the day. He could take his pictures under any weather conditions. And he did not have to locate his studio on the top floor of a building, in order to have access to a vast skylight.

Nakash's ability to give his clients more than a functional record of their visage did not go unnoticed by his peers. When he entered his photographs in international photography competitions in the early 1920s, he won awards and received praise from fellow artists and photographers. To the Royal Canadian Academician Adam Sheriff Scott, Nakash's portrait of Malaky Karwashian was "a supreme achievement of haunting beauty and dignity." And to a visiting art critic from Belgium, "it was impossible for any artist, painter or sculptor, to go as deeply into the psychology of any human being as you have gone," he told Nakash when viewing the results of his portrait.[2] This was the kind of praise that Nakash liked to hear. Capturing a subject's inner personality on canvas had been the central aim of the classical portrait painter. Now Nakash could take pride in the knowledge that he possessed the ability to reveal "the deep characteristic mood of the person" through the medium of the camera.[3]

There were other portrait studios in Sherbrooke—Sears Studio was one—which made good use of electric lights. But the lion's share of the portrait commissions went to George Nakash. With business booming, he needed an assistant. What better way to acquire one than by bringing the eldest child of his favourite sister to Canada?

It may seem surprising that Nakash had difficulty obtaining immigrant status for his young Armenian nephew, Yousuf Karsh, in 1923. After all, in 1915 Canada had joined its allies in protesting against the Turkish atrocities in Armenian Turkey. Five years later, the Canadian government had signed the Treaty of Sèvres, which established the state of Armenia in Soviet Russia. The same year, a group of Canadians had raised $300,000 to assist the destitute Armenians. Even so, Nakash's repeated appeals to the newly established Department of Immigration and Colonization initially fell on deaf ears. After all,

Turkey had been Canada's enemy during the First World War and any national from that region was regarded as an enemy alien. Above all, Armenians—and Syrians—were still on the "non-preferred" list of newcomers. It was not until Nakash travelled to Ottawa in August 1923, and personally set his case before an official in the Department of Immigration, that he managed to get permission to sponsor his nephew's immigration to Canada.

CARRYING HIS WOOL MATTRESS, down comforter, and a few coins in his money belt, fourteen-year-old Yousuf Karsh and his cousin Markram Setlakwe boarded the second-class section of the Faber Line ship aptly called the *Canada* in Beirut on November 24, 1923. Two months earlier Yousuf had left his family in Deir-ez-Zor and travelled for ten hours by bus to Aleppo. There he had lived with a sister of his father and her husband, Jean Hallah, for about two months. Then, once word came that his immigration papers were in order and his uncle George Nakash had sent him a boat ticket, Yousuf took the train to Beirut, where he stayed with some distant relatives. Two weeks later he boarded the *Canada*.

During the voyage from Beirut to Halifax, the *Canada* called at Alexandria and Marseilles, before crossing the Atlantic to North America. By the time the ship arrived in Halifax—more than a month later—it had collected 300 passengers, most of whom were immigrants.

Confined to the second-class deck, Yousuf and his cousin must have had an unpleasant trip. The last part of the voyage was by far the worst. On December 29 a heavy snowstorm swept over the Maritime coast. The forty-mile-an-hour gale that accompanied the storm blew almost every full-rigged sailing ship, two-masted or four-masted schooner, steamer, and passenger liner off course. Remarkably, the 5648-ton *Canada* was brought, or rather blown, into Halifax harbour by Captain Fornier a day early. It berthed at Pier 2 on the last day of the year. But another day had to elapse before "Youssef Kerch, age fifteen years from Aleppo, Syria" (as his "Declaration of Passenger to Canada" form stated) was admitted into the country.[4]

There was only one good thing about arriving in Halifax during the first snow storm of the season: the high drifts of snow covered the devastation that had left the north end of the city in ruins in 1917 when the Belgian Relief vessel *Imo* collided with the French munitions carrier *Mont-Blanc*. This was why the city looked magical rather than grim when Yousuf emerged from the vast concrete transit shed where he and his cousin had spent their first night in Canada before going their separate ways.

"Everything," Yousuf recalled years later, "was beautiful and exciting." There was the pleasure and relief of finding his uncle George Nakash on the dock. There was the new experience of walking through knee-deep snow. And because he arrived during the festive season, to Yousuf the city shone, as he later recalled, with "the sparkling decorations on the buildings and in the windows, a church with people going to early service, the huge American automobiles and the swinging tramways, the shop windows and the crowds of grown-ups walking and children playing." All of this "intoxicated" the young Yousuf with "joy."[5]

There was no less drama during the journey from Halifax to Sherbrooke. The train got stuck in a snowdrift. This meant that the passengers had to spend two nights rather than one on board and that the train's restaurant ran out of food. Even so, George Nakash amused Yousuf by sharing "every experience" with him. And even though Yousuf was hungry and disoriented, he responded with "wild enthusiasm" to everything his uncle told him.[6]

Halifax under snow, the unexpectedly long train journey to Sherbrooke, and the arrival at Nakash's studio-home on Wellington Street were all a far cry from travelling in two-wheeled wooden carts or by donkey and from living in thick-walled stone houses with earthen floors, small windows, and no running water or electricity. No wonder young Yousuf recalled being "naturally impressed" by the comparative luxury of his uncle's life in Sherbrooke.[7]

Nakash did everything he could to prepare his young nephew for his new life in Canada. Aware that citizenship was a marker of identity, that it provided legal status and an entitlement to rights, Nakash insisted that Yousuf apply for Canadian citizenship as soon as he arrived. Knowing, too, that financial security was foremost in the mind of every New Canadian, Nakash took out a small endowment policy on Yousuf's behalf and paid the annual premiums until he reached adulthood. George anglicized Yousuf's name. From now on he would be called Joe. He enrolled his young nephew in the Protestant Cambridge School. And, finally, in order to improve his nephew's virtually non-existent English, George asked his old friend Ellery Read to give Joe private English lessons.

Accepting the prevailing melting-pot theory, politicians and educators were convinced in the early 1920s that the children of non-preferred immigrants could, unlike their parents, be assimilated into the country and thereby provide "the material upon which Canadians as nation-builders must work."[8] This was not, of course, easy for non-French and non-English-speaking New Canadian children to do. There were no special English as a Second Language classes in the community. Few teachers were qualified or had the time to help New Canadian children in the classroom. Most of these children were simply placed well below their grade level and expected to learn English and to absorb the new culture around them by osmosis.

Records at the Eastern Townships School Board show that from January to February 1924, fifteen-year-old Joe Karsh sat with six- and seven-year-olds in grade one. The records also reveal that, during his first two months at the Cambridge School, he was often late for class or absent altogether.[9] Twenty years later, Karsh would recall his first day of school: "I suppose there is no loneliness greater than that of a boy at a new school. And if the school is in a new land of unfamiliar customs and unknown speech, the loneliness is even greater."[10]

Joe's loneliness, his tardiness, and his many absences did not, however, mean that he was an unenthusiastic pupil. Thanks to his mother, Joe possessed a strong desire to learn. It was doubtless due to Bahiyah, and to the Arabic and Armenian cultural traditions, that Joe was also unusually polite by North American standards. Whenever he was addressed in the classroom, he would impress everyone by standing beside his desk and then bowing to the four points of the compass before answering the question. Joe's elaborate manners won him favour among his teachers, who encouraged all of the students to be especially kind to him. No one in Sherbrooke had encountered such exquisite manners—unless they happened to have had their portrait taken at the Nakash Portrait Studio.

By March 1924, Joe was allowed to advance to the fourth grade. Here he was at least with ten- or eleven-year-olds, only a few years younger than himself. It was now that he made friends with Lewis Rosenbloom and Jack Ewing. Rosenbloom and Ewing, along with the other male students in Joe's class, went out of their way to make him feel at home: "At recess on my first school morning the boys played marbles and I had no marbles; they gave me a handful, urging me to play with them—they not only encouraged me to win, but took good care that I *did* win!"[11] It was in the same class that he met his life-long friend Margaret Bradley. "He looked very different with his long black stockings and knee breeches," Margaret recalled. "And he had fuzz on his face because he hadn't started shaving."

The children's friendship began when Joe wrote Margaret a little note in Arabic script. She responded by writing a note to him in English. Joe was the first foreigner that young Margaret, her sisters Moira and Fredericka, and her two other siblings had ever met. Margaret and Moira proudly took charge of their exotic new friend. "We tried to make him skate; he had little thin legs, but he wasn't very good." Chaperoned by the family's maid, they took him to the Casino Theatre for Saturday film matinees. And, as Margaret also recalled, "We took Joe to our home."[12]

It was a short walk from Joe's house to the palatial brick residence that belonged to the local dentist and city mayor, Fred Bradley, and his wife, Mabel. Joe made the walk from Wellington to Wolfe Street frequently. It was not just Margaret and her siblings who made his visit a pleasant one. Or the many Sunday dinners that Joe enjoyed eating in the Bradleys' home. Or the clothing that was passed on to him from the Bradley boys. What attracted Joe more than anything else was the atmosphere of the Bradley home.

There were always guests at the Bradleys' dinner table. Sometimes it was Fred and Mabel Bradley's nephew, the young poet and pianist Ralph Gustafson, who lived next door, and sometimes a local or out-of-town government official, a board member of the Sherbrooke Library and Art Association, or a fellow member of the musical club. There was also music in the Bradley home. Mabel had studied voice in Paris and in Montreal, where she had earned the sobriquet "the Empress of Song." After a successful but brief career at London's Covent Garden, she had married Fred Bradley and moved to Sherbrooke, where she immediately became involved in the city's musical societies. When George Nakash began courting Florence Jarjour, the ties between "these Armenians" (as Florence, George, and Joe were called) and the Bradley family strengthened. This was partly because Florence possessed a lovely singing voice. She and Mabel Bradley often sang duets, and young Joe was there to hear them.

While Mabel Bradley introduced Joe to classical music and her husband introduced him to civic officials, the Bradley children, along with other children at the Cambridge School, introduced Joe to the nuances of the English language and to schoolyard culture. When it rained he was taught to sing "Rain, rain, go away, come again another day." When the Bradley children were served ice cream, he was encouraged to join them in the chant "I scream, you scream, we all scream for ice cream." When he accompanied his friends to Miller's store during school recess, he discovered jaw breakers, yellow and red suckers, humbugs, and jelly beans. If Joe stepped on a crack in the sidewalk, his schoolmates would tell him that he'd broken his mother's back. If a ladybird lighted on his hand, it was a good omen and the children would chant "Ladybird, ladybird, fly away home."

Joe quickly learned, however, that there was no place in the schoolyard for the traditions of the Middle East. Turkish sweetmeats were just as out of place as the Arabic saying "Who resembles each other will get together." So was the Arabic concept of fate, or *jagadakeer* which literally means what is written on the forehead. Joe soon learned that his English-speaking friends had more flexible ideas, less fatalistic than those in the Levant. In keeping with the New World dream, most of the children at the Cambridge School were raised to believe that anything was possible.

Despite the disadvantages of subjecting New Canadian children to what educators referred to as the "direct" or "natural" method of instruction, "the funny little foreigner," as Yousuf later referred to his young self, was soon speaking a halting, if not always grammatically correct, English.[13] He would mix up words like "God" and "dog." He had difficulty distinguishing between "fifty" and "fifteen"—the results could be amusing when asked his age. And, like most new English or French speakers, he took things too literally. Shortly after becoming an apprentice in his uncle's studio, he responded to a client's comment that "I'm afraid I might break your camera" with the reply, "Don't worry, we have another one."[14]

Educators and immigration officials hoped that all newcomers would renounce their native culture and language. Joe Karsh did not, at least in the home. He spoke Arabic with his uncle and with George's sister, Nazlia, whom George had brought to Canada in 1919. The Lebanese shoemaker who lived and worked below their own studio-residence on Wellington Street spoke Arabic with Joe, Nazlia, and Nakash too. And there were frequent visits to and from the homes of the many relatives who, thanks to Aziz Setlakwe, were scattered throughout the Eastern Townships by the time Karsh arrived in Canada.

In 1927 George Nakash married Florence Jarjour, who was a Canadian of Syrian descent whom he had met at Thetford Mines before moving to Sherbrooke.[15] The arrival of Nakash's young bride-to-be gave Joe yet another person with whom he could speak Arabic. When Florence joined the Nakash household, it no doubt meant more Arabic food like *Kubbe nie* (finely ground raw beef, cracked wheat, onion, and spices), exotic vegetables like okra—imported in tins, of course—as well as lamb shish kebab. It also meant that, just like at home, Joe was living in a family where husband and wife went to different churches. With Joe attending the Catholic cathedral, his uncle the Methodist Church of Dr. G. Ellery Read, and Florence the Orthodox Church, things were little different than they had been in his own family, back in their distant Armenian millet in Mardin.

DURING HIS FIRST YEAR in Canada, Joe *saw* before he *heard*. He learned to think in shapes, forms, and mass. He "read" the people around him according to their expressions, their posture, gestures, and other nuances associated with body language. Joe wanted desperately to communicate and he used the only assets he had: his eyes and his good manners. His elaborate politeness not only won him friends among his classmates and teachers. Manners were his armour, his protection from a culture that was so different from the one he had known since birth. His good manners also saved him from blundering and from any embarrassment that might ensue if he misread a gesture or expression. Joe's extreme courtesy continued to be his means of communication and his defence when he began his apprenticeship as a photographer.

Joe was not initially enthusiastic about following the profession of his uncle. This was because Joe — and his parents, who had initially wanted him to become a priest — now hoped that upon immigrating to Canada, he would become a doctor. Yet if Joe had chosen to continue with his studies, it would have been a long uphill climb. He would have been in his early twenties before finishing high school and in his thirties before earning a degree in medicine.

On the other hand, becoming a photographer did not require any previous educational qualifications. A gracious studio manner and a willingness to learn could make up for any educational or linguistic deficiency. Nor was it mandatory for pupils in the province of Quebec to remain in school beyond the age of fifteen. But above all, George Nakash needed an assistant. This was why he had brought his young nephew to Canada. And this was why, in the summer of 1924, after barely four months at the Cambridge School, Joe became his uncle's apprentice.

The prospect of following George Nakash's profession looked even bleaker to Joe, who would have preferred to study medicine, when a friend told him that he would never make a substantial amount of money as a photographer. Joe became visibly glum. "We were making prints and I could tell that Yousuf was upset," Nakash recalled much later. "He said he had almost decided that photography was a field in which he would go nowhere."[16] Nakash gave his nephew three months in which to decide whether or not he wanted to continue his apprenticeship. He also gave him the following advice: "Pick on something that you love and you'll be happy; if you don't make a fortune at least you are happy in doing it." Two weeks later Joe made a decision. Despite the hardships that he knew he would have to endure until he established himself as a photographer, he decided to continue his apprenticeship. "After that," Nakash continued, "he was determined to learn all he could." Indeed, from that moment on, Nakash concluded, his young apprentice "seized every opportunity that came his way."[17]

Joe quickly absorbed everything his uncle taught him. He learned the special language of the studio in the camera room. He listened carefully to the repartee that took place between his uncle and a client. He watched how George Nakash paid close attention to the overall composition of the pose. How he manipulated the direction, angle, and intensity of the spot and floodlights with the least disruption to the client. How he devoted almost as much attention to the light that fell on his subject's hands as on his or her face. And, finally, how by the time Nakash had clicked the shutter he had already formed the finished portrait in his head. "The moment your sitter comes in you take a look, a general look" and, Nakash recalled years later, "you try to remember that mood."[18]

While it was during sittings in the camera room that Joe listened and watched most intently, there was also much to learn in the darkroom. Nakash was relatively unschooled in this area of photography. He used toners and developers more by instinct than according to any scientific method. This did not mean, however, that he was slapdash. In fact, he taught Joe to take great pains when mixing the chemicals, retouching and enlarging the negative, and choosing the grade of paper for the final print. Doing things well was important to Nakash and it would soon become equally important to his nephew.

Children on a
Country Lane Near
Brompton, by George
Nakash, circa 1930

Joe's education did not always take place in the studio. During their long moonlight walks in the surrounding countryside, George Nakash enhanced his nephew's appreciation of the landscape. He also gave Joe his first camera. The earliest surviving photograph taken by Joe was made on the outskirts of the town. It was taken two years after he had received the Brownie box camera on his birthday, December 23, 1924. Joe's "Early Landscape" is similar to George Nakash's "Children on a Country Lane Near Brompton," taken several years later. Both photographs are firmly rooted in the romantic Pictorialist tradition of photography. Both capture the mood, the ambience of the scene, due to some deft manipulation of the negative during the developing process. In presenting an impression rather than a documentary likeness of the subject, both men were demonstrating that there was more to making a photograph than just clicking the shutter or depressing the bulb. Photographers were artists, not technicians. "Instead of using a pencil or brush," Nakash later recalled, "we in photography draw with light." Indeed, he continued, "The artistic possibilities of the camera depend entirely upon the imagination, the actual capacity, the knowledge, skill and technical training of the photographer."[19]

One of Joe's friends was so impressed by his photograph that he asked him for an enlargement of the work. Then, without Joe's knowledge, the friend entered the photograph in a contest at Eaton's Department Store. One can only imagine Joe's pleasure when a cheque, in the amount of fifty dollars, arrived in the mail. Overjoyed with winning first prize, Joe gave ten dollars to his friend and sent the rest of the money to his parents in Aleppo.

However much George Nakash required his nephew's assistance in the studio, by 1928 he knew that he had taught his young pupil all that he could. Joe "learnt quickly," Nakash's daughter Vivian Saykaly recalled, "and my Dad was able to see that...he had to go on to get better. That's why he sent him to [John] Garo."[20] The provincial town of Sherbrooke, as Nakash well knew, was a very limited place for a young photographer to grow in. There was only one thing to do: send Joe to a larger city where he could study under a more experienced photographer than himself.

NAKASH HAD MET THE Boston-based portrait photographer John H. Garo (Garoian) in 1921. Though he shied away from photographic competitions, Garo had been a judge at the 23rd Annual Convention of the Photographers' Association of New England in Springfield, Massachusetts, where Nakash had received Salon Honours. The two men, who had both left Turkish Armenia to make a life for themselves in North America, soon became close friends. And in 1928, Nakash asked Garo if he would take his nephew as an apprentice for a period of six months. Believing, as he told a reporter, "that we all have an obligation to humanity to serve others," Garo agreed to take on the nineteen-year-old Joe Karsh.[21]

Garo's work, like Nakash's, was firmly rooted in the Pictorialist tradition of photography. Compositionally and formally, Garo's photographs also paid homage to classical portrait painting of the eighteenth and nineteenth centuries and to the earlier Old Masters. Neither man was on the cutting edge of photography. Both had been outflanked by the New Objectivity photographers like August Sander, Alfred Stieglitz, and their followers, who dissociated themselves from Pictorialist techniques in their efforts to make a social record of

representative types. Nor did Garo's and Nakash's work possess the innovation and the energy characteristic of the work of the emerging New York School of photographers, who used 35-mm cameras to take their frequently candid, and what some critics deemed as vulgar, photographs of New York City's street life. And, although Garo was a master of the bromoil, platinum, and gum bichromate techniques of printing, when in the developing room he, like Nakash, worked by instinct rather than according to any set formula.

Though clearly past his prime by the late 1920s, Garo had been one of the leading portrait photographers in North America. He was the first American photographer to exhibit his photographs at the Boston Art Club. He was also among the first group of American artists to exhibit paintings with the prestigious London Salon in the galleries of the Royal Society of Water Colour Painters. During the years before and throughout the First World War, it was not unusual to see an entire photography magazine or journal devoted to the work of John Garo.[22]

His reputation as a photographer, just like Nakash's, rested on his ability to size up his subject quickly, then to capture what he felt to be the subject's inner personality in the resulting portrait. Garo was equally known, like Boston's most renowned visiting portrait painter, John Singer Sargent, for knowing how, as he put it, "to make an interesting and beautiful picture of a subject that is not in itself intrinsically beautiful."[23] Thus it is not surprising to learn that presidents, musicians, writers, and wealthy blue-blooded Boston Brahmins all beat a path to the door of Garo's second-floor studio at 737 Boylston Street. They could be certain that John H. Garo would do them proud.

When Garo had begun as a watercolour painter, he had earned his living as a commercial artist. In fact, he did not take an apprenticeship in the studio of a commercial photographer until he was in his early twenties. This was in the mid-1890s, when the emergence of the Box Brownie camera had seemingly turned everyone into a photographer. Once he became a professional photographer, Garo quickly realized that art and photography were separate yet kindred forms of expression. Indeed, he would later insist that "the camera had artistic possibilities and that, in the hands of an artist, the lens is just as efficient means of expression as the brushes and pigments of the painter."[24] Just like Boston's leading pre–World War One portrait painters, Garo also strove to produce the same soft edges, the same filtering or diffused light, and the same shadows in his photographs. Garo was equally convinced that the photographer, like the artist, required a vivid imagination, a knowledge of traditional portrait painting, and an ability to imagine the picture before the shutter was exposed to light.

Garo's affinity with the portrait painter made him indifferent to the increasing vogue among photographers for taking their portraits with the help of electric lights. It wasn't just the worry of blowing a fuse, or of tripping over wires and cords in the camera room, or of being faced with a high electricity bill at the end of the month that made Garo take all of his portraits by natural light. He considered artificial light to be too harsh. This was because he felt that, unlike natural light, it could not move around an object. Or give it the soft edges that Pictorialist photographers and Boston portraitist painters like Gretchen Rogers demanded in their work. This was why Garo continued to pose his distinguished clients under an enormous north-facing skylight, and to manipulate the large roller shades covering it.

Since Garo worked entirely by daylight, he closed his studio each day at 4 p.m. But he did not leave the premises and make the long journey by taxi to his home on the outskirts of Boston. Rather, he transformed his palatial reception rooms — decorated with stag heads, mahogany furnishings, sumptuous Persian carpets, and examples of his own oil paintings and photographs — into a salon, a meeting place for the city's cultured elite.

What became known as the cocktail hour in John Garo's studio was, according to fellow photographer Franklin "Pop" Jordan, "a notable and delightful institution."[25] No invitations were ever issued. It was simply known that after 4 p.m., anyone who wanted good food, good drink — a difficult thing to come by during Prohibition — and good talk could find it at 737 Boylston Street. Drawn by the sheer magnetism of Garo's strong, though not overbearing, personality, artists, musicians, writers, and other members of the city's cultural and social establishment would turn up for friendly discussion on a wide range of subjects. Sometimes Garo would entertain his friends by singing an aria in his splendid baritone voice. At other times a visiting musician would take the floor and thereby entertain Garo and his guests. Whatever form the late afternoon soirees took, Garo enjoyed bringing together as many diverse elements as possible with the idea of challenging the smug and socially stratified community. He also enjoyed the experience of receiving attention from the city's establishment when he had come to the United States as an impoverished immigrant.

For Garo, photography was clearly a medium through which he could "interpret the art of painting, the art of music, the art of classical art." But his greatest canvas, he continued, was "the fine art of living." "I have enjoyed every minute of my life," he told a reporter less than two years before his death in 1939.[26] No one who knew John Garo — and George Nakash knew him very well — would have doubted this.

Garo was not just a bon vivant, nor merely a brilliant photographer who immortalized the great and the good in portraits that flattered his clientele in the Pictorialist mode. Garo helped make photography into a respectable profession and the photographer into a respected artist. Like the British society photographer Cecil Beaton, who was Garo's junior by a few years, he raised the status of the portrait photographer from the man with a black cloth who entered by the back door of his client's house to the man who was asked to stay to lunch or dinner. This was the man to whom George Nakash knowingly entrusted his young, seriously minded, talented, and very ambitious nephew.

The Apprentice

Yousuf Karsh spent two years in Boston under the tutelage of John H. Garo. Every six months, however, Joe rode the Central Vermont train from Boston back to Sherbrooke in order to renew his Canadian visa. The contrast between the two cities must have been striking to the young man. To begin with, Boston was a much larger and certainly a more cosmopolitan city than Sherbrooke. Boston boasted two art galleries with international collections, the Isabella Stewart Gardner Museum and the Boston Museum of Fine Arts. Sherbrooke, by contrast, had recently closed the doors of its Arts Building; its collection of mainly nineteenth-century Canadian paintings, its library, and its scientific exhibits were now scattered throughout the city.

Boston not only possessed a substantial public library. It had two good schools of fine art and design. It also had a wide ethnic mix. At one end of the social spectrum there was the sophisticated Brahmin caste and at the other the culturally rich, though financially impoverished, Italian, Irish, Jewish, Afro-American, and Syrian communities. Sherbrooke had few New Canadians, a fact which had made "those Armenians" popular rather than threatening to the community. And its mill and factory owners, governors of the Eastern Townships Bank, and other functionaries were in a different league to Boston's long-entrenched elite.

When Joe arrived in 1928, Boston still possessed a reputation for being the "Athens of America," even though some of its most notable luminaries—the writers Henry James and T. S. Eliot and the art collector Bernard Berenson—had migrated to Europe (where James had died in 1915). And although the city was hit in 1929, like all other parts of North America, by the Depression, Boston's high blue-collar wages for those still in employment meant that it fared better than most cities in the United States.

Karsh never referred to the deprivation that must have been evident in the city from the autumn of 1929. Whenever he recalled the two years that he spent in Boston, he dwelt on his own sense of fulfillment. Moving to Boston, Karsh said on more than one occasion, marked "the beginning of my education." Garo's studio became Joe's "university."[1] And Garo himself became Joe's Michelangelo. This was why Karsh always insisted that his training as a photographer in Boston and his education as a man went hand in hand.

WHEN JOE ARRIVED in Boston at the age of nineteen, he had had four years' experience in a small but lively photography studio. He had begun to take his own photographs, albeit with a simple Brownie box camera. And, having won first prize in the T. Eaton Company photography competition, he had enjoyed some recognition as a photographer. What Joe had not acquired during the four years of training with his uncle was a comprehensive knowledge of developing techniques or a mastery of the ability to capture the mood of a subject through the manipulation of natural light. Above all, Joe did not appreciate the extent to which portrait photography was derived from traditional portrait painting or the debt that he and his contemporaries owed to an earlier generation of photographers. For instance, he was not yet aware of the work of Julia Margaret Cameron, who, during the latter part of the nineteenth century, had made "beautiful and noble pictures that would elevate the spirit" and, most importantly of all, "describe an idea or a state of mind" that would expose the personality or soul of her subject.[2] All this he still had to learn.

There was something else, less tangible, that was missing from the first four years of Joe's apprenticeship as a photographer. With so little schooling to his credit, he was not as well spoken and as well informed as his clientele. It did not take Joe long to realize that this was how Garo won the respect of his notable clients. This was how Garo put them at ease before the camera. And this was ultimately how he was able to bring out the more favourable features or expression of every subject he photographed. By establishing social parity with his clients, he made them feel that it was a privilege to be photographed by John Garo.

He was determined to improve the halting English — and reading ability — of his young apprentice, so he hired a retired professor from Northeastern University to give Joe lessons. Garo also wanted his young apprentice to be as well read as he was. Joe's education thus began in the Boston Public Library, which was within walking distance of Garo's Boylston Street studio in the centre of town. It was here that Joe worked his way through the classics when he was not assisting Garo in the camera or darkroom. And here, as will be later seen, that he met some of his models.

Moreover, Garo wanted his thirty-years-younger apprentice to have the formal art instruction that he himself had experienced when he took drawing lessons from Ernest Lee Major at Boston's Normal Art School. Convinced that a photographer should possess a knowledge of picture-making as a painter, Garo did two more things. He encouraged Joe to study the works of the great portrait painters reproduced in books of art at the library and exhibited on the walls of the city's two fine museums. And, remembering the benefit that he had received by taking drawing lessons himself, he enrolled Joe in Boston's New School of Design. Founded in 1913 and directed by the portrait painter Douglas John Connah, the school was just up the road from Garo's studio. This was to be the first, and last, formal art-school training that Karsh would ever receive.

After one session at the New School of Design, Karsh knew that he was no artist. Though he had no difficulty capturing light and shadow with his charcoal stick, he had no ability or understanding of how to draw anything in perspective. The instructor, noting his student's difficulty and knowing that he was a student of John Garo, asked Joe to adjust the lighting of the life model. Happy to be released from the drawing board, Joe willingly accepted this task.

Thanks to his training under George Nakash, Joe had already acquired a sound knowledge of electric lighting and of general composition. Indeed, he did such a good job at the New School of Design that the instructor made a point of discussing the effect that Joe's illumination and arrangement of the drapery had on the model. He even asked Joe to help him criticize the other students' work; and they apparently welcomed the young photographer's observations as to how successfully they had captured the effects of light in their charcoal sketches.

The evening class at the New School of Design was not only concerned with studio work. Time was also devoted to discussing the paintings and sketches of the Old Masters. This was one area of the visual arts where Joe could be of no help to his instructor or to his fellow students.

It was generally felt, among photographers, that a knowledge of Old Master portrait paintings would provide a good starting point for any portrait photographer. Julia Margaret Cameron, for example, had learned much from traditional painting, as can be seen in her full-face photographs of the poet Alfred Tennyson and the scientist John Herschel. One of the standard texts on portrait photography, Otto Walter Beck's 1907 publication, *Art Principles in Portrait Photography*, encouraged photographers to "strive to attain the depths, the tactile quality, the logic and the completeness of balance that delight us in masterpieces of drawing or painting in monochrome."[3] Even twenty years after Beck had written his seminal study, educationalists were still advising photographers not to "miss the opportunity of seeing these old-time examples of portraiture."[4] Certainly Garo worked in this tradition. As his friend Franklin "Pop" Jordan told a reporter for the *Boston Herald* in 1937, "His handling of composition, of light and shade, conform to the best usage of the classic arts."[5]

Photographers had much to learn from portrait painters. They could, for example, adopt a low vantage point, popular among portrait painters, in order to make the subject of their work appear more dignified. They could also study the work of Rembrandt, Velasquez, and other Old Masters — as Karsh would later advise his own students to do — in order to learn more about light.

Rembrandt was first and foremost famous for the painstaking way in which he drew or painted with light. He used light — and conversely dark, empty spaces — in order to make the illuminated areas of the face and clothing glow on the canvas. He used light, too, in order to capture a single, sharply focused moment, thereby anticipating the act of photography. Rembrandt used light not only to reveal what he felt was the inner character of his subject, but also to enhance a person's appearance. When painting his own portrait, for example, he would cast a shadow down one side of his face in order to reduce the size of his bulbous nose. This made him appear more refined, more relaxed, and more good looking than he was in real life. Here was another lesson that photographers would use to their advantage, and to the advantage of their less attractive clients.

Rembrandt was not the only Old Master from whom Joe learned. An artist of an earlier era, Hans Holbein, taught Joe the virtue of patiently observing the surface detail of a work, like the texture of the skin, the hair, and fabrics. Titian and his sixteenth-century artist contemporaries brought home to Joe the expressive possibilities that were inherent in the shadow. And the paintings of Velasquez showed Joe the various ways in which light could be employed to unify every element in a work. Yet it would be the paintings of Rembrandt that had the most influence on Karsh, as is testified by his later sobriquet, the Rembrandt of Photography.

Joe's introduction to the portrait paintings of the Old Masters was reinforced by what Garo told him in the studio. His teacher seemed to have the whole repertoire of classical portrait painting in his head. And he impressed Joe with his detailed descriptions of the masterpieces that his student was studying in reproduction at the Boston Public Library and at the New School of Design.

It was through Joe's study of the Old Masters that he learned the value of seeing and of remembering what he had seen; and then of incorporating what he had seen into his work, by manipulating the reflective screens and great roller shades that covered the north window of Garo's studio, or by manipulating the glass plate negative in the darkroom. Thus, as Garo told Joe, a photographer should never leave anything to chance. And as Garo noted in a lecture in 1926, "We can control light and can exercise personal control at every step from the exposure of the film or plate to the production of the finished print and thus can make our results pictorial."[6]

It was also by studying the Old Masters that Joe discovered the source of Garo's belief that the photographer had to be as well informed as his client.

Garo knew, for example, that the Spanish artist Velasquez had not acquired his position in the court of King Philip IV simply through the truthfulness of his naturalist style. Velasquez's access to the European aristocracy was due, as well, to his worldly elegance, his sharp intellect, and his lavish dress. The ideal portrait painter, from Anthony Van Dyck to Joshua Reynolds, had possessed impeccable manners, a keen and penetrating intellect, an excessive charm, a flair for dressing, and a studied nonchalance that signified the artist's gentility. This enabled some to live more like princes than like impoverished painters. This was how they gained access to, and won the friendship of, triumphant generals, kings, and courtiers, and other leaders of society who wanted to have their achievements celebrated in a portrait painting. By immortalizing the famous, moreover, the Old Masters assured the longevity of their own reputations.

Joe quickly realized that Garo's success as a portraitist was based, in no small part, on his ability to converse with significant figures either during the cocktail hour or during a portrait sitting. Yet Garo's ebullient personality, his flamboyant attire — he wore flowing black smocks and colourful, soft silk scarves — would not have been enough to inspire his commissions from the famous. Garo had to conspire in the belief that there was something inherently special that distinguished his privileged clients from less accomplished or less-well-placed mortals. And above all, he had to foster the belief that the photographer was capable of revealing the accomplishments and even the soul of his subject in the finished portrait.

The notion that achievement or position was evident in the face, and hence that the visual commemoration of the soul of a person could be revealed by the painter or the photographer, was not new — and current trends of face psychology have revived this. Greek and Roman artists had sought to establish a relationship in their work between physical appearance and the soul, between beauty and virtue, and between internal and external perfection. During the early years of the fifteenth century, artists of the Renaissance had gone one step further: they connected the cult of personality with the notion of individuality. Their revival of the idea that the soul could be seen in the face prompted them to make a lifelike, albeit frequently idealized, likeness of their subjects.

Inspired by this reasoning, Garo believed that anyone who made his or her mark on society possessed some inherent quality that it was the photographer's gift to reveal. Like Julia Margaret Cameron, whose portraits gave a monumental view of human personality, Garo sought out leading figures in the arts and sciences as well as politicians and patricians because he believed that they possessed greater qualities than others.

Led by Garo, this interpretation of the work of the Old Masters instilled Joe with many lessons. In technique, he learnt how the photographer, too, could make light work for him. In lifestyle, he perceived the necessity of being well attired and well educated in order to win the respect and inspire the complicity of his subject. Moreover, he came to share the belief that the face could express the soul. In the process, Joe indelibly identified his art with the idea that it was the achievers in society who, more than anyone else, possessed an innate goodness, which the photographer could expose by illuminating the soul. This was perhaps easier for Joe to accept because it fit with what he, as a Catholic, had already learned of St. Augustine's doctrine: that goodness and greatness were one and the same thing.

All of these ideas would guide Karsh throughout the rest of his career. And even long after they became unfashionable for most photographers, he would cling to them as ferociously as had the Old Masters and his teacher John Garo. Karsh was hardly exaggerating, therefore, when he wrote, years later, that "the ideas I absorbed there [in Boston] became the measuring sticks by which I came to judge things in later years."[7]

EVEN THOUGH GARO became Joe's spiritual father, he did not allow his student to become his clone. "One day while Mr. Garo was looking through a window," Karsh recalled long afterwards, "he called my attention to an abstract design in the distance—I had difficulty making it out—then he turned to me and said, 'Yousuf you have the same colour eyes that I have,' but I said they do not see the same thing."[8] Garo was pleased with Joe's response. Artists had been consciously putting their imprint, their own personality, into their work since the Renaissance and Garo knew that Joe's work would only possess a freshness, a validity, and a truth if he did not copy his own work. Joe was, therefore, not asked to reproduce the same thing as Garo but encouraged to think for himself. "No matter how much you admire this or that photographer," Karsh would tell a meeting of the Photographers' Association of America twenty years later, "be true to your own feelings…don't be a copyist."[9]

THERE WERE OTHERS besides Garo who supported and influenced Joe during his two years in Boston. Franklin Jordan, an amateur photographer of some merit, the head of a Boston-based printing house, the author of the standard book on photographic enlarging, *and* the editor of the influential journal the *American Annual of Photography*, gave Joe "unflagging interest and good counsel and warm friendship."[10] There were other admirers too. Garo's nephew Francis Eresian marvelled at how the young, ambitious boy absorbed everything to do with photography.[11] Then there were the many people whom Joe encountered during Garo's famous cocktail hour. "I listened to politics, books, sometimes just a chain of funny stories; sometimes music, occasionally a whole opera."[12]

Joe did something else during the cocktail hour in Garo's studio: he tended the bar. There was still Prohibition during the years that Joe lived in Boston and it was his task not only to serve the illegal drinks but also to procure the flavouring. He made frequent visits to the local drugstore to obtain gin, rye, rum, and bourbon essence, which he mixed in the darkroom. As the distinguished guests came to pay court to Garo, he would call out to Joe, "Give Dr. Koussevitsky [the conductor] his favourite drink—nitric acid."[13]

Tending the bar enabled Joe to converse with such luminaries as the opera singer Enrico Caruso, the cartoonist Ralph Sadler, the sculptor Clarke Noble, and the conductor of the Boston Pops, Arthur Fiedler. "As I responded to their personalities," Karsh wrote much later, "I gradually came to realize that photography in general, and portrait photography in particular, was capable of furnishing me with immense satisfaction." It was through Garo's four-o'clock soirees that Joe came to appreciate the extent to which "a human face was a mirror in which, from moment to moment, the subtlest of emotions was reflected."[14]

Joe also received a good portion of his education in the less glamorous darkroom. Garo "was a master technician" and, Karsh recalled years later, "He
drilled me in all the various photo processes."[15] There were many failures on
Joe's part when he attempted to print from the 16-by-20-inch glass plate negatives from which Garo made his prints. And there were many lectures from
Garo during which he told Joe why and where he had gone wrong. It was arduous work becoming the perfectionist that Garo wanted Joe to be. No wonder it
took him eighteen days to complete his first gum arabic print. Garo taught Joe
the importance of taking infinite pains with the most minute details. And this
was how Joe learned patience and discipline.

When he was not assisting Garo in the studio or in the darkroom, or reading in the public library or attending night classes in art or English, Joe took
his own photographs. Indeed, Joe often found his subjects through his other
pursuits. "I would go to the Public Library close by and silently observe the different readers who I was interested in photographing. Then I would introduce
myself saying, 'I'm a student of photography … would you give me the pleasure
of modeling for me?'"[16]

It was in Boston's public library that Joe asked a dark-haired young woman
if she would give him half an hour of her time and accompany him to Garo's
studio. The resulting photograph, titled simply "Early Portrait" (circa 1929) — a
three-quarter-length portrait taken at a low point of view — leaves no doubt that
Joe's art was comfortably situated in the Pictorialist tradition. Compared to the
far more accomplished photographic portraits that Nakash and Garo were taking at the time, this is not a particularly inspired work. But Joe, like his two
mentors, was concerned with capturing the subtle gradations of light, with giving his work a strong sense of sculptural form while, at the same time, avoiding
a sharp focus. Joe was equally intent on allowing his subject to lock eyes with
the viewer — and with the photographer. The woman's gaze in "Early Portrait"
is direct but not harsh. Franklin Jordan pronounced the portrait "beautiful."[17]
Joe was so pleased with his friend's praise that he presented him with the first
gum print that he had ever made.

More ambitious in its use of light and paying less homage to the Pictorialist
tradition was a portrait that Joe made of Garo himself before leaving Boston in

1930. It must have been a daunting task and yet Joe's photograph of his teacher is beautifully composed. It demonstrates how well Joe had absorbed the lessons of Rembrandt and other traditional portrait painters because it is all about light: how light falls on the folds of Garo's flamboyant bow tie, how light illuminates Garo's curls, how it highlights his collar and cuffs, and how light moves around Garo's figure, giving it the solidity of a stone sculpture. Above all, this is a portrait that takes John Garo head on by successfully capturing the sheer energy of the man.

Conversely, Garo had taken Joe's photograph a year earlier. It is a romantically stunning work. Joe is wearing a magnificent turban crested with a feather, which is held in place with a jewelled pin.

There was nothing original about photographing someone in costume. Rendering a subject in fancy dress or masquerade had been popularized by Van Dyck in the 1620s. "Vandyke dress," as it became known, prompted later generations of artists, like the eighteenth-century painter Watteau, to render their subjects in Shakespearean poses, antique garb, or Turkish robes. During the nineteenth century, artists became even more fascinated by what they believed to be the sexually permissive, unfettered, and freewheeling visual culture of the Arab world. Julia Margaret Cameron turned her subjects into Old Testament prophets, for example. And, some years later, George Nakash would dress a handsome bearded tramp, whom he found on the streets of Montreal, in a flowing robe and head dress and call the resulting photograph "Desert Chieftain."

Early Portrait, 1929

With its tension between light and dark, between naturalism and the symbolism, and between a real and assumed identity, Garo's photograph of Joe in a turban shows the romantic Pictorialist tradition at its best. But this portrait is more than this. It is an exercise in transference, paying homage to Joe's and Garo's birth in Turkish Armenia, and to the culture that they were keeping alive by conversing in Arabic.

Joe certainly looks comfortable wearing the lavish turban. He also appears much younger than his twenty years. He looks pleased; after all, he is being photographed by John Garo—a privilege in itself. Joe looks relaxed. And why not? The complicity necessary for the making of a successful photograph was

there. They shared a common heritage: Garo and Karsh had experienced Turkish atrocities, in 1895 and 1915 respectively. They had each immigrated to North America in their mid-teens. And, above all, both men possessed an enormous respect for one another: Joe for the master photographer Garo, and Mr. Garo, as Joe called him, for his young protegé.

By the end of Joe's second year in Boston, the Garo studio had become his second home. He had, of course, worked hard. And because of this, he had not only won the respect of Garo, who made him his assistant during his second year, but also won the affections of many other people. "I'm sorry, that you are leaving us, Joe," Franklin Jordan wrote when he heard that Garo's assistant was to depart, "for you have made yourself a firm place in our affections."[18]

There was never any question of Joe remaining in Boston indefinitely. And however much he credited Garo with being the one man to whom he owed more than any other person, he saw Garo's weaknesses as well as his strengths. When he came to write his memoirs following Garo's death, Karsh criti-

John Garo, circa 1930   cized his teacher for not having enough ambition. "He made portraits that were classics," he wrote of his former mentor, "but he did not even give them the momentum they could have received from one another in a collective showing."[19] There were no exhibitions and no submissions to photographic competitions by John Garo. Nor did he make any attempt, like his contemporary August Sander, who published *Face of Our Time*, to publish his photographic collection in a portfolio or a book. Then there was the matter of Garo's naivety when it came to his friends and acquaintances. In Karsh's view — as well as in many others' — people frequently took advantage of Garo's hospitality. For Garo was generous not only with his drink during the cocktail hour, but with his money. In the end he died a pauper. "Doubtless he suffered financial losses as the result of his own stock speculations," Karsh commented, "but I fear that his speculations on some of his friends must have brought his bitterest setbacks."[20]

There was something else about Garo that met with Karsh's disapproval, and that was his marriage, to Aliée. Karsh had seen how George Nakash's wife, Florence, was an enormous help to him when she decided to manage the financial side of his business. Aliée Garo, who did not enjoy good health, was an accomplished pianist, but this was not enough for the highly critical Karsh

because she made little effort to understand or to contribute to her husband's career. That a woman should be the artist's helpmate was clearly in Karsh's mind when he said of Garo's wife, "I do not mean by this that she was indifferent to his success, but she could not have been the inspiration of it."[21]

Garo was aware of his faults. He knew that his assistant possessed more energy and drive and, most of all, more ambition than he himself had. He knew, too, that young Joe was more shrewd than himself when it came to handling money. But Garo feared one thing: that his young apprentice might allow his ambition and his desire for success to jeopardize the quality and the standard of his work. This is why Garo's parting advice to Joe was to "keep up your ideals."[22]

Years later, Karsh suggested that he would have liked to have moved from Boston to Washington, D.C. There, he would certainly not be treading on Garo's territory, since the latter never travelled and took all of his photographs in the studio. Moreover, in Washington Joe would have had an abundance of important "personalities" to photograph. With this in mind he approached the American immigration authorities. He soon discovered to his dismay, however, that "Washington was out of the question because the immigration quota for Armenians was nil."[23] In any case, he was due back in Quebec. He had promised his uncle that, following his training with Garo, he would return to Sherbrooke and work alongside him in the Nakash Studio.

Young Yousuf in a Turban, by John Garo, circa 1929

And this Joe faithfully did. From April 1930 to October 1931 he put into practice all that he had learned while working with Garo and before that with his uncle. He also began, as he told Garo when he returned to Sherbrooke, to make his portraits with the aid of electric lights.[24] He and his uncle planned a joint exhibition of their work, though it never came to fruition. Nakash continued to exhibit in the United States, but it was clear, as one critic pointed out when Nakash won the grand prize at the Association of New England Photographers for his "Portrait of a Little Boy" in 1932, that his work was "a bit old fashioned in its fuzzy soft focus."[25]

Joe wanted to move beyond the Pictorialist mode that his uncle — and John Garo — still practised. Joe wanted to develop an individual expression of his own. He wanted to have a greater variety of clients. Moreover, he hoped to

expand his social contacts. The first thing he asked Florence Nakash when he returned to Sherbrooke was, "Where is the tennis crowd?"[26] Joe wanted, in short, more than the sleepy town of Sherbrooke afforded him.

Joe began preparing for his exit by asking visiting representatives of the Eastman Kodak Company to let him know if there was an opening in Ottawa. This was how he learned that John Powis was looking for an assistant. And this was why, a year and a half after returning to Sherbrooke from Boston, Garo's restive apprentice put everything he owned into two suitcases and boarded the train for Ottawa, in search of greatness for himself.

IT WAS GEORGE NAKASH who brought young Yousuf Karsh to Canada, Nakash who introduced him to the camera, and Nakash who gave him a sound education in photography. A stylistic comparison of Nakash's and Karsh's mature work shows the extent to which both photographers moved in the same direction throughout their long careers. Karsh's never-ending attempt "to convey the sense of sunlight being spilled over a person's face and hands" and his later boldness in revealing every line on the human face came from Nakash.[27] It was also Nakash who impressed upon his nephew the importance of being well dressed and polite so that he might win the respect of his clients and thereby create a rapport with them. Finally, it was due to the generosity of his uncle George that Joe was able to obtain further instruction and further experience as a photographer at a crucial moment in his career.

These were, however, private debts, privately acknowledged. Karsh would assure Nakash in a letter, "I must pause and pay homage and my thanks to you, my uncle, who gave me the start and taught me the lesson of taking pains and doing things well."[28] Yet when the famous Yousuf Karsh later recalled the first six years of his career as a photographer in newspaper interviews or in his own writings, he gave little public acknowledgement of the four years that he had spent with his uncle. Whenever he talked about his early years in public, therefore, it was Garo to whom he gave the credit for laying the groundwork of his training as a photographer. Indeed, as he told a friend years later, "Everything I have become I owe him."[29]

CHAPTER **FOUR**

Joe Goes to Ottawa

What kind of place was Ottawa when Karsh arrived there in the autumn of 1931? The climate was a problem: horribly muggy in the summer and bitterly cold in the winter. Yet, visiting the city seventy years previously, the English novelist Anthony Trollope had called it the Edinburgh of British North America: "It stands nobly on a magnificent river with high, overhanging rock and a natural grandeur of position which has perhaps gone far to recommend it to those who chose it as the Capital of Canada."[1] Later commentators would admire Ottawa's Gothic-revival Parliament Buildings, its magnificent Château Laurier hotel, and the Victoria Memorial Museum, which brought the collections of the country's national museum and art gallery under one roof.

Yousuf Karsh chose Ottawa as a place to make his own way as a photographer because, as he told a reporter, "it was the capital and would attract the most interesting people."[2] Certainly the state, along with the nobility and the church, had long been traditional sources of patronage for the portrait artist. As the national capital, Ottawa had its fair share of statesmen and, to a much lesser extent, stateswomen. The town's political elite was composed—from the top down—by the Governor General, the prime minister, cabinet ministers, and other politicians, who, along with a myriad of civil servants, made up the bulk of the city's population. Then there were prosperous businessmen from the commercial segment of the population who ran the shops, the lumber and paper mills, the iron works, and the clothing factories.

Karsh also felt that Ottawa was a crossroads. "Many who made the trip to the New World stopped in Washington, and then," he subsequently observed, "came to Ottawa before making the trip back to Europe."[3] (This was true in 1931 and would be true eleven years later when the British prime minister, Winston Churchill, visited the city at a significant moment in the world's history.) But there was a more parochial side to the city. For most residents, Ottawa's virtues lay in its accessibility to the Gatineau Hills — for skiing or hiking depending on the season — and, to the socially minded, in the plethora of skating and garden parties. Indeed, many people who lived there complained that the place was too quiet. There was no professional theatre, no symphony orchestra or opera. People had to be content with an array of amateur cultural activities for their entertainment. For some, there was too much gossip, making the city more like a company town than the nation's capital. Yet living there was comfortable — for those who lived in the right area of the city, of course. Life was uncomplicated and friendly, for those of Anglo-Saxon heritage.

Yousuf Karsh, Self-Portrait, June 1933

But what was it like for someone who left definite and indefinite articles out of his sentences when he wrote a letter? Who spoke English with a thick accent? Or who, even before he spoke, announced his difference by his appearance and his bearing? Along with his exotic demeanour, Karsh had an olive skin and a frail frame — at twenty-two he stood at just over five foot six inches and weighed less than 130 pounds.

Karsh rarely referred to the difficulties that he encountered when he first moved to Ottawa. Even long after he had become one of the world's most respected portrait photographers, he was never allowed to forget that he was different from the "average" Canadian. In 1971, one writer noted that Karsh possessed the face "of an Armenian rug-dealer," that he spoke with a "heavily-accented middle European voice," and that he exhibited a "soft Levantine manner."[4] Though an ostensibly more liberally minded commentator would credit Karsh with having "enough of an accent to be interesting but not difficult"

and possessing sufficient "courteous formality to be appealing but not alarming," the ethnic slur was still there.[5] And it remained there, in one form or another, for the rest of Karsh's life.

No one but an immigrant can imagine what it is like to live in a culture that is so very different from one's own. Though Karsh had been a Canadian resident for seven years and was naturalized on his twenty-first birthday, his move to Ottawa represented the first time since his arrival in North America that he was to live outside of an Arabic-speaking home.

The timing of Joe's arrival in Ottawa could not have been worse. In 1931, Canada was in the midst of an economic depression; by 1933 one-third of the workforce would be unemployed. The situation for New Canadians was particularly grim. They were not only blamed for the unemployment crisis; they were either denied work or, if they were lucky enough to get it, treated with disdain by their employers. The government, under Prime Minister R. B. Bennett, did not help things. It shut Canada's doors to potential immigrants—unless they were willing to work on a farm. It also ordered some 30,000 New Canadians, who in the government's view had become a "burden" on the economy, to leave the country.

Given the inhospitable behaviour of the general public towards anyone who looked or sounded different, it is little wonder that Joe had difficulty finding a place to live when he arrived in Ottawa. Initially he slept in a dormitory at the YMCA. Then he managed to get shared accommodation in a crowded boarding house. It was not until 1935, four years after arriving in the city, that Joe was able to tell John Garo that he had "a very delightful and restful room" at 183 Metcalfe Street, above the Wellington Arms Tea Room. Here he found "a great deal of happiness" because he could be with his own thoughts and enjoy listening to classical music on the radio and reading H. G. Wells's popular book *The Outline of History*.[6] Any chance of getting a place of his own, however, was out of the question. Ottawa's landlords, as Joe's brother Malak discovered when he arrived in the city a decade later, remained reluctant to rent an apartment to anyone who looked different.

Given the level of hostility towards New Canadians, it seemed that there were only two survival strategies available to Joe. He could seek refuge by attaching himself to Ottawa's small Syrian and Armenian community. Or he could renounce his ancestral heritage, improve his English and acquire a demeanour that would be more acceptable to the Anglo-Saxon community. Karsh did not seek comfort by choosing the first option. On more than one occasion, he made it clear that he did not want to become closely associated with the Arabic-speaking community in Ottawa. When his brother Malak was about to embark for Canada in 1937, for example, Yousuf warned him against associating with his Aunt Mansura and the people she was bringing to Canada from the Middle East because "they belong to a much older school...of thought and behaviour."[7] And when it looked as though his former mentor George Nakash would join him in the capital, he did everything he could to discourage him, not welcoming more Armenians on what was now his turf. As he told John Garo, he did not want "an entire colony in Ottawa."[8]

At the same time, Joe did not turn his back on his Middle Eastern roots. After moving to Ottawa, he continued to visit and to correspond with his Armenian relatives in Quebec. Often lonely during his first three years in the city, Joe frequently turned to George and Florence Nakash, along with John Garo, for solace.

Karsh thus sought a middle ground between the two options available to him during the process of making a home and creating an identity for himself in Ottawa. Like Dorothy in the land of Oz, he turned his difference to his advantage. He wore his hair, now rapidly thinning, an inch longer than everybody else. He donned a black smock—à la John Garo—in the camera room. He wore a fedora and a black cape, attire that left no doubt that he was an artist. To differentiate himself from other photographers, Karsh took his photographs with a white camera, allegedly after a child asked him, "Why do you use a black camera?" Likewise, he abandoned the traditional black focusing cloth, choosing instead a colourful gold-lined burgundy fabric. "The cloth gives me a start," he told a reporter for *Maclean's* magazine a few years later. "The sitter comments on its beauty and the conversational opening is made."[9]

Shortly after arriving in Ottawa, Joe reverted to his birth-name, which he chose to spell in the Arabic rather than in the Armenian form. He made no more attempts—as he had done in Boston—to improve his English. And he continued to practise the effusively polite manners that had helped him as a child in Sherbrooke. For example, when Karsh greeted anyone, he would give a little bow, duck his head while shaking hands, then look up with his soft brown eyes. If he happened to meet someone in the street, he would doff his hat. (This habit wore out the crown of many hats at the point where Karsh had repeatedly grasped it.) Few people failed to be charmed by his old-world manners or amused by his flamboyant dress. In a town where most Canadians were a little stiff and distant, Karsh must have been a refreshing, if exotic, presence.

That Karsh was turning his foreignness into a virtue did not go unnoticed. One journalist called him "the Holbein of his day." He also compared Karsh to another expatriate, the German-born composer Handel, "who adapted Germanic charisma to English convention and thereby achieved greatness."[10] Karsh would have been flattered by this comparison because he wanted, more than anything else, to present himself as an urbane, educated, suave, and, above all, acceptable newcomer to Canada. If that meant claiming that his father was a wealthy merchant, denying his Jewish and possibly Syrian ancestry, and keeping aloof from the Arabic-speaking community in Ottawa, so be it. Karsh could not, like Dorothy, return home from his nightmare-dream in the land of Oz by chanting "There's no place like home" three times. With Mardin, Turkey, now out of bounds, there was no home for Karsh to return to, so he invented a new one in the nation's capital.

Doing this was not an easy task. There was xenophobic Ottawa to cope with. There was his loneliness. He missed John Garo. And Garo, along with "the boys" who dropped in for the after-four-o'clock soirees, missed Joe. There was little privacy in his living quarters. He felt guilty because he did not have sufficient funds to help his family in Syria, as was expected of the son who had moved to the New World in order to make his fortune. But above all, Karsh was not happy working for his new employer, John Powis, whose studio at 130 Sparks Street was in the centre of downtown Ottawa.

Karsh was discontented because when his own portraits of débutantes and brides appeared in publications like Toronto's *Mayfair* magazine they were attributed to the studio of John Powis. Karsh was also frustrated because Powis, like Garo before him, seemed to lack initiative. For example, Karsh criticized his boss's failure to take advantage of his accessibility to the Governor General of Canada, whom he had photographed on several previous occasions. Nor did Powis, in Karsh's view, make any effort to build on his connections with other officials in the government. During the Imperial Economic Conference that took place in the summer of 1932, it was only because Karsh sensed that photographing dignitaries could be "a new challenge for Canadian portraiture" that a number of the visiting statesmen, including the British Chancellor of the Exchequer Neville Chamberlain, were invited to sit for their portrait at the Powis studio.[11]

While Karsh was disappointed that none of the photographs he and Powis took at the Imperial Economic Conference made much of an impression on the Canadian public, the exercise had nevertheless been instructive. First, Karsh had discovered how easy it was to gain access to important "personalities," as he and his contemporaries called them. And second, the presence of so many high-ranking visitors confirmed Karsh's belief that Ottawa was the best city in the country from which to launch his career.

IN THE LATE NINETEENTH century two American-based photographers, the Quebec-born Napoleon Sarony and the American Mathew Brady, gave a new dimension to portrait photography. Their claim was that photographs, like traditional portrait paintings, could reveal the inner moral character of the subject and thereby instruct, amuse, and entertain. So great did the American public's demand for photographs of important people become that both photographers found themselves paying "personalities" to sit for them. For example, Sarony paid the actress Sarah Bernhardt a fee of $1,500 for the privilege of taking her photograph.[12]

Karsh openly admitted that, for him, personalities had "a great glamour." As he told an interviewer in 1940, he possessed an enormous respect for "the people who accomplish things; who are more interested in giving than receiving."[13] He claimed that his desire "to photograph the great people of this earth" came from his experience of the Armenian massacres that "intensified my feelings for the suffering," and, he continued, "taught me *something* of the depths of life and the heights of life."[14] It was Karsh's sense of empathy that prompted him to believe that he had the ability to reveal the soul of his subject through the medium of photography. "There is a brief moment when all that there is in a man's mind and soul and spirit may be reflected through his eyes, his hands, his attitude," Karsh maintained in 1966. "This is the moment to record. This is the elusive moment of truth."[15]

As his early scrapbooks show, Karsh had long studied the photographs of actors, politicians, and other people of achievement whose images appeared at regular intervals in publications like *Vanity Fair*. He not only felt that photographing these individuals would enable him to celebrate, as he put it, "the people who make things happen."[16] He also knew that photographing a famous person was more lucrative than recording a baby, a débutante, or a wedding party. Moreover, establishing a reputation as a photographer of the famous would allow him to distinguish himself from the run-of-the-mill studio photographers around him. Susan Sontag may have been right in claiming that a photograph confers importance on the individual being photographed,[17] but Karsh knew that in photographing a "personality" he also conferred importance on himself.

Although Karsh developed a degree of independence while working for John Powis, he nevertheless needed a break if he was to follow in the footsteps of photographers like Brady and Sarony. His break came in the autumn of 1932 and it happened at the Ottawa Little Theatre.

BY THE MIDDLE OF the 1920s, there were little theatre groups in every city across the country. Some produced plays by Canadian playwrights, others focused on the English and French classics, while still others stuck to the more popular drawing-room comedies. These amateur dramatic societies had little interaction with one another until April 1933. That year the winners of the annual regional drama festivals met in Ottawa and, using the premises of the Ottawa Little Theatre, competed for the Bessborough Trophy.

Conceived in 1932, the Dominion Drama Festival was the brainchild of Lord Bessborough. The Governor General wanted to do two things through this annual event. First, raise the standards of amateur theatre in Canada by hiring British dramatists to adjudicate the regional and national competitions. And second, help define and contribute to Canada's national identity by encouraging Little Theatre groups to produce Canadian plays.

During the week-long festival the regional groups not only staged plays, they also had a good time. They saw as many productions as possible, they attended tea and cocktail parties, and, on the final evening, they donned their dinner jackets or long evening dresses and joined the festival's officials for dinner at Government House. As one observer caustically noted, the festival was the "grand social affair of the year rather than...a review of the country's work in the theater."[18]

There is some evidence to suggest that, even before the founding of the Dominion Drama Festival, Powis was taking photographs of the Ottawa Drama League's performances, which were staged on a regular basis at Ottawa's Little Theatre. Certainly, by 1932, Karsh had become acquainted with the Drama League, which occupied Ottawa's former Eastern Methodist Church. In the autumn of that year a friend, either Lysle Courtenay or another photographer, Johan Helders, had taken him to a performance of *La Belle de Haguenau*.

Karsh's introduction to the Ottawa Drama League marked the turning point—some might even say the real beginning—of his career. For one thing, he was introduced to the city's elite. Among its performers, designers, directors, and audience were the Governor General, Lord Bessborough, the former prime minister, Sir Robert Borden, and other past and present high-ranking officials in the government. As one observer in Montreal noted sarcastically, "the average citizen of Ottawa knows very little of the Drama League, except that it is a 'highbrow,' and...snobbish organization for the edification of the 'creme de la creme.'"[19] Other commentators were critical for different reasons: in their view, the Ottawa Drama League mounted nothing but mediocre, workmanlike and, above all, safe, non-controversial plays.

On his first visit to the Little Theatre in the autumn of 1932, Karsh not only met some of Ottawa's most illustrious citizens. Following the performance of *La Belle de Haguenau* he was taken backstage where he met the production's leading lady—and his future wife.

This is how Karsh later recalled his encounter with Solange Gauthier in her dressing room: "There reclined an attractive young woman, with one foot pointed towards the ceiling as she pulled on a stocking. She threw a gay smile at her friend, and also at the funny foreign-looking boy who accompanied him, and being Solange, shouted in her rich accent: 'Well, if you *will* come into my dressing-room when I'm pulling on my stockings —' and went right ahead with the other one in her uninhibited fashion."[20]

Solange Gauthier was Karsh's senior by eight years. She could claim illegitimate descent in an earlier generation from the French writer Anatole France. Solange, along with her parents and her brother, had left Tours, in the Loire region of France, when she was a young girl. According to Karsh, once Solange arrived in Canada she boarded in convents until, at the age of fourteen, she moved to an English-speaking high school in Ottawa. It was at this point that her mother's friend, the well-known journalist Madge Macbeth, introduced the teenager to the Junior Drama League. And it was from this group

Les Soeurs Guedonec
(Solange on left), 1936

that Solange progressed to Ottawa's Little Theatre, where she not only acted in but directed several plays in her native tongue.

When Yousuf met Solange in 1932, her father had recently died and her mother, Héloise Gauthier, was teaching French at Ottawa's prestigious Elmwood School for Girls in the leafy suburb of Rockcliffe. Solange herself was earning her living as a secretary to one of the Members of Parliament from Quebec. She had been married, briefly, but now lived with her mother.

Solange had reputedly turned down offers of a career in the professional theatre and in films because "French girls of good families in those days didn't go on the stage!"[21] Yet, even though she was an accomplished actress and stage director she was not, according to one friend, outstanding. Nor did the diminutive and very energetic woman possess the looks that would have enabled her to become a star. Solange realized that she was no beauty but fully appreciated how to dress and present herself. She wore loosely fitted flowing garments and knew how to use her elongated grey-blue eyes and even her unattractive hands to best advantage. No one who met Solange Gauthier failed to be impressed. George Nakash's young daughter, Vivian, found Solange to be "an exciting woman."[22] Karsh's later assistant, Peter Miller, singled out Solange's "deep and

rather hoarse" voice, which enabled her to "coo like a dove or speak in a tone that stings like a whip."[23] And Karsh's cousin, Raymond Setlakwe, praised not only Solange's cooking but also her wit, intelligence, and social skills.[24]

It is not surprising that Karsh, as Solange came to call him, became good friends with the lively actress. They were both New Canadians who wanted to be accepted by the establishment yet were determined to maintain their difference rather than assimilate into the Anglo-Canadian norm. (Although proud to be a Canadian, Solange was fiercely proud of her French ancestry.[25])

Both Yousuf and Solange had something else in common: they liked people, particularly important people, and knew how to get to them and to make them their best friends. Moreover, they were less interested in amassing a fortune than in seeking fame. Like so many other New Canadians, what Solange and Yousuf wanted more than anything else was to be accepted by their adopted country. If Karsh became the most famous photographer in the country, and if he and Solange associated with the famous, this could be achieved.

Before their marriage Karsh wrote to a friend that Solange had "no claim to beauty nor prettiness."[26] After it, he noted that she possessed all of the attributes that he most admired: she was an individual, an eccentric who possessed an expressive face.[27] If Karsh had continued to say why he was attracted to Solange, he might have added that he liked her "flair for fun," her unfailing interest in people, and her sound business sense, all of which she would eventually put to good use in the Karsh studio.[28] He would probably have also agreed with Solange's friends who called her "a first class snob" yet admired her for treating everyone, no matter how important or humble, with equal courtesy.[29]

From the moment she met Karsh in October 1932, Solange claimed that she had "the greatest belief in him."[30] She also saw that there was a dark side to Karsh's personality. He was often glum and depressed. And he was a loner. Solange later told Karsh's brother Jamil, "So few people really know him."[31] Solange also knew that, just like herself, Karsh was no looker. By the time she met him he had lost most of his hair. Moreover, he was short compared to most Anglo-Canadian men, though taller than Solange's five-foot-two. He wore thick-lensed glasses to read and to adjust the focusing lens on his camera. None of his features, Solange also noted, were perfect. And yet when Karsh smiled, Solange recalled, "you will think he is the most charming man you have ever met."[32]

Karsh's appealing demeanour, along with his enormous potential and unrelenting ambition, made the sophisticated older woman take immediate interest in the young photographer. She introduced him to the actors, directors, and board members of the Ottawa Drama League, among whom were the Governor General and his young son, Viscount Duncannon.

One false step that Solange took was to encourage Karsh to tread the boards himself, in a play called *See Naples and Die*. His performance was let down by the fact that although the role demanded him to do little more than play a game of chess, it became clear to the audience that the young actor knew nothing about the game. Worse, at the end of the play, when Karsh and his chess partner were scripted to shoot a general, his partner's revolver got lodged in his pocket with the result that he shot *himself* in the leg.

More promising by far was another of Solange's initiatives. It was she who made it possible for Yousuf to become the official photographer of the Ottawa Drama League in 1932. As Karsh told an interviewer in 1945, one of the first Ottawa Drama League productions that he photographed, shortly after meeting Solange, was *Hamlet*.[33] Lord Duncannon, on vacation from Cambridge University, had taken the leading role, alongside the Ottawa socialite and amateur actress Julia MacBrien. Exercising his interest in the theatre, and his position as the honorary president of the league, Lord Bessborough designed the spare module stage sets and attended most of the rehearsals. And Karsh, most likely under the aegis of John Powis, took photographs of the actors during the rehearsal.[34]

In supporting the Governor General's hobby, Karsh acquired unique access to him on easy terms — unique, at that time, for an Armenian immigrant. During the league's rehearsals, Karsh often sat with Lord Bessborough. The Governor General "advised him about theatrical photography techniques."[35] As Karsh told members of the Montreal Women's Club in 1943, "I, upon his suggestion, made notes of the exact lines which I felt would be photogenic." Then, during the interval, Karsh would ask the actors to recreate the "photographic moments" that he had noted in his written cue. In the league's production of *Romeo and*

Juliet in the autumn of 1933, this was how Karsh captured the moment when, upon entering the Capulets' tomb, Romeo uttered the words "Thus I enforce thy rotten jaws to open."[36] In this way Karsh was realizing Bessborough's intentions as much as his own.

In April 1933, Karsh became the official photographer for the debut of the Dominion Drama Festival. He now met the country's future and first Canadian-born Governor General, Vincent Massey. Karsh was also introduced to the provinces' lieutenant-governors, the prime minister, the leader of the opposition, and provincial premiers, all of whom sat on the festival's board. Karsh never made much money in his capacity as the festival's official photographer. His fee — one dollar per print — hardly covered the printing costs. Moreover, it was hard work. He had to attend as many evening and matinee performances as his studio schedule would allow. He spent many late evenings developing prints of that day's performance in order to provide the country's newspapers and weekly magazines with photographic copy the following day.

Romeo and Juliet,
1933

If he was lucky, as with the Dominion Drama Festival photographs he sent to *Mayfair* in 1933, his photographs would appear with the byline "Photographs by Karsh, Ottawa." If he was not, as was the case when he submitted photographs to *Saturday Night* during the same festival, his photographs were attributed to the studio of John Powis.[37] (*Saturday Night* did, however, publish one photograph under Karsh's name in 1933. It was a portrait of the British adjudicator, Rupert Harvey, and the festival's first president, Colonel Osborne.[38])

When Karsh photographed Duncannon in the leading role of *Romeo and Juliet* for *Saturday Night* several months later, things were different. Thanks to *Saturday Night*'s social editor Adéle M. Gianelli, Karsh was brought to the attention of the magazine's editor. B. K. Sandwell, who, along with Vincent Massey, was a leading cultural nationalist, told Karsh that he was "delighted with the photos."[39] Karsh was not only happy with the praise. He liked the magazine's high-quality glossy stock paper and the way in which his five photographs were laid out. He also liked the accompanying text, which described his work as "excellent photographic glimpses."[40] Above all, Karsh was pleased to have all of the photographs explicitly attributed to himself.

Following the publication of the photographs from *Romeo and Juliet* in January 1934, Karsh was given a large order from Government House for additional prints. In Sandwell, he had come to the notice of one of the most influential editors in the country, and, as Karsh proudly told John Garo, it looked as though his photographs would be published "all over the continent."[41]

Karsh was hardly exaggerating. Two of his prints from the play were about to be published in the popular British magazine *The Sketch*.[42] This was a fitting venue for a photograph of Duncannon because, like *The Tatler* and *The Illustrated London News*, *The Sketch* featured "photographic glimpses" of the British aristocracy at plays, masked balls, hunts, and society weddings. And when Karsh's photographs appeared, they were accompanied with the byline "Karsh, Ottawa" or "Karsh—Ottawa." This was, of course, the sort of exposure that Karsh needed if he was going to distinguish himself from other local—and, indeed, from other international—photographers.

When the second Dominion Drama Festival came around in 1934, Karsh was commissioned to take photographs of twelve plays. As in the previous year, *Saturday Night* did not allow one of its staff photographers, "Jay"—Thomas George Jaycocks—to dominate the photograph section of the magazine with candid shots taken with his 35-mm Leica camera. Rather, Yousuf Karsh and his 8-by-10-inch studio camera got the lion's share of the work. Sandwell published Karsh's photograph of the festival's adjudicator, James T. Grein, and five other photographs in a special feature. This time Karsh's name was not consigned to the bottom of the photographs. "Camera Study by Karsh, Ottawa" indicated that this article was as much about the photography of Karsh as about the plays his photographs captured. Karsh's festival debut in *Saturday Night* did not end here. In mid-May, his work dominated the magazine again: along with a formal portrait of the directors of the festival were photographs that captured no fewer than seven performances.[43] And in June, *Mayfair* published even more of his festival photographs.

KARSH WAS CERTAINLY not the first or the last photographer to benefit from his exposure to the theatre. Britain's Cecil Beaton and, later, Lord Snowdon, and

America's Richard Avedon, all owed a debt to the theatre. Even the Flemish portrait painter Rembrandt enhanced his understanding of light and of character by making his apprentices perform theatricals.

Like that of many photographers, Karsh's association with the theatre was due, in part, to the increasing popularity of the cinema. In an effort to reclaim their audience from the growing popularity of the movie theatre, professional and amateur theatrical companies all employed photographers to take "stills" of the actors and to take "highlights" of the dramatic action. These publicity photographs were published in the program, they were used for display in the lobby of the theatre, and, in order to advertise the play, they appeared in the press.

Photographers quickly discovered that not only did they have a new outlet for their work, but the very act of taking pictures during a theatrical performance introduced a new visual language. For one thing, by the 1930s most theatres were using dimmers, tungsten lights, compact consoles, and light boards. The intensification and distribution of stage lighting revealed forms, produced shadows, gave the illusion of nature, and contributed to the dramatic action. Every photographer who worked in the theatre quickly came to appreciate the extent to which the dark areas of the stage were as significant as the illuminated areas. And to see the various ways in which light could alter the actor's projection of a character by reflecting, absorbing, highlighting, selecting, transmitting, and refracting. And how placing a spotlight directly above an actor's head could give the face a skull-like appearance. And, conversely, how floodlights—particularly tungsten lights—could make a face look gaunt or emaciated.[44]

Another crucial factor for any photographer who worked in the theatre was the presence of the audience—the third eye of any photograph. Equally relevant was the extent to which dress and costume, along with the instruction of the director, could transform an actor's projection of a character. It was in the theatre that Karsh not only learned that a good picture was dependent on the photographer's skillful manipulation of the lights, the camera lens, and the negative in the darkroom. It was here, too, that he came to see how the subject and photographer interacted during the sitting.

Karsh gave various accounts of the ways in which his introduction to the Ottawa Drama League and Dominion Drama Festival changed his life. Talking to a reporter in 1947, he claimed that he "became enamored with the great possibility of stage lighting and it is from this that I have developed my present technique of lighting subjects."[45] Speaking to a group of photographers at a conference a few years later, he said that he "was amazed to see what a clever stage director could do with lights."[46]

Admittedly, George Nakash had introduced Karsh to some basic electric lighting techniques in the mid-1920s. But as Karsh later claimed, "the theater was my introduction to the use of artificial light."[47] Writing in his memoir in the early 1960s, he reinforced this point by noting how he discovered that "Mood effects could be created, selected, modified, [and] intensified" by the use of light.[48]

During the last decade of his life, Karsh underplayed these earlier claims when he told the art historian Lilly Koltun that he had had to adapt theatrical lighting to his own system because it did "not translate well alone for general pleasure" and thereby required augmentation.[49] That Karsh was using natural, in conjunction with artificial, light in the studio long after being introduced to the theatre, however, is almost certain. As he told a reporter in 1942, the absence of a skylight would have made the camera room look like "a padded cell."[50]

Lysle Courtenay, 1933

Taking photographs at the Dominion Drama Festival also introduced Karsh to new ways of seeing. A comparison of Karsh's 1933 portrait of his friend Lysle Courtenay with the much-reproduced photograph of Romeo and Juliet taken a few months later shows how, within a very short period of time, Karsh had moved from being a devotee of the Pictorialist style, practised by Garo, to being a practitioner of the New Objectivity. That style eschewed the Pictorialist tendencies — both compositionally and formally — which made photographic images mirror the qualities of a painting, etching, or drawing. Rather, the followers of New Objectivity were concerned with sharp definition, stark contrasts, and what the Pictorialists felt was an austere presentation of whatever subject was to be captured.

Taking photographs in a theatre where the lights had been set by someone else also made Karsh ask questions — and find answers — as to how the director and his lighting assistants got the effects they did. As he said much later, he

had been "impressed by the versatility of the director's being able to create moods with the use of spotlights and filters and floodlights."[51] Watching the director during the rehearsal of a play was equally instructive. It made Karsh realize that he had to become more of a participant than an observer in the camera room. Thus photography was not only about adjusting the lights and focusing the camera lens. It was about creating a rapport with the subject. It was also, as Lilly Koltun has eloquently noted, about valuing the "immediate, instantly transparent message, communicated on the surface unambiguously, delivering a narrative moment through face, gesture, eyes, hands and body."[52]

Karsh showed that he was capable of doing all of these things when he made a formal portrait for *Saturday Night* of Julia MacBrien, who had played Duncannon's Juliet and his Desdemona at the Ottawa Little Theatre.[53] An accomplished actress, MacBrien knew how to respond to a director's instructions. And when she posed for Karsh, who "directed" her in the autumn of 1933, she helped him produce a stunning portrait.

Julia MacBrien, 1933   Karsh became so accomplished at directing his subjects that he got a reputation for being somewhat of a bully. But bossing people around in order to get the results he wanted usually worked, because his instructions were always couched in his famous charm. "They talk to him much as they would talk to their doctor," a reporter observed in 1942, adding, "He talks to them the way most doctors wouldn't dare and there are no hard feelings because it's all in the interest of art."[54]

The theatre not only taught Karsh how to get the best out of his subjects. It also gave him a greater appreciation for the middle tones of a print. It taught him how to infuse his portraits with a sense of drama by juxtaposing light and dark areas of the print in order to create a tension that would not otherwise be there. This high-contrast approach to photography would become Karsh's trademark, his signature for the next thirty years.

BY THE MIDDLE OF THE 1930s, Karsh's theatrical photographs were appearing regularly in newspapers and magazines in Britain as well as in Canada. They were displayed in the windows of stores like T. Eaton Company in Toronto. And

drama groups, like Toronto's Hart House Theatre, bought Karsh's photographs of their productions in order to have a record of their performance.

Although working as a photographer for the amateur theatre was hardly remunerative, it was rewarding. Karsh built a large audience for his work. He met the woman, Solange Gauthier, with whom he who would share the next twenty-eight years of his life. In the process, his formal portrait work acquired a sharper focus, a greater delineation of detail, and more tonal contrast and Karsh himself gained a better understanding of the tension that existed between the photographer and the subject. Above all, as he told John Garo in 1938, "meeting these personalities and the prestige one gains makes it well-worth doing."[55] Karsh had thus succeeded in establishing connections with his future patrons and his future clientele. After his first year in Ottawa, there was certainly no doubt in his mind that his relocation to the capital of Canada had been a good move.

Court Photographer

Being a professional portrait photographer in the early 1930s was not unprofitable. Employees with secure jobs—and that meant most of the professional classes in bureaucratic Ottawa—had more spending power for small luxuries and services. So, in spite of the Depression, there was a never-ending demand for photographs of children, brides, débutantes, and graduates, and to commemorate other events that marked the various stages of North Americans' lives. In addition to this, the public was hungry for visual images of its heroes, be they royalty, statesmen and stateswomen, athletes, scientists, or film stars. And since magazines now had better layouts and used a better quality of paper and more sophisticated forms of reproduction, photographers were scrambling to get their work published. As a writer for *The American Annual of Photography* observed in 1927, professional photography had become "a large industry with many branches and as many specialists as there are fields."[1]

In May 1933 Yousuf Karsh made a short visit to Boston. He wanted his former teacher's blessing—and possibly even his advice—for a new enterprise. John Powis was retiring and Karsh wanted to take over his business. John Garo was supportive. And when Karsh returned to Ottawa, he thanked his former mentor for his "inspiration and enthusiasm."[2]

Karsh borrowed $1,200 from his Quebec-based cousins, Michel and Cali Setlakwe, and set up his photography business in John Powis's former studio. Located in the centre of town, the studio at 130 Sparks Street was close enough to the Parliament Buildings for Karsh to hear the carillon strike the quarter hour. He had enough money to cover the first month's rent and utilities and to pay for photographic equipment. This included an enlarger, chemicals and trays, spot and floodlights, film, various grades of papers for printing, and, most important of all, an 8-by-10-inch camera. But the loan from Karsh's cousins left nothing to pay for the cost of furnishing the small reception room that was located on the second floor of the building, right below his studio. Solange came up with a very inexpensive solution: orange crates could be transformed into furniture if they were covered with monk's cloth. As Karsh later recalled in his memoir, this gave him "some attractive but hardly either elegant or substantial furniture."[3]

By July 1933, after only three months in business, Karsh told George Nakash that he was "absolutely broke." Not only was it hard to find the landlord's rent, but other people were "after their money" too.[4] Hoping for some financial assistance from his uncle, Karsh made a trip to Sherbrooke. Nakash was sympathetic. He realized how very difficult it was to begin a business during the depths of the Depression. And, even though he could barely afford it, he advanced his twenty-two-year-old nephew a modest loan.

Three months later, Karsh learned to his dismay that the Sparks Street building was about to be demolished. He had sufficient funds to set up a temporary studio in nearby Metcalfe Street during the construction of the new building. Moreover, taking advantage of this initial inconvenience, he set out to design a studio to his own specifications.

Occupying two floors above Wright's flower shop, the new Karsh Studio consisted of a top-floor, skylighted camera room, a small reception room, finishing and developing rooms, and a small dressing room. Anyone who walked along Sparks Street would have known that a photographer had just moved into the new building because adjacent to the stairs leading to the second floor was a small display case with examples of Yousuf Karsh's work.

Initially, Karsh was the receptionist, the photographer, the developer, and the printer. No wonder he told his uncle, two months after visiting Sherbrooke, that he was "extremely busy."[5] Yet a look at Karsh's Studio Register during his first six months in business indicates that he had 139 sittings, barely one for every working day. Among his clients were businessmen, débutantes, brides, people wanting passport photographs, and his first diplomat, the Chinese consul, C. Chou. Karsh charged one dollar for a finished print—a bargain, when his competitors were asking up to four dollars. This fee covered the cost of materials and the time involved in taking the photograph and producing the finished print. If a client wanted an additional print or a photograph of another pose from the sitting, the cost was the same: one dollar.

Though Karsh complained to Nakash that his returns were "very limited," his gross income after just six months in business was over a thousand dollars. While this was enough to enable him to hire a secretary—at seventeen dollars a week—it would be some time before he could afford to employ a full-time assistant. When he needed extra help in the darkroom during the seasonal rushes, he simply hired a printer on a part-time basis.

At the end of 1933, after nine months in business, Karsh's Studio Register indicates that he had accumulated a respectable number of clients. The sitting fees, along with the royalties from selling his photographs to newspapers and magazines, had yielded a gross income of $4,000. This comprised total receipts, not net profit, but, generated during Karsh's first year and in the midst of the Depression, the sum represented a healthy turnover for a new business.

Karsh knew that he had to work hard if he was going to pay back the loans so kindly provided by his relatives and if he was going to keep up with the local competition. Out of the thirty-four Canadian photographers listed in the prestigious international publication *Who's Who in Pictorial Photography*, five were from Ottawa alone. Among the eleven portrait photographers based in the city, there was the long-established Ottawa Photographic Studios, a stone's throw away from Karsh's Sparks Street studio. There were also a host of other prominent photographers, including F. G. Ashton, E. W. Jackson, Clifford M. Johnston, Harold F. Kells, and Karsh's friend J. Alex Castonguay. With their long-standing clienteles and solid reputations, these photographers posed a direct challenge to the newly established Karsh Studio.

Yet Karsh was undaunted by the competition. When John Powis had set up his studio, he had taken over the clientele of the well-established William James Topley, who had photographed former prime minister Sir John A. Macdonald as well as several governors general. During Karsh's first two years on his own, he reminded government officials and magazine editors alike that his previous employer had photographed these and other local dignitaries. Similarly, in his newspaper advertisements introducing "Modern Photographs by Karsh" to the Ottawa public, Karsh declared that his studio was "now occupying the one-time studio of John Powis."[6]

In 1927, the prestigious journal *The American Annual of Photography* had rightly noted that there were many branches of photography that a budding photographer could pursue. When Karsh set up his Sparks Street studio, he had a clear idea of what kind of photographer he wanted to be. As one who left nothing to chance in the camera room or the darkroom, Karsh felt that documentary photography — in the style of such emerging photographers as England's Bill Brandt or France's Henri Cartier-Bresson — was not for him. And although his scrapbooks from the early 1930s are filled with magazine clippings of fashion photographs by the British photographer Cecil Beaton among others, this line of photography was not for Karsh either. First, it would have been difficult for him to operate as a fashion photographer from his Ottawa base. And, second, the independently minded Karsh would have had to dance to someone else's tune — in this case the design editor's.

From the time of his apprenticeships, Karsh had wanted to become a portrait photographer. And the way in which he now chose to advertise his new business indicates what kind of people he hoped to attract to his studio. He did not attempt to drum up business by using one of the popular catch slogans of the day: "Someone, somewhere, wants your photograph" or "Photographs live forever" or "Photographs never grow up."[7] Rather, Karsh chose to present himself to the public by promising to give them a modern, inexpensive, good, and, above all, pleasing portrait. "Entrust the details of your Bridal Portrait," went one advertisement in 1933, "to one who reveals the charm and beauty of the subject."[8]

From the outset, therefore, Karsh wanted to attract a higher class of clientele to his studio than did many of his competitors. By 1934, when he had photographed a number of the débutantes who had been presented to the Governor General at Rideau Hall, Karsh boasted, in another advertisement for the studio, that his photographs had "the distinction that is inseparable from their Excellencies' Drawing Room."[9]

Karsh not only sought to attract the well-heeled by advertising in the local newspaper; he also took a more direct approach. When he learned of a forthcoming society wedding or the presentation of a young woman to the Governor General at Rideau Hall, he asked the bride-to-be or the débutante for the privilege of commemorating the important event with a portrait. When la Comtesse de Dampierre moved to Ottawa in January 1937, Karsh wrote to her in prose that matched his polished manners: "Ever since your arrival in Ottawa, I have looked forward, with anticipation, to the honour of making some photograph studies of you and I hope that I may be so favoured in the future."[10] And when Karsh learned that Major M. F. Gregg, vc, had just been promoted, Karsh took "the liberty of suggesting that a most fitting memento of your appointment would be a modern, artistic photograph."[11]

Although Karsh did not like photographing children, he never missed an opportunity to do so. It was not beneath his dignity to remind a mother that her child was now old enough to sit for a portrait. Enclosed with his letter to the mother of one prospective client was a folder containing some examples of his photographs of infants. This, he told Mrs. Atwood, was offered in order to give "some idea of the type of work I enjoy doing of babies."[12]

Karsh's direct approach to prospective clients usually yielded positive results. Indeed, during his first decade in business, the bulk of Karsh's clientele were brides, débutantes, and babies.

Every client who climbed the stairs to the second-floor reception room at 130 Sparks Street was made to feel that his or her patronage was worth having. After the initial greeting, Karsh would attempt to set his clients at ease by talking about the portraits that hung on the walls of the reception room. This led to some general remarks about the prominent personalities he had photographed. This seemingly informal repartee enabled Karsh to discover how his client was going to react in the camera room. It also enabled Karsh to assess how he was going to capture the essence of the subject's personality in a single image.

During the course of the sitting itself, Karsh never allowed the conversation to flag. "My main object," he subsequently observed, "is to keep the sitter interested for the duration of the sitting."[13] If his client daydreamed or looked bored, Karsh would wave his brilliantly coloured focusing cloth over his head — a gesture that rarely failed to provide another point of conversation. Then he would re-emerge from his cover, lift his finger — he never said, "Hold it" — to indicate that the subject should maintain the pose. At this point all conversation would cease until the click-click of the shutter announced that the camera lens had opened and closed and the contours, the areas of light and shadow, and the grey tones in between had been recorded on the negative. Only then would Karsh allow conversation to resume — until, of course, he lifted his finger again.

Two Young Girls
with Doll and Glass
Ball, circa 1934

Observing Karsh in the camera room a few years later, a reporter told how the photographer skillfully "fascinated his sitters by his own conversation and display of energy to such an extent that it is impossible for them to be apathetic in front of his camera...While conversing fluently, telling stories, drawing out the subject, releasing him from his timidness," Karsh would literally leap around his camera and lighting equipment, "shifting and adjusting the focus and rise of the lensboard, touching, gesticulating and never betraying the slightest evidence of indecision."[14] Karsh did all of these things with no sense of urgency. In fact, the greater the pressure, the slower he performed his tasks.

Karsh made himself known to the Ottawa public not only in the camera room when he set up his business in the spring of 1933. In line with the view that exhibitions of photographs made the public better appreciate the artistic nature of the craft, Karsh took advantage of his introduction to the Ottawa Drama League. In the autumn of 1933, he got the league's permission to mount an exhibition in the foyer of the Little Theatre. Karsh was thrilled by the large attendance: within three days 1,500 people, including the former prime minister Sir Robert Borden, had viewed his work. He was also pleased, as he told his

uncle, that "much enthusiasm was expressed."[15] Two years later, in April 1935, Karsh exhibited another series of "Portrait Studies" in the same venue with the hope that it would bring in more business.[16] And a year after that the T. Eaton Company in Toronto gave him his first exhibition outside of Ottawa when they put on a modest display of Karsh's work from that year's Dominion Drama Festival, pronouncing them "among the finest theatrical photographs we have ever seen."[17]

These early exhibitions introduced Karsh's photographs to a wide range of people in the city. They brought him more prestigious clients like former prime minister Borden. And the reviews that Karsh received in the local press gave him free advertising. For example, one critic who attended Karsh's April 1935 exhibition pronounced the show "a stimulating display by a photographer who has a distinct flair for the medium of his expression and who obtains notable results by his skill in characterization." Though Karsh might not have been pleased with the reviewer's suggestion that it was "towards children's" photography that the photographer's "warmest inclinations" lay, this was, nevertheless, an astute observation.[18] The fact was that two years later, Karsh's portrait of an Ottawa infant was selected from some 90,000 photographs of babies in a competition in New York. Karsh attributed winning first prize to "luck" rather "than sheer artistry."[19] Whether he liked it or not, as a portrait of two young children holding a doll and a glass ball shows, he had as much ability to bring out the best in children as in adults.[20]

FROM THE MOMENT he set up business in the spring of 1933, Karsh was determined to put his name and his work in front of a national audience. He had already enjoyed seeing his photographs published in such Toronto-based national magazines as *Mayfair* and *Saturday Night*. And, according to his Studio Register, he continued offering his society portraits to other magazines and newspapers in Canada. This gave him tremendous exposure. As the American photographer Edward Steichen wrote of his monthly contributions to *Vogue* and *Vanity Fair*, "I have an exhibition every month that reaches hundreds of thousands of people through editorial and advertising pages."[21]

Karsh also continued to cultivate his friendship with the editor of *Saturday Night*. B. K. Sandwell not only published Karsh's photographs on a regular basis, he also introduced the young photographer to many dignitaries. In 1938, Sandwell sponsored an exhibition of Karsh's portraits outside of Ottawa. (Held initially at Robert Simpson Company department store in Toronto, the "Exhibition of Portrait and Pictorial Photography" by Yousuf Karsh then moved to the Convention Hall in Ottawa's Château Laurier Hotel.) And the same year, Sandwell commissioned the Ottawa-based writer Madge Macbeth to write a feature article on the twenty-seven-year-old photographer.

Madge Macbeth did Yousuf Karsh proud. It may have helped that she was a friend of Solange's, prompting sympathy for the new man in her life. In just a few hundred words, Macbeth told her readers about Karsh's dramatic escape from Turkey with his family. She noted his credentials: he had studied with his uncle in Sherbrooke, Quebec, and then with "the great Garo" in Boston. She told how, following Karsh's move to Ottawa, he had photographed theatrical productions, become an associate member of the Royal Photographic Society of Great Britain, and photographed "practically all the prominent people living in or passing through the Capital during the past five years." She made a stab at describing Karsh's "sensitive hands, and fine eyes, in which shadows of tragedy lurk." She noted how he became "as nervous as a prima donna before an important sitting."[22] If anyone doubted Karsh's skill as a photographer, they only had to look at the accompanying portrait by Karsh of Madge Macbeth. With its decorative background, its play on light and dramatic pose, the portrait gave the British society and fashion photographer Cecil Beaton a run for his money.

Karsh's exposure through the national press not only gave him a regular "exhibition," it also got him more clients. What débutante could refuse to engage the services of the man who had photographed Miss Diana Clark, the daughter of the British high commissioner and Lady Clark, for *Saturday Night* in 1934?[23] Certainly the message was clear: If you planned to attend the ball celebrating the opening of Parliament, you could do worse than to stop by the Karsh Studio in order to commemorate the event.

It should not be thought, however, that Karsh's published photographs were confined to portraits of women and children. He produced portraits of

successful politicians, businessmen, and other notables for the *Canadian Who's Who* and for the *Montreal Standard*'s "The Man of the Week" column.

What Karsh felt were his "first really important pictures," however, were taken in the late spring of 1935.[24] The subject was the Governor General, Lord Bessborough, whom Karsh had photographed a year earlier when he had taken a group portrait of the organizers of the Dominion Drama Festival, as well as taking the photographs of Bessborough's son in *Romeo and Juliet*. But Karsh wanted a private sitting with Bessborough and his wife. And Karsh wanted the sitting to take place in his Sparks Street studio, where he could control the light and create a setting that would be appropriate to his subjects' office.

Writing to Rideau Hall's comptroller in March 1934, Karsh noted that his previous employer, the recently retired John Powis, had photographed previous governors general and that Karsh wanted to carry on that tradition.[25] The comptroller asked Karsh to submit his curriculum vitae. Karsh followed his instructions. Then nothing happened for several months.

The Bessboroughs were the first vice-regal couple to agree to have their portraits made in a photographer's studio. Karsh clearly had a lot at stake. A successful outcome might allow him to use the words "By Appointment of Their Excellencies the Governor-General and Countess of Bessborough" in his advertisements and on his letterhead. It might induce other high-ranking officials and diplomats in the city to beat a path to his door. And it could also result — as with his portrait of Lord Duncannon — in international coverage in the press.

Lord and Lady Bessborough, 1935

Karsh willingly complied with the instructions he received from Rideau Hall before the sitting, in the early spring of 1935. Their excellencies required separate dressing rooms to change into their formal clothes. So Karsh dipped into his pocket and employed a carpenter to erect a wall within the existing one. They also needed a setting that was appropriate to their status. Karsh designed a curved set of stairs that his carpenter added to his list of work.

As Madge Macbeth had noted in her article for *Saturday Night*, Karsh was always anxious before an important sitting. This occasion was no exception. He was rightly nervous about his poor English — after photographing the

Governor General, Karsh asked him to "please *recline* in the reception room with my secretary" while he photographed Lady Bessborough. Karsh was also worried about getting the right camera settings, something he always did more by instinct than by any preconceived method. Indeed, Karsh was so nervous during the sitting that he failed to focus the camera properly. After developing the negatives, Karsh discovered to his horror that the photographs "were a complete fiasco."[26] Karsh wrote an apologetic letter to the Governor General in which he attributed his failure to nerves and requested another sitting. Lord and Lady Bessborough graciously agreed to visit the Sparks Street studio for a second time. Once again, a small crowd gathered at the entrance to the studio in order to catch a glimpse of the vice-regal couple. Once again Karsh lost a night's sleep. And, once again, he was nervous during the sitting.

This time, however, the results—full-length portraits of the couple together and individually—were successful. Standing on the first step of Karsh's modernist spiral staircase, the couple might have looked out of place. But they did not. Karsh drew on traditional forms of representation that had their origins in antiquity. Portrait artists often placed their subjects on a dais in order to raise them up above the normal viewing level. Equally, artists depicted royalty in full or, at the very least, three-quarter-length pose. Karsh did both of these things. He took full-length portraits from a low viewpoint—a perspective the Old Masters had reserved for reigning sovereigns and other nobility. He also departed from his sharply contrasting form of illumination and bathed their excellencies in light.

Karsh's photographs got the hoped-for reception. As with the previous photograph of Viscount Duncannon, the individual portraits of Lord and Lady Bessborough appeared in the British press. This time *The Tatler* gave Karsh's "excellent portraits" a full page.[27] He also got something that he had asked for the previous year: patronage as the official photographer of Canada's governors general.[28]

It is not surprising that when the next Governor General arrived in Ottawa, in 1936, their excellencies Lord and Lady Tweedsmuir were soon posing for Karsh. The interest previously shown in his photographs of the nation's most exalted dignitaries was repeated. And just like Karsh's "friendship" with Bessborough, he became a "friend" of Tweedsmuir's. Indeed, just a couple of weeks before Tweedsmuir's death in 1940, Karsh was to help the Governor General choose photographs for his autobiography, *Memory Hold-the-Door*.

Karsh plainly believed that he had much to gain from taking portraits of high-ranking statesmen and stateswomen; and he exploited his access when the opportunity arose. After learning that President Roosevelt and his son were about to visit Prime Minister William Lyon Mackenzie King and the new Governor General at the Citadel in Quebec, Karsh wrote to the comptroller of the household at Rideau Hall and requested a sitting.[29] Already a known quantity in the right circles, Karsh was allowed to travel to Quebec as a member of the press corps.

It was a splendid summer's day in July and after enjoying a state luncheon, the dignitaries walked outside the Citadel without their overcoats. The photographers jostled for space while taking their photographs. Karsh had hung back from the crowd. When the press photographers left he asked the dignitaries if they would pose again. The small group resumed their stiff pose. This would not do, however, for Karsh. So he pretended to take a photograph; then, just when they thought he had finished, they relaxed. This is when Karsh pressed the shutter of his camera. The result was stunning. The ailing American president, who was leaning discreetly on the arm of his son Elliott, had dropped his awkward demeanour. Canada's prime minister was laughing. And Lord Tweedsmuir, who was in the midst of telling the other three men a joke, was animated. The resulting photograph was published in newspapers throughout North America. And it received first-class marks from Karsh's mentor John Garo.

This success appears to have encouraged Karsh to experiment during his next engagement with Lord Tweedsmuir, whom he had previously photographed in formal Windsor dress. In 1938, Karsh told his friend Lysle Courtenay that he "felt the need of introducing something less stagy and less dramatic for court photographs" than the spiral staircase and fluted pillars.[30] Shortly after writing this, Karsh photographed Tweedsmuir without an imposing setting, without vice-regal dress, and without the harsh light that had eliminated every blemish from the faces of Lord and Lady Bessborough.

Karsh was emboldened to make a warts-and-all portrait on this occasion because he was not presenting his subject as the Governor General, but as John Buchan, the author of such thrilling detective novels as *Greenmantle* and *The Thirty-Nine Steps*. In this portrait, therefore, Buchan wears a comfortable-looking tweed jacket. Every line on his face, including the large, oval scar that dominated the left side of his forehead — the result of a fracture to the skull at the age of five — is depicted. And even Buchan's large-knuckled hands, which compete for the viewer's attention with his face, become a dominant feature of the portrait.

Karsh's portrait of John Buchan is an early example of what might be called vintage Karsh. All the traits that would distinguish his later work — the dark background, the high tonal contrast, and the sharp focus — were there. The only element remaining from his earlier vice-regal portraits was the low viewpoint. And this was necessary because it transformed Buchan, who weighed less than 130 pounds, into a powerful, rugged-looking man of action, thus matching the fictional heroes in his novels.

Lord Tweedsmuir,

W. L. Mackenzie King,

President Roosevelt, and

His Son, Elliott, 1936

PHOTOGRAPHING PERSONALITIES like Bessborough and Buchan helped to make Karsh's name known across Canada and introduced his work to the British public. The resulting sales of these portraits to newspapers and magazines added to his pocket book. But these kinds of commissions did little to build his reputation as an "artistic photographer," as he chose to describe himself to the editor of *Mayfair* in 1933.[31] This could only happen if Karsh won the respect of his peers.

Although, as his future wife Solange had observed when they met in 1932, Karsh was a loner, he did make an effort to acquaint himself with the local photographers in his midst. He became friends with the photographers Johan Helders, whom he photographed in his Sparks Street studio in 1938, and J. Alex Castonguay, who had photographed him in the same venue in 1933. Karsh became an active member of the Ottawa Camera Club, an organization that

since 1896 had brought professional and amateur photographers together to listen to visiting lecturers and to discuss one another's work.

But Karsh wanted wider approval for his work. He submitted what he felt were his "artistic photographs" to exhibitions and salons around the world. In 1935, for example, he proudly told Florence Nakash that he had several photographs accepted for display at the London Salon.[32] Equally, Karsh not only contributed to photographic society exhibitions in Canada and abroad, he also saw to it that his work was displayed in leading photography indexes and trade journals such as *Photograms of the Year* and *Popular Photography*.

Karsh had an opportunity to exhibit his work alongside that of prominent photographers from around the world. In 1934, he exhibited in the National Gallery of Canada's International Salon of Photographic Art. The inauguration of the annual exhibition was an important event for Karsh and other Canadian photographers. By having their work shown in an institution devoted to fine art, they received approval from the nation's foremost art gallery.[33]

John Buchan (Lord Tweedsmuir), 1938

Moreover, by showing his work with the art of local photographers like H. F. Kells and C. M. Johnston and one of the country's most imaginative photographers, Vancouver's John Vanderpant, not to mention international photographers like New York's Nicholas Haz, the twenty-five-year-old Yousuf Karsh demonstrated that he could hold his own ground against these and other, more established photographers. Because even though one critic felt that his contribution to the exhibition, "Outcast," was "rather somber as a whole," he had to admit that Karsh's photograph was "among the best of the nudes, notable for its perfect lighting."[34]

However complimentary the reviews, Karsh was not satisfied to let only the critics comment on his work. Whenever he had the opportunity, he did so himself. But Karsh knew that he was not a polished public speaker. He was aware that his knowledge of the English language was limited. So he took a novel approach to presenting his work in public.

Supported by the acting and linguistic skills of Solange Gauthier, Karsh presented his ideas in a short skit. *Photography—Your Side and My Side* was performed in May 1935 before a group of photographers in Toronto.[35] In the skit, Karsh demonstrated how he placed his female clients in a receptive mood in

order to get the best photographic results. During a mock appointment with a female client—Solange—he told his audience how he wanted a woman to present herself for a sitting. She should not arrive at the studio after having just visited the beauty salon or having put too much rouge on her cheeks. She should not wear a patterned dress. And, although women seemed to think that black made them look slimmer, black, in Karsh's view, was inappropriate for a portrait sitting. In fact, as he told a reporter for *Maclean's* magazine a few years later, black gave a haggard look to any woman, "whether she is 18 or 80."[36] Finally, no woman should ever come to his studio with the expectation that he would make her more attractive than she was.

A year later, in response to an invitation to speak at Ottawa's Rotary Club, Karsh solicited the help of Solange and her young friend the dancer Betty Low. Karsh began the skit, *The Kindly Eye of the Modern Camera*, by claiming that photography was "the most widely used and most progressive of all the arts of the present day." In order to reinforce his point, he talked about the various uses to which photography could be put by the medical and educational professions, not to mention the magazine and newspaper industries. Addressing his own specialty, portraiture, he told his audience that it was his aim "to be able to get behind the outward appearance of the man, to reach his mind and soul." "The conscious photographer tried, as much as possible," he continued in his introductory remarks, "to make the photograph convey all that and, in order that he may be sure of the results, the sitter must share all of the interest which the photograph holds for him."[37] Then, calling on his two assistants, Karsh demonstrated "the trials and tribulations," as a journalist attending the event put it, "which beset the path of the professional photographer"—especially while photographing a female client.[38]

Karsh pushed the limits of satire even further two years later when he and Solange performed another skit at a conference of photographers in Scranton, Pennsylvania. The skit revolved around a conversation between a photographer and his assistant as they prepared for the following day's work. A female client, whom Solange felt "must have been very good-looking at one time," but was now "fat, fair, and fiftyish," had asked if she could wear a black dress and pearls for her sitting. "Couldn't you tell her this could be alright for a tea party,"

Karsh replied, "but not suitable for a photograph?" Another woman was to sit for her portrait after an interval of ten years. Although Karsh remembered her as charming, it was "going to be a hard sitting" because his client had "a new crop of wrinkles and more flesh."

While women clearly offered Karsh the biggest challenge, he and Solange made it clear during their skit that men were not always easy subjects either. For example, a businessman who sat for his "Man of the Week" portrait had "several rolls of fat under his chin." Then there was another difficulty with male clients that had more to do with the photographer than with the subject. Karsh told his audience that photographers had a tendency to over-light their male subjects. And, he concluded, when photographers came to develop the print, they had "a tendency to be frightened of shadows and so the result is flat."[39]

In the various skits that he and Solange performed in Eastern Canada and the United States, Karsh revealed that he possessed a playful and sometimes wicked sense of humour; that he was a showman; that he had clearly defined expectations of his clients; and that his clients had expectations of him. He also demonstrated that he had a good grasp of the history of photography and of the many uses to which it could be put. The writer Louis Paul Flory had claimed in 1927 that photography had taken its place as a fine art.[40] Yousuf Karsh took the same view, and clearly thought of himself as an artist.

Even though Karsh presented himself as a portrait photographer, he wanted, as he told John Garo in 1935, "to devote more time to the artistic side of photography."[41] Certainly a work like his nude study "Outcast," which found its way to many exhibitions and salons, was of a more experimental nature. But doing more work of this sort required time. It also meant that Karsh had to expose himself to the experimental work of other photographers. He was, of course, familiar with the work of the photographers at the local camera club. But in 1934, Karsh was introduced to a broader range of work available to him through the National Gallery of Canada's annual exhibitions of photographs and through visits with the modernist photographer John Vanderpant, who always found his way to Karsh's studio when he was in the national capital. Even so, Ottawa was hardly a major centre of photography. But New York, a day's journey by train, certainly was, and in the spring of 1936 Karsh set out for New York City.

Karsh couldn't have visited New York at a better time. The Museum of Modern Art was holding a stunning exhibition of abstract art. Thanks to the New Deal's sponsorship of artists like Thomas Hart Benton, the city's post offices and other public buildings were decorated with murals depicting the history of the United States. Dorothea Lange had just taken her seminal photograph "Migrant Mother" in Nipomo, California, while she was creating images of dispossessed rural labourers for the United States Farm Security Administration. Photographers of a very different kind — Alfred Stieglitz and Paul Strand, among others — were, like Canada's John Vanderpant, turning mundane objects like fences and cabbages into serene, multilayered abstract pictures. New York's magazine industry was giving photographs more space than ever before in its publications. Indeed, by 1930, 80 percent of America's advertising agencies were using photographs in their work. Some magazines, like Condé Nast Publications' *Vogue* and *Vanity Fair*, were paying their photographers hefty fees — especially if the photographs were of personalities or fashion models. (The American photographer Edward Steichen could ask up to $1,000 for one of his spare and elegant fashion portraits.) Finally, the Museum of Modern Art admitted photographers to its galleries with the exhibition Murals by American Painters and Photographers, as Canada's National Gallery had done two years previously.

New York was not only the centre of photography. During the week that Karsh spent in the city, Katharine Cornell was acting in George Bernard Shaw's play *Saint Joan* at the Martin Beck Theatre. The Boston Symphony Orchestra, under the direction of Serge Koussevitzky, was performing the work of Jean Sibelius at Carnegie Hall. The famous conductor Leopold Stokowski was conducting the Philadelphia Orchestra at Carnegie Hall. The violinists Jascha Heifetz and the much younger Yehudi Menuhin, along with the pianist Artur Rubinstein, were about to give concerts. And an exhibition of tapestries designed by the French artist Georges Braque was on show at the Bignou Gallery. Little did Karsh know, as he walked around New York City, that all of these people would, within a few years, be sitting in front of his camera.

Armed with letters of introduction from John Garo and from the New York photographer Nicholas Haz, whom he had met in Ottawa two years earlier, Karsh visited the first photographer on his list. Pirie MacDonald was of French nationality but lived in New York. His letterhead indicated that he was a "Photographer of Men." In his capacity as the president of the Oval Table Society of New York, MacDonald was a frequent speaker at exhibitions of photography. Although Karsh found MacDonald to be "very impressive and interesting," he was disappointed that MacDonald did not show him his camera room. MacDonald did, however, show Karsh a number of his 11-by-14-inch prints, which he had made with glass-plate negatives. He also regaled the young Karsh with stories about photographing such personalities as Theodore Roosevelt and Edgar Wallace.

Karsh next met up with the artist, teacher, writer, and modernist photographer Nicholas Haz. Even before previously meeting Haz at the National Gallery's salon in 1934, Karsh had read his articles in the prestigious journal *Popular Photography*. Like many American-based photographers, Haz supported the notion that paintings were not the country's "best means of self-expression as a nation." Rather, it was, he continued, only through photographs, motion pictures, and architecture that "we can express ourselves best."[42]

When Karsh met Haz at the Master School of Photography in Rockefeller Plaza where he taught, the Hungarian-born photographer told him about the scientific and mechanical progress of photography. A devotee not only of the modernist movement but also of what Karsh called the "miniature camera," Haz was different from MacDonald, who believed that the best photographs were made with a large-format camera and a glass-plate negative. Haz arranged for Karsh to meet Martin Munkasci, a fashion photographer at *Harper's Bazaar*. Much to Karsh's surprise, Munkasci also took his own photographs with a 35-mm camera. Karsh was not, however, impressed with Munkasci's photographs, which he thought looked better in reproduction than they did when he examined them in the photographer's studio.

The high point of Karsh's visit to New York City was undoubtedly his meeting with Edward Steichen. Pirie MacDonald had written the letter that introduced Steichen to John Garo's former student. This was an important meeting for Karsh, who had admired Steichen's photographs since his student days in Boston. "It was like necessary food," he later recalled, "to turn to his pages in *Vogue* for inspiration."[43]

When Karsh visited Steichen's studio in April 1936, the Belgium-born photographer was the world's most famous portrait photographer. Yet this was not all. He had transformed the fashion industry by placing his models against uncluttered and blatantly artificial settings, and then photographing them by using innovative lighting. In 1932, he had produced a forty-foot-long enlargement of skyscrapers, dams, bridges, tunnels, and railroads for the Center Theatre at Radio City. In the same year, his photo mural of the George Washington Bridge was exhibited at the Museum of Modern Art. If all of this wasn't enough to impress the young Yousuf Karsh, Steichen was the highest-paid photographer in the world. When Karsh met him, he had an annual income of over $100,000. Most of this came from *Vanity Fair*, for his portraits of prominent people, and from *Vogue* for his fashion photographs.

Steichen greeted Karsh dressed in a khaki shirt and trousers and wearing his bedroom slippers. "I made very slow progress with him," Karsh told Garo after the meeting, "because I feel he is a man who has far more work than he can take care of, and therefore, interviews such as mine are a regular nuisance."[44] Though Steichen's time was clearly limited, he did not shortchange the young photographer. Convinced that photography was a means of self-expression, he cautioned Karsh against following the "painter's point of view"—at least until he had a good grasp "of the optical, chemical and scientific side of photography."[45] He talked about the "psychology" of portraiture: the photographer not only had to understand his or her subject but had to put them at ease.[46] He told Karsh how to go about meeting the famous personalities. (Steichen was a consummate self-promoter and adept at constructing identities for his clients.[47]) He entertained Karsh with stories about some of the people he had photographed. And, finally, he left no doubt in Karsh's mind that the camera was a suitable medium for artistic expression.

Karsh not only listened to what Steichen told him, he also asked questions. He asked if a young photographer like himself should take on what he called "photography publicity." "While magazines may give you some help with technical information," Steichen replied, "their main purpose is to create the desire and curiosity to experiment on your own—and that is what really counts!"[48] Even so, Steichen insisted that the artistic side of photography was not necessarily out of kilter with commercial work. After all, he had furthered his own reputation—and his marketability—in the commercial world because the advertisers who employed him felt that the effectiveness and the sincerity of their advertisements were enhanced by the very fact that Steichen was an artist.

Karsh returned to New York City two years later, in the spring of 1938. He met Steichen for a second time. He travelled to Rochester, New York, and visited the Eastman Plant and the Defenders Plant, which specialized in one area that Karsh hoped soon to explore: colour photography. And he spent two days with Nicholas Haz.

The two men had obviously hit it off during Karsh's first visit to New York, because a few months later Karsh arranged for Haz to give a lecture, "Portraiture and Figure Photography," at the National Gallery of Canada. Taking advantage of Haz's presence in Ottawa during the autumn of 1936, Karsh also took lessons from him in "Abstract Designs."[49]

Karsh insisted that his second trip to New York was "very inspiring" even though he left almost no record of the visit.[50] Both visits to New York, however, had a profound influence on his work. He produced experimental photographs like "Elixir" and "The Fringe of Winter's Mantle." And, following his short study of abstract art with Haz and his second visit to New York, he produced "City of Straws," which demonstrates that even if Karsh did not attend the exhibition of abstract art on show at the Museum of Modern Art in the spring of 1936, by the end of the decade he had grasped the principles of non-representational art.

Picasso said that "a true artist never copies nature; neither does he imitate it. He merely allows imaginary objects to dress themselves with the appearance of things real."[51] "City of Straws," which Karsh produced in 1940, did just that. "My first glimpse of New York," was, Karsh wrote, "something between a wondrous dream and a terrible nightmare; something unreal." Four years later, Karsh found a way of portraying these mixed feelings when a member of his staff placed a box of straws on the table. Karsh began pulling one, then another, straw out of the box. "Before I realized it I was…evolving my own interpretation and just the upper structure of a great and ephemeral metropolis."[52] Karsh then took the box to the camera room, set up his lights, and pressed the shutter. The resulting photograph transformed the box of soda-fountain straws into a dignified and powerful abstract image. As one writer noted when he viewed the photograph, there were not too many nor too few straws; they were not centred nor too near to the edges of the photograph. The tone values which went from grey and black to white were rich. The depth and volume were good and the rhythm was free.[53] Karsh produced his final print on glossy paper. This brought out the waxy texture of the straws and revealed something of the haunting mystery that he had felt when he first saw the skyscrapers in New York City.

Making photographs like "City of Straws" reinforced Karsh's efforts to become an "artistic photographer." His visits to New York, where he had rubbed shoulders with the most successful photographers in the business, made him feel that he was part of a wider community of photographers. These kinds of contacts would have an enormous impact on his career. His use, for example, of grey and black vertical background panels, his later involvement in commercial photography, and his experimental works like "City of Straws" were

City of Straws, 1940

all inspired by what he saw in New York or learned from Nicholas Haz. Even Karsh's 1941 portrait of Winston Churchill was influenced by his encounter with "the Great Steichen," who had photographed Churchill in 1933. It was not just flattery that prompted Karsh to tell Steichen that the meeting was "a great inspiration for a young man to build his career upon."[54] It was the truth. Steichen had given Karsh confidence and reassurance that he was on the right track.

Marriage

Karsh could afford to devote more time to his experimental work and take time off to visit New York because, during the last four years of the 1930s, business was booming. The early volumes of the leather-bound order books in which he recorded the sittings (from back to front, in Arabic style) show that by 1936 twice as many people climbed the stairs to his Sparks Street studio as in 1933. And they were paying more for the privilege of being photographed. A single print by Karsh now cost $3.15 instead of one dollar, and by 1938 that fee would triple again, to $9.50 for a 5-by-7 ⅓-inch photograph; if a client wanted an 8-by14-inch print in 1938, the fee was $35.00. And while residents in Ottawa got their photographs at a reduced price, Karsh was reluctant to lower his fee for anyone else (as J. M. Smith of Brigdens Ltd. in Toronto discovered when he asked for a discount in 1937).

In 1934 Karsh's net profit (or taxable income) was already a decent $3,000. The next year, however, it rose to over $4,000, with a gross income of $10,000 and costs of running the studio at $6,000. As the bulky ledger books that reconciled every balance to the last penny indicate, his income was to remain at that level for the next four years.

With money to spare, Karsh hired a female and a male assistant to join the secretary, Jean McJanet, whom he had engaged in the early 1930s. He paid off the loan from his cousins, adding 5 percent interest to the original amount. He increased the sum of money that he had been sending to his parents in Aleppo, Syria. And he gave financial assistance — as well as sympathetic recognition — to the two men who were most responsible for his success: John Garo and George Nakash.

In September 1936, John Garo's wife was ill and her husband found himself "in a temporary jam."[1] Karsh came up with $200. A year later, Garo himself was ill and general business, as he told his former apprentice, was "still rotten as usual."[2] Karsh dipped into his pocket once again.

Then there was Aziz George Nakash. In the middle of the 1930s, he relocated from Sherbrooke to Montreal, where he hoped to establish a photography studio. The move cost him "great anxiety," Karsh told Garo, because Nakash was "not the man for the big city."[3] Using his connections with the editor of *Saturday Night*, Karsh asked B. K. Sandwell to commission his uncle to take society photographs for the weekly magazine. He also made use of Solange Gauthier's connections with Members of Parliament from Quebec, encouraging them to seek out his uncle in Montreal.

By 1937 Nakash was back on his feet. Initially, he was employed in T. Eaton Company's photography department, where he took an incredible thirty-five portraits a day. Not happy working for someone else, he opened his own studio again, first on fashionable Sherbrooke Street, then on Ste. Catherine Street. Nakash ran The Nakash Studio — Artistic Portraits until 1974. He was over eighty when he closed the doors of the studio.

Though Karsh frequently complained that his own finances were often strained during the 1930s, there were sufficient funds to enable him to upgrade the facilities in his Sparks Street premises. "Now I have a very practical and efficient studio," he told John Garo in December 1936, shortly after taking possession of his renovated workplace.[4]

Karsh was aware, as J. Vincent Lewis noted in the 1927 issue of *The American Annual of Photography*, "that the livelihood of the professional photographer depended upon his customers and that if he was to attain any degree of success in his business he had to please them."[5] Until the middle of the 1930s, Karsh worked within the Pictorialist tradition of photography, often romanticizing his images. He also knew, from having studied the paintings of the Old Masters, that most portrait artists had followed one of two routes. Either, like the seventeenth-century painter Anthony Van Dyck, they had produced flattering images that invariably pleased their clients. Or, they had produced immensely vital, immediately convincing, albeit decidedly unflattering, realistic studies in the manner of Hans Holbein. When Karsh told an interviewer in 1940 that his work was directed towards bringing out "the strength and personality" of his male clients and "the charm and beauty" of his female subjects, there was no doubt as to which camp he inhabited.[6]

Such artistic aspirations depended on technique for their fulfillment. In the autumn of 1936, Karsh approached Siegmund Blumenfelt, who worked for the famous William Notman Photographic Firm in Montreal, to help him with a task that he had previously performed himself: retouching negatives. The process was time consuming. Working directly on the negative, the photographer would increase areas of density with a pencil or brush — thus eliminating blemishes or shadows — or conversely reduce areas of density by scraping the negative with a sharply bladed knife.

"I do not like very fine retouching," Karsh told Blumenfelt, to whom he offered fifteen cents for every negative he retouched. And Karsh added, "under no circumstances should the character be wiped out."[7] Karsh never stooped, like Cecil Beaton, to reducing waist lines in the retouching room or to adding eyelashes that the client had failed to flutter to the camera. Karsh knew all too well that a heavy-handed retouching job could contaminate a photograph and thereby vitiate the verisimilitude that he was after. Even so, he did believe that with sufficient skill the "optical 'intruders,'" as he chose to call them, could be eliminated.[8]

Blumenfelt was thus free, for example, to delete any lines on the neck or tone down any highlights that struck the shoulder. (Using a black-inked pen, Karsh had indicated the areas to be corrected on the proof.) But Blumenfelt was not to eliminate the lines that appeared around the nose or the lips or under the eyes — unless, of course, Karsh had told him to do so. And if Blumenfelt was uncertain as to whether a negative needed more retouching than Karsh indicated on the proof, he was to leave that decision to his boss.

Blumenfelt evidently possessed the light touch that Karsh wanted, because he was soon offered a permanent position in the Karsh Studio. The initial agreement was that he be paid twenty-five dollars a week. The significance of Blumenfelt's contribution, however, is shown by the fact that before long he was given a raise of 30 percent, putting him on the handsome salary of $1,680 a year, little short of half of what Karsh himself was earning. Karsh evidently realized the foundations of his new-found prosperity.

Success did not come without stress. Karsh was a worrier. He fretted when business was slow. He complained to Nakash when outside photographers appeared to be "grabbing" all they could during the opening of Parliament.[9] And he worried about all of the people — Garo, Nakash, and his family back in Aleppo — who had a financial claim on his hard-earned profits.

Not one to rest on his laurels, Karsh continued to work hard. So did his employees. They were on the premises from 8 a.m. to 6 p.m., six days a week. Indeed, the only time that they ever seemed to relax was during the airing of Karsh's favourite radio program. "If he was in town," his future sister-in-law Barbara Karsh recalled, "he would come up and work with the prints and so on when *The Happy Gang* was on."[10] Generally, however, Karsh kept his distance and his worries from his staff.

Although he did not have as many sittings a day as his uncle, Karsh was frequently tired to the point of exhaustion. Vacations were few and far between. And they were never taken for more than a few days. In the winter, Karsh travelled to a little farmhouse a few miles from Ottawa where he did nothing but sleep, eat, ski, and take long walks in the mountains. In the summer he found relaxation at the Hotel La Clairere in Quebec. Here he maintained a strict regimen. The day began with a swim in the nude. Before lunch he played a game of tennis, his favourite sport and one in which he excelled. After lunch he took a nap, then did a little reading until it was time for dinner.

DESPITE BEING CHRONICALLY TIRED, Karsh told Garo in September 1935 that he was "happy about everything that I do." But, as he had confided a few months earlier, "aside from business I always find myself alone."[11]

With the studio on a solid financial footing, Karsh was in a position to do something about his loneliness and about his heavy workload. He had long talked about bringing one of his brothers to Canada. In 1936, he told his brother Malak, who was living in Aleppo with their parents, that he had enough money to buy him a ticket to Canada. Karsh hoped that his eight-years-younger brother would not only give him much-needed company but also become the much-needed manager of the studio's printing department.

Malak's departure saddened Bahiyah and Massih Karsh. Yet, according to the youngest brother, Salim, "it gave us the hope that one day we would be there."[12] Moreover, having two members of the Karsh family earning North American salaries would, as Karsh well knew, provide his parents "with happy means of livelihood."[13]

Assisted by George Nakash, who knew his way around the immigration department bureaucracy; Karsh secured permission from the director of the Department of Immigration, F. C. Blair, to bring his brother to Canada. When Malak sailed to North America in the autumn of 1937, Yousuf had secured him a second-class ticket. This was because Karsh wanted his brother to mix — as he himself had when he came to Canada in 1923 — with a better class of passengers than would have been the case in third class. But, unlike Yousuf, Malak arrived in Canada with a high school diploma and with work experience — following his graduation he had worked as an accountant.

Karsh was delighted when he embraced his brother on the dock in Montreal. "I cannot describe to you," he told his friend Lysle Courtenay, "the amount of satisfaction and pleasure derived from the first moment of encounter."[14] After settling Malak into his rooming house above the Wellington Arms Tea Rooms, Yousuf took his brother for a hike in the Gatineau Hills, which lay to the north of the city. In an effort to improve Malak's spoken English, Yousuf arranged for his brother to have private English lessons. And, with a view to giving him more confidence and making him more independent, Karsh enrolled Malak in New York's prestigious Clarence White School of Photography.

By the time Malak left Ottawa to study in New York in June 1939, he had spent over a year spotting and finishing photographs in the back rooms of the Karsh Studio. And, in the course of listening to his brother speak to the members of the Ottawa Camera Club, Malak had come to appreciate the mastery of light and brilliant composition that made Yousuf's portraits different from everyone else's in Canada.

Malak had not begun to take photographs himself until a few months before leaving for New York City. When he did begin, however, he showed that another member of the Karsh family had considerable talent. During the visit of King George VI and Queen Elizabeth to Canada in the spring of 1939, for example, Malak captured the enthusiastic reception that Canadians gave to their sovereign. One of Malak's photographs recording the royal visit even appeared in *Saturday Night.*

The one-month-long course at the Clarence White School of Photography was, in Malak's view, "disappointingly short."[15] But it did expose him to the technical and theoretical sides of photography. It introduced him to the various branches of photography, namely, documentary, fashion, and portraiture. And in line with the school's advanced thinking—"We will give you all the rules we know, but your success depends on how well you can break them"—he gained the confidence to experiment.[16] Indeed, within a short time, Malak was capable of creating expressive unconventional photographic compositions. Always modest and deferential to his older brother, he gave Yousuf the credit. "That is your influence on me," Malak reported in one of the missives that allowed his brother to be a vicarious participant in the course.[17]

Karsh got more than he bargained for when Malak joined him in Ottawa. As he proudly told John Garo, his brother not only fulfilled all of his expectations in the studio but also possessed "a vein of humour (which I do not) and which I think adds spice to life."[18]

Malak did have a wonderful sense of humour. He knew how to make his frequently depressed older brother laugh. Naturally, he spoke Arabic, and staff members remember that this was how Yousuf and Malak conversed in the

studio. Malak was also good company outside of the studio. He and Yousuf
spent many happy hours listening to records, sharing sweetmeats imported
from Syria, and discussing the latest trends in photography.

Given Malak's aptitude and ambition, it was a natural step for him to set up
his own photography studio in 1941. While Yousuf felt no threat from his talented younger brother, he did ask him to refrain from using the Karsh family
name, so Malak's first name became his byline. And even though Malak was
"very interested in the human face, in human attitudes," he stuck to what he
called "commercial photography and pictorial journalism" in deference to his
older brother.[19] Yousuf was determined to reserve the Karsh brand name for
his own use, and was later adamant that no other member of the Karsh family
should follow his and Malak's line of work. When the second-youngest brother,
Jamil, asked if he could join his brothers in the photography business, he was
told to stick to his medical studies.

It was not long before Malak's photographs of Ottawa and many

Malak Karsh, 1951   other cities and landscapes across Canada were a regular feature in

Toronto's *Star Weekly* and *Saturday Night* and in the *Montreal Standard*. Though Karsh had himself taken documentary photographs—in 1935 he
produced the photo-essay "Camera Glimpses of Ottawa" for the *Ottawa Journal*—
he was happy for the moment to leave this area of photography to his younger
brother—providing, of course, that Malak stayed away from portraiture.

Though off to a good start, Malak's career was to be cut short when he contacted tuberculosis in the winter of 1943. For the next eight years he would be in
and out of the Ottawa Sanatorium, leaving his newly married wife, Barbara, to
care for and to support their young family and run the studio. After he fully
recovered, Malak would go on to become one of Canada's most distinguished
documentary photographers.

SOMETIME IN 1936, Solange Gauthier left her job as secretary to a Member of
Parliament from Quebec and joined the Karsh Studio. She became, as Karsh told
Garo in 1937, "my private secretary or better still my interpreter."[20] When Karsh
wrote his memoir years later, he insisted that Solange was "my teacher, my

expression, my conscience."[21] This was not mere sentiment. "He was doing his beautiful work," their mutual friend from the 1930s Betty Low recalled, "but it was her ideas; she was the driving force, raising him up from being a court photographer." It was also Solange, according to Low again, who "cultivated Yousuf and gave him culture."[22]

Although Solange was to become Karsh's wife three years after joining the studio, she was initially an employee. "My job," as she told an interviewer for the *Canadian Home Journal* in 1951, "is to see that bills go out and that money does come in."[23] But Solange did much more than this. She oversaw the other employees, smoothing things over when Karsh lost his temper. "My little man is on his high horse today," was her frequent refrain to the staff.[24] She took dictation, then rewrote Karsh's letters because "'*unfortunately* he sometimes swallows part of the dictionary without chewing it.'"[25] And she did preparatory research on every important client, so that Karsh could ask a series of questions that would impress and flatter his subject during the sitting.

Knowing that most of Karsh's clients were nervous when they entered the reception room, Solange went to great lengths to put them at ease. Just before the sitting commenced, she drew on her experience in the theatre and applied makeup. If a woman had shadows under her eyes, Solange used a light foundation to hide them. If a broad nose or a double chin was the problem, she applied dark makeup to make these features less prominent. Similarly, if a man had blond eyebrows or a fair moustache, she darkened them with mascara. This, Karsh insisted, was "not to make them appear artificial" but simply "to make them show up as clearly in the portrait as they did in real life."[26]

Once in the camera room, Solange kept up a friendly banter with the client until Karsh had finished adjusting the lens on the camera and the lights. When he was ready to depress the shutter, Solange either left the room or stood stock still in the corner of the studio. If the client was famous, Solange prepared, for posterity, a typed transcript of the conversation that had taken place between Yousuf and his important subject.

If all of this were not enough, shortly after joining the studio Solange became Karsh's favourite model. Possessing more character than beauty, she provided a contrast to the débutantes, who exuded charm and youth. She was also different from women who, like her, were on the cusp of middle age, because she had no preconceived ideas of how the finished print should look. Being an actress and former ballet dancer, Solange knew how to project the expressive qualities that Karsh sought to bring out in everyone he photographed. Finally, Solange was willing, for the sake of Karsh's art, to remove her clothes in the camera room.

Karsh had first photographed Solange in 1934 on the stage at the Ottawa Little Theatre. Then, she posed for him in formal evening dress, cuddling her beloved black Persian cat, Atia, then as a European intellectual, as the dance mistress to the young Betty Low, and finally as a refugee. Karsh also captured Solange's natural exuberance in a series of experimental out-of-doors shots: Solange dancing among the spring blossoms and willow trees; Solange pushing her bicycle along a country lane on the outskirts of Ottawa. And, this time indoors, Solange in the nude—although he took care never to show her face— in "Outcast," "Female Nude," and "Elixir," among other nude portraits of her. Many of these photographs were submitted to exhibitions of photography; one, "Solange Under the Willows" (1938), was displayed wherever Karsh happened to be living.

From the outset, Solange was obviously no ordinary employee. When she met Yousuf Karsh in 1932, she had sensed that he possessed enormous talent. Once she joined the Karsh enterprise, she discovered how impatient he could be with his staff, how inefficient he was at managing the financial side of the business, and how prone he was to depression following a difficult session in the camera room.

In Solange Gauthier, Karsh not only had someone to run his business. He had a muse. He had someone to soothe his frequently shattered nerves. He had someone who gave him "continuous inspiration" and, he continued in a letter to a friend, someone who made him work harder.[27] Above all, Solange helped Yousuf make connections with the right kind of people. As Betty Low put it, Solange knew "who would be good for Yousuf—what would be good for Yousuf."[28]

Karsh only had to glance at his heavy ledger books to realize what an enormous difference Solange Gauthier's business acumen made to the studio's financial health. But he was unlike Malak, who confessed to his business manager and future wife, Barbara Holmes, that "I just can't live without you" when she threatened to join the Nursing Corps during the Second World War. Karsh was less interested in romance, less emotionally dependent, than his younger brother. Indeed, when Solange made it clear in December 1938 that she wanted more than a business relationship with her boss, Yousuf initially recoiled.

It was customary for men in the Middle East to marry later in life than North American males. It was also common for them to choose a much younger spouse. Bahiyah Karsh was more than ten years younger than her husband. Solange, by contrast, was eight years older than Yousuf. Still, Yousuf's father, Massih, had married Bahiyah when he was thirty, the same age as his eldest son was in 1939. It was not, however, Yousuf's own—or Solange's—age that was the problem here. There was something else that made Yousuf write Solange the "most sincere and difficult letter I have ever written in my life" on January 5, 1939.

Female Nude

(Solange), 1935

It is clear that Yousuf had first agreed to marry Solange but then panicked and wrote the letter. In it, he professed his admiration for her "charming qualities" and his appreciation for her "great kindness." Yet he wrote, "Our marriage cannot succeed, because I cannot love you in the way you should be loved." The problem, he hinted, was not with Solange but with himself. "I speak to you of my gratitude," he confessed, but "we must not mistake it for what is so fundamental in marriage, or love." Though Yousuf admitted to being "grieved" by the prospect of hurting Solange, he could not deceive her into thinking that he loved her when he clearly did not. There seemed to be only one solution: they should not meet until "we both have become more quiet inwardly." Hence his heartfelt conclusion: "It is well to part now, before we realize the hopelessness of our association, which would demand of me what I feel entirely unable to give—my unselfish and unbounded love."[29]

How can we make sense of this? We know that Madame Héloise Gauthier objected to the liaison and had asked George Nakash to discourage his nephew from marrying Solange. Nakash made an attempt to do this, not because he disliked the vibrant and intelligent Solange but because he feared any further

contact with his nephew's prospective mother-in-law.[30] But this discouragement was not decisive. Nor, as a Roman Catholic, did Karsh appear to be troubled by Solange's status as a divorced woman. Rather, a more plausible explanation for his change of heart can be found by looking at Karsh himself.

Karsh was single-minded in his determination to succeed. Like many men from the Middle East, he had been conditioned to preferring and to feeling more comfortable in the company of men than of women. Above all, the tragic nature of his childhood experiences, first in Mardin, then in Syria, and to a lesser extent in Canada, had turned him into a very private individual. It seems likely that Yousuf Karsh was simply too busy, too preoccupied, too introverted, and too sexually inhibited to share his life with someone who would most certainly make demands that he would be unable to fulfill.

And yet, less than four months after receiving his letter, Solange Gauthier had become Mrs. Yousuf Karsh. One reading is that Yousuf's realization of his dependence upon Solange had gradually overcome his qualms. Another is that they simply came to some sort of understanding that accommodated their different expectations of marriage.

Solange on a Bicycle, 1935

After their wedding in Ottawa on April 27, 1939, the couple travelled to Boston so that Solange could meet her husband's mentor, John Garo. Swept up in the marriage of his apprentice, who now signed his letters to him "your loving son," Garo photographed Solange and Yousuf. He also allowed Karsh to take a few feet of moving picture of him in the studio. During the evening Mrs. Garo played one of her compositions for them on the piano. Then, the following morning, they saw the newlyweds off to New York, where the couple spent the rest of their honeymoon.

No relatives had been invited to the wedding. Karsh's own family in Aleppo only heard of the marriage when Yousuf and Solange wrote to them from New York. "Come, come," Massih Karsh beckoned his second-youngest son, Jamil, when his wife read him the news, "your brother has got married." Bahiyah wept tears of joy when she heard the news. The marriage of the eldest son was a very important event in the life of an Armenian family. This was because it represented more than an alliance between two individuals. It was an alliance between two groups. The groom's bride became a member of her husband's

family, just as the groom became a member of the bride's. Speaking on behalf of the whole family, Jamil congratulated his brother on his choice and wished him "a happy long life with the bride — a life based on mutual understanding, having the same aims and the same interests."[31]

While there is little evidence about whether Héloise Gauthier ever fully accepted her son-in-law, there is no doubt that the Karsh family embraced Solange and that she embraced them. For example, she called Malak, Jamil, and Salim her brothers — just like the Karsh brothers addressed one another. She used the Arabic word for mother and father when addressing Bahiyah and Massih Karsh. And, finally, she took over the role of corresponding with the Karsh family in Syria.

"NOBODY THOUGHT OUR marriage would work out, we are so different," Solange told Karsh's young assistant Peter Miller in 1954.[32] And yet, according to Betty Low, Solange and Yousuf were the ideal couple. It is true that they had quick tempers. But "their flare-ups," Miller recalled, were "hot but brief."[33] These conflicts were outweighed by the support they gave to one another during their mild bouts of depression. As Karsh later recalled, "Solange was a buffer for my emotions, and I was for hers."[34] In all sorts of ways, they were well matched. They both enjoyed dressing well. Karsh wore beautifully tailored suits. Solange wore clothes that Yousuf had chosen for her and flamboyant hats designed by a milliner based in Toronto. They also both enjoyed eating good food — whether they were dining at their favourite Chinese restaurant, the Canton, or eating Solange's wild duck à l'orange, which she brought to the table in a halo of blazing brandy. Above all, Yousuf and Solange shared the same goal: to make Karsh the biggest name in the world in portrait photography.

Solange and Yousuf, by John Garo, 1939

Solange knew that this could only be achieved if she made her life subservient to her husband's career. Following their marriage, she gave up acting at the Little Theatre. According to her friends, Solange now had greater fun playing Madame Karsh than any role she had played on the stage. Solange had been an occasional contributor for the local newspaper. This activity did not stop, it simply took second place to the demands of her "Lord and Master," as she sometimes

called Yousuf. "His work is the important thing," she recalled years later, "and so I submerge myself in it."[35]

It was not only in the studio that Solange worked hard to promote her husband's career. During the 1940s, she gave a series of lectures to a number of Women's Canadian Clubs in southern Ontario. "The insatiable Solange, who is as sure of her Yousuf's destiny as Clara Wieck was of Robert Schumann's," as one journalist put it, knew no modesty when talking about the merits of her photographer husband.[36] In one talk, Solange referred to Karsh's "unknowing genius," in another to "his phenomenal psychological intuition."[37] And in still another address, titled "Karsh, You've Monopolized Me," Solange exposed the less public — and less flattering — side of her husband's personality to her female audience. He was both "kind and thoughtless... He says some very mean things when he is tired — I'm his safety valve — then says the loveliest and most loving words." He was also untidy: "he strews his clothes all over the place; comes in from a walk with muddy feet, which he tracks all over the house; and leaves the bathroom looking like a nightmare." Solange also revealed that she and Yousuf slept in separate bedrooms.[38]

The message that Solange transmitted to her female audience would not have been foreign to them. It fitted the artist-genius cliché. Karsh was a "child" who clearly needed looking after. And Solange was therefore not only Yousuf's helpmate, she was his surrogate mother.

After their marriage, Yousuf moved into Solange's apartment on Somerset Street West. A few months later they moved into the Duncannon at 216 Metcalfe Street. Built as a luxury apartment block, the Tudor-revival building, with its leaded-glass windows and imposing foyer, was home to several Members of Parliament as well as the speaker of the House of Commons. Within walking distance of Parliament Hill and the Karsh Studio, the Duncannon was an ideal location for Yousuf and Solange.

Although the apartment was large enough to accommodate Malak, the recently wedded couple wanted a house of their own — and no doubt more privacy than their Metcalfe Street apartment offered. Driving their newly acquired Plymouth into the outskirts of Ottawa, they scoured the area for a suitable lot on which to build. Within a year they had found four acres lying adjacent to the Prescott Highway. Located on a bend in the Rideau River, the property offered privacy and a gently undulating landscape comprising a wooded ravine, a creek leading into a little bay, and an abundance of wildlife. Best of all, the property was only a twenty-minute drive away from Karsh's downtown studio.

Solange charted the construction of the house in a column, "The Diary of a Dream House Come True," which appeared in *Canadian Home Journal*. By late 1940, the small, round, pink stucco house was complete. And by the middle of the following summer, the property came into its own. Its flat roof offered Solange and Yousuf a place to escape the hot and humid summer nights. They slept on the roof just as Yousuf and his family had done in Mardin, Turkey. The rich soil allowed Solange to grow a large variety of vegetables and herbs, like night-blooming white tobacco, which she planted under their bedroom windows. And, located on the flight path of hundreds of migrating birds, their new home gave them a new hobby: birdwatching.

It was here that Betty Low remembers being photographed next to the stream in a negligee, then drinking dark rum with Yousuf and Solange. It was here that Karsh played tennis. It was here that Solange and Yousuf counted over fifty varieties of birds and named the house "Little Wings." It was here that they would often end the day by dancing in front of the large plate-glass windows. And it was here, finally, that they entertained, flattered, and fascinated a large number of visitors.

Solange and Yousuf possessed a rare talent for being able to talk about the famous people they encountered at the studio without, one reporter noted, "making anybody want to scream." This was because "they look upon everyone, with or without a crown, simply as a person."[39] It was also because, by professing no political affiliation, they remained on the outside and could therefore not be labelled. As Solange put it, "being old country–French born, I have made it a rule to have nothing to do with politics."[40] It was the same for Yousuf. He had photographed J. S. Woodsworth, the leader of the Cooperative Commonwealth Federation, in 1938 and would go on to photograph Tim Buck, the leader of the Communist Party, in 1943, as well as every leading figure in both the Liberal and Conservative parties.

It was not just high-ranking politicians (of all political persuasions), civil servants, and diplomats who were entertained at Little Wings and, before that, either at the studio à la John Garo or at the Duncannon. People from the cultural and entertainment industries, along with businessmen, theologians, and university presidents, were also wined and dined by Yousuf and Solange. Some of their guests were clients. Others were casual acquaintances who would almost certainly end up sitting before Karsh's camera.

As noted above, it was Solange who made sure that Yousuf photographed any personality who passed through Ottawa. On the first day of King George VI and Queen Elizabeth's royal tour of Canada in 1939, Solange ensured that Yousuf, and no other photographer, photographed them at a tea party hosted by the premier of Quebec and the Canadian prime minister at Spencerwood. It was Solange, too, who brought the Afro-American baritone Paul Robeson, the New York photographer Nicholas Haz, and the director of London's Tate Art Gallery, John Rothenstein, to the Karsh Studio.

Little Wings under Snow, circa 1942

Even Solange was not able to get everyone to come to the studio, as one bizarre incident in February 1936 demonstrated. The trouble arose with the supposedly Native-born conservationist known as Grey Owl, then at the height of his fame following a successful lecture tour in England. Yousuf and Solange had to exercise a great deal of patience in their dealings with "Mr. Grey Owl" during his visit to Ottawa. Karsh arranged a dinner party at the studio but long after the guests—among whom were writers, cabinet ministers, and journalists—had arrived, it became obvious that the guest of honour was not going to make an appearance. Karsh excused himself from the party and ran down the street to the hotel where Grey Owl was staying. In the midst of "raising a drunken row in the bar," Grey Owl indicated that he had no intention of yielding to his host's entreaties to grace the studio with his presence.[41]

Instead, a day or so later, Karsh returned to the hotel. This time, although Grey Owl was sober, he sported several stitches below his left eye—the result of a recently removed cyst. Unfazed by the blemish, Karsh set up his camera and lights. When he later developed the negative, he cropped it so that Grey

Owl's face, along with the brim of his hat, dominated the photograph. Karsh did not, however, remove the scar. Indeed, it, along with the close cropping, gave Grey Owl a sense of gravitas, thereby reinforcing what Karsh believed to be the rugged nature of the man before his camera.

A couple of months following the sitting, Karsh sent Grey Owl complimentary copies of the photograph, for which the editor of *Year Book of the Arts*, William Deacon, had paid Karsh handsomely. "It is a rare treat," Yousuf dictated to Solange, who no doubt put her own spin on his words, "to meet a man of courage, determination and frankness which you revealed to me at the time of my visit to your hotel. These qualities, if I may say, are captured in the portrait I made of you."[42]

After Grey Owl's death in 1938, Karsh, along with the rest of the world, discovered that the conservationist was not Native at all but the British-born Archibald Belaney. Karsh agreed that his attempt to celebrate "the gaudy impostor" had been "a serious mistake." Nevertheless, he included Grey Owl's portrait in his 1978 publication *Karsh Canadians*, insisting that "His false identity cannot, however, diminish his achievements as one of Canada's earliest conservationists."[43]

Grey Owl, 1936

FOR A MAN WHO HAD been in business for less than ten years, by 1939 Karsh had certainly made a name for himself within Canada. As one journalist noted in March of that year, Karsh had recorded "the features of nearly all of Canada's great and near-great."[44] Whether he knew it or not, by doing this he had given Canadians—and the governing class in particular—a flattering image of itself for its own edification. Yet Karsh was not satisfied. As he told John Garo a year before his mentor's death in the autumn of 1939, "I hope that in the next five years I will have done some creative work that will justify the great schooling and ideals you imported to me when I was with you."[45] Though Garo did not live to see it, here was a prophecy that would be fulfilled, on schedule, and with an abundance that even the ambitions of Yousuf Karsh had not anticipated.

PART TWO

THE CROWNING

OF A

CAREER

Annus Mirabilis

If there is one image that stands out among the fifty thousand portraits that Yousuf Karsh took during his long career, it is his famous photograph of Winston Churchill. It was taken at a crucial turning point in the Second World War—and in Karsh's career, as it turned out. Under the sobriquet "The Roaring Lion," this was the photograph that made Karsh a household name and one of the most sought-after portraitists of the twentieth century.

Likewise, if there is one anecdote that almost everyone knows about Karsh, it is of how the photographer, then just thirty-three, had the audacity to remove Churchill's cigar from his lips just before clicking the shutter. "I did not feel that I wanted to make just another of these cigar pictures," Karsh told W. Dawson of the *Canadian Home Journal* a few weeks after the photograph was taken on December 30, 1941.[1] And it is part of the Karsh myth that, until that moment, he was an obscure and unknown photographer. As a writer for *Maclean's* magazine noted of the uncharacteristically short sitting, it made Karsh "internationally famous in exactly five minutes."[2]

The story surrounding the making of the Churchill portrait is far more complex than myth or anecdote would suggest. We need to ask more skeptical and more searching questions. What were the circumstances under which Karsh came to produce the photograph? How did Karsh's photograph of Winston Churchill come to be published? Why did it, rather than any other visual image of Churchill taken before or after December 1941, come to represent the definitive portrait of the British prime minister? And finally, what made "The Roaring Lion" one of the iconic images in the history of twentieth-century photography?

IN SEPTEMBER 1939, within days of Hitler's invasion of Poland and less than four months after Solange and Yousuf's marriage, Canada declared war on Germany. Suddenly everyone in Ottawa wanted his or her photograph taken—particularly men and women in the services who were going abroad or had found themselves posted to the capital. Moreover, for those who had jobs in the booming war economy, there was money to spend on small luxuries, at least until the government introduced wage and price controls in December 1941. It was under these conditions that a host of professional photographers in Canada and elsewhere began taking very different kinds of pictures.

Yousuf Karsh, Self-Portrait, 1938

In 1940, the society and fashion photographer Cecil Beaton captured the aftermath of a London air raid. The resulting photograph appeared on an American Red Cross poster and was featured on the cover of *Life* magazine, in an effort to prompt American participation in the war. Another English photographer, Bill Brandt, photographed the blackout, rather than the destruction resulting from the Blitz. France's Brassaï and Henri Cartier-Bresson found war-related subjects for their cameras too. So did the American photographer Margaret Bourke-White, who took an uncharacteristically jovial photograph of Joseph Stalin while on assignment in the Soviet Union for *Life* in August 1941.

Such opportunities put a premium on colour photography, in which Karsh had had little experience. True, he had earlier approached John Garo about learning more, but it was not until June 1940 that Karsh was able to report to his uncle in Montreal that "I got what I wanted but have not had the time to practice it—namely, how to make colour prints from transparencies." Karsh found the colour process to be "very difficult and complicated and extremely expensive."[3] By the following year, however, he was submitting colour photographs

to magazines. Karsh seldom derived "true artistic satisfaction" from working in colour, holding that it left nothing to the viewer's imagination, but by 1943 he would on occasion make the time during a sitting to take colour as well as black-and-white photographs.[4]

Canadian photographers enjoyed new attention in wartime. They helped give newspapers, magazines, and government propaganda agencies like Canada's War Information Board and the National Film Board a much-needed impetus and a new relevance by recording the home front. As Karsh put it later, "the whole scene changed" in 1939. "There were no more Governor's Drawing Rooms where enchanting debs made their formal bow with Prince of Wales feathers in their hair," but instead, he explained, "the young soldier...just going overseas...and the General, who for the first time was weighed with the terrible responsibility of command and guardianship of all these young lives."[5] Karsh clearly shared the military's sense of mission. In a talk given to the Photographer's Association of America in 1951, he not only recalled feeling like "a young crusader" who must project "the good side" of the war, he declared his motto: "To tell the truth in terms of beauty."[6]

Karsh's line of thinking was very much in step with that of many others in Canada's artistic community. "Beauty — in the form of paintings and sculpture," R. S. Lambert noted in *Maritime Art*, "could help to restore the mind to health by giving us a sense of poise, proportion and serenity."[7] According to another article in this magazine, exhibitions like Britain at War, which toured Canada in 1941, demonstrated "how the visual arts could be integrated into a country's social fabric and how the artist, as any other public servant, could perform a worthy social task."[8]

Malak Karsh recorded wartime activity in Ottawa, on the Maritime coast, and in Newfoundland for periodicals in Canada, Britain, and the United States. Yousuf's Studio Register shows that during the early years of the war, squadron leaders, group captains, air commodores, and ordinary soldiers and seamen made their way to his studio. He met a request from his recently engaged picture agency, Pictorial Press in London, for "a set of about 10 pictures showing the principal ministers of the present Canadian Cabinet."[9] Inspired by his brother's success with American newspapers, Yousuf sent a long list of his personalities to

C. M. Graves for publication in the *New York Times.*[10] Finally, Karsh produced a colour photograph of a young CWAC woman and another of a group of RCAF men in what he called a "dramatic" or heroic pose for the *Canadian Home Journal.*[11]

Prior to the war, Solange had made it possible for Yousuf to meet a number of dignitaries through her contacts in the Ottawa Little Theatre and her secretarial job on Parliament Hill. After the outbreak of hostilities, she drew on these contacts once again. Within the first year of the war, she saw to it that Yousuf photographed virtually every leading civil servant and the head of every branch of the armed forces, along with diplomats, high commissioners, the Governor General and, most important of all, the Canadian prime minister.

Karsh had of course photographed Mackenzie King in 1936, along with President Roosevelt and Lord Tweedsmuir, at the Citadel in Quebec. On that occasion the prime minister is said to have told Karsh, "Oh, but I have admired your work for so long."[12] Yet it was not until August 1940 that Karsh secured a private sitting with Mackenzie King, at his summer residence in Kingsmere, outside of Ottawa.

Mackenzie King was not an easy man to photograph. Not only was he squat, dumpy, and unimpressive looking, he was also vain and fastidious, and disliked spontaneity. Whenever he was near a camera, he assumed a stiff pose that made him look rather silly and self-satisfied. He was mistrustful of journalists, who, overlooking the enormous stamina and endurance that kept him in office for over twenty years, enjoyed portraying him as a comic figure. Indeed, with the outbreak of the war in Europe, it was all the more important that he was presented to the Canadian people — and to the other Allied heads of government — as a strong, statesmanlike leader. So when he agreed to sit for Ottawa's most famous portrait photographer on a late summer day in 1940, it was clear how Mackenzie King hoped to be portrayed.

When Yousuf and Solange arrived at Kingsmere, they found the prime minister dressed in comfortable tweeds — fitting attire for a man who was spending a weekend in the country. Taken for the most part out of doors, Karsh's photographs were informal: Mackenzie King and his seventeen-year-old dog, Pat, looking over their domain; Mackenzie King sitting on a swing in the garden; strolling across the lawn; or walking down the steps in front of the impressive house. Readers of Toronto's *Star Weekly*, which commissioned the photographs, were therefore given a less pompous, more humane man than they were used to seeing in the press.[13]

As Mackenzie King got to know Karsh, he discovered that there was much to admire in the young photographer. Karsh was polite. He was a perfectionist like Mackenzie King himself. He was well dressed. He appeared to be trustworthy. And he was accommodating. During the Kingsmere session, Karsh had agreed to include the much-loved Pat in almost every shot. And afterwards, when Solange was writing the captions to accompany the photographs, she tactfully deleted her repeated observations of how Pat had invariably sat between his master's legs.

Karsh was a master at ingratiating himself with an important personality, and Mackenzie King was no exception. During this first sitting, Karsh had been "greatly taken with the beauty of Kingsmere," as Mackenzie King noted in his diary, and he had seemed "quite awed and inspired with the view from the Abbey ruin which he thought...would be a beautiful spot for a Shakespearian play."[14] Following subsequent sittings with Mackenzie King, it was not unusual for Karsh to tell him that he had "thoroughly enjoyed the honour of photographing you, and I hope some of these proofs will convey my feelings for you."[15] And to see that the prime minister got the proofs within twenty-four hours. "Great relief to have these promised photographs duly presented," Mackenzie King wrote as his train was pulling out of the CPR station in the summer of 1941.[16]

Mackenzie King
at Home, 1940

But there were other reasons why Mackenzie King was anxious to cultivate the young photographer. The photographs from the sitting at Kingsmere became Christmas presents for the prime minister's friends and presentation gifts for visiting dignitaries. Karsh's photographs of famous people had begun to appear in the American press and Mackenzie King wanted to be photographed in the company of statesmen from the United States. He regretted, for example, that Karsh had not photographed him alongside the king and queen during their royal tour of Canada in 1939. Indeed, Mackenzie King was so eager to have Yousuf Karsh take his photograph that a story circulated around

Ottawa that it was not unusual to see the Canadian prime minister carrying Karsh's camera bags.

Although Karsh was seen by many as Mackenzie King's court photographer, producing a satisfactory photograph of the prime minister was not easy. Part of the problem, Karsh noted much later, was that "King wished me to depict the man he visualized himself to be."[17] Another difficulty was Mackenzie King's very set ideas about how he wanted to be portrayed. "He tries to co-operate," a frustrated Karsh noted in 1946, "but camera-consciousness invariably creeps into the sitting."[18] Though Karsh felt that he had "completely failed" during every photo session with Mackenzie King, the prime minister thought otherwise: "Hardly a week passes that someone, either by word or letter, does not express some commendation of the latest portraits... You will never know what this means to me," he continued, "particularly in the light of the problem that pictures of myself seem to have presented to photographers of the past."[19]

By the time Yousuf and Solange visited Kingsmere in the summer of 1940, the Karsh Studio had a turnover of $20,000 — exactly twice as much as in 1936. This produced a net income for Yousuf and Solange of $8,000 a year. Yet, while the exigencies of the war and the patronage of Mackenzie King had filled the coffers of the studio, this intense activity extracted a price. During the first two years of the hostilities Karsh was working so hard that in the spring of 1941 he ended up in Ottawa's Civic Hospital for a "rest."[20] During the same year he had been forced to retreat to his favourite lakeside resort, the Hotel La Clairere. "My darling, of course, we are going to do a great deal of creative work when you come back," Solange encouraged her exhausted husband from Ottawa, "and it will all be so much easier because of your good rest."[21]

Karsh was not only overworked, he was frustrated. Despite his access to virtually every visiting dignitary in Ottawa and to every high-ranking government and military official in the country, the bulk of the studio's clientele — and therefore its earnings — still came from taking portraits of brides, graduands, businessmen, and women of a certain age. Moreover, as Yousuf told George Nakash in April 1940, he and Solange had not yet produced "the great masterpieces that we dreamed about."[22] A year and a half later Karsh got his chance, when Winston Churchill arrived in Ottawa.

MACKENZIE KING HAD been thinking about asking his favourite photographer to make a portrait of himself and Churchill when Karsh contacted the prime minister's private secretary, Walter Turnbull. There was nothing unusual about Karsh asking Mackenzie King for help. Earlier that year the prime minister had made it possible for Karsh to photograph Princess Juliana and her two daughters, Beatrix and Irene, who, having fled the Netherlands, were spending the war years in Ottawa. Moreover, Karsh no doubt sensed that Mackenzie King was as eager to be photographed with his British counterpart as Karsh himself was to photograph Churchill. Indeed, the sitting would be advantageous for both men. Karsh would have an opportunity to produce a portrait that would give him national, and maybe even international, exposure. And Mackenzie King would be photographed in the company of the man who had led the British Empire through its "finest hour." But there was one factor that neither man considered when they made their arrangements: would the British prime minister agree to the sitting?

Winston Churchill was as fastidious as Mackenzie King about how he dressed, what he ate, and how he was represented in the press. Conscious of his image, he often gave photographers a difficult time. He had intimidated Cecil Beaton when "he glowered into the camera," during a sitting in the autumn of 1940.[23] Churchill had been an equally difficult subject for Margaret Bourke-White, who was commissioned to photograph him on his sixty-eighth birthday. And yet there is little evidence in the resulting portraits that Churchill did not enjoy being photographed. Indeed, whether he was portrayed holding a Tommy gun (in Felix H. Man's well-known photograph), watching a mock battle, meeting dignitaries, showing off his "siren" jump suit, giving the victory sign, or holding up his Havana cigar, he was invariably smiling.

This benign image, however, represented only the public side of Churchill's personality. Although he could be a captivating conversationalist, most people who worked with him quickly discovered that he was a bully and a workaholic who demanded as much commitment from everyone else as he imposed on himself. Yet until December 1941, only one photographer, Cecil Beaton, had revealed this side of the British prime minister's personality. Seated at his cluttered desk in the Cabinet Room, there is no doubt that Churchill was upset by the intruding photographer.

Beaton's photograph of a stern and brooding Churchill thus presented a different man to the readers of the *Daily Telegraph*, where it appeared on December 23, 1940. At least one member of the Churchill family thought that Beaton had produced a representative portrait, since Churchill's son, Randolph, chose it as the frontispiece for the North American edition of his father's speeches, *Blood, Sweat, and Tears.* Yet Beaton's portrait was not in keeping with the public image of Churchill. Consequently the anomaly was largely ignored. Newspaper editors wanted Churchill to give their readers a reassuring smile. Even when the cartoonist Sidney Strube put Churchill's head on the body of a bulldog in 1940, the British leader still looked benign. Sternness and defiance were expressions for Hitler, Mussolini, and their generals, not for the British prime minister.

Churchill's tenacity was not projected through the visual media but rather along the radio waves. Delivered in the House of Commons, and then broadcast around the world later the same day by the BBC, Churchill's speeches conveyed his vigour and toughness. When he told the British public, "I have nothing to offer but blood, toil, tears and sweat," it was an inspiration for everyone who heard his words.

But during the winter of 1941–42, Churchill needed more than words with which to fight the Germans and the Italians. The previous May, Greece had been occupied by Hitler's forces; in June, the British offensive against Rommel in North Africa had failed; and in August, Churchill's meeting with President Roosevelt on their respective battleships off the coast of Newfoundland did not bring the United States into the war as the British leader had hoped it would. All of this changed, of course, when the Japanese bombed the American naval base at Pearl Harbor on December 7, 1941.

Churchill literally danced when he learned that the United States had declared war on Japan and that Germany, in turn, had declared war on the United States. He was jubilant because, as one historian would observe, for the last two years the sixty-seven-year-old prime minister had been carrying "the world on his shoulders."[24] With the United States now in the war, there was an ideological need to unite the English-speaking peoples behind strong political leadership. And there was, equally, a need to give the public a strong visual image of their leaders.

WINSTON CHURCHILL WAS not a well man when he risked being attacked by U-boats as he crossed the Atlantic to North America in December 1941. Mackenzie King, who was in Washington to meet him, noted how "flabby and tired" he looked.[25] Sir Charles Wilson, who attended the British prime minister when he suffered a minor attack of angina shortly after arriving in the American capital, recalled how a concerned Churchill kept asking him to check his pulse.[26] With President Roosevelt needing to be propped up due to his own disability and Churchill looking unwell, too, Mackenzie King "could not help thinking of what a terrible thing it is that the fate of the world should rest so largely in the hands of two men to either of whom anything may happen at any moment."[27] Indeed, a photograph of the two leaders that appeared in *Saturday Night* made Churchill and Roosevelt look more like two elderly friends on a day's outing from a nursing home than men who could face down both Nazi Germany and imperial Japan.[28]

Despite his precarious health, Churchill hit the right note when he spoke to a joint session of the American Senate and House of Representatives that December. And by the time he departed for Ottawa in the company of Mackenzie King, he had been assured by President Roosevelt that the United States' number-one priority remained the defeat of Germany.

When Churchill arrived in the Canadian capital on December 29, the RCMP had difficulty holding back the crowds who had come to meet him at the train station. "He thoroughly enjoys meeting the crowds," Mackenzie King noted that evening, "and adopting characteristic poses with cigar in his mouth, hat on end of cane, making the sign 'V' with his two fingers, and generally stirring up enthusiasm like a ten year old."[29]

Churchill was no stranger to Canada. In 1929, he had travelled the breadth of the country, staying at a ranch in Alberta and at the Château Frontenac in Quebec City. He had admired "a new machine called the Combine" in Manitoba, and revelled in the lushness of the vegetation on the Pacific Coast and "the twenty Switzerlands rolled into one" as he described the Canadian Rockies in a letter home to his wife, Clementine. "Everywhere," Churchill continued, he was "welcomed in the warmest manner…The sentimental feeling towards England is wonderful…The US are stretching their tentacles out in all directions, but the Canadian National spirit and personality is becoming so powerful and self-contained that I do not think we need fear the future."[30]

Nor was Winston Churchill a stranger to the Canadian prime minister. The two men had known one another since the early part of the twentieth century, when Churchill had made a lecture tour of North America following his participation in the Boer War in South Africa. And even though he was often irritated by Mackenzie King—Churchill's physician could not "help noticing Winston's indifference to him after the wooing of the President in the White House"—publicly, at least, the British prime minister spoke with warmth and affection of his long friendship with the Canadian prime minister.[31]

Churchill was in Canada for barely three days before he returned to Washington for further talks with the American president. During that time he kept up a prodigious pace. He reviewed the troops and met with publishers and press photographers, Chiefs of Staff and members of the Conservative opposition. He also visited an air-training field, where he avoided slipping on the icy tarmac, and dined at Government House, where he was made a member of the Canadian Privy Council, and at the prime minister's private residence, where he was reunited with his own friend, First World War flying ace Billy Bishop. In addition to all of this, on December 30, midway through his visit, Churchill addressed the Members of Parliament and senators in the Canadian House of Commons.

On the morning of Churchill's speech, Mackenzie King rose at his usual hour. After doing his exercises, he read a little, then worked on an address to welcome the British prime minister to the Canadian parliament. After finishing his speech, he ate lunch, then arranged for an honour guard to greet the distinguished visitor on the steps of the Parliament Buildings and for a glass of water to be placed next to the podium where Churchill would speak. Finally, before proceeding at 3:25 p.m. to Parliament Hill, Mackenzie King took a twenty-minute nap.

Winston Churchill had worked on his speech the previous evening. After excusing himself from a large dinner party held in his honour at the Governor General's residence where he was staying, he looked over some notes he had drafted in Washington. He knew that he had to set the right tone in his speech if he was going to persuade Canada to contribute more supplies and troops to the war effort. He had to compliment Canadians on their participation in the hostilities to date. He had to underscore the fact that, now that the United States was in the war, Canada occupied "a unique position in the British Empire because of its unbreakable ties with Britain and its ever-growing friendship and intimate association with the United States."[32] Above all, Churchill had to come up with the kind of stirring rhetorical language that the Canadian public — and the rest of the world, to whom the speech would also be broadcast — expected to hear from the great orator.

Churchill continued to work on his speech the following morning. When the final draft was finished, the Governor General's secretary typed it on pocket-sized sheets of paper. When she had done this, Churchill slipped the pages into the left-hand pocket of his jacket and left Rideau Hall for Parliament Hill.

Yousuf Karsh had even less sleep than Winston Churchill the previous night, because he did not sleep at all. This left him feeling "upset, tense" and, Solange further observed, "nervous."[33] Nevertheless, he did not cancel his morning appointments. When the last client left the studio at just after 2 p.m., however, Karsh skipped lunch and, with one assistant in tow, walked up to the east side of Parliament Hill, to the Speaker's Chamber.

The previous afternoon, Karsh had instructed a House of Commons steward to remove the heavy furniture from the room and the gilt-framed historical paintings from the dark, oak-panelled walls in order to make the room compatible with his camera room. Then he had set up his 8-by-10-inch Agfa view camera with its 14-inch Ektar lens, adjusted his bank of six floodlights (taking the place of the old north window), his two spotlights (which provided accents), and his background light. And after doing this, he asked another steward, whose physique was not unlike Winston Churchill's, to pose on the spot where the photograph was to be taken. Karsh also obtained permission to watch the British prime minister give his speech. Thus, when Churchill and Mackenzie

King walked into the House of Commons to a large round of applause the following day, Yousuf Karsh was in the press gallery, a prime vantage point.

Normally the Canadian House of Commons, as *Saturday Night* reporter Margaret Lawrence noted, was "a dim hall—dark green dark brown, neutral grey, a little somber old gold." Moreover, the exaggerated height of the ceilings seemed to dwarf everyone in it. But on Tuesday, December 30, things were very different. There was a microphone, which allowed Churchill's speech to be broadcast around the world. There were cinematographers from the War Pictorial News with their large cameras and "terrific blinding lights." There were press photographers, who added to the unnatural illumination by popping their flashbulbs throughout Churchill's speech. According to Lawrence, they "had not before been able to turn so much light upon Churchill or to shoot away to such an extent." And, finally, there was "the darling of the camera folk," as Lawrence called the British prime minister, who knew "that the world loves pictures; and that people like to see faces." When Churchill stood up in the House of Commons "to receive the homage of Canada, he took care that the cameras had a chance and enough time" to photograph him.[34]

Churchill began his speech by giving a general account of the war and noting how important was Canada's contribution. Drawing upon his rhetorical skills, he went on to entertain the House with a great deal of humour—and bathos. He spoke of the "Hitler tyranny, Japanese frenzy and the Mussolini flop." Towards the end of his speech, Churchill brought the house down when he recounted how, after the fall of France in June 1940, the French generals had said dismissively, "In three weeks England will have her neck wrung like a chicken." Churchill then commented sarcastically, "Some chicken"—pausing for applause as he looked to the right side of the House—"some neck"—a crescendo of applause.[35] This was the point at which Karsh, who had been observing Churchill's gestures, his posture, and his facial expression from the press gallery, claimed that he got his "moment of inspiration."[36]

Before everyone had finished singing "God Save the King," which marked the end of the special session, Karsh had left the House of Commons and was in the Speaker's Chamber. He had a long time to wait for his subject to appear. After leaving the House, Churchill drank a scotch and soda, while Mackenzie

King sipped a cup of tea. Then Churchill was introduced to members of the opposition in the Conservative Party. Finally, he met with publishers and editors from across the country and answered their questions, according to Mackenzie King "in an astute and clever way."

Mackenzie King also noted in his diary how "immensely relieved and pleased" Churchill was with having his speech out of the way.[37] Churchill was indeed relieved. But he was also tired. He had been unsuccessful in persuading Mackenzie King to turn off the glaring spotlights in the House of Commons. Churchill had also been bothered by the incessant popping of the photographers' flashbulbs while he spoke. But his speech had gone well. Now he was looking forward to the informal dinner party that Mackenzie King had arranged that evening at Laurier House. It was therefore with relief that he followed Mackenzie King towards the Speaker's Apartments where he had left his overcoat. At this point, however, the Canadian prime minister and his entourage guided Churchill towards the Speaker's Chamber instead.

When Karsh heard footsteps and muted voices in the corridor, he switched on his spot- and floodlights. The next thing he knew Churchill had entered the room and was exclaiming, "What's this, what's this?" There was a nervous laugh from Mackenzie King and the others. Everyone, it seemed, knew about the sitting with Yousuf Karsh except Churchill.

The British prime minister did not join in the laughter. The last thing he wanted was to confront another set of glaring lights. Sensing his distress, Karsh stepped forward: "Sir, these photographs may be the ones which will serve as a constant source of hope and inspiration which you have created in the heart of the civilized world."[38]

It seemed that Churchill had no choice. Grudgingly, he agreed to allow Karsh to take just one photograph. The entourage stepped aside. Karsh checked the focus on his lens; it was sharp, and the lighting and the composition were perfect. But when he removed the viewing cloth from his head, Churchill still had the Havana cigar between his lips. Determined that he was not going to photograph Churchill with this theatrical prop, Karsh walked towards the British prime minister and said, "Sir, I have an ashtray all prepared for you." Churchill gave no indication that he was going to remove the cigar from his mouth, so Karsh did it for him.³⁹ "By the time I got back to my camera," Karsh recalled years later, "he looked so belligerent he could have devoured me."⁴⁰ It was at this point that Karsh exposed his 8-by-10 Super XX Panchromatic film to the light for one-tenth of a second. It was now, too, that one member of the party surreptitiously pocketed the reluctantly abandoned cigar from its ashtray.

Amused that the young photographer had had the audacity to remove the cigar from his lips, and aware that the Speaker of the House, J. L. Glenn, was in the process of lighting him another cigar, Churchill told Karsh that he could take one more photograph. By this time the British prime minister had relaxed and was smiling. Karsh took a second exposure. Then, after Churchill had joined the rest, Karsh took a third photograph. This time he pointed his camera towards the entourage, in hopes of photographing the two prime ministers together. Anxious to end the session, Churchill broke from the group, walked towards Karsh, shook his hand and said, "Well you certainly can make a roaring lion stand still to photograph him."⁴¹

The Roaring Lion
(print of untouched
negative), 1941

Karsh knew that Mackenzie King had looked forward to being photographed with Churchill. But Karsh was not thinking about the candid shot he had taken of both prime ministers when he packed up his equipment, left the Speaker's Chamber, and walked down Parliament Hill to his Sparks Street studio. He was thinking about the two photographs that he had taken of Winston Churchill, which had captured the two sides of Churchill's personality: the first, resolute and defiant—a pose that Churchill had taken for photographers since childhood—and the second, jovial and benign.

Karsh was anxious as he hurried back to the studio. There had been no opportunity to establish the rapport with his subject that was normally crucial to the way he worked. No opportunity to give more definition to the prime minister's features with the application of a little makeup. And above all, no opportunity at the end of the formal sitting to produce more than a candid photograph of Mackenzie King and Churchill.

On the other hand, Karsh knew that chance played a part in every photograph he took. "Sometimes you find things on the film that you did not realize you were getting," he subsequently told a reporter for the *Milwaukee Journal*.⁴² Equally,

Karsh knew that the making of a portrait did not end with the click-click of the shutter. As a writer noted of Karsh a few years later, "Who says retouching is unjustified when this master uses it so cleverly and to such advantage?"[43]

When Karsh arrived at the studio, Solange recalled that he looked "very tired and rather green" but, she added, he was "excited."[44] While his assistants prepared "just the perfect developer," Solange made Yousuf sit down, smoke a cigarette, and tell her what had happened during the sitting. Then, Solange recalled, Yousuf "closeted himself in the darkroom and I waited."

Years later, Karsh asked his young assistant, Herman Leonard, if he would like to develop the negative of "The Roaring Lion." As Leonard explained some sixty years later:[45]

> Smiling Churchill, 1941
>
> Karsh's technique was to develop by inspection not so much by time, the inspection was done against a green light that was so dim and so feeble that it took ten minutes to even see that there was a green light there and he would take a negative and hold it up against the green light for a second or so and see whether the density pleased him and then put it into the developer or put it into the stop bath. Apparently he was a bit nervous and pulled it a bit too soon—maybe a minute—and the negative was a little bit thinner than he would have liked it.

It was several minutes before Karsh had completed the developing process and Solange heard his voice from the floor above, "telling me to come and see the two negatives." It was a good sign. "I knew that he had succeeded," she reported later, adding that "there was much rejoicing and yet much humility in his bearing for I have noticed that Yousuf Karsh is always most humble when he has succeeded in a difficult task."[46]

WHEN KARSH SAW the first image in the developing room, he knew that his work was far from over. He also knew that he needed more than a pristine negative. Much had to be done during the washing, drying, retouching, and other stages of the developing and printing process. He had to make Churchill look less

tired and less haggard. He had to heighten the tension that had arisen between the unwilling sitter, who had been deprived of his cigar, and the cocky photographer, who had taken it from him. He had to give Churchill more strength and gravitas by giving him more solidity. He had to crop Churchill's elbow and much of the chair from the negative in order to emphasize the pyramidal composition of the picture. He had to bring the buttons on Churchill's coat into focus and give a sharper definition to the ring, watch chain, handkerchief, the top button of his shirt, and the notes that protruded from Churchill's pocket. He had to improve the tonal gradation of the picture and deal with the overexposed areas of the negative that had been burned out into white. Finally, he had to give more strength to Churchill's smooth, soft, feminine-looking hands that had astonished Cecil Beaton during his session with Churchill a year earlier and had "shocked" Karsh during his own sitting with the British prime minister.[47]

Karsh adjusted all of these things. He cropped the negative. This eliminated a blemish at the top. It pulled Churchill to the front of the picture plane. It helped to reduce Churchill's corporeal bulk, and gave him a commanding, heroic presence that was almost superhuman.

During the retouching, Karsh added a wider range of middle tones to Churchill's face and hands. He also toned down the area behind his head. He gave the back and side lighting a greater sense of direction. Finally, he exploited the subtlety and the fine, sandpaper-like finish of the matted silver paper he used for printing. The paper made the watch chain and ring glow. It enhanced the three-dimensional quality of the photograph. And it made the white areas of the print luminous — the collar and cuffs, the handkerchief, and speech in the pocket.

With its pyramidal composition, its dramatic intensity, and its dark, subtle "palette" broken by crisp highlights and stunning luminosity, Karsh's portrait now emerged. It drew on the sensibility of the classical portrait paintings of the Old Masters as well as that of Edward Steichen's seminal 1903 photograph of the American banker J. Pierpoint Morgan and his 1932 portrait of Winston Churchill.[48] There was no sense in Karsh's finished print that Churchill was concerned about the precarious state of his health, or downcast at having just

heard the news that Malaya was likely to fall to the Japanese, or anxious about the dangerous voyage that he faced on his return journey to Britain. Just like the Old Masters who made kings and queens appear more beautiful or more powerful than they were, Karsh had used artful manipulation to transform an unpromising negative of a tired, overweight, sick, and slightly annoyed man into a photograph of a heroic figure who had just told the world, "If anybody likes to play rough, we can play rough too."[49]

Karsh manipulated the second, smiling negative of Churchill in a similar way. But the resulting print was pedestrian compared to "The Roaring Lion." There had been no tension between the photographer and the subject when Karsh clicked his shutter a second time. Moreover, because Churchill was posing, the results were not dissimilar from virtually every other photograph of him. Indeed, in Karsh's smiling portrait of him Churchill looked more like a jovial figure on a Toby jug than a powerful statesman.

YEARS AFTER TAKING his seminal photograph of Churchill, Karsh claimed that when he looked at the negative he immediately knew that it "was an important picture, the first really important picture that I made."[50] But did he really think this at the time? The day after photographing Churchill, Solange sent both photographs to the editor of *Saturday Night*. Had Karsh's—and possibly Solange's—political naivety prevented them from realizing that it was the first, not the second image, that was the winning photograph? Indeed, it was only when Karsh learned that the more politically astute B. K. Sandwell had chosen the defiant photograph for the cover of *Saturday Night* that Karsh sent $2 to the registrar of copyrights in Washington, D.C.

Karsh insisted that he was only prompted to take the second photograph of Churchill because "in the [first] portrait he had given me was a very dour and solemn one." The smiling portrait had, therefore, initially been Karsh's favourite of the two photographs, because Churchill had worn "a smile of confidence— confidence in the righteousness of a great cause which could not be lost and God helping him he would see it was not lost."[51] Following the publication of the first exposure in *Saturday Night* on January 10, however, Karsh received "so many letters from people saying thank you for giving us Churchill that," as he told the editor of the *Canadian Home Journal*, "I have the feeling, perhaps, that I have given them a Churchill they wanted and Churchill the smiling one will give them even more so the Churchill of Victory."[52]

What Karsh had accomplished in his first exposure was certainly not lost on newspaper editors across the country—and indeed around the world. As Madge Macbeth noted in February 1942, "Yousuf Karsh has raised the art of photography…to the art of painting."[53] She might have added that Karsh had also given documentary photographers a run for their money. Few of them had ever been given a credit line for their photographs. Few of them had ever been given adequate time to adjust the lighting or to "pose" their subjects. And few of them had been given an opportunity to append a story to their photograph. But, unlike Karsh, they were not drawing on the classical tradition of portrait painting when they took their photographs. Nor were they determined to turn statesmen into heroic figures.

Karsh, the twentieth-century court photographer, was different. He had given the world a visual analogue of the Augustan language so familiar in Winston Churchill's speeches. It is no coincidence that, when *Saturday Night* published "The Roaring Lion," it was accompanied by excerpts from Churchill's Ottawa speech. Presented together, Churchill's words and Karsh's picture were like facing pages of a book, classical and heroic in the way that they complemented each other.

PM and the *Herald Tribune* were among the first American newspapers to publish Karsh's defiant portrait of the British prime minister. On February 2, *Life* printed a large-format version with the byline "This is one of the most remarkable portraits ever taken of this humane and violent man." This was echoed on February 28, when the more ambitious *Illustrated London News* brought out a slightly sepia centrefold version, claiming it was "one of the most remarkable portraits ever taken of this most remarkable man!"

Alongside the photograph of Churchill in the *Illustrated London News* was Karsh's description of how he had removed the cigar from the British prime minister's lips. According to Madge Macbeth the story of how Churchill had been "trapped" into posing when Karsh removed the cigar was almost as significant as the image itself.[54] If every picture tells a story, this was the story that Karsh's photograph of Winston Churchill prompted.

Mackenzie King was disappointed when he saw the results of Karsh's third exposure. Karsh had only managed to capture the profiles of the two prime ministers. However, Mackenzie King was not so much concerned by the unposed nature of the photograph as by the expression on their faces. He and Churchill had been laughing about the persistence of the thirty-three-year-old photographer, and Mackenzie King did not want their jovial expression to appear in the photograph. Even so, even he admitted that Karsh's portrait of Churchill could not have been better. Indeed, Mackenzie King was so pleased with the results that he saw to it that Churchill received copies of Karsh's two portraits before he returned to Britain. Mackenzie King also presented the photographs to President Roosevelt. Then, hoping for a similar portrait, he immediately arranged for Karsh to photograph himself again. Mackenzie King adopted a pose similar to Churchill's — vainly, in more senses than one. The result, which did not appear in *Saturday Night* until October 1943, did not produce the masterpiece for which Mackenzie King had hoped.[55]

Upon returning to England after his short visit to North America, Churchill found that his popularity had gone up by 10 percent. He also discovered that, thanks to Yousuf Karsh, the press had an image that matched his defiant speeches. Despite the shortage of paper, Churchill put both photographs to good use. "The Roaring Lion" was reproduced on a poster-sized broadsheet alongside excerpts of his speeches. A cropped version of the second, smiling portrait was illustrated on a poster to encourage the British public to invest in victory bonds. And even though Churchill's family did not like the first image — his daughter, Mary, felt that "it was rather cheeky for him to take the cigar from Papa" — Churchill used it himself.[56] A cropped version of "The Roaring Lion" appeared on the cover of a volume of his war speeches, *The Unrelenting Struggle*, in 1942. And when Churchill later wrote his history of the Second World War, Karsh's famous image was used on the sixth volume, *Triumph and Tragedy*, in 1954.

"Unless we are greatly mistaken," a journalist wrote in the *Calgary Herald* on February 11, 1942, "it will be this portrait by Karsh that will go down through the centuries to give future generations their most accurate idea of the physical appearance of Winston Churchill at the moment when three quarters of the people of the world had their hopes largely based on him." What the journalist could not have predicted, however, was the extent to which Karsh's portrait would represent Churchill for the rest of his life. It was reproduced on letterheads and on postage stamps, on the covers of books, on doors and on marquees. In 1965, newspaper editors around the world chose Karsh's portrait for the front page of their newspapers to announce the former British prime minister's death. And up to this day, Karsh's portrait is given pride of place in the White House.[57]

With one shot, Karsh had created the definitive image of Winston Churchill. At the same time he had established himself as the world's most famous iconographer and image-maker. From now on, whenever he took a photograph there were expectations on the part of the person being photographed, and of Karsh himself, that he would do likewise. Like Cartier-Bresson's decisive moment, Yousuf Karsh's definitive image had become part of the dominant visual idiom of the twentieth century.

CHAPTER EIGHT

Mission to Britain

Life was hectic for Solange Karsh after *Saturday Night's* publication of Karsh's defiant portrait of Churchill on January 10, 1942. She was anxious to settle into the home that she and Yousuf had recently built on the outskirts of Ottawa, yet found herself spending more and more time in the studio. Many other newspapers and magazines in North America and in Britain wanted to publish "The Roaring Lion" and the smiling portrait of Churchill too. Solange engaged New York's British Combine Photography to sell the photographs in the United States and Miller Services Limited of Toronto to handle sales in Canada and in Britain. Not everyone was happy with this arrangement. Britain's Pictorial Press felt out of pocket because up to this time it had had sole responsibility for placing Karsh's photographs in British newspapers.

Solange not only supplied Karsh's agents with multiple copies of the Churchill photographs but also gave them an accompanying text. Titled "Now It Can Be Told About Churchill's Portrait," the document provided everyone who published the photograph with the story of how Yousuf Karsh had removed the cigar from Churchill's mouth in order to take the famous picture.[1]

What Yousuf and Solange had not expected was the extent to which "The Roaring Lion" would disrupt what Karsh called "the even tenor of our days at the studio."[2] For one thing, by February 1942 Solange was getting "so tired of answering letters about Churchill" that she was "beginning to wonder if there is anything else in our life."[3] Besides the demands from Karsh's agents, there were requests from the public. Uncertain what to charge for "The Roaring Lion," Karsh sought the advice of B. K. Sandwell. The editor suggested a retail price of $3 for an 8-by-10 and $15 for a 16-by-20-inch print; this is what anyone who asked for the portrait paid. There were also many letters of congratulations. Most fell into the category of fan mail and were answered by the secretary, Jean McJanet. But some, like the congratulatory letters from Karsh's English teacher in Sherbrooke and from his brother Jamil in Syria, required Solange and Yousuf's personal attention. Adding to this correspondence were letters from budding photographers, all of whom wanted to apprentice with Karsh. These applicants were turned down, albeit in the gracious manner that characterized the "two person letters" that Solange wrote under Yousuf's name.[4]

Although the response to the Churchill portraits disrupted life in the studio, Solange made time to capitalize on her husband's success. She asked Karsh's Toronto agent, Hamilton Miller, to approach Eastman Kodak, which had supplied the lens, the film, and the lights that Karsh used for the sitting, on the grounds that "this photograph of Churchill has a great deal of advertising value for Eastman Kodak."[5] Within a month, Kodak's Toronto store was displaying Karsh's photograph of Churchill in its window. Solange also encouraged every major magazine that had not yet published either portrait of Churchill to do so. "As I know you are a wide-awake magazine, I am quite sure that you have seen Karsh's portrait of Churchill," she told the editor of the American-based *Cornet* magazine. "Perhaps you would be interested in reproducing some of Yousuf Karsh's work?"[6] Finally, whenever a magazine or newspaper failed to print the byline "Karsh, Ottawa," under "The Roaring Lion," they could expect to receive a letter from Solange demanding that an apology appear in the next issue.

Besides doing all of these things, Solange saw to it that whenever a dignitary visited Ottawa or a nearby city, Yousuf was there to photograph him or her. For example, when the Quebec Conference was held in Quebec City in 1943, Solange made sure that Karsh was given an opportunity to commemorate the event,

which brought together what Peter Clarke has called the "Not-So-Big Three" —
Mackenzie King, Roosevelt, and Churchill.[7]

Solange's involvement in the Karsh Studio did not end after she had typed a letter or made arrangements for a sitting with a dignitary. Following Karsh's session with Madame Chiang Kai-shek in June 1943, for example, Solange thanked Mackenzie King for making the sitting possible. She encouraged B. K. Sandwell, whose magazine was a beneficiary of Karsh's portraits of famous personalities, to thank the prime minister for making the sitting possible. She also asked "Dr. Bunny," as she called Sandwell, to ask Mackenzie King "whether it would not sometimes be possible to assign a more restful moment for Mr. Karsh's operations."[8]

Sandwell agreed to put pressure on the prime minister, largely because Karsh had been disappointed with the results of the portrait he had taken of Madame Chiang Kai-shek. In spite of her playful manner with Karsh and Mackenzie King — as Karsh was about to click the shutter, she exclaimed, "I am sorry, gentlemen, I do not smoke cigars!" — the sitting lasted only a few minutes. Karsh had had little time for conversation that might have helped him get beneath the heavy makeup that covered Madame Chiang Kai-shek's unsightly skin condition and made her face look like enamel. Two years later, during the summer of 1944, Karsh produced an equally unsuccessful portrait of General de Gaulle. Karsh complained that he only had five minutes with the leader of the Free French before the press photographers had their go at the general. As a result, de Gaulle looks stiff and anything but engaged with the photographer. Given that Karsh had had even less time with Winston Churchill, it is a miracle that the portrait of the British prime minister turned out the way it did.

As Solange noted, the attention given to Karsh's photograph of Churchill made her husband more humble than proud. Indeed, success did not find Karsh resting on his laurels. With Jean McJanet looking after the secretarial side of things and two other employees doing the developing, the printing, and the touching up, "the Maestro," as they called Karsh, was free to spend most of his time in the camera room. He had up to six one-hour sittings a day, broken only by lunch with Solange at their favourite Chinese restaurant. Even so, half of the people in Ottawa who wanted to be "Karshed" were turned away.

After December 30, 1941, Karsh's priorities began to change. He knew that he could keep his name before the Canadian public by publishing his portraits of visiting dignitaries in magazines like *Saturday Night* and by addressing luncheon clubs and photographers' conventions. He knew, equally, that he could double his income by raising his fees and by increasing the number of people he photographed during the course of a day. But he wanted more than money and recognition within Canada. He wanted to build on the international recognition that he had gained after photographing Winston Churchill. However, this was not an easy thing to do in wartime Canada.

It was Karsh's brother Malak who offered him a way through. Having long supplied photographs to British newspapers through Pictorial Press, Malak had become, by the autumn of 1942, that agency's representative in Canada. After December 1941, Pictorial Press encouraged Yousuf Karsh to send them photographs too, "so that we can keep your pictures and your name before the eyes of those who manage the big society magazines here."⁹ The British publisher George G. Harrap was equally interested in making Karsh's name known outside Canada. In the autumn of 1942 he offered to publish a book devoted to Karsh's portraits. Karsh jumped at the opportunity and promised to supply Harrap with no fewer than seventy portraits of personalities and seventy 150-word captions.

Karsh was hardly in a position, however, to expand his list of personalities and thus meet the requests from Harrap and Pictorial Press for more portraits. He had already photographed virtually every resident dignitary in Ottawa. There were no royal tours during the war and visits from foreign dignitaries and entertainers were few and far between. And even if he could have afforded to travel abroad, Europe was obviously out of bounds, and so was the United States: only those Canadians whose work was of an official nature could secure permission to leave the country during the war. It did not look like things would change — until Karsh's old friends B. K. Sandwell and Mackenzie King came to his rescue.

JUST LIKE PRESIDENT ROOSEVELT, Mackenzie King was distrustful of the totalitarian implications of government propaganda. He had only reluctantly agreed to attach Canada's wartime propaganda agency, the Bureau of Public Information—later absorbed into the War Information Board—to his own office in 1940. And he had balked at the idea of hiring Canadian artists to record the home and war fronts as they had done during the First World War. It was only through the intervention of Vincent Massey, then the Canadian high commissioner in London, that fifteen artists were attached to the army, navy, and air force in the spring of 1943.

On the other hand, Mackenzie King did not object to letting the established media—the National Film Board and the Canadian Broadcasting Corporation—influence public opinion. Nor was he against commemorating the war though tablets, sculptures, and memorials, provided he had a hand in writing the inscriptions, in creating the designs, and in choosing the place where they would be installed. Above all, he liked official portraits, particularly when he was the subject, as every visiting dignitary to Laurier House discovered when Mackenzie King showed them photographs of himself, of his mother and—to the horror of President Roosevelt—of Adolf Hitler, whom Mackenzie King had met shortly before the outbreak of the war.

It is not surprising, therefore, that when Sandwell approached Mackenzie King with the idea of sending Karsh to England in order to make portraits of the leading actors in the war, the prime minister jumped at the idea. The publication of Karsh's portraits in the national and international press would show the rest of the world, and Britain in particular, that Canada was doing more than her share of the fighting. Equally, if Karsh's portraits were deposited in the Canadian archives, they would not only serve as a memorial to every leading participant in the war but also provide military scholars with visual documents of wartime leaders.

In the early spring of 1943, Sandwell began compiling a list of personalities whom Karsh could photograph if he were to travel to England. Solange began collecting what would amount to thirty-two letters of introduction in anticipation of Yousuf's visit too. Yet, she need not have bothered, because Karsh's anticipated visit was being arranged by the Canadian prime minister in concert with the War Information Board and the Department of External Affairs. Towards the end of the spring, Karsh met with the under-secretary of state for External Affairs. Norman Robertson gave the young photographer $350 towards the cost of his equipment and guaranteed his passage to England. Robertson also assured Karsh that, once he had arrived in the British capital, the Canadian high commissioner himself, Vincent Massey, and the prime minister's London-based personal assistant, Leonard Brockington, would help him photograph as many personalities as possible during his sixty-day visit.

In the eyes of the Canadian government, Yousuf Karsh was clearly the right man for the job. He had an ability, as one reporter noted in 1942, "to determine character almost in a flash."[10] He had a reputation for not wasting the time of busy people and for being able to adapt his equipment to any situation that he encountered outside the camera room. He was a known quantity. By 1942 he and Mackenzie King had become friends. Leonard Brockington, who supported the prime minister's decision to send Karsh to England, had recently become Karsh's lawyer. And while Vincent Massey and Norman Robertson could not claim to know Karsh well, they were nevertheless familiar with his work.

Karsh was also attractive to Canadian government officials because there was little possibility that the publication of his portraits of wartime leaders would create disharmony among the Allies. Clearly, Karsh could be relied upon to produce a positive, even flattering, portrait that would make the public not only more familiar with but also more sympathetic to their leaders.

B. K. Sandwell had as much to gain from Karsh's visit to Britain as the Canadian government. Sandwell knew that the public wanted to see what their wartime leaders looked like. This was why *Saturday Night* advanced Karsh $1,000 for the right to publish any black-and-white photographs that he took in England. This was also why the editor of the rival *Maclean's* magazine, Napier Moore, bought the rights to every photograph that Karsh produced in colour. (Karsh would receive $250 if a photograph appeared on the front cover of *Maclean's* and $150 if it was published inside the magazine.) Finally, when

Pictorial Press and British Combine heard that Karsh was about to travel to England, they began negotiations with the *Illustrated London News* and *Life* magazine, respectively.

However Karsh's trip to Britain turned out, he was not going to be out of pocket. The Canadian government had agreed to cover his travel expenses, on the condition that copies of his photographs were deposited in the Canadian public archives. The national and international press had offered him a hefty fee for the right to publish his black-and-white and colour photographs. And a prominent British publisher had already paid him a handsome advance on sales when he had signed a contract with the company a year earlier.

Suddenly, therefore, Karsh was not only about to have an opportunity to expand his list of personalities and thereby enhance his reputation at a time when it was difficult to do so. He was also about to move into a higher income bracket. Above all, he was being given a chance to make "a small contribution in my own way and according to my own special training and tal-

Princess Elizabeth,   ents, to the outcome of the struggle."[11]

1943

IN EARLY SEPTEMBER 1943, Solange accompanied Yousuf—and 750 pounds of photographic equipment, which was neatly packed in black cases and cardboard boxes—as far as Montreal. Then she returned to Ottawa.

Although Solange reported to Jamil and Salim that their brother was going "on the greatest adventure of his life," she was anxious.[12] Yousuf was going away for two months and, given that he had so completely dominated her life since their marriage, she was not looking forward to being alone. Moreover, he had little experience of world travel. "See that he gets the necessary ration cards and advise him about many British manners," Solange told Pictorial Press. And Yousuf, though thirty-four, was not used to travelling on his own. "I don't know how he will even find a telephone number (he has never had to do it)," Solange further explained.[13]

Solange's anxiety proved to be well founded. When Karsh reached Halifax, where almost twenty years earlier he had first set foot on Canadian soil, he

discovered that his ship, the *Queen Mary*, had left without him. This meant that he had to forsake the luxury of sailing to England on one of the fastest liners on the ocean and instead travel by convoy.

Years later, Karsh recalled that the crossing to England was relaxing and peaceful, although dull. During it he learned how to put on a Mae West life jacket in thirty seconds flat. He made light conversation with the other seven passengers on board their Norwegian freighter. But most of the time he worried about his irreplaceable equipment, which had been stored in the hold of the ship. Upon arriving in England he discovered that his concern had been justified, because unknown to Karsh and his fellow passengers the ship had been loaded to the gunwales with explosives.

Once Karsh and his equipment reached London, there was less to worry about. After checking into the Savoy Hotel, he walked down The Strand to Canada House, where he was greeted by the Canadian high commissioner.

Vincent Massey had known of Karsh's work ever since the founding of the Dominion Drama Festival in 1933. Like Karsh, Massey believed that visual images were the best means of commemorating the war and of letting the public know what was happening on the home and war fronts. This was why Massey gave Karsh two assistants, put a car and a driver at his disposal, and assigned the Canada House press relations officer, Campbell Moodie, with the task of looking after the photographer during his visit to London.

The charming and resourceful Campbell Moodie introduced Karsh to the personnel in the publicity section of the British Ministry of Information. He put the Canadian Army's darkroom facilities, located in the basement of Canada House, at Karsh's disposal. He got permission from the British government to allow Kodak to exceed their quota of rationed paper when it came to Karsh. And, most important of all, Moodie persuaded various dignitaries to sit for the Canadian photographer.

Before he left Canada, Pictorial Press had warned Karsh that it might be difficult to photograph everyone on the list that he and Sandwell had compiled. Yet thanks to the well-connected Vincent Massey and the persistence of Campbell Moodie, few doors remained closed. Indeed, Karsh was so successful that other professional photographers, according to Leonard Brockington, were far from being in love with the Canadian photographer because he got all of the sittings.[14]

Unlike the British photographer Bill Brandt, who was taking pictures of wartorn London for the Ministry of Information, Karsh was not in Britain to photograph the people he saw lying on two-tier metal bunks in the London tube stations. Or the children who told him how they had hidden under a table when their house had been partly destroyed by a blast. Or the burnt-out bomb sites that were rapidly becoming covered with rosebay willow-herb and fireweed. Or the defiantly unsilenced orators who entertained Karsh in Hyde Park. Or the smashed docks that he saw in London's East End. Or the casualties whom he met from the Sicilian campaign and who were now in a hospital on the outskirts of London. Or the "beautiful court" that he admired at Oxford's Magdalen College, where he spent a peaceful hour. Or the colourful military personnel — French sailors with their red pom-poms and striped shirts, Polish officers with their dragoon-like mortarboards, and British nurses with their scarlet-lined cloaks — whom he saw parading around London.[15] None of these subjects came within Karsh's remit. He had come to Britain to take portraits. And thirty-six hours after arriving in London on September 12, Karsh was on the job.

Lord Wavell, who was preparing to leave Britain in order to take up his post as Viceroy of India, was Karsh's first subject. Following the sitting, which had taken place at the Dorchester Hotel, a reporter told readers of the London *Star* that Yousuf Karsh was in their city to photograph fifty Allied celebrities for "the Ottawa War Gallery." And Karsh told the reporter that Lord Wavell had possessed "a fine, strong face," which would surely make the resulting portrait of him "another Churchill."[16]

Being well briefed was essential to the success of every portrait that Karsh made in England. One person who helped him do this was the Pictorial Press's Tom Blau. Like Karsh, Blau was a refugee — in his case from Nazi Germany. Like Karsh again, he possessed old-world charm and old-world manners. He also shared Karsh's exquisite taste in clothing: when the two men met for the first time in London's Trafalgar Square, each confronted virtually a mirror image of himself.[17] Meeting every other evening at the Savoy Hotel, Blau left Karsh laden with potted biographies and press photographs of the people he was about to photograph. "These informal pictures," Karsh later recalled, "were very helpful in their revelation of characteristics, and greatly assisted my own interpretation of these personalities when I came to portray them."[18]

In addition to receiving assistance from Tom Blau, Karsh was helped by a circle of friends whom he described in a letter home to Solange as "little Canada."[19] Among the Canadians whom Karsh met at the Savoy were officers who had transformed a riverside suite into a club where they could relax while on leave. There were Canadian civilians too, like Leonard Brockington, with whom Karsh often shared wartime austerity dishes such as Woolton pie and tarte de Gaulle in the Savoy's Grill and River Room.

Brockington and the other Canadians at the hotel also briefed Karsh on the people he was about to photograph. His friends also encouraged him to give impromptu exhibitions of his proofs in his hotel room. They helped him make connections with non-political subjects such as the dramatist George Bernard Shaw. And they gave him an account of the progress of the war. The "marvellous talk" of his Canadian friends reminded Karsh of the lively and informative discussions that he had listened to in John Garo's studio more than ten years earlier.[20]

There was much for Karsh to absorb. Three days before he arrived in Britain, the post-Mussolini Italian government had surrendered. During his visit, the Canadians, along with the British and American armies, had begun to inch their way up the boot of Italy. The Allies had also commenced their round-the-clock bombing of Munich, Frankfurt, and Hanover. And, on the eastern front, the Russians had opened a new offensive against the Germans.

Mindful of the censor, Karsh said little in his letters home about the exigencies of the war. His upbeat missives told Solange how much he liked the food and how he even liked the blackouts: "It brings to me many happy recollections of my childhood using the small torches in the dark of night reminds me of Christmas time when my father led us children at midnight mass."[21] In an effort to introduce some normality into Yousuf's life, Solange told him about the Siberian maples, tamarack, mountain ash, and honey locust at Little Wings, which were ablaze with colour. She assured him that she was holding the fort at the studio. She also told him that she missed him to such an extent that she was "almost afraid to admit it."[22]

Karsh never complained about the long queues for food, or told Solange about the hour-long drone of the Allied bombers that blackened the sky on their flight to Germany every night, or about the air-raid sirens that sent people scurrying for shelter in the London underground especially when, on October 9, fifteen German planes dropped thirty tons of bombs on London. Of more concern to Karsh was the possibility that he might put a wrong foot forward by committing a grammatical error or by breaching British rules of etiquette. This was why, shortly after arriving in London, he composed a "Daily Prayer": "Oh Lord, Help me to keep my big mouth shut until I know what I am talking about."[23]

Karsh evidently need not have worried about his manners or about making a grammatical faux pas, because he seems to have impressed everyone he met. Leonard Brockington and Vincent Massey were charmed. Karsh "has quite enchanted Canada House which normally is a very reserved, taciturn organization," Tom Blau told Solange in late September.[24] And Blau was charmed too. "It is unique," he told Solange in another letter, "the way he manages to catch people's names, repeat them as he focuses from the waist and then comes up, focussing them closely with a friendly courteous smile."[25] Blau was equally impressed by Karsh's "unfathomable shrewdness." "His lovely baroque manners almost succeed in covering it up," Blau continued, "but I was aware of it from the first."[26]

It should not be thought, however, that things always went smoothly. Sittings usually had to be squeezed between conferences or meetings. This made things difficult for someone who described himself to a London-based Canadian journalist as no "hit and run photographer."[27] Not only was the time allowed for a sitting too short, but it often took place late at night or in the early hours of the morning.

There were also problems of another kind. Karsh had to reduce his bulky photographic equipment to a minimum since it, along with himself, his two assistants, and driver, had to fit into the army jeep. Once Karsh arrived at his destination, the lack of standardized electrical outlets posed another challenge. Sometimes he had to work without the aid of artificial light or use a combination of artificial and natural light. Then there was a lack of space in which to take a photograph. Much to the horror of his clients, Karsh ordered his assistants to move furniture, lamps, and, when he was at Buckingham Palace, a massive chandelier. Having to take photographs outside the controlled environment of the studio was taxing. Most studio photographers would have collapsed from exhaustion under these conditions. Not so Yousuf Karsh. According to Tom Blau, Karsh's capacity and appetite for hard work had—just like his polished manners—to be seen to be believed.

In sixty days Karsh had more than sixty sittings. And of the resulting portraits, he felt that at least forty-two were "major portraits."[28] It was a remarkable feat to get to so many high-ranking dignitaries to make time for a sitting with Yousuf Karsh. Besides photographing virtually every leading official in the British government and armed services, he also had sittings with many foreign dignitaries, including the president and the prime minister of Czechoslovakia, the commander of the French Army in North Africa, the crown prince of Norway, the prime minister of the Polish Republic, and the prime minister of South Africa, Field Marshal Jan Smuts.

David Low, 1943

In an effort to expand his list of personalities, Karsh arranged sittings with the playwright Noel Coward, the author H. G. Wells, and the cartoonist David Low. He photographed old friends like Susan Tweedsmuir, now living on the outskirts of Oxford. He also photographed the new friends that he made, like the commander of 1st Canadian Corps in Britain, General H. D. G. Crerar, with whom he spent a restful weekend at his country house.

Most of the people who sat for Karsh were cooperative, if short of time. King George helped him hang the army blanket that served as a backdrop for his portrait. The future queen, then Princess Elizabeth, gave Karsh tips on how to photograph her mother: "'Do you think that is the right expression, or should it be more smiling?'"[29] Noel Coward gave Karsh a drink—something that was not always easy to come by in wartime London. And the cartoonist David Low threatened to draw a cartoon portrait of him.

Only a few people turned Karsh away. When the sculptor Jacob Epstein saw him, his two assistants, and the mountain of photographic equipment on his doorstep, he refused to let the men into the house. Others had to be coaxed into

Noel Coward, 1943

Lord Beaverbrook, 1943

cooperating with the ever-demanding photographer. Lord Beaverbrook insisted that he be photographed with his thumbs through the lower loops of his braces, because "'Everyone sees me that way.'"[30] Karsh was not going to be told how to pose his subject, however. He made Beaverbrook take a less aggressive, more reflective pose by engaging the former minister of aircraft production in a discussion about post-war commercial air travel.

The sitting with the eighty-seven-year-old Nobel laureate for literature, George Bernard Shaw, seemed equally unpromising. Karsh insisted that the furniture in Shaw's house had to be rearranged before the sitting could take place. Shaw's secretary made it clear that no furniture could be moved. The matter was settled in Karsh's favour only when he confronted the playwright: "'Mr. Shaw, if your hands were tied behind your back and your mouth sealed and then you were asked to write your best play, what would you do?'"[31]

Karsh had his favourite subjects. Lord Louis Mountbatten, the ladies' pin-up during the war, was judged the most handsome. To underscore this point, Karsh gave a debonair touch to the portrait by asking Mountbatten to wear his naval officer's cap slightly off centre. The young Gurkha subahdar Lalbahadur Thapa, who had just been awarded the Victoria Cross for his bravery, brandished a long knife during the sitting, which the photographer likewise braved. The actor and playwright Noel Coward was the most elegantly dressed and, unlike the deputy prime minister, Clement Attlee, who made it a point of pride to wear his old suits during wartime clothes rationing, the most vain. Finally, the king, whom Karsh attempted to portray as "a man who has felt the war," was tactfully saluted as his most gracious sitter.[32]

King George VI, 1943

Karsh was determined to make everyone whom he photographed represent the deeds or the station that had put them on his list. But did he? He certainly transformed an otherwise timid-looking King George into a commanding figure. Since Karsh told Solange that photographing the king was "the big event, or rather, one of the biggest events of my life," he took extra care to make sure that the photograph turned out the way it did.[33] Conversely, Karsh made Princess Elizabeth appear to be as carefree as any other eighteen-year-old woman, when in fact she was as serious-minded as her father. Lord Wavell and Herbert

Morrison each had only one functional eye, yet in Karsh's portraits of them there is no suggestion of this disability. The future British prime minister Clement Attlee, who, according to one biographer, was famous for his "extraordinary ordinariness," was made into a dynamic, if mysterious, figure in Karsh's portrait of him.[34] Noel Coward looked his suave, confident self; George Bernard Shaw his most impish; and David Low his most whimsical. Although there was never any doubt about the force of personality or the ability of the minister of aircraft production, Lord Beaverbrook, in stature this Canadian from New Brunswick was short and squat. Yet in Karsh's portrait of him, Beaverbrook appears to possess a large and commanding physique.

Including hands in almost every portrait that he took while in England gave Karsh's work a dynamic quality. He knew that a person's hands could, as he said on more than one occasion, "be as expressive of a person's character as the face."[35] This was why he had made the gnarled knuckles of John Buchan as prominent as his lined face in his 1938 portrait. Karsh knew that a photographer could make a subject's hands look like claws if they were placed against the face. Or make them appear clumsy if the broad, flat view of a hand was turned towards the camera. Or introduce a sense of disorder in the photograph if the fingers were interlocked. Karsh avoided every one of these visual traps. Indeed, whether sunk into pockets, clasping a lapel, resting on the hip or on the back of a chair, or holding a cigarette, the hands in Karsh's portraits were as important a feature as a raised eyebrow or the suggestion of a smile.

George Bernard
Shaw, 1943

AT THE OUTBREAK OF THE WAR, Karsh had made it his mission to tell the truth in terms of beauty. Once in England, however, he saw what he called his "Mission to Britain" in military terms.[36] "I am a photographer on the offensive," he wrote shortly after arriving in London. "I first reconnoiter the territory by gathering as much information as is obtainable about my sitter; then in meeting him, I engage him in light skirmishes until I have got the situation in hand…Then and only after I am satisfied that I have secured a clear mental picture of my subject," he continued, "do I launch operations in earnest."[37] When Karsh returned

to Ottawa following his successful trip, he continued to feel that his "portrayal of the men who shape our destinies is a small contribution in my own way" to the running of the war.[38]

On his first morning back in Ottawa in late November 1943, Karsh had a visitor from Toronto who helped him put his war aims into practice. Having bought the rights to Karsh's British photographs for *Saturday Night*, B. K. Sandwell was there to welcome him home—and to see his proofs. Sandwell need not have worried about the quality of Karsh's work. Blau, who had seen the uncorrected proofs before they were sent to Canada by diplomatic mailbag, found them to be up to Karsh's high standard.

Over the next two months, Karsh and his assistants transformed his closely guarded negatives and marked-up proofs into finished prints. After they had done this, Sandwell introduced Karsh's British photographs to the Canadian public on January 29, 1944 with a portrait of the king on the cover of *Saturday Night*. During the next twelve months Sandwell published several other portraits from Karsh's "Mission to Britain" on either the cover of his magazine or heading the "Name in the News" column. *Maclean's*, which still had the publication rights to Karsh's work in colour, published his British portraits on its cover two days after its rival, *Saturday Night*, had begun publishing its own.

Canadians had an opportunity to see the results of Karsh's trip to Britain in yet another form when, in February 1944, seventy-five portraits were put on display at the Château Laurier. During the eight-day-long exhibition nearly 26,000 people—all anxious to see how the local photographer had portrayed their wartime leaders—lined up to view Karsh's portraits. The collection was then put on show at Simpson's department store in Toronto. "Each is a brilliant and memorable masterpiece of Karsh's great Genius," went one advertisement in the *Globe and Mail*, "for Karsh photographs great men as they have seldom been photographed."[39] After Toronto, the exhibition moved to Montreal, and then to Winnipeg, where it met with equal success.

In Toronto for the exhibition, Karsh took the time to address a gathering of the Women's Canadian Club at the Eaton Auditorium. Dramatizing his work with a practised technique that he and Solange had long mastered, he told stories about the personalities he had photographed in England. He revealed that he had begun "to feel rather sad and unhappy" about his wartime work. "Had I been able to show just what made these personalities great?" he asked his audience. But then, whether opportunely or opportunistically, he read out a letter that had recently appeared in the *Montreal Standard* for February 12, 1944. The French-Canadian man who had written the letter not only insisted that Karsh's portrait of King George had made him feel proud to be a Canadian, he suggested that "this brilliant piece of photography, if displayed in every Canadian home, could be a real incentive toward racial harmony" and thereby "do more than the most convincing politician to dispel and eradicate that absurd wave of wartime opportunism and demagoguism which has infested our political life."[40] It is hard to imagine that Karsh was unaware of the effects that he created, at the lectern as much as in the darkroom.

IN ACCORDANCE WITH copyright law in 1943, every portrait that a photographer took—with the exception of those of the royal family—could be published only once. After that, permission had to be secured from the subject. Tom Blau helped Karsh do this. And Karsh's British and American agents were free to sell the photographs to anyone who wanted to publish them.

The editors of the *Illustrated London News* chose Karsh's black-and-white photographs for their magazine. From January 8 to May 20, 1944, they appeared under the heading "The Men Who Shape Our Destinies." Mackenzie King, who found himself featured in the company of King George and other luminaries in the British magazine, was pleased. So was Karsh, who received more coverage in the British press than ever before. And so was Tom Blau, who had not only sold the photographs to the *Illustrated London News* but also found clients for Karsh's work in other newspapers in Britain as well as in France, Switzerland, and Sweden.

Karsh's British photographs were popular because, as with the famous photograph of Winston Churchill, they could be used to reinforce wartime patriotic rhetoric. For example, according to the *Sunday Times*, Karsh's portrait of the South African leader General Smuts expressed "the resolution of a man of Empire, great soldier and world statesman, whose untiring work is cementing the bonds of the British brotherhood of nations as now being furthered at the Empire Conference in London."[41]

It was the same with the *Life* article "Leaders of Britain." Published on February 4, 1944, it was devoted to the men "who in this hour of war truly stand for England." This time, however, Karsh's photographs of figures like Lord Louis Mountbatten, King George, and George Bernard Shaw were accompanied by a text that told how Karsh had taken every photograph. According to *Life*, "the brilliance of Karsh's portraits depends a good deal on what he has just said to the sitter." It also depended on the skillful way in which Karsh had drawn his subjects into argument and, the writer added, on the way in which he had brought out his subject's character through his ingenious lighting. Most of the dignitaries featured in "Leaders of Britain" did appear to be engaged with the photographer. And most of them did, as Karsh hoped they would, look like men of action on whom the public could rely.

With the publication of his work in *Saturday Night*, *Maclean's* and *Life*, Karsh had the satisfaction of being not just a one-photograph man. He was equally pleased that, even after he had left England, his art was being put to the service of the war effort. As he proudly told the editor of *Life*, "The Canadian Government officials most definitely feel that my sympathetic presentation of 'Leaders of Britain' had done a great deal to help further mutual and international understanding."[42]

Photographing so many dignitaries during his "Mission to Britain" had, Karsh recalled years later, other benefits. It enabled him to lay the foundations of his international portfolio "in the most satisfying fashion possible."[43] It also established a reliable way of presenting a photograph by Karsh to the public. From now on, every important subject that he met would have a story. And every story that Karsh told would have a photograph. Karsh thus satisfied the public by telling as well as showing. At the same time, he kept his name before the public. After Karsh returned from England, the central figures in his portraits were no longer only the subjects portrayed, but also the man who stood behind the camera.

CHAPTER NINE

On Assignment

By 1942 Yousuf Karsh should have been enjoying real prosperity. The studio's net profits were over fourteen thousand dollars, compared with an annual average of eight thousand dollars during the three previous years. Yet, Karsh had now become a victim of his own success, mainly because earning more money pushed him into a higher bracket of wartime taxation. That year he not only had to pay a "normal tax" of $894 on his personal income, but was also hit with a "graduated tax" of $5,600. Moreover, any part of the Karsh Studio's profits deemed to exceed "standard profits" for 1936–39 was hit by the introduction of the Excess Profits Tax (EPT) in 1941.

The combined effect was piquant. In 1942, the difference between his own personal income, allowed as "salary of owner," and the total profits of the studio was subject to EPT, levied at a punitive rate of 100 percent. This difference amounted to nearly $1,400, bringing the total paid in taxes to nearly $8,000. Compared with 1939, the studio's net profits in 1942 had nearly doubled, but Karsh himself was left with a net disposable income of only $6,291 — a thousand dollars less than he had had three years before.[1]

No wonder Solange brushed Jamil Karsh's request aside when he asked for $500 towards the cost of his study at medical school in Beirut. "We hear of the

fame of Yousuf and even we see the pictures he photographs as that big photograph of the great man Churchill," Jamil wrote to Solange and Yousuf in June
1942. But the hoped-for assistance was not forthcoming. As Solange told her
brother-in-law by return mail, "You will have to do as your own brother Yousuf
did and achieve what you want out of life by working for it."[2]

Solange attempted to alleviate the taxation woes of the Karsh Studio when, in
October 1944, she appeared before the Income Tax Department's Board of Referees.
"I was definitely told," she recalled a few years later, "that Yousuf Karsh might be
an artist, but that as far as they're concerned he was a photographer earning his
living with his photography." This meant, Solange explained, that "for taxation
purposes all photographers were businessmen and not professionals."[3]

While Yousuf was happy to let Solange represent his financial interests before
the Board of Referees and was always reluctant to discuss fees with his clients—
that was left to Solange and his private secretary, Jean McJanet—he was as
shrewd as his illiterate father about financial matters. Yousuf knew that he had
to keep his name in the international arena if he was to maintain his high profile and his growing income, which was increasing due to the sales to publishers
of photographs of prominent statesmen. In 1944, for example, Tom Blau suggested that Karsh should spend a few weeks every year in London because, in his
view, no advertising campaign would be better than the week-by-week exposure of Karsh's British portraits in the illustrated press.

Karsh believed success possible because he possessed a unique ability to
establish an instant rapport with and win the confidence of powerful statesmen
(and, less often, stateswomen), people in the media, be it B. K. Sandwell at *Saturday Night* or Floyd Chalmers at *Maclean's*, and agents like Tom Blau in London.
Even though it was always more satisfying to work in his own studio, Karsh
understood that his business depended partly on his ability to take a good picture in any venue.

Karsh was entering the world of photojournalism at the right time. While
large-format picture magazines had been around North America since *Illustrated
America* hit the newsstands in 1890, new technologies and the public's increasing
demand for visual images of every noteworthy event and every important person saw a new generation of photographers prosper through their association

with the illustrated press. For example, Sandwell could never get enough photographs of prominent leaders for *Saturday Night*. And, although *Life* magazine had its own photographers in the field during the Second World War, it also bought pictures from freelance photographers or hired them for specific assignments.

All of this augured well for Karsh. *Saturday Night, Life, Collier's Weekly, House Beautiful, Fortune,* and *Esquire,* not to mention magazines and newspapers in Britain and continental Europe, published Karsh's portraits on the front covers of their magazines. Impatient with depending on what came to them through his agents, some even commissioned him to produce portraits.

It was a stroke of good luck that Karsh's first photo assignment in the United States was with *Life*. Launched in 1936, and modelled on France's *Vu* and Britain's *Picture Post, Life* was the leading picture magazine in America. No wonder journalists and photographers scrambled to sell their words and their pictures to the publication, which at its peak claimed a weekly readership of more than twenty million people.

With leading photographers like Margaret Bourke-White and W. Eugene Smith working for *Life*, Karsh was in good company. Unlike most of the photographers, he was assured that his portraits would be accompanied with his byline. Moreover, like White and Carl Mydans among others, Karsh was allowed to bring another dimension to his portraits by providing written copy to accompany his visual images. This is not to suggest, however, that *Life* never altered Karsh's captions — written largely by Solange — to fit the magazine's conservative ethnocentric view of the world and thereby reflect Henry Luce's "messianic belief in America and the American way of life."[4] Or that the magazine's editor would not set the tone of a sitting beforehand by providing Karsh with a list of "human interest" questions to ask his subject.

Even before *Life* published "Leaders of Britain" on February 7, 1944, its editor, Wilson Hicks, asked Karsh if he would consider travelling to Washington, D.C., in order to photograph seventy American dignitaries. Karsh told Hicks that he liked the idea of spending the spring of 1944 in the United States. After all, the country was about to host an international conference at Dumbarton Oaks, in Washington, in order to discuss the founding of what would become the United Nations Organization. There would be not only a significant number of important American dignitaries in the nation's capital, but international statesmen and women too.

Moreover, Karsh knew that *Life*, from whom he had received $3,500 for his "Leaders of Britain" photo essay, paid well. Hoping to receive an even higher fee than his previous commission, Karsh told his American agent, J. E. Lewis of British Combine Photography, that he would only accept the assignment if *Life* would give him $100 a day plus expenses. Lewis, who was negotiating the commission, passed this information on to Wilson Hicks. When Hicks heard what Karsh was asking for, he nearly fell backwards over his chair, exclaiming that the suggestion was too rich for his blood.[5] But *Life* wanted Karsh. And Karsh wanted the job. The two parties therefore compromised: Karsh agreed to accept the handsome fee of $7,500. This was just $1,500 shy of what he had asked for in the first place.

The editor of *Life* was not the only person who was eager to see Karsh in Washington. When officials at the American Embassy in Ottawa got wind of Karsh's forthcoming visit to the United States, they asked one American senator to "extend to Mr. and Mrs. Karsh any courtesies which you may be able to do," adding that Karsh was "unsurpassed in his art."[6] The Ottawa-based British high commissioner, Malcolm MacDonald, hoped that Karsh would have time to photograph British officials who were arriving in Washington for the Dumbarton Oaks conference. "No doubt you hate having your photograph taken," MacDonald told Field Marshal Sir John Dill and Lord Halifax, "but I hope, not only as an act of personal kindness to Mr Karsh, but also in the interest of posterity that you will agree."[7]

Canada's Department of External Affairs and War Information Board were not to be outdone by their strongest allies. Karsh's "Leaders of Britain," according to one official at External Affairs, had "done a great deal to help further mutual and international understanding."[8] And, even though the Canadian agencies were reluctant to jump on the cultural diplomacy bandwagon, they were nevertheless convinced that "the publicity value of his [Karsh's] work places him in a somewhat different category from most other businessmen."[9]

External Affairs thus saw to it that Karsh had the full cooperation of officials at the Canadian Embassy in Washington, D.C., and the Canadian War Information Board in New York. The department offered to transport, by means of diplomatic mailbag, his proofs back to Ottawa or anywhere else that Karsh wished to send them. It lent him photographic and developing equipment. And it offered to help him make portraits of several Canadians who were living in the United States. The list of prospective subjects included government officials and cultural figures like the band leader Guy Lombardo, whose Royal Canadians had played in New York's Roosevelt Grill since 1929, and the Canadian tenor Edward Johnson, who was the director of New York's Metropolitan Opera.

WHEN KARSH LEFT for New York and Washington in March 1944, his "Leaders of Britain" article had recently appeared in *Life*. He had secured a large fee from the same magazine for another assignment. And Solange was at his side. It was Solange who oversaw the travel arrangements; Solange who, in preparation for a sitting, darkened eyebrows and temples with mascara and put the client at ease with her lively and informal conversation; Solange who made sure that before the sitting took place, Yousuf showed his client the leather-bound portfolio containing his favourite portraits.

Seeing photographs of George Bernard Shaw, Paul Robeson, and Winston Churchill, among other notables, assured Karsh's clients that they were in good company and, even more important, that the photographer might do them equal justice. This exercise also gave Karsh a segue into conversation. No client could remain mute after hearing the story of how Karsh had taken the cigar from Churchill's lips or how Shaw, when he had discovered that Karsh was Armenian, exclaimed, "I have many friends among the Armenians, but to keep them strong and healthy they should be exterminated every little while."[10]

Solange was not Karsh's only assistant on this trip to Washington. *Life* made the services of *Time* magazine's Washington bureau available to him. The Washington staff not only gave Karsh potted biographies of the people he was going to photograph, they also gave him questions to ask his clients and they made the appointments for the sittings. They also saw to it that the 700 pounds of equipment that the couple had brought with them on the train from Ottawa was not only transported around Washington but set up to Karsh's satisfaction before every sitting.

Once Solange and Yousuf had installed themselves in separate rooms at the Wardman Park Hotel, they embarked on a gruelling schedule. The mornings and afternoons were spent travelling between government buildings, hotels, and embassies for the sittings. During the evenings, Karsh transformed his hotel bathroom into a developing room so that he could provide his clients with proofs the day after their sittings. It took Karsh three months to complete over seventy portraits of politicians, military figures, diplomats, justices of the Supreme Court, and high-ranking civil servants. He also fulfilled a number of private commissions; at $350 a sitting, these were lucrative. He took photographs of the Pentagon building, the Senate, and the White House for his London agent, Tom Blau. And while Karsh did not manage to photograph any of the Canadians that had been suggested to him by officials at External Affairs, he did make good use of the diplomatic mailbag to transport his film and his proofs back to Canada.

Yousuf Karsh in Washington, May 1944

Karsh had been tired when he arrived in Washington. And with the inevitable loss of a night's sleep before each sitting with an important personality, he became even more exhausted. There were other factors that contributed to his deteriorating physical state. During the sitting itself, he had to work under considerable pressure. "How long will this take?" was the refrain that usually greeted Yousuf and Solange before a session. This was because the people Karsh was photographing were not only busy, they were used to the quick-snapping press photographers who took little of their time. Karsh's worries did not end here. Once the session was over, there was always the fear that the portrait he had just taken would not be up to his high standard.

For the most part, however, Karsh's portraits did turn out and his clients were pleased with the results. As in London, Karsh presented the dignitaries he met in Washington in the best light. When he photographed the British ambassador, he avoided showing the public that Lord Halifax had a withered arm. Indeed, according to the American director of war information, Elmer Davis, Karsh had injected more dignity into his portraits of British personalities "than God ever intended." Not surprisingly, Davis warned Karsh, "Be careful in Washington or we'll never recognize ourselves."[11]

Though never short of conversation or charm during a sitting, Karsh did become withdrawn and silent when he was not on the job. "Although I am by his side," Solange told Jamil Karsh, "there are times when he seems rather far away."[12] Solange knew that Yousuf needed time to gather his energy for the next session. This was why she found it easier to communicate with Yousuf by letter. "Perfect that we can be silent for so long each with our thoughts—it does show real understanding," she wrote from the adjacent hotel room. "But," Solange continued, "when my thoughts are so busy they are always about you while I know that when you seem deep in thoughts you are preoccupied about your work."[13]

Solange was eager to talk to Yousuf on that occasion partly because she wanted to know what he had been thinking about during that day's sitting with the notoriously cantankerous secretary of the interior, Harold Ickes. The session had not been easy. As Karsh recalled years later, "Mr. Ickes had become so inured to news photographers that he had developed a technique of letting his body sit for them to shoot at while his thoughts proceeded unruffled about their business."[14] Karsh had been unable to shake Ickes out of his absent-minded expression, until Solange, who was better-informed about the secretary of the interior than her husband, asked Ickes what he thought about the proposal to build a pipeline through Western Canada. Her question made Ickes's benevolent mask fall. It was at this moment that Karsh clicked the shutter and produced a portrait that captured the secretary's ruthlessness.

Harold LeClair Ickes, Secretary of the Interior, 1944

During their three-month sojourn in Washington, Yousuf and Solange made repeated trips to New York. It was here, in her capacity as Yousuf's business manager, that Solange used her charm to turn every business acquaintance into a friend. "Both Yousuf and I felt that we had known you for years," she told the editor of *House Beautiful*, Elizabeth Gordon, after their first meeting. "Fee plus expenses is correct," she continued in the next paragraph, before indicating that she hoped *House Beautiful* would find enough celebrities to make working for the magazine worthwhile.[15] It did. Over the next few years Karsh photographed such notable figures as Canada's ice-skating diva Barbara Ann Scott and Chicago's famous if eccentric architect Frank Lloyd Wright. Elizabeth Gordon and other business acquaintances provided Yousuf and Solange with a

circle of friends who helped to lighten the demanding pace that the Karshes set for themselves in New York.

In both New York and Washington Yousuf and Solange were caught up in a whirlwind of early evening cocktail parties and weekend visits to country houses up the Hudson River and on Long Island. They went on shopping sprees: to Bloomingdale's to buy Karsh's silk underwear and to Brooks Brothers to buy his shirts. They attended plays and concerts, at which Yousuf fell asleep out of exhaustion. And they visited the Metropolitan Museum of Fine Art and the Museum of Modern Art.

Although Yousuf's appointment book, which he wrote in Arabic, was riddled with complaints about being tired and exhausted, this was the kind of milieu in which he and Solange flourished—and made lots of money. Too flamboyant for sleepy Ottawa, they seemed more at home in New York and Washington than anywhere else.

DURING KARSH'S TIME in Washington and New York, *Life* began publishing his colour photographs. A fresh-faced portrait of Princess Elizabeth commemorating her eighteenth birthday and a less successful portrait of Charles de Gaulle were among the photographs featured on the front cover. Yet it was not until the spring of 1945 that *Life* published Karsh's Washington photo essay featuring twenty-seven portraits of men who had worked closely with President Roosevelt. Titled "Roosevelt's Men," Karsh's photographs appeared the week after the president died.[16]

In spite of the props—pipes, glasses, pens, cigarettes, and even a cigar— Karsh presented every one of "Roosevelt's Men" as confident, capable, and very much in charge. As with his portraits of British statesmen, Karsh conveyed these qualities not only through his subjects' facial expressions but also through their hands. "Almost unconsciously," Harold Dingman observed that spring in *Magazine Digest*, "the hands of his subject had become as much a signature of Karsh's work as the neat script in the corner."[17] Karsh echoed this observation almost word for word in notes for a memoir that he began at this time. "Hands have been so important for me; you might say that they are almost a signature," he wrote. "They show tenseness and empathy; they show poise and dignity; they show taste and vulgarity; they show happiness and sadness."[18]

No women were included in Karsh's essay, but if there had been then one woman would certainly have been among them. Eleanor Roosevelt was as accomplished as any of the statesmen in "Roosevelt's Men." She wrote a syndicated newspaper column six days a week. She held press conferences and, as the assistant to the director of the office of civil defence, an office in the government.

People told Karsh that he would not be able to make a satisfactory portrait of the first lady. It is true, as the political cartoonists made clear, that Eleanor Roosevelt was anything but beautiful. Yet it seemed incredible to Karsh "that such a vital personality could not be photographed."[19] He did not attempt to transform Eleanor Roosevelt into a beautiful woman when he photographed her in the White House's Rose Room in the autumn of 1944. Rather, he gave her expressive hands and gestures as much attention as her face and thereby conveyed the dynamic personality of the first woman to bring a president's wife into the public sphere.

Karsh notably tried to photograph another woman—and one who did have a claim on beauty—during the autumn of 1944. Yet the resulting portrait of Clare Booth Luce, who was not only the wife of *Time-Life*'s Henry Luce but also a congresswoman, playwright, editor, and critic, was not successful. This was because Karsh had clearly not engaged with his subject, whom he chose to photograph in profile and at a distance. Consequently, he captured neither Luce's beauty nor her ebullient and sometimes frustrating personality. Not surprisingly, it was the portrait of the less attractive Eleanor Roosevelt that found its way into Karsh's "calling-card" portfolio.

ALTHOUGH *LIFE* TOOK almost a year to publish a significant number of Karsh's Washington portraits, the editor did not forget about the Canadian photographer. In the spring of 1945 the magazine's commissioning editor, Wilson Hicks, assigned Karsh to join an army of 2,635 other journalists and photographers who were heading to the United Nations Conference on World Organization in San Francisco. Karsh immediately agreed to photograph nineteen conference

delegates in San Francisco and twelve other personalities in Washington, D.C., and New York before he got to San Francisco. It promised to be a lucrative assignment. Karsh would receive $4,079.34 plus expenses for one-and-a-half months' work. Once his portraits had appeared in *Life*, his British, Canadian, and American agents were free to sell them to other newspapers and magazines. And because he maintained the copyright on every photograph he took, photographing "the big boys," as Karsh called the conference delegates, would provide more photographs and more stories for the hoped-for book of portraits. Equally, as with his "Mission to Britain" he hoped that his photographs of international leaders would serve history and the war effort by promoting "mutual understanding among the peoples."[20]

When Karsh arrived at the United Nations Conference on April 25, the Second World War was not yet over. By the time the conference ended two months later, Hitler had shot himself; the Germans had surrendered at Rheims; the Russians had established themselves in Berlin, Vienna, and Prague; and, although the war with Japan was not over, the Americans would shortly close that front by dropping two atomic bombs on Hiroshima and Nagasaki in August.

Eleanor Roosevelt, 1944

The night before he died, Franklin Roosevelt had prepared some words to set the tone for the San Francisco conference: "If civilization is to survive, we must cultivate the science of human relationships — the ability of all peoples, of all kinds, to live together and work together in the same world, at peace."[21] Two weeks later, when the young, flamboyant, gum-chewing head of the American delegation, Edward Stettinius, declared the conference open before 282 delegates representing 50 countries, there was a degree of optimism in the air. Everyone seemed determined to create a new world order by finalizing the charter that Roosevelt and his wartime allies had drafted at Dumbarton Oaks the previous summer.

According to the Canadian diplomat Charles Ritchie, most of the delegates who gathered at the Opera House in the Veterans' Memorial Building above San Francisco Bay looked "as if they were here for the Elks Convention."[22] There were exceptions, however, like the closely body-guarded Russian delegates, whose nearby warship, rumour had it, was loaded with equal quantities of caviar

and champagne. And the decoratively attired Saudi Arabian minister of foreign affairs, Prince Faisal ibn Abdul Aziz, who looked more like the silent film actor Rudolph Valentino than a diplomat.

Solange stayed at home. So, before the sittings took place, Karsh had to apply the mascara to temples and eyebrows, and put the delegates at ease by showing them his portfolio of portraits. *Life*'s staff did help by arranging the appointments and giving him potted biographies of the people on his list to be photographed. *Life* also provided Karsh with two assistants, albeit of an unusual kind—Boy Scouts.

It is amusing to visualize the suave and elegant thirty-seven-year-old Yousuf Karsh rushing from his appointments at the Mark Hopkins Hotel, the Fairmont Palace, the Whitcomb Hotel, and the St. Francis Hotel, where the conference delegates stayed, then to his makeshift studio in the director's room at the Bank of America, and back to his own hotel, the Sir Francis Drake, with the two Boy Scouts in tow. It is not difficult to see the boys listening, wide-eyed, as Karsh regaled Canadian journalists with stories of how he had taken some of his more famous photographs. It is difficult, however, to imagine how Karsh trained the two adolescents to unpack and then set up his equipment and to hang the old, grey Canadian army blanket that he had first used in London as a backdrop. Or to envision the mid-teen Scouts following the quick-stepping Karsh around Chinatown in search of a gift for Solange.

Prince Faisal ibn Abdul Aziz, 1945

One of the Scouts, a fourteen-year-old boy nicknamed Skippy, left an amusing account of the seventeen days that he spent as Mr. Karsh's assistant. The sittings, of which there were rarely more than two a day, varied. They could be anywhere from five minutes to half an hour long, providing the delegate showed up in the first place. Karsh spoke Arabic to Prince Faisal and French to Joseph Paul-Boncour— who could not speak English. Karsh was undaunted when, in the middle of a sitting at the Fairmont Hotel with Ivan Subasic, the Yugoslav minister's secretary rushed into the room and announced that the Nazi armies had just quit Italy. And, as Skippy further observed, Karsh had the temerity to ask the head of the Russian delegation to help him secure an official invitation to the Soviet Union.[23]

By this stage in the war, the Russians had won enormous respect among their allies for helping to bring about Germany's demise. Not surprisingly, there was always a large crowd outside the St. Francis Hotel hoping to catch a glimpse of the square-headed, self-conscious man who led the Russian delegation. Karsh's sitting with the Russian foreign minister, Vyacheslav Molotov, was as exciting for the photographer as it was for his young assistants. Shortly before Karsh had left Canada, Tom Blau told him, "Your work in the Soviet Capital would have the effect of finally putting Stalin, Molotov, Kaganovich and Kalinin on the map. None of these men and none of the great Russian Army leaders have been done justice in photographs and the psychological impact of the portrait studies of these great personalities of the twentieth century would be tremendous and far reaching."[24] After Karsh returned from Britain in 1943, officials at the War Information Board told the secretary of the Canadian section of the Permanent Joint Board of Defence, H. L. Keenleyside, "Now to Russia to photograph Russian military and political leaders and also our Ambassador, Mr. Wilgress."[25] And two months before Karsh arrived in San Francisco, the Canadian secretary of state for External Affairs had asked his ambassador in Moscow, L. Dana Wilgress, to approach Soviet officials about sending Karsh to the Soviet Union.[26] When Karsh arrived in San Francisco, there was encouragement from another quarter too. Britain's ambassador to the Soviet Union, Lord Inverchapel, assured Karsh that Stalin's noble head and penetrating eyes would make good photographic copy.

Karsh had already applied for a visa to the Soviet Union, with the intention of photographing the man who ruled his country through an interlocking system of terroristic and terrorized bureaucracies controlled by the police, the party and the army. Yet it seemed highly unlikely that Karsh was going to photograph Stalin until after the sitting with Molotov. Speaking in French and exuding old-world charm, Karsh got more than the five minutes that Molotov's assistants had promised for the sitting. He had enough time to tell Molotov about the difficulties he was having securing an entrance visa, to which Molotov replied, "Why not, why not? By all means."[27]

Confident that a visa would now be forthcoming, Karsh told a Canadian newspaper reporter that a trip to the Soviet Union was imminent.[28] He must have also conveyed this to Solange. Addressing the Women's Canadian Club in

London, Ontario, during Karsh's absence, she told her audience that "As a result of his appointment with Molotov, Mr. Karsh is pretty sure that he is going to be allowed to take his camera to Russia."[29]

Karsh was clearly on a high when, a month before the conference ended, Skippy and the other Boy Scout helped him pack up his equipment for the last time and then joined him in a farewell lunch. There was much for the trio to celebrate. The two Scouts had met almost every leading statesman — for Karsh always made a point of introducing his assistants to his client. And not only had Karsh taken three times as many portraits as *Life* had commissioned, he had also squeezed in a few private portrait commissions, of whom George Mardikian, the chef-owner of the Omar Khayyam restaurant, was one. Karsh had also photographed Britain's deputy prime minister, Clement Attlee, for the third time — on this occasion wearing the new suit he had bought for the conference. Karsh had produced a sensitive portrait of Molotov, challenging Charles Ritchie's view that he looked more like an employee in a *hotel de ville* than the leader of the Russian delegation. And, finally, Karsh had, he believed, secured Molotov's support for a trip to the Soviet Union.

The only thing that Karsh had not managed to do in San Francisco was to photograph his fellow countrymen. *Life* had not included any Canadians on its list of prominent personalities. Admittedly, Mackenzie King had left the conference early, and Karsh had already photographed many of the other high-ranking Canadian delegates at home, but the Department of External Affairs had hoped that he would photograph the distinguished ambassador to the Soviet Union, Dana Wilgress. And yet there is no evidence to suggest that Karsh had any contact with the Canadian delegation while he was in San Francisco. This was a pity, because the Canadian delegation had proven themselves to be the best prepared, the most thoughtful, and more active than any other middle-ranking country at the conference.

The fact of the matter was, Karsh was no longer interested in using his portraiture to help construct Canada's national identity as he had done during the 1930s and early 1940s. This is not to suggest that he was not interested in producing portraits of modern-day heroes whose accomplishments met his criteria of greatness, or that after San Francisco he was less determined "to try in some tangible way to help peoples of the world to a better knowledge of each other."[30] But there were bigger fish to fry than Canadians. After all, as Bruce Downes wrote in the prestigious journal of *Popular Photography* that May, Karsh was "the most sought after portrait photographer in the world." He continued, "There is no question that Karsh dramatizes his subjects always seeking to make them as dignified and imposing as possible." Nor was there any question that "there are those who see nothing in him but luck, publicity and a certain measure of bluff" and claim that "his work was showy rather than great." But, Downes insisted, one could not ignore the fact that the Canadian photographer had restored portrait photography "to its old state and dignity and respectability" at the moment when the critics feared that it had "fallen to a level of a dubious psycophantic [*sic*] trade." And this was why, Downes concluded, Yousuf Karsh had become "as renowned as his subjects."[31]

AFTER VJ DAY, on August 14, 1945, most people wanted to forget about the Second World War. Portraits of sportsmen, musicians, businessmen, and, above all, Hollywood stars suddenly became more popular than portraits of generals, diplomats, statesmen, and others who had been instrumental in winning the war. After the summer of 1945 a new kind of hero emerged: the celebrity. Film stars, athletes, musicians, and others in the sphere of leisure-time activity fell into this category. It was in response to this consumerist heroism that in January 1946 the editors of *Life* offered Karsh an assignment of a very different kind: to travel to Hollywood for the purpose of taking the portraits of twenty film stars.

Hollywood was booming when Yousuf and Solange arrived at the Beverly Hills Hotel later in January. With some eighty million Americans going to the movies each week, 1946 was to prove the best year that the film industry would ever see. After that year, things changed. First, the congressional investigation by the House of Representatives Committee on Un-American Activities tore the community apart in its search for alleged communist infiltrators. And, second, "the box," as that piece of furniture that took pride of place in the corner of the living room was called, began to challenge the cinema's dominance of the moving image.

Karsh was convinced that he could get beyond the artificially constructed glamour portrait if he photographed the stars in their homes. By merging actors' screen roles with their off-screen personalities, movie magazines were already showing their readers that the stars were ordinary folks just like them. The Hollywood photographer John Engstead had been photographing his celebrity clients out-of-doors and in their homes since 1942. And, a year before Karsh arrived in Hollywood, the Polish-born American photographer Weegee (Arthur Fellig) had shown that just as the photographer could confer stardom, the photographer could also take it away. But film stars did not appreciate being caught unawares in a candid shot which might feature the grotesque movement of their mouth or the graceless gesture of their hands. Nor did the studio bosses and publicity agents, for whom the unblemished image of their clients was the principal commodity in marketing their films to the public. Not surprisingly, Weegee was soon back in New York.

Greta Garbo did not mind fans adoring her on-screen image: "They pay to see it and I respect that covenant."[32] But she refused to maintain the screen myth off the set. Most stars, as Yousuf and Solange quickly discovered, were different, however. They wanted the best of both worlds. This was why Bette Davis allowed Karsh to photograph her at a beach-side cottage at Laguna Beach. Why Peter Lorre invited Karsh to his farm, and Gregory Peck to his cozy home above Beverly Hills. And, finally, why Sydney Greenstreet chose to be photographed surrounded by a clutter of figurines and curios; Peter Lorre among his collection of old keys and tools; Boris Karloff at his private club; and fourteen-year-old Elizabeth Taylor with her menagerie of pets.

But did film stars meet Karsh's category of greatness? They had no claim on goodness. They had performed no heroic deed nor held any public office that would set them apart from the rest of society. Were Hollywood stars just famous for being famous? But Karsh was not looking for heroes when he and Solange arrived in Hollywood in January 1946. He was looking for new subjects because the editors of *Illustrated London News* and *Life* were tired of his wartime heroes.

Even so, Karsh was determined to avoid portraying "Hollywood as a glamour factory."[33] And even if he had been set on doing this, other Hollywood-based photographers like George Hurrell, Philippe Halsman, Clarence Sinclair Bull, and

George Hoyningen had already made actors from Joan Crawford and Greta Garbo to Clark Gable into glamorous stars. This was why Karsh wanted to separate the stars "from the moving picture make-belief and," he continued in an article for *Photo Arts*, "to try to portray the essential human being in all of them."[34]

Photographing film stars in their homes allowed Solange to offer "a delightful word picture of her many interesting meetings with the more famous Hollywood personalities" to the *Ottawa Citizen*. Thus, according to Solange, Robert Montgomery was "a very happy family man." Gregory Peck was "more interested in discussing his family than talking about movie making." The child actor Dean Stockwell was "just a real boy." And Dana Andrews possessed "a plain, friendly and gracious manner."[35]

Were the stars really as charming as Solange made them out to be in her interview with the press? This is hardly the impression conveyed by Yousuf's private notes and Solange's letters to the studio's secretary, Jean McJanet. For example, Solange did not warm to Humphrey Bogart, because he

Margaret O'Brien, 1946

evidently thought that he was irresistible to women. "I'm sorry," she told McJanet, "but I couldn't fall for a guy like that."[36] Solange and Yousuf were critical of Judy Garland, whose face was covered in "enough make-up to be scraped off with a rake or a bulldozer." Sydney Greenstreet was "not as interesting as expected." Lionel Barrymore, who was confined to a wheelchair, looked much older than he claimed to be. And Greer Garson "shocked" Yousuf and Solange because "there was not a bit of naturalness" and she "acts on and off the stage." This was not a problem that Karsh experienced only with Garson. "It is immensely difficult to keep an actor from acting," Karsh reflected later, in his memoirs, "especially when the camera is present."[37]

Yousuf and Solange were not, however, disappointed with everyone they met. Bette Davis was much prettier and much younger than she looked on the screen. "Both of us have gone completely overboard about her," Solange told McJanet, who was eager for news about her favourite stars.[38] "Yousuf purred the whole time," Solange continued, during his visit with Peter Lorre. They both found Elizabeth Taylor to be "a perfect gem," another child star, Margaret O'Brien, to be "beautifully mannered and affectionate," Dana Andrews (despite experiencing

domestic difficulties) to be "very nice," and Gregory Peck to be "very charming."[39] And, finally, Angela Lansbury and Ingrid Bergman both impressed Solange and Yousuf by showing up for their sittings without makeup—and being beautiful enough to be photographed without it.

However determined Karsh was to avoid producing the celebrity portrait, he and Solange were certainly treated like celebrities themselves during their month in what many called the dream factory. The film stars invited them to cocktail parties, to brunches, to lunches, and for dinner. And the owners of the major studios—Fox, Warner Brothers, MGM, and RKO—invited Yousuf and Solange to tour their studios, join them at lunch and dinner, and attend private screenings. The private screening of *The Maltese Falcon* at Warner Brothers with three of the actors Karsh had photographed—Greenstreet, Lorre, and Bogart— was particularly exciting.

When the photographer Baron de Meyer had arrived in Hollywood, the movie stars refused to sit for him unless he could guarantee that the photographs would appear in a major American magazine. By contrast, *Life* had employed Karsh, and the stars had agreed to sit for him because he could be relied upon to produce a flattering image. Karsh would never follow Weegee's example of catching a star off guard in order to produce a sensational portrait. Thus the stars knew that Karsh not only had the backing of the most popular magazine in the country but also possessed a trustworthy track record. This was why, once Yousuf and Solange had settled into the Beverly Hills Hotel, their telephone never stopped ringing.

This kind of attention was new to Karsh, who had often needed to work hard to get a sitting with a personality. Moreover, most statesmen and other high-ranking individuals had been unfamiliar with his work. They had always been in a hurry. And they would never have invited Karsh to lunch or even offered him a cup of tea. (The Queen Mother was an exception. But Karsh refused her gracious offer of tea, fearing that it would break his concentration.) Though few individuals whom Karsh photographed lacked vanity, the reputations of public dignitaries did not depend on the outcome of Karsh's portraiture.

In Hollywood things were different. Every film star knew about Karsh. Gregory Peck even envied him for having the opportunity to meet so many of the other film stars. And they and their publicity agents and film producers all cared about how the portrait would turn out. This was why Bette Davis, who felt that her hair had not been right and her mind had been on other things, asked for another sitting when she saw the proofs.[40] This was why no film star or studio boss was ever short of time. "The difficult we do at once; the impossible takes a little time," as Karsh noted in his diary.[41] He and his new friends in Hollywood were in the same business: entertainment. Consequently they both had a stake in the outcome of the portrait.

However much Karsh was admired, the studio bosses soon discovered that he could not be bought for a lunch at the Beverly Hills Club or the Brown Derby, or for a private screening of *The Maltese Falcon* or *National Velvet*, which was currently elevating Elizabeth Taylor to star status. Nor could he be persuaded to photograph Lauren Bacall. "We hear she is a devil and a b——," Solange told McJanet.[42] Nor convinced that Humphrey Bogart was a worthy subject. "They will have to say pretty please several times before we consider doing Bogart," Solange wrote after having lunch with Jack Warner.[43] Warner Brothers did. Five days later the portrait was made. Karsh changed his mind about Bogart. He eventually changed his mind about Lauren Bacall too, but she had to wait ten years before being "Karshed" by the famous photographer from Ottawa.

According to one observer, searching "for the star's true identity 'behind' or 'underneath' the media-constructed facade" was a fruitless task.[44] Karsh knew that it would be difficult photographing people whose stock-in-trade was knowing how to look good both on and off the screen. The "most difficult part of the assignment," he recalled later, "was impressing upon them the fact that I wanted to photograph them as people — not as movie stars."[45] But did he get behind the image, the trademark, the big name, as he hoped to do? Or were the portraits that he made in Hollywood, like the text that accompanied them when they appeared in newspapers and magazines across North America several months later, sanitized versions of their subjects?

There is no doubt that Karsh maintained total visual control over every aspect of the photographs he took in Hollywood: from setting up the camera and lights, to posing and capturing the subject, to developing and then touching up and cropping the negative. It should not be surprising that some of the portraits that he produced in Hollywood possessed characteristics—tonal contrasts, a dark palette, and dramatic gestures—that had been his signature since his days as a photographer for the Ottawa Drama League and the Dominion Drama Festival. Nor that his portraits resembled those of an earlier Hollywood photographer, George Hurrell. Nor that Karsh showed in his portraits that he was familiar with the skills of the cinematographers who were involved in the increasingly popular film noir genre best illustrated by *The Big Sleep*.

Even though he felt that Sydney Greenstreet, Peter Lorre, and Boris Karloff did not, in real life, resemble their unsavory screen personae, Karsh was unable to get beyond the screen image just as the stars were unable to pose in front of his camera out of character. Lorre, Karloff, and Greenstreet each looked like the villain of the piece in Karsh's portraits of them. Not so Humphrey Bogart. In his portrait of Bogart, Karsh challenged "the rugged, lowbrow villain" who appeared on the screen. He portrayed Bogart's features to best advantage by securing a modulation of tone and by lightening his palette.[46] Focusing on Bogart's expressive hands, Karsh placed the ever-present cigarette in his right hand rather than in the corner of his mouth. Although doing these things did present Bogart as a more benign figure than the tough-minded Philip Marlowe character he portrayed in the movie theatres, the resulting portrait of Raymond Chandler's fictional hero was anything but charming.

Karsh's portraits of Elizabeth Taylor, Ingrid Bergman, Angela Lansbury, and other female stars were less dramatic, more highly lit, and not overtly sexy. He wanted Bergman to look like "the young mother who had just been playing with her child" and Lansbury the "very sweet and unaffected" woman whom he had just met.[47] The fourteen-year-old Taylor, who begged her mother to allow her to wear a grown-up dress for the sitting, looks years older than her age, while the other child star whom Karsh photographed then, Margaret O'Brien, who pulls her pigtails into the air, looks younger.

Virtually every star was eager to sit before Karsh's camera in the hope that he would produce a definitive image. Yet no portrait that Karsh took in Hollywood came to stand—like his photographs of Winston Churchill and Eleanor Roosevelt and George Bernard Shaw had—for the person they portrayed. Hollywood photographers and the silver screen had got there first. Nor, as the *Ottawa Citizen* had promised its readers, did Karsh reveal "the deep human side of its people" and thereby give "the unglamorized version" of Hollywood.[48] Nor, as George Hurrell had done in the 1930s, did Karsh set a new standard for the Hollywood portrait as *Life* no doubt hoped that he would. Photographing the stars at home did not work. The film stars had too much at stake to let their hair down. And Karsh had too much at stake to make his subjects anything other than glamorous.

If he had relied less on the dramatic contrasts of light and shade, and if the film stars had been willing to experiment, Karsh might have offered *Life* something new. But he was not going to experiment on the job. Nor was it his intention to produce the kind of warts-and-all portraits that had made John Buchan's gnarled knuckles and Lord Beaverbrook's deeply lined face the subjects of their portraits. Karsh and the film stars admired one another and were dedicated to achieving a common result. Above all, they were fellow professionals who stood on either side of the camera.

Elizabeth Taylor, 1946

WHAT HOLLYWOOD GAVE Karsh was a new kind of hero: the celebrity. It also gave him the satisfaction of photographing personalities who were not removed from him by wealth, status, or power but were his social equals.

As the critic Bruce Downes made clear, Karsh had established a niche within a genre—formal portrait photography—that, due to the popularity of the candid shot and the documentary photograph, had fallen out of favour. During the first half of the 1940s, he had done so by seeing to it that his portraits appeared on magazine covers around the world. By submitting his portraits of Eleanor Roosevelt, George Bernard Shaw, Noel Coward, and, of course, Winston Churchill to exhibitions of photographs from St. Louis to Detroit and Chicago, from Calgary, Edmonton, and Montreal to Los Angeles, California, and London,

England. By giving his collection of great men and women visual images to match their achievements. By expanding his repertoire to include film stars. And, finally, by giving magazines and their readers a story of every important person he photographed.

In less than fifteen years after setting up his studio, Karsh had become internationally acclaimed. Yet, in spite of his trip to England in 1943 and to California in 1945 and 1946, he was not well travelled. He had not been to continental Europe or to Asia. He had not even seen much of Canada or the United States. But when Karsh returned to Ottawa from California, all of this was about to change.

Faces of Destiny

While he was in Hollywood, Karsh made the most of his opportunities. He did not restrict his clientele to the movie stars he was commissioned to photograph for *Life* magazine. For one thing, some of them, like Bette Davis, had already been featured on the cover of *Life*, so if Karsh wanted to photograph them he had to make private arrangements to do so. Angela Lansbury and Elizabeth Taylor were not on *Life*'s list either, but Karsh photographed them for their studio bosses. Moreover, his work was not confined to Hollywood itself.

Life also wanted Karsh to produce a portrait of Thomas Mann, so Solange and Yousuf made their way to Pacific Palisades, where the German writer had been living in self-imposed exile from Nazi Germany. Though flattered by the idea of being photographed by the "Kanadischen Meister photographer" who had made the famous portrait of Winston Churchill, Mann, who was in the process of finishing his novel *Doktor Faustus*, was ill.[1] Fearing that Mann's condition might be revealed by a formal portrait, Karsh supplemented it with a photograph of the author's hands. When Mann viewed this unconventional study months later, he found it to be "a highly remarkable piece of work," which reminded him of a famous drawing by the sixteenth-century German artist Albrecht Dürer. And while the more traditional portraits that Karsh took did reveal Mann's "ailing character," the writer nevertheless found them to be "true masterpieces."[2]

A few months before Karsh arrived in Hollywood, *Life*'s editor, Wilson Hicks, had commissioned him to make a series of portraits of business executives. The proposed photo essay, "Captains of Industry," would reinforce Henry Luce's belief that every dollar a businessman made was "a patriotic contribution to the national debt."[3] It foreshadowed the founding of Luce's magazine *Fortune*, which would chronicle the activities of the country's leading businessmen. And, for Karsh, the commission would prompt many companies, like General Electric, to have him make a portrait study of their leading executives too.

Karsh began photographing the twenty-two business executives for *Life* while on a trip to New York in the autumn of 1945. Later, on his way to Hollywood in January 1946, he stopped in New York once again and photographed more. In Hollywood itself, he chalked up Donald W. Douglas, who ran Douglas Aircraft; Union Pacific Railroad boss William Martin Jeffers; and movie mogul Jack Warner. Karsh also travelled north to San Francisco and captured Henry Ford II.

The assignment from *Life* was challenging. Almost all of the business executives who sat for Karsh appreciated the value of good publicity. And, because of this, they—and their personal assistants and publicity agents, whose job it was to promote their bosses—collaborated until, Karsh sarcastically noted, they almost stood on their heads.[4]

Martin R. King, who had a chance to observe Karsh's sittings with high-ranking executives at General Electric, told the story from the other side. The evening before the session, Karsh studied the biographies of the subjects, surveyed the location of the shoot, and then dined and relaxed. Before the session began the next day, King noted how Solange obtained further details from General Electric's publicity agent about the subjects to be photographed while Karsh set up his camera, adjusted the angle of the lights, and focused his lens on his sit-in assistant. When the technical side of the shoot was in place, Karsh brushed his hair with his palms, spread his legs apart, and folded his arms, before saying, "Yes, Solange." Solange then gave him any further biographical details that she had managed to obtain from the subject. After this, the General Electric executive was led into the studio. Solange immediately engaged him in flattering or relaxing conversation. Standing to one side, Karsh silently observed his subject's physique, his movements, and his gestures and noted any imperfections on his face. "He was mentally beginning to form the picture," King further noted, "that he would have his mechanical slave camera duplicate." It was at this point that Solange would retreat to a corner of the room and the "exclusive performance of the artful genius, Yousuf Karsh, would begin."[5] Though Karsh had centre stage from this point on, it was clearly Solange who had set the scene for his performance.

Executives, just like Hollywood's film stars, were among America's new heroes. But whereas film stars were made by the media and exuded sex, businessmen were made by money and exuded power. Indeed, as the American commentator Vance Packard would later observe, business executives had become the country's social models because they embodied "the greatest material rewards we can offer, and some of the greatest rewards of prestige."[6]

None of this was news to Karsh. Businessmen, along with brides, babies, and politicians, had been his stock-in-trade from the moment he founded his studio in 1933. He was particularly well suited to provide flattering photographs of business executives because, as Bruce Downes had earlier noted in *Popular Photography*, Karsh's portraits of men conveyed a "command to look."[7] Besides, Karsh had a natural affinity to businessmen. After all, he was one himself, as the Canadian tax department made all too clear. Like most successful business executives, he was driven and decisive; he was adept at self-promotion and sophisticated in appearance; and he knew how to handle people, how to gain their trust, and then get the best out of them.

When it came to his own employees, Karsh, like many business executives of his generation, demanded total allegiance. His assistants were forbidden to ski lest they break a leg. They were required to live within walking distance of the studio so that they could arrive on time.[8] Like many business executives, Karsh also exhibited a kind of gruff paternalism towards his employees. Joyce Large, who joined the studio at the end of the Second World War and remained until the early 1970s, discovered that her new boss "was very short-tempered" and always impatient. Though Large felt privileged to be working for Karsh, she also felt that he should feel privileged to have her working so hard for him.[9]

Large, along with the studio's other four employees, often worked through their lunch hour. They worked from 9 a.m. to 6 p.m. rather than 5, and they were frequently on the premises during the weekend.

Karsh rarely directly expressed his appreciation to his staff for their hard work. Indeed, one of the few times he let down his guard was at Christmas. The handwritten notes he appended to his employees' Christmas cards told his staff what Karsh found it difficult to say in person: how very grateful he was for their commitment to the Karsh Studio. Tangibly reinforcing this point, every Christmas card was accompanied by a generous bonus. Some of his employees even saw a rise in salary on an annual basis. Although distant and taciturn, Karsh did know the value of having good people work for him and was willing to pay for it.

Solange did much to make up for Yousuf's inability to fulfill the paternalist ideal. If she noticed that her employees' children showed a flair for drama, she enrolled them in the Ottawa Little Theatre. If an employee's child wanted to learn French, Solange's mother, Madame Gauthier, was conscripted into giving them private lessons. And if staff members were ill, it was Solange who made sure that they had access to the best medical treatment in town.

Marion Anderson, 1945

IF IT WAS NOT ENOUGH of a challenge to be photographing image-conscious film stars alongside publicity-seeking business executives, Karsh took on another assignment at this time. RCA Victor needed portraits of its musicians for album covers and general publicity, and in the autumn of 1945 Karsh began to produce them. Musicians—like music itself—were already dear to Karsh's heart. His 1941 portrait of the Afro-American singer and actor Paul Robeson had a special place in his calling-card portfolio. And the equally successful portrait of the contralto Marion Anderson was usually among the four or five works that Karsh submitted to group photograph exhibitions around the world. In 1945, RCA Victor was giving him another opportunity to photograph musicians: not two but twenty-four performers, composers, and conductors.

The assignment from RCA Victor proved to be so much to Karsh's liking that he wrote several articles about it. In the *American Annual of Photography*, Karsh told his readers that he had expected musicians to be temperamental because they were "so accustomed to having their audiences look upon them as little less than gods."[10] Yet much to his delight the sittings took less out of him than he had expected. This was because, as Karsh told his readers in *Saturday Night*, musicians were "more poised and have a really greater sense of drama than even film stars."[11] And, while film stars did not know what to do with their hands during a sitting, musicians clearly did. In fact, as Karsh further noted in the *American Annual of Photography*, their hands were in such constant and expressive movement that "their every act and gesture" suggested endless possibilities for the camera.

The sales manager at RCA Victor had asked Karsh to make portraits that were "true character readings, perfectly natural and informal."[12] Yet Karsh's portraits of musicians—male and female alike—were anything but natural, for the obvious reason that he chose to photograph them in a professional context. The New York photographer Arnold Newman, who like Karsh had a gift for formal design, had been photographing musicians and artists in their milieu since 1941. In line with what became called "environmental portraiture," Karsh photographed Artur Rubinstein playing the piano and Eugene Kash performing on the violin. Likewise, Arthur Fiedler, of the Boston Pops, conducts; the violinist Jascha Heifetz and the conductor Sir Thomas Beecham study a music score; and Jeanette MacDonald is in full song. What Karsh had to say about these musicians in the text that he produced to accompany the portraits was almost otiose. His pictures had said it all and really were, as the cliché goes, worth a thousand words.

GIVEN THE COMMISSIONS from *Life* and RCA Victor, it is not surprising that the entries in Karsh's and Solange's diaries frequently noted their physical fatigue. "Yousuf Karsh, dead tired and put to bed," Solange wrote from New York on November 2, 1945. Other entries tell the same story: "nerve wracking sitting," and another "very long and difficult"; "dead tired," and "completely exhausted."[13]

It was not only Yousuf who was exhausted. As the business manager for the Karsh Studio, Solange had to continue managing the accounts when they were on the road. (The meticulous records that she maintained show that their most expensive item while travelling was not postage stamps, fuel, or gas mileage but their favourite drinks, brandy and scotch.) Solange also had to meet Yousuf's agents, publicity managers, and magazine editors, from whom she negotiated fees and secured assignments. She also saw to it that galleries like the Museum of Modern Art and the Brooklyn Museum of Art were presented with copies of Yousuf's favourite photographs for their permanent collections. Solange had to do all of these things, as she told the Women's Canadian Club in 1948, while looking smart, exuding charm, and being efficient and businesslike.

While Solange looked after the business side of things when they were on tour, Yousuf took the portraits—he rarely had more than two sittings a day—and then developed the negatives in the hotel bathtub. As already noted, he also accompanied Solange to cocktail parties and breakfast meetings, and to concerts and musical performances. This demanding schedule sometimes resulted in carelessness. Karsh once left his coveted portfolio of portraits in a New York taxi (though the treasure was later recovered). The arduous routine also resulted in long bouts of exhaustion, which prevented him from enjoying an evening's entertainment because when the lights dimmed in the theatre he invariably fell asleep.

When Yousuf and Solange were on the road they did not forget about the Karsh Studio back in Ottawa. Yousuf carried the heavy double-decker cheque book so that he could mail end-of-the-month cheques to his staff. And Solange kept abreast of what was going on back home through the daily reports that Joyce Large sent to wherever Solange and Yousuf happened to be. If a problem arose that Joyce could not handle, she would often end up writing to Solange twice a day. Asked if she ever called them, Joyce Large replied, "He would have killed me if I'd picked up the phone."[14]

Large modestly recalled that she only dealt "with the mundane stuff" in the office. Even so, this entailed making sure that "the Maestro" had biographical information for an upcoming sitting with an important personality; doing the bookkeeping; sending out the bills; arranging appointments for further sittings;

and answering fan letters, requests for prices and sittings, and orders for prints. Confident that Joyce Large also wrote "very warm" letters, Karsh rarely bothered to scrutinize the correspondence that was written under his name.[15]

The visits to New York, Washington, and Hollywood during the winter and spring of 1945–46 were all the more exhausting for Yousuf and Solange by being interspersed with trips back to Ottawa. This was when Karsh caught up with his local clientele, who kept him busy with four sittings a day. This was when he made sure that his technicians had developed the negatives and retouched and spotted the proofs according to his handwritten instructions. This was also when he secured permission to publish the portraits of his more important personalities. This, finally, was when he made plans for further trips and re-examined his fees. If you wanted to be "Karshed" outside of Ottawa in the mid-1940s, you had to pay $300 for the sitting and around $400 for a set of finished prints. If, however, you were lucky enough to be a resident of the capital, you could get your portrait done for two-thirds of this price.

It was on these trips back to Ottawa that Karsh also caught up with government commissions. Whenever a new Governor General came to Canada or hosted a ball, Karsh—and his camera—was invited to Government House. When the Department of External Affairs discovered that Karsh's portrait of its minister, Louis S. St. Laurent, was a popular feature in Canada's foreign embassies, Karsh was asked to send additional prints, albeit at a reduced fee. Karsh continued to cultivate W. L. Mackenzie King. In 1947 Karsh produced a colour photograph of the Canadian prime minister for *Maclean's*. He also kept the prime minister informed about any conversation he had had with a foreign dignitary. Following a sitting with the future American president General Dwight D. Eisenhower in 1947, for example, Karsh sent Mackenzie King an account of their conversation, for which the prime minister was grateful. Mackenzie King clearly appreciated having someone with whom he could discuss "the wisdom of my attempting to continue much longer in the position of leadership of my Party and of the Government." "I feel that I should seek retirement before very long," he told Karsh in January 1948, "and give the Party a chance to select a new leader."[16] A few months later he did so. At the ensuing Liberal leadership convention, the party duly elected Louis St. Laurent as Mackenzie King's successor.

Life in Ottawa was not all work for the Karshes. Yousuf played a great deal of tennis, both at home and at the Rideau Lawn Tennis Club. Solange enjoyed watching him on the court, although gardening, cooking, and feeding the birds at Little Wings were also among her recreations. If Karsh happened to be in town during the Dominion Drama Festival, he would still act as its official photographer. (In 1948, for example, he photographed no fewer than thirteen plays.) Karsh also made time to attend openings at the National Gallery of Canada, film previews at the National Film Society, and lectures at the National Geographic Society and the Canadian Club. And in 1947, he and Solange travelled to Toronto to attend a dinner celebrating the winner of the Leacock Medal for Humour. During the evening Karsh competed with five other men to see who could give the funniest and wittiest speech in six minutes. Karsh did not win, but the fact that he was chosen to participate in the first place shows that more than a few people now knew him to be an entertaining speaker.[17]

Solange and Yousuf also made time to entertain at Little Wings, where they had a full-time housekeeper-cook and a gardener-chauffeur. They were generous hosts to their friends, like Madge Macbeth and the civil-servant poet Duncan Campbell Scott, but according to a writer for the *National Home Monthly*, most of the people who found their way to Little Wings were more likely "to be people it is profitable to know."[18]

Karsh closed down the studio for two weeks every August but he and Solange rarely took a vacation away. If they did, it was only to the nearby Laurentian Mountains or to the home of Uncle George Nakash in Montreal.

UP UNTIL THE SPRING OF 1946, Karsh ran his business — like his life — in a simple and straightforward manner. But this was now no longer feasible, because the Karsh Studio had an annual turnover that had quadrupled during the war, reaching $44,000 by 1944.

The situation in 1943 illustrates his difficulty. There is particularly full documentation for that year because of a negotiation with the Department of National Revenue over Excess Profits Tax (EPT), settled only after Solange appeared at a hearing in October 1944. The issue remained the same as it had been in 1942:

EPT in effect confiscated any amount above "standard profits" (as compared with pre-war profits.) The settlement was generous to Karsh, in that "standard profits" were agreed at $14,000, and since actual net profits in 1943 amounted to $16,921.50, EPT of $2,921.50 was payable. Together with income tax, this meant that Karsh had a total tax bill of $9,582 — nearly 60 percent of his net profit for the year.

Admittedly, EPT was a temporary wartime measure and the level of personal taxation then fell. Still, something clearly had to be done if Karsh was to reap the full benefits of the high earnings derived from his lucrative assignments in the United States, the sale of his photographs, and his private commissions.

Yousuf, Solange, and their obliging accountant at Davis, Boyce and Company came up with a sophisticated solution. In the spring of 1946 they set up another company. Solange was designated the president of Little Wings; she and Yousuf were the principal shareholders. Capital stock was 500 shares at $100 a share, making $50,000 in total. The new company handled advertising and publicity. This separated the marketing of Karsh's work from its production in the Karsh Studio, which continued to function on the old basis. Yet there was little except the financial distinction between Little Wings and the Karsh Studio. Both businesses shared the Sparks Street premises, and the books of both companies were kept in tandem, with a portion of the wage costs being attributed to Little Wings.

It was a clever arrangement to minimize the taxed profits of the Karsh Studio and maximize the legitimate tax expenses of Little Wings. The year that Little Wings was set up, the two companies had a combined turnover of $84,000. Did this increase represent new business? Yes and no. It becomes obvious from examining the accounts, which form a large part of the Karsh archive, that much of the increase was derived from the same source, with more than half of the business being put through the books twice. What Little Wings was marketing was what the Karsh Studio was producing. Thus what the Karsh Studio showed in the revenue column as "sales" (and thus as income) was shown in the Little Wings accounts column as "expenditure." But since turnover is measured by adding income and expenditure, the combined turnover of both companies together obviously exaggerates the real volume of business. Little Wings was, in fact, creaming off a retail marketing profit on stock that it had bought wholesale from the Karsh Studio.

The intimate links between the two companies likewise generated a double income for the Karshes. This gave Solange a substantial salary while not putting this directly on the payroll of the Karsh Studio, which might have generated ill feeling among other employees. Moreover, the arrangement allowed each of them to claim large sums in business expenses. And large they were. After 1946, Solange and Yousuf travelled first class. Moreover, they rarely travelled alone.

From now on, the tall and good-looking British-born photographer Monty Everett—and after him a succession of other photographer-assistants—would accompany Karsh whenever he was out of Ottawa. Having someone to help carry and set up his equipment gave Karsh an easier time on the road. "I am learning to be patient," Yousuf reported to Solange when he and Everett were in Hollywood again in 1948, "and take things in my stride."[19] Karsh was not exaggerating. With Monty Everett changing the film during a sitting, Karsh was able to keep up a friendly banter with the client—until, of course, he raised a finger. It was at this point that all conversation would stop and Monty Everett froze until Karsh had depressed the bulb.

Giving Solange a much-deserved salary was the main objective of Little Wings, since the new company was not intended to produce large profits. Initially her salary was $5,000 a year; then, in the 1950s, it doubled to $10,000. She could thus claim her own personal tax allowances and expenses. Although Solange did not go in for expensive jewellery, she could now afford to acquire a unique collection of hats created by Edgar Noffke, and dresses and suits designed for her by Madam Martha of Fashion Creators of Canada in Toronto. In 1947 she oversaw the home extension of Little Wings. In 1948 she took a cruise around the West Indies. And in 1949 she paid the enormous sum of $500 for a black opossum fur cape.

Yousuf used his new-found wealth in much the same way. He drank the best brands of scotch and cognac. His suits and his shirts were tailored. He joined Solange on holiday. The Pink Beach Club in Bermuda was a favourite

destination. Though the place was calm and restful, it was full of prominent personalities like the film star David Niven, who made Pink Beach his home. Not surprisingly, Karsh always moonlighted in Bermuda—or wherever else he happened to be "on vacation."

The decision to set up Little Wings came at the right time for the Karsh Studio. The company was able to take advantage of large profits earned from high-paying magazines like *Saturday Night* and *Life* as well as from the largest advertising agency in North America, J. Walter Thompson. It was the Thompson agency that had secured Karsh the RCA Victor assignment in 1945; the Thompson agency that had arranged sittings for the Playwrights' Company with Maxwell Anderson, Kurt Weill, and Robert Sherwood, among other dramatists, a year later; and the Thompson agency for whom Karsh had produced twenty colour portraits of politicians for the covers of *Newsweek* and *Esquire* magazines in 1948. It was also the Thompson agency that sent Karsh back to Hollywood for a second visit, during which he photographed Clark Gable, Joan Crawford, the Marx Brothers, and four other screen stars for *Col-* Joan Crawford, 1948 *lier's Weekly.* And it was the Thompson agency that handled the many requests from Canadian and American companies that wanted Yousuf Karsh to photograph their top executives. Finally, it was the Thompson agency that commissioned Karsh to produce his first photo essay featuring prominent women.

When the photographer Franklin "Pop" Jordan saw the results of "Women of Achievement" in *Collier's Weekly*, he was impressed with the various props that his friend Karsh had used in order to symbolize the twelve women he had photographed. The ice-skating champion Barbara Ann Scott is caught in a silver cloud reminiscent of a spray of ice, the blind poet Helen Keller "reads" Braille, and the writer Clare Luce sits at her typewriter. The old grey army blanket that had been a backdrop for kings, politicians, and other prominent personages was abandoned—at least on this assignment.

Thanks to the Thompson agency, 1948 turned out to be a bumper year for the Karsh Studio. Sales rose to an astounding $82,000. This gave Karsh a net profit of $41,600—double that of the previous year. And while Little Wings suffered a net loss of $4,300, this was after Solange had deducted her salary and

her expenses—the real point of the company's existence. These high earnings were not coupled with a decline in quality. In 1948 Karsh produced some of his most memorable portraits, and to help him do this he took on a young American, Herman Leonard, who had just graduated from Ohio University with a degree in photography and who was prepared to apprentice with Karsh for no salary.

When Karsh met Albert Einstein at Princeton in 1948, the renowned physicist had reached his peak more than thirty years earlier when he had provided a new description of the physical universe, which won him the Nobel Prize in 1921. Yet it was the older Einstein, with his crumpled clothing, his sockless shoes, his wild hair, and distracted expression whom photographers and cartoonists alike had made into a visual icon. Now retired from his academic post and suffering from an abdominal aneurysm—a clear indication of syphilis—Einstein nevertheless spent a few hours every day in his office at the Institute for Advanced Study, where he was working on the third edition of his 1949 book, *The Meaning of Relativity.*[20] This was where Karsh found him, photographed him, and, following the sitting, captured his voice on a tape recorder.[21]

Albert Einstein, 1948

Few people knew that Einstein was lonely: "It is strange to be known so universally and yet to be so lonely," he told a friend in 1952.[22] And that his colleagues at the Institute for Advanced Study like Robert Oppenheimer now saw him as more of a landmark than a beacon.[23] And, finally, that Einstein regretted that the public had linked his work to the development of the atomic bomb when the concepts and discoveries that had led to its creation involved a different kind of physics and a different cast of scientists.[24]

Most portrait photographers had portrayed Einstein as the wild-eyed scientific eccentric whose incomprehensible theories had supposedly brought havoc upon the world. Not so Yousuf Karsh. He wanted to capture the enlightened, other-worldly, and what he thought was the saintly visage of the peace-loving genius.

Einstein had worn a wool jacket for the sitting. Not satisfied with this garment, Karsh sent Herman Leonard to fetch something else. Leonard returned with a sweater. When Einstein put it on, the young man recalled, "his hair was sticking out so I offered him a comb." "I never use one," Einstein replied, and no one dared to suggest that he should.[25] The sweater might have reinforced the image of the eccentric scientific genius in anyone else's hands, but its soft texture, along with Einstein's contemplative pose — and Karsh's gentle lighting — made the sixty-nine-year-old man look benevolent. Indeed, what Karsh captured was the natural openness and genuine humility that made people listen to Einstein whether he was calling for the founding of a world government or advocating better relations with the Soviet Union.

After Karsh's portrait of Einstein appeared in publications and exhibitions around the world, future clients, notably Ernest Hemingway, also wanted to wear a sweater for their portrait. When Karsh arrived in Cuba in 1957 to photograph Hemingway, he had expected "to meet the author, the rugged hero of his novels." And when Hemingway asked Karsh what he wanted to drink, Karsh ignored the fact that it was 9 a.m. and, thinking that he would please his subject, answered "Daiquiri, Sir," to which Hemingway replied, "Good God, Karsh, at this hour of the day?"[26] To Karsh's surprise, Hemingway also told him, "I don't drink while I write, for you cannot write serious stuff and drink." The man whom Karsh encountered exhibited a "peculiar gentleness," which led Karsh to call Hemingway "the shyest man I ever photographed." Shy Hemingway might have been, but as Karsh's portrait of the author's line-worn face also revealed, he was "a man cruelly battered by life but seemingly invincible" — or almost so, because four years later he would take his own life.[27]

Ernest Hemingway, 1957

GIVEN KARSH'S GRUELLING schedule during the years following the Second World War, it is no wonder that Solange counselled him in 1948 from the West Indies, "Darling, please don't overtire yourself…one pays a dreadful penalty."[28] Karsh did not heed her advice. Almost a year later, "the dear boy" (as Solange told his friend Pop Jordan) was "killing himself more than usual."[29] Karsh had never slowed down before and there was no indication that the forty-year-old man would do so now. Moreover, he could not slacken his pace if the promised book of portraits was ever going to be published.

Commissioned by the British publisher George Harrap in 1943, *Faces of Destiny* was scheduled for publication the following year. But Karsh had failed to meet this deadline. He claimed that he needed more portraits. Yet even after he got them following his trips to New York, Washington, and San Francisco in 1944 and 1945, he continued to stall. Harrap was not pleased. As he told Solange, "It is one of those tragic things that men, however great they are in their time are soon forgotten."[30]

Karsh ignored this warning because a new problem had arisen. Harrap could not afford to use the photogravure method of reproduction that would make Karsh's portraits faithful to the original prints. Karsh was so concerned about the production quality of the illustrations that, as Solange told Harrap, "He would rather wait years than risk the publication of a book with inferior reproductions."[31] Then there was the matter of producing a 150-word essay to accompany each photograph. Pop Jordan came to Karsh's rescue in the spring of 1945, but even though the editor of the *American Annual of Photography* was well qualified to help Karsh produce the essays, Jordan found it difficult having to work from Karsh's fragmented notes. "I had to add a lot of stuff to make it up to the minimum of 150 words," he told Solange, whom he hoped would be pleased with his effort.[32]

Karsh was pleased with Jordan's revisions but he continued to stall the publication. This was because he wanted an American firm to co-publish the book. In September 1945 the Chicago publisher Ziff-Davis agreed to print the book in the United States and, due to post-war paper shortages in Great Britain, to send George Harrap three thousand unbound copies for publication six months later. But the book was unable to meet Ziff-Davis's publication deadline, because Karsh had failed to submit the foreword on time.

Thinking of the preface that the American poet Carl Sandburg had written for Edward Steichen's recent publication *Road to Victory*, Karsh hoped that George Bernard Shaw would do the same for him. But Karsh's London agent, Tom Blau, quashed the idea: "Mr Shaw might not remember you with sufficient clarity." And even if he did, Blau continued, it was doubtful whether the eighty-nine-year-old playwright "would like to write a preface to a book he has not seen."[33] The Canadian author and literary journalist Merrill Denison was then asked to write the foreword and edit Jordan's essays accompanying the portraits. Denison agreed to do this and was paid a generous fee of $1,200.

By September 1946, Denison had placed the text for the book in the American publisher's hands and printing began. When Karsh saw the proofs of the book, however, he dragged his feet yet again. The quality of the reproductions—printed in halftone—did not meet his high standards. The sharp contrasts and subtle gradation between light and dark were lost. The black areas were flat and lifeless. The white areas did not sparkle. Not only were the illustrations unfaithful to their original facsimiles. Karsh also wondered if he had chosen the best photograph to represent each personality depicted.

Karsh knew that the public's understanding and appreciation of his work was conditioned by where and how the portraits were presented. Most of them had been produced for private display in the home or for illustration in the mass media. Putting them between the covers of a book was another matter. His readers—and his critics—would get more than a passing glance at the seventy-five portraits. And what would they find? According to Karsh: repetition, retrogression, and unevenness.

Karsh always insisted that he worked by instinct, that a portrait was the product of what happened between him and the subject. "I seize each sitting and this challenge spontaneously," he wrote in his awkward English when asked for his "secret."[34] However, creating portraits that gave his viewers the feeling that they had been given "the most graceful introduction possible to a great personality" was not entirely dependent upon Karsh's spontaneity.[35]

Karsh knew that there was much more to making a photograph than this. He knew better than anybody else that the sharp definition and gradation of illumination from light to dark that gave the middle tones of his sitter's face a third dimension was achieved by the way in which Karsh positioned his flood and spotlights during a sitting and the extent to which the detailed instructions he wrote for the spotter, the proofer, and the developer were carried out.

Working to a formula presented a danger to every portrait photographer. And this was surely why Karsh feared that the poor quality of the reproduction along with the repetitiveness and the poor selection of images might work against him when the seventy-five examples of his work were brought together in a book.

These concerns would have stalled the publication even further if Solange had not waded in to assuage Karsh's "doubts and fears." "To be a perfectionist in your own work is divine," she told him in September 1946; "to try to be one in a field which is not yours only means disturbances." Moreover, by 1946 many of the portraits were three years old and, she further noted, "people will have lost all interest in most of your personalities." Thus "the time is now for this one book or NEVER."[36] Yousuf took Solange's advice. *Faces of Destiny, Portraits by Karsh* appeared in late 1946, in time for the Christmas market in North America.[37]

George Harrap need not have feared that people would not be interested in looking at portraits of their wartime leaders. Admittedly, five businessmen, one architect, and an actor, along with three women — Eleanor Roosevelt, Madame Chiang Kai-shek, and Princess Elizabeth — shared centre stage with the politicians, diplomats, and royal leaders. Nor need Harrap have worried that people would be reluctant to purchase a book of illustrations because they were used to getting their pictures through the less expensive illustrated weeklies. And the American publisher need not have feared that Karsh was not sufficiently well known to attract American readers. *Faces of Destiny* was an instant success. It sold over 13,000 copies in North America, and, when it appeared in Britain six months later, it sold 3,000 more.

The only people who questioned the overwhelming success of *Faces of Destiny* were Yousuf and Solange. They were unhappy that the book had not been more widely reviewed in Britain. "We cannot these days obtain the lengthy and numerous reviews we would like owing to the small size of our newspapers and the consequent restriction of space available for literature and cultural matters," was the reasonable reply Solange received from Harrap Publishers regarding the lacunae in British reviews.[38]

Yousuf and Solange also complained about the distribution of the book in North America. Yet their Canadian distributor at Ambassador Books felt that his company had "done a damn good job of distribution."[39] It was also disappointing that Karsh had refused to help promote the book: he would not attend autograph sessions at bookstores in Toronto, Montreal, and Ottawa. "I know that it is done a great deal in the States," Solange told Ambassador Books' employee H. R. M. Clee, "but it hardly seems dignified enough for Karsh in Canada."[40] Finally, even though Karsh had written in the foreword that he felt that he had succeeded in portraying the famous "both as they appeared to me and as they impressed themselves on their generation," he remained unhappy about the quality of the reproductions.[41] This was why he refused to allow Ziff-Davis to print a second edition of the book. It is also why Karsh quashed the idea of following up *Faces of Destiny* with a book of portraits devoted to musicians, actors, and writers.

This grudging reaction seems quite unwarranted by either the sales figures or the critical response to Karsh's first book. In June 1947, Karsh was hailed as "one of the world's greatest photographers" by a writer for the *British Journal of Photography*.[42] Walter Harrap went even further in his praise when he told Karsh that *Faces of Destiny* had firmly established him "as the premier camera portraitist in the world."[43] There was no doubt about such claims in the minds of other people who reviewed the book or among Karsh's friends. Pop Jordan was intrigued with the portrait of Shaw: "this is the softest print I have seen of this subject." He marvelled at the balance Karsh had achieved between the tonal qualities of the face and those of the figure and clothing in his portrait of the Canadian Governor General Viscount Alexander of Tunis.[44] Mackenzie King, who was flattered to be included in the book, praised Karsh for having "made a fine contribution to the art and literature of our country."[45] There was also praise from an unexpected quarter.

A writer for the Armenian publication the *Hairenik Weekly* was thrilled that Karsh had not missed the opportunity "to advise the world" that he was an Armenian and "to acquaint the world of the great injustice" that he had suffered as a young Armenian in Anatolia.[46] Another Armenian, the photographer Housepian Tzolag, told Karsh how popular *Faces of Destiny* was among members of the Armenian community in Baghdad.

Though Merrill Denison had written the foreword to the book, Karsh had supplied the biographical details and scrutinized the final text. It told the story of Karsh's birth in Mardin, Turkey, his expulsion by the Turks from "the reign of horror," and his subsequent immigration to Canada. The foreword contained some curious distortions, however. It misrepresented the status of Karsh's illiterate father, Abdel al-Massih, failed to give George Nakash credit for teaching "Joe" the rudiments of photography and helping him set up his studio in Ottawa, and exaggerated the length of time that Karsh had studied with John Garo in Boston. No credit was given to the American photographer Edward Steichen, whose instruction on "how to meet the different personalities" had been an "inspiration" to Karsh on his 1936 visit to New York.[47] But the significant point for the Armenian community in Canada and abroad was that one of their own had become famous and had used his fame to draw the world's attention to the Armenian genocide by the Turks.

The popular and financial success of *Faces of Destiny* had a lot to do with the positive reviews it got at home and abroad, and with the public's curiosity about their leaders. But there was another reason why the book struck a chord, especially with North American readers.

Karsh's "contemporary historical documents," as he called them in the foreword, included a group of portraits ranging from the humble Afro-American clerk in the White House to Eleanor Roosevelt, General Dwight Eisenhower, and the American President Harry S. Truman. These were the people who were creating a new world out of the ruins of Europe. Some would be occupying a place in the newly created United Nations Organization, whose home would not be London, Paris, or Rome but New York. Others, the architects and the businessmen, would be equally important in bringing the new world's message to the old. "For many years European thinkers have been telling us that the age we live in is decadent," the Canadian author Hugh MacLennan claimed in *Maclean's*. "But we and the United States are no longer dominated by Europe....[and] Karsh shows us that whatever else our society might be, it is not decadent."[48] Karsh thus supplied the visual images that carried this confident message to a wide and receptive public. The irony, however, is that, still unhappy with the quality of the reproductions of his work and with the lack of reviews in the British press, Karsh did not appreciate the full extent of his own achievement.

Karsh Dancing with
Young Mary-Ann, 1963

Back to Europe

On April 28, 1949, the Ottawa *Journal* announced that Yousuf and Solange Karsh had just left Montreal by air for Europe. According to Solange, Yousuf had possessed "a very roving foot" ever since photographing the wartime leaders in Great Britain.[1] Now, six years later, he was returning to Europe to capture, as the Ottawa *Journal* put it, "the new spirit which pervaded postwar Europe."[2]

Karsh's trip represented a departure from his travel plans because during most of the 1940s his sights had been set on Moscow, not on London, Paris, or Rome. This was because Karsh had been desperate to photograph Joseph Stalin. But in 1949 it seemed unlikely that the opportunity to do so would arise without help from Canada's Department of External Affairs. That department was generally reluctant to support cultural activity. In its view, Canadian culture was not "sophisticated enough to be relied upon in a program of cultural relations."[3] Nonetheless, External Affairs had shown itself eager to help Karsh photograph Stalin—at least until a cipher clerk from the Soviet embassy in Ottawa revealed that a spy network was operating in Canada. Even after the subsequent defection of Igor Gouzenko in September 1945, and the revelation of the Soviet Union's espionage activities to the Canadian public the following spring, Karsh still wanted to travel to Russia. And during the remaining years of the decade he continued to tell reporters that he was on the verge of photographing Joseph Stalin.

What did seem feasible for Karsh was a trip to Great Britain and to the western part of continental Europe. After all, Tom Blau had been encouraging him to return to London since 1944. Nicholas Haz had warned him that he was in danger of becoming stale: "Your problem now is not so much to still improve yourself," the New York photographer told Karsh in 1946, "but to keep on an even keel and avoid retrogression."[4] Moreover, by the end of 1948 Karsh was running out of subjects. Visiting Europe would enable him to add more dignitaries to his stock of celebrity portraits. It would be inspiring. "One always leaves the presence of great personalities somewhat humble," he had told the Art Association and Camera Club in Bermuda in 1948, "and yet stimulated and feeling a better human being for their meeting."[5] And, with a commission from *Newsweek* magazine in the offing, the visit might even be lucrative.

A rival to Henry Luce's *Time* magazine, *Newsweek* was already a known quantity to Karsh. In 1948 he had made "an impressive collection of scalps" in colour for *Newsweek*.[6] At $500 a sitting plus expenses, the assignment had been profitable. Moreover, the magazine had been so pleased with the results that it had redesigned its cover in order to set off Karsh's photographs and, as an inter-office memo put it, thus "provide the note of distinction which we like to think that *Newsweek* deserves."[7]

The kind of attention that *Newsweek* had given to reproduction values was important to Karsh, particularly since his colour work was not always shown at its best. In the autumn of 1948, for example, *Collier's Weekly* had commissioned him to make portraits of the American presidential candidates—the Republican Thomas E. Dewey and the Democrat Harry S. Truman—in the forthcoming election. When Karsh saw the results in January 1949, he was horrified. So was Pop Jordan, who had viewed the proofs before publication. "I suppose the money is some recompense for your wounded feelings," he commiserated, "when you see such horrible reproductions of your beautiful work."[8]

Karsh could not be consoled. He blamed the magazine's editor for the poor quality of the reproductions. The editor, Oscar Dystel, in turn blamed Karsh for providing *Collier's Weekly* with a colour transparency of Truman that was "not up to the usual standards as far as exposure is concerned."[9] To make matters worse, Dewey's press relations chief, who somehow got his hands on a copy of the transparency, gave it to *Life*. When *Life* published the photograph of Dewey, Karsh was caught in an awkward position between *Collier's Weekly*, who maintained that they had exclusive rights to the transparency, and *Life*, who had no right to use it at all.

Working for *Newsweek*, however, had been different. Proud of the three-dimensional quality of his colour transparencies, Karsh was pleased with how the magazine had reproduced them. And even though *Newsweek*'s editors thought that one of the Washington portraits was too dark for the cover of their magazine, they were satisfied enough with the quality of the other portraits to offer Karsh another assignment. What *Newsweek* wanted were portraits of men like President Vincent Auriol of France, Premier Alcide de Gasperi of Italy, and four other Europeans including Paul-Henri Spaak and Jean Monnet, who were working towards European unity. And the magazine not only wanted Karsh to produce colour transparencies of these people, it wanted him to produce a written account of what took place at each sitting.

Newsweek promised to get Karsh an hour with every subject, to put the magazine's bureau chiefs in London, Paris, and Berlin at his disposal, and, most important of all, to pay him a handsome fee plus travel expenses. It was an attractive offer for a travel-hungry photographer who needed to update his stock of dignitaries. And even though Solange insisted that they would have preferred to have made a trip to Europe without having to work, it is difficult to imagine Karsh forfeiting a chance to photograph the great and the good at someone else's expense.

With only a small number of portrait sittings to complete for *Newsweek*, Karsh could also take on other work. Casting Karsh's net beyond the political arena, Tom Blau offered to arrange sittings with the philosopher Bertrand Russell, the writer J. B. Priestley, the artist Henry Moore, the scientist Julian Huxley, and with the Paris-based French playwright and poet Jean Cocteau. And the New York-based advertising agency J. Walter Thompson commissioned Karsh to produce images that would be suitable for Christmas cards: a painting of the

Madonna, a carved religious sculpture, a set of church bells, a flight of stairs leading to a famous shrine, a person kneeling in a prayerful attitude.[10]

Karsh also made his own contacts. He asked Pix Incorporated of New York to handle the distribution of his European work in the United States. Pix agreed to do so on the condition that they would take a 30 percent cut on all sales. Working through the Department of External Affairs, Karsh gathered letters of introduction to several Canadian ambassadors. Most were eager to meet the famous photographer. At Canada's legation in Oslo, for example, D. M. Cornett felt that Karsh "would provide us with the opportunity of securing some favourable publicity for Canada in Norway."[11] Karsh also sought help from European ambassadors in Ottawa, all of whom were on his Christmas card list. Finally, he contacted several people whom he had photographed during his 1943 trip to England. Sir Stafford Cripps was one. With the help of his old friend Leonard Brockington, the British chancellor of the exchequer agreed to pose for the Canadian photographer again. Karsh also approached Shaw. "Mr. Karsh's portraits have had a great success," the playwright replied through his secretary, Miss Patch, but "I shall not let him try to improve on them."[12] Undeterred, Karsh wrote to Shaw again, but it was no use. "Mr. Shaw directs me to say in answer to your letter," was Miss Patch's final reply, "that he will not sit again to Karsh as he is now a very old man, undistinguished from any other old crock with a white beard."[13]

EUROPE WAS A VERY different place than it had been when Karsh visited England in 1943. Countless millions of civilians as well as soldiers had lost their lives during the hostilities. The economies of most European countries were in disarray. So were many of their governments. Between 1946 and 1958, France had twenty-four prime ministers. There was no political continuity after the war in defeated Germany or Italy. And there was an iron curtain across Europe: in response to the Allies' establishment of a West German government in June 1948, the Russians had cut off rail, highway, and water access routes to Berlin.

When Yousuf and Solange arrived in Europe in late April 1949, West Berlin was in the midst of an airlift mounted by the western Allies; when the Karshes went home in early August, the Allies had flown some 250,000 missions transporting two million tons of goods to the blockaded city. Things were little better in Britain than in the former German capital. Though the country had won the war, it was the world's largest debtor nation in 1945. There was food and gasoline rationing; the British Empire was shrinking, notably when Britain had given "the jewel in the crown"—India—its independence in 1947.

None of this made travelling around Europe trouble free, still less congenial. Especially if you were driving a large, gasoline-consuming Chrysler loaded down with 250 pounds of camera equipment and crammed with three passengers in the front seat. Especially if your only languages were French and English. Especially if you were unaccustomed to filling out forms, dealing with officious customs officials, queuing for food, or concerning yourself with a plethora of other difficulties evident in post-war Europe. And especially if you were used to being treated with great respect by people who knew your worth.

Monty Everett had now been recruited, initially when Karsh had persuaded him to take a short sabbatical from running a photography and lithography studio that he had established the previous year in Ottawa. The twenty-four-year-old Royal Canadian Air Force veteran accompanied the Chrysler and the camera equipment by ship from New York to Liverpool and had a pleasant enough crossing to the country of his birth. More pleasant, at any rate, than Yousuf and Solange. During their day-long Trans-Canada Air Lines flight via Gander, Newfoundland, and Shannon, Ireland, to London, Solange was suffering from a cold. Her condition did not improve once she and Yousuf installed themselves in the luxury of London's Savoy Hotel. Their plans to start their European journey in sound health—they had spent the early spring resting in Barbados—had come to naught when Solange's cold turned into a severe case of sinusitis.

Karsh had planned to visit eleven countries. Due to Solange's poor health, however, he ended up visiting only six: England, France, Italy, West Germany, Belgium, and, at the last moment, Finland. Even so, with Monty at the wheel of their ostentatious car, they managed to clock over 10,000 miles. During their three-month sojourn, Karsh completed most of the assignments for *Newsweek* along with the sittings arranged for him by Tom Blau. In the first two weeks alone, he photographed Air Marshal Tedder, Admiral Lord Frazer, and six business executives. When Karsh returned to England from continental Europe in mid-July, twenty-three individuals—from the sculptor Henry Moore and the composer Ralph Vaughan Williams to the British prime minister, Clement Attlee—agreed to pose in front of his famous white camera. And during the weeks in between his two working visits to England, Karsh photographed sixteen dignitaries on the continent.

SOLANGE HAD NOT BEEN in France for some forty years. She lovingly recorded their first meal at La Pomme d'Or in Abbeville: they ate bisque de crevettes, then steak and pommes frites, followed by a green salad—all for the equivalent of less than ten dollars. But things had changed since her childhood. "The noise in Europe is unbelievable," she told the secretaries back home, "something like Times Square…Paris was one long hell—and very nearly a complete fiasco." Moreover, Solange "had to sleep in a Chinese dressing gown to keep from freezing completely."[14]

Karsh had problems in England as well as on the continent. First there was the difficulty of getting his equipment through customs during an era of tight import restrictions. He threatened to take fifteen minutes out of the promised hour-long sitting with the chancellor of the exchequer, Sir Stafford Cripps, in order to tell him "what a terrible customs department they have."[15] Then there were problems with the electricity. Karsh purchased a dozen different plugs to cope with the multiplicity of sockets, only to discover that his collection often fell short of what was required. It was not just the variety of electrical outlets that posed a problem but also the lack of power. After he and Monty had hauled their equipment up six flights of stairs for the sitting with the Roman Catholic intellectual François Mauriac, they discovered to their dismay that the electricity had been turned off. Desperate for a photograph, Karsh sat Mauriac in front of a set of French doors which led onto a small balcony. He asked Monty to hold a white bed sheet to serve as a reflector. Then Karsh took his picture. The resulting photograph, which was pared down to an absolute minimum, was too dark for the cover of *Newsweek*. But Karsh came to think that he had nevertheless captured Mauriac's "dark despondency about human affairs."[16]

Many people, like Mauriac, were living close to the poverty line. And those who were not did not want to advertise the fact. When Karsh arrived to photograph Averell Harriman, the American ambassador, in his palatial Paris residence, Harriman insisted that they choose another setting lest he cause offence.

Karsh faced another kind of problem, too, in Europe: lack of the recognition he felt was his due. True, in Britain the press wrote extensively about his visit and in London the well-known photographer Baron invited several of his colleagues to meet the man who had been such an influence on his own work. "It was a tribute to Karsh's eminence how eager they all were to meet the master," Baron recalled in his memoir.[17] But on continental Europe things were different. There were no notices in the press to announce Karsh's arrival. No photographers were eager to meet and to entertain Yousuf and Solange.

Many of the Europeans Karsh photographed had simply never heard of him. The German composer Richard Strauss had to be persuaded to sit for Karsh and, even after agreeing to pose, was uncooperative. François Mauriac, 1949 It is true that Karsh's lack of German prevented the two men from engaging in conversation. It is also true that Strauss—who died two months after the sitting—was far from well. But even if Karsh had spoken German and Strauss had not been ill, the Canadian photographer would have still been an unknown quantity rather than an honoured guest in the home of the famous composer.

Karsh had naively expected that his book, *Faces of Destiny*, would have made him a household name on continental Europe. When he realized that this was not the case, he was "distressed and embarrassed."[18] This represented a failure of comprehension about the impact of the war. Even Winston Churchill could drive through Berlin in an open car without being recognized at the time of the Potsdam conference in 1945. "I had forgotten," recalled Lord Moran, who had accompanied Churchill to Potsdam, "that the press and the cinema, which have made his face as familiar to the Canadian lumbermen as to the Russian peasant, have in Germany by neglect brought him to earth and made him anonymous."[19] In this context, the man famous for having photographed Churchill could hardly expect to trade on his fame in Germany.

It was only when Yousuf, Solange, and Monty reached Italy that things improved. "For the first time on this misguided trip," Solange told Joyce Large and Betty Cookson, "things are looking up."[20] Visiting the great cathedrals in Rome was, Karsh later told Charles Prilik of J. Walter Thompson, "a most stirring experience."[21] It was the Canadian ambassador in Italy, Jean Desay, who was responsible for this pleasant turn of events. He invited Yousuf, Solange, and Monty to his home for a drink, and then took them out to dinner in a restaurant where they were serenaded. The stroll through Rome's narrow, twisting streets following dinner made this "an out of this world evening," as Solange called it in her letter to the secretaries back at the Karsh Studio; she declared in awe that words failed when she attempted to describe the ruins of the Forum by moonlight.

Jean Desay not only entertained the Canadian party with an open hospitality that Karsh would come to expect when he was abroad, Desay duly arranged Karsh's sittings with the Italian prime minister, Alcide de Gasperi,

and with the foreign minister, Count Sforza. Above all, it was Desay who enabled Karsh to have one of his most memorable — and lucrative — sittings.

Karsh already had a letter of introduction to Pope Pius XII from Cardinal Francis Spellman, whom he had photographed in Boston the previous year. But Desay's sponsorship was crucial. Before the session took place, the Pope blessed the religious items that Yousuf and Solange had brought with them. And when they returned to Canada in mid-August, the colour transparency that Karsh had taken of the Pope was transformed into fifty thousand lithographs. Commissioned by the Vatican, Karsh personally delivered fifteen thousand copies the following spring.[22]

The post-war expansion of Canada's embassies throughout Europe not only meant that there were ambassadors to help Karsh make contact with his subjects. Embassy staff also helped to courier Karsh's precious negatives back to Canada in the diplomatic mailbag. This was why, even before he returned to Ottawa, the portrait of the scarlet-robed Supreme Pontiff had been developed in the Karsh studio by Karsh's assistants, Peter Kuzyk and Paul Desmarais, and sent for publication. "Great news this morning when I arrived at the studio," Betty Cookson reported to

Solange, Yousuf and Monty over a month before they returned to Canada. "Joyce, Peter and Paul were looking so smug and handed me the morning *Journal*—on the front page: 'Karsh photographs Pope in the Vatican.'"²³

Before leaving Canada, Karsh had been determined to photograph the men who were "shaping the destinies of Europe."²⁴ And despite the difficulties he encountered on the trip, Solange was convinced that Yousuf had nevertheless taken "some mighty fine things."²⁵ By early August, Karsh had photographed not only three prime ministers, a pope, and an archbishop but also writers, artists, an actor, philosophers, film moguls, composers, and businessmen—many of whom were seeking to create a new world out of the ruins of the Second World War. When he photographed these individuals, Karsh incorporated every one of his stylistic devices and approaches to date. For example, the portrait of the British film producer J. Arthur Rank harkened back to the photographs that Karsh had taken for the Dominion Drama Festival in the early 1930s. Karsh's portraits of Bertrand Russell and Jean Cocteau focused as much on the hands as on the face and were as dramatic as the portraits he had made of the Hollywood film stars. And the improvised portrait of François Mauriac showed what Karsh could do without the help of his spot- and floodlights.

Bertrand Russell, 1949

Yet these stunning photographs were not among Karsh's favourite studies resulting from his trip. Rather, it was the portrait of Jean Sibelius that would go into Karsh's coveted calling-card portfolio, that would be shown in exhibitions around the world, would appear in future publications of his books, and would be the focus of newspaper articles and a subject for discussion in radio interviews and lectures.

Sibelius, as Solange reported to the secretaries in the Karsh Studio, was initially "as temperamental as all get up."²⁶ But that was before two Shell Oil magnates, whom Karsh had photographed in London, managed to convince the composer to sit for him. And when Karsh visited Sibelius's Finnish retreat some thirty-eight kilometres from Helsinki, the composer's view of the young Canadian photographer changed.

Karsh's visit to Sibelius's home at Järvenpää became a story that the photographer never tired of telling. How the fastidiously dressed eighty-six-year-old

recluse had met him at the garden gate of his house, Ainola, which, like Little Wings, was surrounded by birches, meadows, and water. How Sibelius had asked the power authorities to run a line from the road to his house so that Karsh would have sufficient voltage to illuminate the five floodlights and the five-hundred-watt spotlight that he had brought with him from London. How the two men had shared cognac, cigars, and good food between the poses. How Sibelius had agreed to let Karsh return for another sitting: "You are fantastic, one does not get tired working with you for you are generating energy."[27] All this led up to Karsh's remarkable statement (so he told Solange, who had remained in London) that he would like Sibelius to adopt him as his son.[28]

When Karsh met him, Sibelius had not published any new music since 1929. Moreover, his most famous work, *Finlandia*, had been written some thirty years before that date. Yet in North America and in Britain, Sibelius's reputation had never been stronger. In 1938 a festival devoted to his music had been sold out in London. During the Nazi occupation of Finland, Malcolm Sargent had conducted a symphony that Vaughan Williams had dedicated to the Finnish composer. (Sibelius had surreptitiously listened to it on the BBC.) And Karsh was able to tell Sibelius how, during the Russo-Finnish war, the spirits of despondent Finnish-Canadian lumbermen had been raised when their foreman piped a recording of *Finlandia* over the loudspeaker system.

Jean Sibelius, 1949

Given all this, how did Karsh depict Sibelius? In his closely cropped portrait, the large, bald-headed man appeared haughty and distant. In fact he possessed an Olympian detachment which reinforced his reputation as a recluse. Karsh also conveyed the great mass of the man "so that in years to come, sculptors who might wish to create a statue of the composer could see his whole figure in its true proportion."[29] Missing from the portrait is any hint that Sibelius was a chronic alcoholic and a notorious womanizer. That his hands shook. That a button on his otherwise beautifully tailored jacket was missing. That he felt that the world of music had left him behind. And that, contrary to Karsh's interpretation of the granite-faced man, Sibelius was a warm, immediate, and spontaneous individual. For Karsh, however, Sibelius was a hero as well as a celebrity.

WHILE POSING FOR Karsh in 1942, Solange had wrapped herself in a shawl and assumed a tortured expression on her face. Karsh hoped that the resulting portrait, which he called "The Refugee," would represent the sufferings of people in wartorn Europe. Seven years after producing this portrait, Yousuf and Solange were "saddened" by much of what they saw in "the Old World."[30] It is true that the four continental cities that they visited—Venice, Rome, Brussels, and Paris— had suffered less bomb damage than many other cities in Europe, including London. Yet no European city was without its share of displaced people, whether in Germany, France, Finland, or Italy. During Karsh's sitting with de Gasperi, the prime minister told him to persuade the Canadian government to allow five million Italians into the country in order to solve Italy's refugee problem.

Nor could Yousuf and Solange have failed to notice the despondent mood that prevailed among ordinary citizens and statesmen alike. When, for example, Karsh asked the British prime minister if the world was a better place since the establishment of the United Nations in 1945, Attlee quickly replied that it was "not much better."[31] Averell Harriman's response to Karsh's question as to whether Europe could expect to reclaim its former place in the world was equally negative.

Karsh had agreed to speak to Ottawa's Canadian Club as well as to several other organizations in Canada and the United States upon his return from Europe. It was the Europeans' sombre mood that Solange attempted to convey when she wrote "the speech you want" for Yousuf on the voyage home on the *Empress of Canada*.[32] Working on the text in her stateroom, adjacent to his, Solange began on an upbeat note: "Never before in history was Europe so keen to welcome Canadians." In France they remembered Dieppe and the heroic part Canadians had played in the invasion of Normandy. In the Netherlands they remembered how Canada had looked after Princess Juliana and her two children in Ottawa. In Norway—another country that neither Solange nor Yousuf had visited on their trip—they remembered how Norwegian airmen had trained in Canada. The Italians were grateful for Canada's part in the Sicilian landings. And the British remembered how Canadians "had stood by her in her hour of need." Finally, "all Europe," she continued, "likes us for the size of our country with its untold potentialities." Canada was a favourite with the Europeans because, though the Americans were both "admired and feared," Canadians could be "trusted implicitly."[33]

Solange then proceeded to demonstrate the extent to which both she and Yousuf had felt as though they had been "living in a lost world" during their trip.[34] Weaving the observations that she had noted during every sitting into the text of Yousuf's speech, Solange supplied the requisite anecdotes. How Attlee had told Karsh that there was little possibility of a woman ever becoming prime minister of Great Britain. How Bertrand Russell had told him that there would never be a great female philosopher. How Karsh had been fixated by the Pontiff's translucent hands during his eighteen-minute sitting. How, conversely, Solange had been horrified by what the British sculptor Henry Moore had done to the female form: there were "holes carved in for breasts and abdomen."[35]

What Solange carefully did not convey—in this or in any of the other talks that she wrote for Yousuf on their return to Canada—was the extent to which the trip had, in many respects, been a disappointment. "Remember," she wrote to Yousuf on board the *Empress of Canada*, "it was not a very funny trip from my point of view."[36] This was hardly an exaggeration. Solange returned to Ottawa suffering not only from sinusitis, anemia, vitamin deficiency, and bronchitis; she was also physically and mentally fatigued. Though Yousuf, like Solange, was also in need of a long rest, his problem was not fatigue but in not having had either the time or the contacts to produce portraits of Charles de Gaulle, the writer Evelyn Waugh, the composer Benjamin Britten, the Germans Ernst Reuter and Dr. Eberhardt, and others commissioned by *Newsweek* or suggested as subjects by Tom Blau. Finally, like Solange, he, too, had been homesick.

"If you bums don't think we miss you," Solange had written to Joyce Large and Betty Cookson from Italy, "you're crazy...we do."[37] Yousuf and Solange were not only happy to greet the staff at the office when they returned to Ottawa in late August 1949; they felt, as Karsh told Charles Prilik of J. Walter Thompson, "infinitely glad to be back on this North American continent which is our home."[38]

YOUSUF KARSH HAD good reason to feel at home, despite the infestation of cater-pillars that greeted him and Solange at Little Wings. Two years earlier, in January 1947, he had participated in the National Citizenship Ceremony. The event celebrated the passing, a few months before, of the Canadian Citizen Act, which declared that Canadians were no longer British subjects but Cana-dians in their own right. Karsh had been chosen to represent the province of Ontario. When he later watched a newsreel of the proceedings at Ottawa's Regent Theatre, he was proud to see himself on the podium with the prime min-ister and the architect of the act, the minister of national health and welfare, Paul Martin.

"Immigrants," as Peter Newman has observed, "want nothing more desper-ately than to ingratiate themselves into the core of their adopted country, having previously been consigned to its fringes."[39] Even after the passing of the Citizen Act and Mackenzie King's admission that it was wrong to treat certain categories of potential immigrants as inferior to other applicants, Armenians were still classified as Asiatics and thus on the non-preferred list of immigrants. Although Yousuf Karsh spent a good deal of time trying to fit in, he was never allowed to forget that he was an Armenian.

During his early years in Ottawa, Karsh had been treated in a less gracious manner than he would have liked because he looked and spoke differently from almost everyone else. True, his image was somewhat exotic; to the (highly sym-pathetic) British photographer Baron, Karsh resembled "an Eastern potentate."[40] Following his success in 1941, the press noted those physical characteristics and mannerisms that made him different from other, Anglo-French Canadians: his small stature and swarthy complexion, his heavily accented English, his crin-kly black tonsure, and his effusive manners and subtle flatteries.

Whenever Karsh crossed the American border, his papers were closely scru-tinized. On one occasion in early 1952 he would certainly have been denied entry to the United States if his lawyer, Ross Tolmie, who happened to be on the same train, had not intervened: "This man is going to the United States to pho-tograph your president."[41]

Nor did the Armenians themselves let Karsh forget his origins. He received dozens of letters from compatriots who had followed his career with, as one correspondent put it in 1944, "a great deal of pleasure and pride."[42] Then there were the many requests from those Armenians who were desperate, like the singer Charles Aznavour, to immigrate to North America, which "in the eyes of Armenian immigrants...stood for a new, rich life in a land of milk and honey."[43]

It was always painful for Karsh to receive letters about the plight of Armenians, because there was little he could do to help. The only way Armenians could enter Canada, provided the government had not exceeded its annual quota of "non-preferred" immigrants, was if they had a relative who was willing to sponsor them. Karsh was thus in a position to do something only for his parents and his two youngest brothers, who were still in Syria. But until the winter of 1947, he made no effort to do so.

It is difficult to understand why Yousuf and Solange were so reluctant to help the Karsh family immigrate to Canada. Karsh was well aware of the political situation in Syria. In 1939 Jamil had told Malak that the country was "in a state of trouble and confusion."[44] After the occupying French forces left Syria in 1946, anti-Christian feeling increased. And when Lebanese and Syrian troops invaded Israel in 1948, things got worse for the Karsh family because it looked as though Jamil was about to be drafted into the Syrian army.

Karsh knew that his parents, Massih and Bahiyah, had always expected to join their two eldest sons in North America. After Malak immigrated to Canada in 1937 and "the family started to break up," there remained the hope, as the youngest son, Salim, recalled, "that one day we would be there."[45] Nor were Massih and Bahiyah enjoying the high standard of living that Karsh's description of his father as "an importer and exporter of the world's goods" in the foreword to *Faces of Destiny* suggested.[46] As Salim told Malak in 1943, "My father's work [as a commissioner] is very little especially during the war" and, he continued, "Father is getting very tired for he works very hard."[47]

Given the fact that the eldest son should, as Salim put it, "be an example," why did Yousuf do nothing to help his family in Syria for so long?[48] They often felt ignored. "Three years passed and we received only two letters from you,"

Salim reminded Yousuf and Solange in June 1942.[49] By early December 1946 Karsh had still not answered his family's letters. It was then that George Nakash, who was the unofficial head of the extended Karsh family, insisted that Karsh should write to his parents. "In North America time seems to slip by more readily as the tempo of living is so fast the pressure of work so constant," was the answer that Karsh gave his family for not writing "as often as I would like."[50]

It is not good enough to say that Karsh may not have appreciated his family's desperate situation because he so rarely corresponded with them. We know that he did receive news of the family through Uncle George in Montreal, through his aunts Lucia and Nazlia, who had settled in Ste-Marie-de-Beauce, and from Malak, who, unlike his older brother, was a good correspondent. But this does not fully explain why Karsh failed to respond directly to his proud mother—"Your fame has spread to the entire East," she told him in 1947—when she asked for first-hand news of her eldest son.[51] When Yousuf told his mother that he was simply too busy to write, it may have been true but hardly the whole truth.

Did Karsh want to protect his family from being an object of the negative stereotyping that he had experienced? In one of his rare letters home, Karsh had told Jamil how Mackenzie King's praise of *Faces of Destiny* had made him "forget that I am a stranger in a new land, a feeling, I am convinced, no one can forget having once leaving his place of birth."[52]

Things came to a head in 1947 when George Nakash and his sister Lucia offered to sponsor the Karsh family's immigration to Canada. "I know that Solange and probably Yousuf are definitely against it," Jamil told Malak.[53] When Yousuf learned, however, that his uncle was about to sponsor his parents' immigration to Canada, he finally moved into action.

In December 1947 Karsh approached Hugh L. Keenleyside. Karsh's stock with the deputy minister of the Department of Mines and Resources was high. Karsh had photographed him in 1944. Keenleyside knew that he was a friend of Mackenzie King, among other high-ranking politicians, and that Karsh had played a major part in the National Citizenship Ceremony. Consequently, barely two months after approaching the deputy minister, Karsh was informed that the government had passed a special Order-in-Council "providing for the admission to Canada of your father and mother and two brothers."[54]

Solange now professed herself as eager as Yousuf to have the Karsh family on their side of the Atlantic. In preparation for meeting Yousuf's family, she reminded Salim and Jamil, "I am definitely your older and eldest sister, but I am very French...I talk where English people remain silent...I am neither young nor old...beautiful, pretty nor ugly...I am myself...and I love you all." Solange was not exaggerating when she concluded in her letter that she and Yousuf were "more than happy that you are in Canada and that we shall do everything we can to see that Mother and Father are happy."[55] As Nakash's daughter Vivian recalled when she greeted the family in Montreal, "it was a joy to see them...the family were so happy to be in this country."[56]

There is a photograph of the Karsh family taken shortly after Yousuf and George Nakash had met them on the docks in New York and then flown them to Montreal, where they spent their first night in Canada before travelling to Ottawa. It is a balmy day in late June and the family sit or stand among the birches. Behind them are the beautifully tended lawns at Little Wings and copses of deciduous trees that Solange and Yousuf have planted over the last seven years. The group makes a lovely family tableau. The beautiful expectant mother, Barbara, holding her two-year-old son, Sydney. Solange, wearing a white sun dress, posing gracefully beside her sister-in-law. Yousuf, who has probably just set up the camera and then joined the group before the automatic shutter clicked, standing to one side and gazing at the ground. Everyone else — Massih, Bahiyah, Malak, Salim, Jamil, Aunt Lucia, George Nakash, and his wife, Laly — looking at the camera. Everyone is happy. But no one more so than Karsh.

Within a few days Massih, Bahiyah, and Salim would begin their new life in Ste-Marie-de-Beauce. Jamil would commence his internship at the Ottawa Civic Hospital. And Nakash and Laly would return to Montreal. But before this happened, they would be royally entertained by Yousuf and Solange — in a mixture of French, Canadian, and Armenian traditions. And Bahiyah, in turn, would teach her two daughters-in-law how to make yogurt and other Middle Eastern dishes.

"All that Parents desire is to see their children and relatives and," Jamil had told Solange and Yousuf shortly before leaving Syria, "to pass the rest of their life in some comfort, which relatively speaking will be a luxury for them — they who have passed a long life in very hard work and many a time in extreme poverty and suffering."[57] Although Karsh had been an errant correspondent, this did not mean that he renounced his sense of responsibility towards his parents. Now, with Massih and Bahiyah safely in Quebec, he did everything he could to fulfill their desire for a comfortable life. Although it was George Nakash who had initiated their immigration to Canada and purchased their modest house in Ste-Marie-de-Beauce, it was Yousuf, Salim recalled, "who was like a father to us."[58]

If Massih and Bahiyah Karsh had a single regret, it was that Yousuf and Solange had not produced a child. But Yousuf and Solange, who was now in her mid-forties, had long ago decided not to have children. With the acquisition of their blue-cream Persian cat, whom they called Al Nica Rollingswood of Little Wings, they had a surrogate child. Moreover, as Karsh told a radio audience a few years later, "I like to think that every picture I make is a new child."[59]

Whenever Yousuf and Solange found the time, they visited the family in the Beauce. Yet it was Salim who made sure that his father had enough cigarettes in his pocket and that his mother wore low-heeled shoes and was careful when she crossed the road. And it was Salim who, following his eldest brother's instructions again, made contact with one or two of the younger priests in the small town "for intellectual companionship."[60] Even though he would have liked to have lived in a bigger city, Salim remained with his parents in the Beauce. He married a French-Canadian woman, Thérèse, and helped run the Setlakwe fashion and craft store which their cousin, Camil Darac, now owned.

The transition for Salim's parents was not so easy. "Father is lonely" and, Jamil reported to Yousuf a month after their arrival, "mother has high blood pressure."[61] Massih spent most of his time looking out the window of their house and listening to the Arabic news and music that was broadcast from

London and the United States. Bahiyah, who spoke a little French, soon became involved in the community. Shortly after arriving in Ste Marie she entered a pair of knitted stockings in the fall fair and won third prize.

During what remained of their lives, Massih and Bahiyah took an interest in their sons' careers. Jamil had a brief internship, thanks to Yousuf, at the Ottawa Civic Hospital and then made connections with other medical institutions in Ontario before moving to the United States. When Massih and Bahiyah arrived in Canada, Malak was enjoying a respite from his recurrent bouts of tuberculosis. Although he had promised Yousuf in 1946 that he would move his business to another town within a year, he remained in Ottawa where he built up an extensive collection of scenic, pictorial, and industrial images which he sold to newspapers and magazines throughout Canada and the United States.

It was in 1949 that Massih and Bahiyah Karsh had even more evidence of Yousuf's success, when he and Solange returned from Europe. The newspapers were full of articles on "How I Photographed the Pope," "How Karsh Photographed Europe's Great," "People Who Influence the Peace," and "Great Leaders Inspire People." Here was evidence that their eldest son was trying, as a writer for *Popular Photography* cogently put it, "in some tangible way to help peoples of the world to a better knowledge of each other" in order to further peace and make a better world than the one that they had left behind them in Syria.[62]

CHAPTER TWELVE

Branching Out

In the autumn of 1949, Karsh's most steadfast American supporter, Franklin "Pop" Jordan, wrote to him and Solange. "I don't know what other thrills can await you," he exclaimed, "after pushing around such characters as The King of England, President of the U.S....and now the Pope."[1] A year and a half later, *Maclean's* magazine, formerly *The Busy Man's Magazine*, answered Jordan's question. The magazine's editor, Ralph Allen, asked Karsh to choose his favourite photographs—and to recount his favourite stories to go with them. Predictably, Karsh chose his portraits of Churchill—both sombre and smiling—along with photographs of actors, the mayor of Tokyo, an industrialist, and a First World War hero. But three other images that he wanted to include were not what the conservative, lower-middle-class readers of *Maclean's*, or anyone else who knew Karsh's work, had come to expect from the country's most famous portrait photographer.[2] Did images of automotive workers, a goose, and the interior of France's Chartres Cathedral mark a new departure for Yousuf Karsh? Or were these "favourite" photographs some kind of a joke on the magazine's subscribers?

A year after "The Secret Loves of Yousuf Karsh" appeared, *Maclean's* commissioned ten photo essays featuring Canada's major cities. Since 1945, Karsh had wanted to produce something that would bring the country's physical features together with its people. Now, seven years later, he had the opportunity to do "something entirely new," as he told *Maclean's*, "and it was a challenge I simply had to accept."[3]

Some readers of *Maclean's*, especially those who lived in any of the cities to be featured, might have known what Karsh was up to long before the photo essay of their city appeared. This was because his 1952 tour to take the photographs had itself become an event.

When Yousuf and Solange arrived at the airport in Vancouver, for example, they were met by city officials who royally entertained them in the hope that Karsh would represent their city in the best light. Before setting up his white tripod and camera in Vancouver, Karsh could be seen soaking up the city's atmosphere and noting locations for shots. After commencing the shoot a few days later, he was invariably surrounded by autograph hunters, policemen, newspapermen—who duly noted his progress in the press—and photographers—who took his picture. Whenever the city had a camera club or a professional photographers' association, Karsh agreed to tell its members how he had taken some of his most famous photographs. And, if the opportunity arose, as it did during the Calgary Stampede on a subsequent trip, he held an exhibition of his work.

Karsh put on a good show when he and Solange headed West in the spring of 1952. In Edmonton he climbed onto a hydraulic lift attached to the back of a truck in order to photograph the friezes that decorated the facades of the city's churches. On the outskirts of the city, he tramped through miles of gumbo in the oil fields and then lay on his back in the mud in order to get a dramatic shot of a drilling rig. In Vancouver he climbed ladders and perched on the edges of roofs. And in Winnipeg he took a Byelorussian dancer in his arms and twirled her in a circle around the floor in order to demonstrate how he wanted her to pose.

Karsh was paid well: he got $1,500 plus expenses for every photo story. The assignment, which began in the spring of 1952, took him to Vancouver, Winnipeg, Regina, Edmonton, Ottawa, Toronto, Montreal, Saint John, Halifax, and Charlottetown. Visiting these cities gave Karsh a "deeper appreciation of Canada and Canadians."[4] But, as Solange exclaimed to Joyce Large, in words that would be unacceptable today, "We're working like *niggers* and it's very hard."[5]

Part of what made the assignment so difficult was that Karsh did not want to produce a detailed record of every city he visited. Nor did he want to present the tourist-bureau view of a place. "Call it instead," he told *Maclean's*, "a Karsh's-eye view of Canada."[6]

But would the photographs that Karsh was about to take really represent, as the magazine promised its readers, "his personal impressions of metropolitan Canada?" Or, as Solange promised the magazine's editor, convey the city's mood?[7] Above all, would Karsh's photographs show ten of Canada's major cities and their inhabitants, like the subjects in his portraits, in the most favourable light?

Before Karsh left on his ten-city tour, *Maclean's* provided him with notes in much the same way as Solange provided him with a verbal briefing of his subject before every portrait sitting. Pierre Berton prepared Karsh's "notes" on Vancouver. The associate editor of *Maclean's* and future historian of Canada told him to look out for the "folksy" Maritimer Norman "Larry" Mackenzie, who was the president of the University of British Columbia; the mayor, Fred J. Hume, "who drinks"; and the lumberman H. R. MacMillan, who could look down from his panelled office in the Marine Building and see his own ships loading his own lumber destined for foreign ports, then look up the inlet to False Creek where his own mills were casting a hazy smog over the city. Berton also drew Karsh's attention to many of the subjects that eventually found their way into his "impressionistic" photo essay of Vancouver: to the fishing boats and grain elevators in the harbour; to the thousand-acre virgin forest, Stanley Park, in the centre of the city; to the garish neon lights that illuminated the heart of the downtown core; to the bearded and turbaned Sikhs; to the totem poles—"some of these are fakes, but not all."[8]

In Maritime Canada Karsh was briefed in the same way. *Maclean's* assistant editor Ian Sclanders prepared an essay indicating that Saint John, New Brunswick, offered "a depressing collection of slums, had 'no architectural beauty,'" but nevertheless revelled in its past. Sclanders told Karsh that Halifax had slums too, though they were offset by many fine buildings. Finally, as for Prince Edward Island, it was "one big farm" and the people from the premier, Walter Jones, down were "agricultural types."[9]

Karsh was not only given specific subjects to photograph; *Maclean's* also gave him a theme for each city. In Vancouver the theme was timber. In Halifax it was the sea. In Montreal it was the vibrant nightlife and the perceived harmony between the city's French- and English-speaking inhabitants. In Edmonton the subjects were oil and air travel. And in Winnipeg it was the city's diverse ethnic community that Karsh was encouraged to capture on film.

There was nothing new about giving a photographer a shopping list before an assignment took place.[10] Germany's magazine editors had been doing it since the late 1920s. This is how one of that country's most distinguished photographers, Felix H. Man, had captured Canada during his world tour in the early 1930s; how *Saturday Night*'s photographer "Jay" Jaycocks had created his photo essay on Canadian cities in 1937; how Malak Karsh and the still photographers who worked for the National Film Board of Canada had been producing their photo stories since the end of the Second World War. But similarities between these photographers' work and what Yousuf Karsh was producing for *Maclean's* ended here. This was because they were working in the tradition of famous documentary photographers like Britain's Bill Brandt and France's Henri Cartier-Bresson. And they were producing photographs that captured the accidents of human expression: curiosity, boredom, frustration, enthusiasm, and wonder.

Horses and Farmer in Potato Field, P.E.I., 1952

Not so Yousuf Karsh. Unlike most documentary photographers, he rarely left anything to chance. He liked to have the image he wanted on the final print in his head before he clicked the shutter. Sometimes that image, as in his photograph of the Prince Edward Island farmer and his horses, had its source in the work of an Old Master—in this case the sixteenth-century Flemish artist Pieter Brueghel the Elder. Generally, however, Karsh employed skills that he had acquired in the studio. Indeed, he claimed that "taking the portrait of a city was not very different from photographing a person."[11]

If most of the photographs that Karsh took on his tour of Canada looked posed, it is because they were: from the ballet dancers in front of Vancouver's famous hollow tree, the woman scrubbing the floor in Ottawa's Parliament Buildings, the newly arrived Chinese immigrant and her son at the Edmonton airport, and the artist sketching on the Market Slip in Saint John, to the lovers

sitting on a bench in Regina's civic park. Working out each shot in advance ensured for Karsh that every photograph he took was perfectly balanced, had well-modulated tonal gradations and, above all, presented a positive image of the subject represented. It also ensured that there were no candid photographs, no accidents. This was what *Maclean's* was paying him for: beautifully composed and aesthetically rich photographs that had been taken by an artist.

There were, however, some marvellous exceptions. The bone-chilling photograph of a child in an iron lung at the "Sick Kids" hospital in Toronto. The stark image of an unidentified Inuit woman recovering from tuberculosis in an impersonal ward of an Edmonton hospital. The ominous photograph of Saint John's Chapel Street slum children watching a parade. The compassionate image of an unattractive, middle-aged New Brunswick woman whose bulky figure contrasts with the delicate posy she clutches in her hands. And the portrait of eighty-year-old Daniel Makaois, who patiently waits for a plane to carry him back to his northern Native reserve following an eye operation.

Inuit Woman in
Sanitarium, 1952

None of these photographs are posed. All of them brilliantly capture the decisive moment that made the work of Henri Cartier-Bresson so famous. Yet not one of these images found its way into *Maclean's*. Photographs of the poor, the unattractive, and the infirm, and shots that revealed the desperate situation of First Nations Peoples, had no place in a magazine that was devoted to convincing its readers that Canada had returned to normality following the Second World War and was now enjoying unprecedented commercial and cultural prosperity.

If there was one theme that ran through Karsh's photo essays, published in *Maclean's* between the autumn of 1952 and the spring of the following year, it was the diverse ethnic makeup of the country. "Canada," he wrote a few years later, "is not a melting pot, it is an alchemy of racial qualities," which sometimes mingled, sometimes flew apart, or boiled up turbulently.[12] While this was clearly Karsh's view of Canada, it was not necessarily the view of those who subscribed to *Maclean's*. In response to Karsh's photo essay on Edmonton, for example, one reader asked, "Is the population made up entirely of Indians, Eskimos and Orientals?"[13]

Readers were equally unhappy when Karsh did not present them with the tourist board's view of their city. "Skid row pilings, a fishing wharf, a butt end of a poor piece of timber" were hardly representative, according to a reader from Vancouver, of "the most beautiful city in Canada."[14] "We have more than slums and broken-down wharves," another reader protested from Saint John.[15] "What is Karsh trying to prove?" was the only comment that H. Hyslop could come up with in response to Karsh's photo essay of Toronto, which placed building sites, crowded streets, and a meat-packing plant alongside photographs of a board meeting, a fashion show, and a television studio.[16]

Not every letter selected for the magazine's "Mail Bag" was negative. To Ola Stech of Montreal, Karsh had shown "Canada as it really is, not as someone would like to see it."[17] A reader from Saskatoon wrote that she could "fairly smell the salt air and hear the fog horns" in Karsh's photographs of Saint John.[18] For a former resident of Vancouver, Karsh's images evoked "the delightful smell of freshly cut lumber, the Sikhs, the North Shore Mountains."[19]

Children Watching
Parade, Saint John,
New Brunswick, 1952

Ironically, it was not Karsh's images but the text that got him into the most hot water. The lengthy captions that Solange transformed from her notes proved "too starry-eyed" for the magazine's editors, who ended up writing their own.[20] These were not the cause of the trouble, however, but rather the essays accompanying each group of photographs.

In Prince Edward Island, for example, *Maclean's* told how Solange and Yousuf had eaten one of the worst meals of their lives. The dinner had begun with a seafood cocktail that had neither sauce nor lemon and was not fresh. The jellied chicken consommé that followed had lumps of commercial gelatin floating in the broth. And the "rare" beef tenderloin that came next was not only less than one-quarter of an inch thick but was overdone. It was the potatoes Florentine that came in for the most criticism.[21] When they were placed before Karsh, he had buried his face in his hands. Equally disgusted, Solange offered to write a pamphlet for the premier, Walter Jones, on "One Hundred Ways to Cook Potatoes." The premier responded by suggesting that there was only one way to cook a potato and that was to boil it.[22]

Criticizing one of the province's most cherished crops was too much for Prince Edward Island's director of tourism, George Fraser, who, during the busiest season of the year, had devoted three days and three nights to showing Yousuf and Solange around the island. It was too much for the staff of the government-subsidized restaurant-hotel where Yousuf and Solange had eaten their meal. And too much for the writer of a local newspaper, who called Karsh "a big-feeling foreigner, now Canadian," who might be better eating "the savoury dishes of Arabia, or what have you, to which he had been accustomed before coming to this unsophisticated land of Canada."[23]

Even more abuse was hurled towards Karsh by the Conservative Member of Parliament representing Queens, W. Chester S. McLure. When the Prince Edward Island fur farmer raised the matter in the House of Commons, he recited a poem entitled "By Gosh." "Some Photos by Karsh," went the doggerel verse, "Can really be harsh / So say cattle owners / Near Fullerton's marsh." After referring to Karsh as a "doubtful Canadian," McLure then warned him that if he were ever to return to Prince Edward Island he would be "as welcome as a skunk in a nudist colony."[24]

These words may have made little impact outside of the country's smallest province. The real hurt was that no one rose to their feet to defend Karsh publicly until Parliament met three days later. Coming belatedly to the photographer's defence, a Member of Parliament for Ottawa, G. J. M. McIlraith, noted that the implications of McLure's attack were "of real consequence" in a country that had been "built up of persons coming from many different lands." McIlraith continued, "I have known Mr. Karsh for many years…[and] I think it was unfortunate that he [McLure] made that statement." Moreover, "while this great Canadian photographer may be a small man physically, he is a man of very real stature."[25] The Conservative leader, George A. Drew, joined the debate the following day. Speaking out of both sides of his mouth at once, he made a feeble attempt to defend his colleague, Chester McLure, while assuring the House that Karsh was a distinguished Canadian who had not only brought honour to the country but resisted many inducements to make his career abroad.[26]

Many readers of *Maclean's* found McLure's remarks, which were reported in the press, to be "unkind, unthinking, insular and stupid."[27] Karsh also received support from the editor of the Montreal-based workers' paper *Canadian Labour Reports* and from the writer and editor of the *Peterborough Examiner*, Robertson Davies: "We are all foreigners, in some way or other, in Canada."[28] One resident of Prince Edward Island, J. Arthur Clark, consoled Karsh by telling him that he had eaten "many poor meals for which we felt overcharged at the same hotel."[29]

The editors of *Maclean's*, however, extended little sympathy. They felt that the essential thing for any artist was to be talked about. Solange and Yousuf thought otherwise. "You've no idea what repercussion it has had in Ottawa," Solange told the magazine's assistant editor three days after McLure had attacked Karsh in the House.[30]

The fact was that Karsh had been publicly insulted not just for his remarks but also because he was not Canadian born or from one of the country's founding nations. Had Karsh been of British or French ethnicity, McLure's attack would have hurt less. But Karsh belonged to a group, the Armenians, who were still classified — despite his own continued efforts to lobby cabinet ministers to repeal Order-in-Council PC 2115 — as Asiatics. And it seemed that however much he attempted to embrace the country as his own, neither he nor his family were fully accepted. Moreover, it was not just the slighting remarks that Karsh himself had to endure. Two years earlier his brother Jamil had failed his oral medical examination, allegedly because one of the examiners, when he had discovered that Jamil was not Canadian born, had "set out to buck Jamil's chances."[31]

On the other hand, Solange's and Yousuf's remarks about the food in Prince Edward Island showed how out of touch they were with the country. Unlike most Canadians, the couple had, from 1952, a live-in cook-housekeeper and chauffeur-gardener. They travelled first class. They stayed in the best hotels and, when service was not up to scratch, their complaints usually put things straight. Moreover, it is doubtful whether they would have eaten a meal in some of the less savoury locations that they photographed: the slums in Saint John, skid row in Vancouver or the steel workers' canteen in Hamilton, where they might have had something more unpleasant to complain about. Furthermore, *Maclean's* had no doubt made things worse by identifying Karsh as "a gourmet of some note." All told, Yousuf and Solange were insensitive in disparaging a crop on which the farmers of Prince Edward Island proudly depended for their livelihood.

But every cloud has a silver lining. "The Karsh Incident" prompted Karsh to become involved in the Canadian Citizenship Council on Immigration Integration. During the early 1950s he chaired one of its sub-committees; although this needed a co-chairman due to his frequent absences, Karsh nevertheless did his bit whenever he was in town. Small potatoes, McLure might think, but it was one way in which Yousuf Karsh could help other immigrants, three decades after his own arrival, to integrate and adjust into Canadian society.

The assignment for *Maclean's* also showed other magazine editors that Karsh was willing to expand his repertoire. In the summer of 1953, for example, Yousuf and Solange flew from Norman Wells to Herschel Island. The bench seats in the small aircraft were uncomfortable and it was a "very bumpy flight." When they arrived in Aklavik they found that the Hudson's Bay Company staff house where they were to stay was surrounded in mud and had no running water — they had to use a chemical toilet. Even so, the photographs that Karsh took of northern wild roses, fireweed, arctic cotton, chickweed, daisies, and Indian paint brush, which Solange preserved between the pages of her notebook, show that the assignment for *Time* magazine was worth enduring the hardships of travelling in the Arctic.[32] And though the food in the only restaurant was "very greasy," the Karshes were too prudent to offer further comment.

Great Lakes Paper
Company, Lakehead, 1953

WHEN *MACLEAN'S* PUBLISHED a second series of Karsh's photo stories of Canadian cities, things were different. This time little attention was devoted to the ethnic makeup of Canada's population. No letters praising or criticizing Karsh's photographs of Fort William–Port Arthur, Victoria, Quebec City, Hamilton, Calgary, and St. John's, found their way into the "Mail Bag." But Karsh was paid even more money. For every photo story he received $2,000 rather than the $1,500 he had earned on the first assignment.

While the work that Karsh produced for the second series was tame and unimaginative compared to the first, he nevertheless created some memorable images: the man perched on a great roll of paper at the Great Lakes Paper Company while eating his lunch; cowboys herding cattle in the foothills of Alberta;

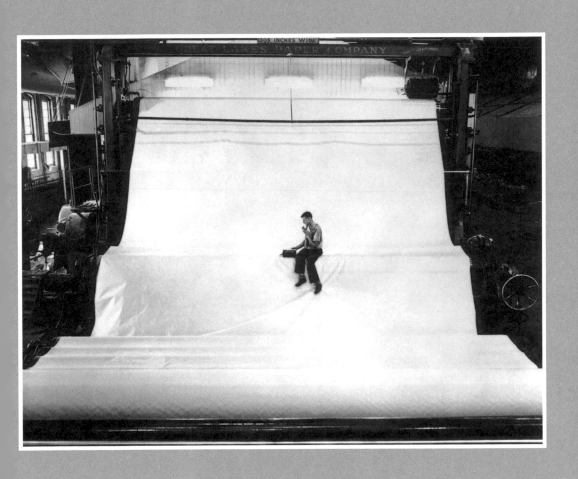

and bronco busters at the Calgary Stampede. Indeed, Karsh had enough confidence in his photographs of what the Victorians of an earlier era had pejoratively called "people of less importance" to submit a number of them to his old friend Edward Steichen, who was organizing an exhibition at the Museum of Modern Art.

Karsh had maintained contact with the man whose work he had admired since his days as a student in Boston. And Steichen had kept up with him too. After Steichen became the director of the Museum of Modern Art's department of photography in 1947, he invited Karsh to contribute three works to one of the first exhibitions that he curated.[33] Karsh's chances for inclusion in a subsequent exhibition that Steichen was curating in the mid-1950s, The Family of Man, therefore looked good. Karsh accordingly submitted photographs from his *Maclean's* photo essays, only to find them sent back by return mail, and without explanation as to why they were judged unsuitable.[34]

Without knowing which photographs Karsh had submitted to the jury, it is difficult to know why his work was rejected. What is known, however, is that most of the world's leading photographers, from newcomers like Diane Arbus to veterans like W. Eugene Smith, Brassaï, Bill Brandt, and Henri Cartier-Bresson, were included in the exhibition. Three Canadian photographers—Richard Harrington, Ronny Jaques, and David Brooks—were among the exhibitors, while the man now widely known as "the Rembrandt of photography" was not. It is also known that although Steichen professed admiration for Karsh's work, he believed that it was impossible for any photographic image to capture the whole person as Karsh often claimed it did. Steichen clearly felt that Karsh's achievement as a whole was more significant than his individual portraits.[35]

Steichen wanted the photographs in the Family of Man exhibition to reflect "the universal elements and emotions in the everydayness of life."[36] He also wanted the exhibition to unite the disparate cultures of the world into a universal human culture, albeit one conceived in and reflecting American terms and values. For someone like Steichen who had come to view the photograph as a social document, there was clearly no place in this exhibition for the portraits of a myth-maker like Karsh who celebrated the heroic individual and worshipped greatness.

To be rejected by a man whom he respected, to be excluded from a show that included so many great photographers, to find other photographers from his own country preferred over him—all this was humiliating for Karsh. This is surely why he never admitted publicly that he had been excluded from The Family of Man, which found its way to the National Gallery of Canada in 1957. This was also why Karsh teamed up with the writer John Fisher a few years later to produce *Karsh & John Fisher See Canada*, which featured many of the photographs from Karsh's city series.[37] And this is surely why Karsh took pains in his memoir to rationalize his absence from what he admitted was an "unforgettable" exhibition.[38]

HOWEVER MUCH KARSH chose to distance himself from the Family of Man exhibition, "persons of less importance" had become part of his oeuvre. And not just with the photo essays that he created for *Maclean's*. A few years before these two assignments, Karsh had entered the world of commercial photography and, by implication, the universalization of human culture to which his hero Edward Steichen was so devoted. In 1941 Karsh had been annoyed when the Goodrich Rubber Company used his wartime photograph of a Royal Canadian Air Force bugler for an advertisement in a newspaper. Yet within a few years, Karsh was photographing wooden bowls for Steuben Glass, cigar smokers for White Owl Cigars, beer drinkers for Brading Breweries, and models for Madame Martha's Fashions. And to help him get some of these and other commissions, Karsh had used the most powerful advertising agency in the United States, J. Walter Thompson, which had already arranged for Karsh's more formal portrait commissions.

From the mid-1940s to the late 1950s, Karsh worked for Thompson and other aggressive advertising agencies, like Walsh Advertising Company of Montreal, as well as for publishing companies like Charles Francis Press, all of which were looking for a new angle for their promotional campaigns. Karsh was certainly not the first studio photographer to clinch a deal over lunch at the Pavilion, the "21" or the Laurent, which were all within walking distance of Madison Avenue's advertising agencies and publishing houses. Moreover, as a writer for the

British Journal of Photography claimed, "it was natural that a local portraitist should aim to secure a share of commercial business."[39]

Although Edward Steichen had given up commercial photography in 1938, this was what Karsh had seen him doing when he first visited him in New York in 1936. And this was certainly what Karsh's business manager wanted him to do when, as the Second World War faded into history, Tom Blau's newly established firm, Camera Press, and New York's Pix Incorporated found it difficult to sell Karsh's portraits of politicians and military men to newspapers and magazines. "All these companies spend countless millions on advertising," Solange told Yousuf, "so let us see what they will do for 'out of this world photography.'"[40]

Money was certainly an incentive. Karsh could ask — and get — two or three times more for a commercial photograph than for a studio portrait. At the same time he could expect to be treated as a portrait artist. This was partly because, as Solange told one advertising executive in 1950, she was "completely against Karsh being treated like an ordinary commercial photographer at their regular rates."[41] It was also because the Thompson agency knew what they were buying when they first approached Karsh to take portraits for the White Owl cigar campaign in 1944.

The J. Walter Thompson agency was not just wooing a famous photographer when they invited Karsh to visit their palatial offices in the Graybar Building next to Grand Central Station in New York. Like Steichen, who was the first photographer to forge an alliance between the fine arts and the corporate world, Karsh always presented himself as an artist and his photographs as works of art. Moreover, Karsh's portraits, which created an idealized vision of the world where success, wealth, and, above all, social mobility were there for anyone who wanted them, were safe. Karsh's photographs were also beautiful. No stray hair, awkward gesture, or unpleasant expression ever intruded. Above all, Karsh's portraits fitted into a form of advertising that Thompson had developed with Edward Steichen's photographs of hands for Pond's Cream: the testimonial or personal endorsement of a product by a well-known person.[42]

Karsh repeatedly insisted that he was no advertising man. Yet in dress, temperament, and manner, he was not unlike the admen — and they were usually men — who worked on Madison Avenue. For example, he dressed in a way that might be called colourful conservative: Brooks Brothers shirts, eye-catching silk ties, well-tailored suits, and a Borsalino hat. When he spoke, he mixed courtesy and flattery with scorn and boastfulness. He exuded an air of prosperity yet also of insecurity. He was overworked and overstimulated.

Moreover, like all advertising men, Karsh was assertive. Under no circumstances were hands to be cropped or deleted from his photographs. When the Thompson agency suggested that he use models for the White Owl ad, Karsh said no and the agency had to find real cigar smokers to pose for him. When his name did not appear in the right-hand corner under the photograph or was not scrawled across the print, a reprimand could be relied upon from himself or Solange. "What do you think people buy," she told the Thompson agency in response to one misdemeanour, "they must be able to see it is a Karsh portrait."[43] And when it was suggested that Karsh think up situations for a Brading Breweries advertisement, he expostulated, "As you know I am not an advertising man but a photographer and I don't think that it is part of my work to think up situations which may or may not meet with the approval of your clients."[44]

At the same time, Karsh aimed to please, provided his artistic integrity was not threatened. At the height of the Cold War, in 1955, he cooperated in the production of a series of photographs for Canadair Limited of Montreal, the manufacturers of the supersonic jet and guided missiles, whose aim was to stress "a need to be ready morally, spiritually, and physically to defend our freedom against communism."[45] During the course of photographing executives for Northwestern Mutual Life Insurance's testimonial advertising campaign, Karsh agreed to lighten his palette. He willingly gave a lighter feeling to his portraits for the White Owl campaign. "This does not mean it cannot have darks in it to help our dramatic quality which we want," the art director, who had asked Karsh to do this, reassured him.[46]

Karsh also accepted the fact that not every photograph that he submitted for an advertising campaign would be suitable. Finally, like for all top admen, there was virtually no person or subject in which Karsh could not become interested—for a price. This was important when, in 1950, he embarked on an assignment that took him into very new territory: the industrial heartland of Canada at Welland and Windsor, Ontario.

KARSH HAD BEEN photographing company executives ever since setting up his business in 1934. By the late 1940s, he had more portrait commissions than he could handle when General Electric, Dupont, IBM, Shell, INCO, General Foods, and virtually every other major company in the United States and Canada hired him to photograph their leading executives.

Big business had thrived during the Second World War, particularly in the United States. American and Canadian companies had not only prospered financially, they had also made moral capital out of providing the sinews for national defence in the cause of freedom. After the hostilities in Europe ended, many large corporations tried to sustain their favourable images. But it was not easy. They were accused of being inefficient and monopolistic. Workers' unions put pressure on senior management for higher wages and better working conditions. At the same time, the advent of the Korean War in 1950 and the rise of McCarthyism the same year strengthened anti-Communist sentiments, giving capitalism—and big business—an opportunity to present its more attractive face.

Karsh helped companies do this by producing positive, powerful images of their executives for publication in annual company reports and for distribution to the press. But big companies needed more than portraits of their leaders if they were going to win the goodwill of their workers, their customers, and the public in general.

As early as 1900, the father of scientific management, F. W. Taylor, had shown the extent to which "human problems stood in the way of production."[47] But it was not until American labour unions expanded during the wartime boom that big corporations set up public relations departments within their own firms and commissioned advertisers and publishing companies to help them establish better relations with their workforce. This was why the president of Atlas Steels, Roy H. Davis, hired the director of the development division of Charles Francis Press to promote better relations between Atlas's workforce and management. And this was why Yousuf and Solange travelled to New York in the early spring of 1950 to meet the press's development director, A. Earle Higgens.

According to Solange's notes from that meeting, Higgens's client wanted "black and white photographs of sweating steel workers at the job; authentic stuff with furnaces."[48] Charles Francis Press had previously hired fine artists to portray these themes. But the client, Atlas Steels, wanted a less expensive way of doing this in Canada, so Higgens turned to Yousuf Karsh.

For Atlas Steels, paying Canada's most famous photographer $2,000 for six images was a bargain. For Karsh, who had never previously taken his camera into an industrial plant, it was a challenge. Solange felt that industrial photography should always represent a money-making proposition, "otherwise, I feel that it is a waste of valuable time, energy," but here the money was good.[49] The commission was lucrative for Karsh's agent, Earle Higgens. His company would get 25 percent of Karsh's fee. It would also receive a hefty sum for designing and printing Atlas Steels' annual calendar and company report as well as for promoting the company to the public through the Canadian and American media.

Karsh, Solange, and Monty Everett travelled to Atlas Steels, at Welland Canal on the Niagara Peninsula southwest of Toronto, in June 1950. Higgens had already briefed Karsh on the history of the company. This was how Karsh learned that not only was Atlas Steels the largest steel plant in the Commonwealth but that it had just installed a new stainless steel rolling mill enabling it to produce everything from pots and pans to car mufflers.

Karsh spent his first day at Atlas Steels walking around the plant. He spent his second day interviewing the fourteen men whom the company had chosen as possible subjects for his photographs. During the third and fourth days Yousuf, assisted by Monty Everett and Solange, set up his camera.

The plant was dirty. Solange's nose got smudged with smut. The heat was intense. Monty had to hold a shield in front of Karsh's face in order to protect him from the fierce heat of the open furnace. The process was noisy. The molten steel crackled as it snaked across the steel plates and the big forge's massive hammers made a deafening sound as they pounded the metal into huge ingot moulds. The dust and the smoke made it difficult for Karsh to see what he was photographing. The vibrating machines interfered with the focus on his lens to the extent that at one point production had to be stopped for twenty minutes.

And, finally, the overflowing ladles of molten metal, which produced a shower of sparks when it hit the floor, made the job anything but safe.[50]

Karsh seemed oblivious to the hazards during his two visits to Atlas Steels in the summer of 1950. Monty was, of course, there to help. While Solange took notes, he set up the tripods, cameras, and three thousand-watt spotlights and photo floods. Monty also replaced the bulbs in Karsh's flash camera after they had popped. And, whenever Karsh needed shots of a subject from two different angles, Monty was no longer an assistant, he became a fellow photographer.

The trio from Ottawa must have looked out of place amidst the smoke, dust, noise, and heat. Karsh donned a hard hat and, when necessary, a pair of protective goggles, but insisted on wearing one of his best suits. Solange wore a stylish dress and, uncharacteristically for her, running shoes. Yet there is no suggestion that the workers, whose hands Karsh invariably shook before clicking the shutter and whose names he took pains to remember, found anything but mild amusement in the visitors from Ottawa.

The interest that Karsh took in the workers was more than incidental. As he wrote to an executive at the Thompson agency following the assignment, "I was asked to portray and place emphasis on the men so that the machines they make would be subservient."[51] Moreover, as Karsh told a reporter for the Vancouver *Province*, he had been determined "to glorify the industrial worker and to give recognition to his skill and craftsmanship."[52]

For someone else who was accustomed to photographing the great men and women of the world, this plan might have presented a problem. Not so for Karsh. "I have taken the portraits of some of the most celebrated men and women of our time," he wrote in the promotional article that Higgens produced for distribution to the press. "I tell you," Karsh continued, "these steel workers are the peers of those men who are better known." Indeed, for Karsh the men at Atlas Steels were "the aristocrats of industry and of steel." This was because they were independent. They worked with their brains as well as with their hands and took a quiet pride in their work. Above all, as Karsh further observed, they were "politically mature, devoted to God, their families, and their country."[53]

There was, of course, a long-established tradition among artists and photographers of portraying the workplace.[54] During the Second World War, the

Montreal artist Frederick Taylor had shown the extent to which industrial workers offered infinite and inspiring subject matter when he had taken his sketching equipment into the Canadian Pacific Railway's Angus Shops and the United Shipyards.

Working at Atlas Steels, Karsh used every trick in his repertoire—and that of many other photographers and artists like Taylor—to transform the men he was photographing into "aristocrats" and the place where they worked into a unified sculptural whole. The converging lines and diagonal shafts of light evident in Karsh's Dominion Drama Festival photographs found their way onto the floor of the steel mill. So did Karsh's dark background—which forced the eye to focus on the subject—and the strongly contrasting tones and subtle gradations that appeared in the grey areas of the print.

In some of Karsh's industrial photographs the men seemed to be an integral part of the machines they were operating. In others, the machine, not the worker, was the subject of the photograph. Most often, however, it was the human figure that dominated. As one writer noted, Karsh's photographs told the "authentic story of the men and machines behind the product."[55] However, nothing was left to chance. One worker, Gabor Stork, had to go through two boxes of matches before Karsh got the right shot of him smoking his pipe. Moreover, although the Hungarian-born man was a sweeper, Karsh threw away his broom and posed him against a stack of finished steel rods.

Karsh's photo shoot at Atlas Steels gave a highly idealized rendering of the workplace. The workers are presented as heroes. They are the masters, not slaves, of their machines. Above all, they appear to be functioning in an environment where noise, vibration, dust, danger, and heat are absent.

Karsh was familiar with his brother Malak's industrial photographs, which he began producing in the early 1940s. In them Malak had used multiple images and melded the worker and the machine, in order to give a dramatic rendering of the workplace.[56] Many of Karsh's industrial photographs were, likewise, "composed" in the printing rooms at the Karsh Studio when he returned to Ottawa. This entailed superimposing two or more negatives in the desired register before placing them in the enlarger in order to make them into a single print.

Karsh got a lot of mileage out of his visit to Welland, Ontario, in 1950. His photographs appeared in the company's annual reports and calendars as well as in the *Atlas Employees News* and *Atlas Steel News*. The photographs formed the core of the Higgens press release that found its way into newspapers in Canada as well as the United States and Germany, exposing Karsh's work to over sixteen million people.[57] The Atlas Steels photographs were treated as works of art when they were exhibited at the Charles Francis Press Gallery in New York and later at Kodak House in London, England, and at several other locations across Canada.

The project was a tremendous success from a public relations point of view. To see portraits of themselves, rather than of their bosses, in the company's publications helped boost the morale of the workers. The company's products—especially those produced by the new stainless steel plant—were made known to the public throughout North America. The text that accompanied the photographs in the annual reports assured potential investors that Atlas Steels, and its workforce, possessed values that were in keeping with the anti-Communist rhetoric of the period. And the publicity material that Higgens produced for the press made it clear that Atlas Steels had hired an artist to do the job: "Just as a Rembrandt or a Van Dyke bear the stamp of their masters, so does all of Karsh's work."[58] The publicity campaign was an acknowledged success. "I wish we had come up with the same idea that you developed for the Atlas people," an executive from General Electric told Karsh, "and I want to say that it's one of the smartest things I have seen from a public relations point of view for some time."[59]

Karsh had enjoyed the shoot. Solange told Atlas Steels' president that she and Yousuf were "wondering why we have received any remuneration for an experience which has proved more than worthwhile, intensely interesting and completely rewarding."[60] And rewarding it was. Within months Karsh was offered a further industrial commission at Ford of Canada's plant in Windsor, Ontario. As Higgens had predicted, many more commissions would come from the United States too.[61]

When Karsh was approached by Ford of Canada's Windsor plant, Higgens demanded a fee of $10,000 for Karsh—and got it. Yet this was not a case of

Assembling Generator at Westinghouse Plant, 1953

Karsh sacrificing his artistic aspirations for commercial gain. During the two-week shoot, he produced some of his best industrial photographs. And at the end of it Ford produced an illustrated booklet, "The Men of Ford of Canada," and saw to it that twenty-seven of Karsh's photographs were displayed at Toronto's 1951 Canadian National Exhibition and were shown in ten other cities across Canada.

Drawing on the techniques that he had seen in Malak's industrial photographs, Karsh used multiple negatives during the exposure process to create the finished photograph of Terry Wasyke and Morris Lehoux, who were spray-painting a car. The result was not an authentic depiction of the workplace but pure drama. In one half of the print, the arcs of spray paint, the oblique and raked lighting, along with the diagonal shafts of light and sharp tonal contrasts, are the subject. In the other half of the print, it is the men who take centre stage.

Terry Wasyke and
Morris Lehoux at
Ford of Canada, 1950

Here, as Karsh admitted, he tried to make Wasyke and Lehoux look more like brain surgeons than mechanics. But the results were far different. The image is sexually charged by a homoerotic tension that is suggested between the two men, an effect that was probably not evident on the floor of the plant but created in the Karsh Studio by the juxtaposition of the two negatives.

Karsh's portrait of another young auto worker, "Rear Window," has become a classic. And this is not just because the photograph of Gow Crapper is tightly composed and beautifully lit. It is because the image predates the working-class counterculture heroes that actors like James Dean and Marlon Brando would come to exemplify a few years later.[62] The only thing missing from Karsh's portrait is a pack of cigarettes tucked under the sleeve of Crapper's T-shirt.

By using the rear window of the car to frame his subject and by allowing a background light to spill over Crapper's right shoulder and illuminate the right side of his face, Karsh isolated Crapper from the noise and the dust of the assembly plant. Karsh thus ensured that the eye of the viewer would not stray beyond his subject. Indeed, Crapper's muscular arms, his youth and, not least of all, his smouldering sexuality are the subject of the photograph.

Though "Rear Window" was the most sophisticated photograph that Karsh took during his two-week-long visit to Ford of Canada, the public relations department did not use it in their annual report. Nor was the photograph incorporated into any of their other publicity material. Perhaps Ford's publicity department sensed the erotic tension that pervades the work. Or perhaps there was another reason why they avoided the photograph.

When Karsh walked onto the floor of the assembly plant, communist elements within one faction of the United Automobile Workers Union, to which every worker belonged, were stirring up trouble among the men on the floor and senior management. In "Rear Window" Karsh made no attempt to turn an industrial worker into an aristocrat. Instead he made him look more like an angry young figure from the proletariat, hinting at the threatening dissidence of a Brando or a Dean. For a company that had already had its fill of difficulties with organized labour, the image of any worker who might look "rebellious" was clearly not acceptable. The photographs that Karsh took of the older workers, of young scientists, and of senior management were more to Ford's liking—and perhaps to Karsh's too. He never chose to exhibit or to publish "Rear Window," a photograph in which he may have expressed more than he consciously intended, making an aesthetic statement more ambitious than his brief.

Rear Window (Gow Crapper of Ford of Canada), 1950

Chasing Shadows

The 1950s proved to be an important decade for Yousuf Karsh. It was not just that he expanded his repertoire by taking his camera into industrial plants and by undertaking more advertising assignments. Nor just that he had a second sitting with Princess Elizabeth, nor that he photographed more celebrities, artists, scientists, and businessmen than ever before, nor even that he produced a second volume of photographs, *Portraits of Greatness*.[1] It was not the quantity or the diversity of subject matter that made the 1950s a crucial decade for Karsh, but rather the quality of the work that he produced. His portraits of Ernest Hemingway, Georgia O'Keeffe, Pablo Picasso, and John and Jackie Kennedy, among so many others, confirmed his status as a master of the art of portraiture. For the Rembrandt of photography, however, the 1950s had a more sombre personal significance. This was to be the last decade when he would have his help- and soulmate, Solange Karsh, at his side.

The decade certainly began on a more positive note than it ended. Admittedly, with the death of Mackenzie King in 1950 Karsh had lost the patronage of his greatest supporter. But Karsh had long cultivated officials in the Department of External Affairs and possessed the confidence to approach—and the stature to be accepted by—virtually anyone he wished to photograph.

When Karsh learned that Princess Elizabeth and the Duke of Edinburgh were planning a visit to Canada in 1951, he contacted the royal household and got permission to photograph the couple before they left London. Due partly to the photographs that Cecil Beaton had taken in 1939, the royal family was, by the early 1950s, beginning to project a less stuffy, more relaxed, and informal image of itself than was previously the case. Following Beaton's example, Karsh saw to it that the princess and her consort were not the only members of the family to sit in front of his camera. Prince Charles and Princess Anne, then aged three and one, also participated.

Karsh arrived for the sitting at Clarence House armed with gifts purchased from Hamley's famous toy store on Regent Street. When he presented Prince Charles with a musical ball, the young prince, who had just emerged from the garden, duly presented Mr. Karsh with a daisy. The gesture set the tone for the ensuing ninety minutes. The princess and the duke agreed to pose in formal and informal dress. They sat individually and together. Karsh took a double profile of the couple, a composition he would repeat when he came to photograph Grace Kelly and her husband, Prince Rainier, Jacqueline and John F. Kennedy, and Bill and Hillary Rodham Clinton. The royal couple also posed with their children. Karsh was so pleased with the colour portrait that he took of Princess Elizabeth and her daughter, Anne, that he and Solange used the image for their Christmas card.

Karsh worked through the night developing the negatives so that the Princess would have the proofs the following day. "Delicious" was her response to the nine colour and twelve black-and-white photographs.[2] Princess Elizabeth was equally complimentary when she viewed the finished prints a few weeks later. She had good reason to be pleased. Karsh had instructed his technicians to eliminate every line and blemish from her face, and from the duke's, and conversely to highlight every other detail in the portrait. The result, in one critic's view, was "disastrous" because the character of the royal pair had been sacrificed to the attention given to his uniform and her dress.[3]

It would perhaps have been more surprising if Karsh the flatterer, the idealizer, and the romantic had not turned the diminutive princess into a flawless monumental figure. Or if he had not transformed her consort into everyone's idea of the handsome prince charming. No wonder a critic noted the similarity between Karsh's portraits and the serene and elegant paintings that the nineteenth-century German painter Franz Winterhalter had made of Princess Elizabeth's great-great-grandmother Queen Victoria.[4]

Because these were official photographs, Karsh got almost as much international exposure for them in the press as he had received for his portraits of Winston Churchill ten years earlier. No singular incident had occurred during the royal sitting that served to distinguish one photograph from the other, but Karsh's comments about the well-behaved Prince Charles, the dignity and graciousness of the royals, and the relaxed atmosphere of the sitting room at Clarence House provided the magazines and newspapers with adequate written copy. One of Karsh's portraits of the princess

Princess Elizabeth, 1951

also gave the Post Office an image for a 5-pence stamp to commemorate her coronation in June 1953. And a year later, the Bank of Canada used the same image on the first new bank note it had produced in seventeen years.

KARSH'S VISIT TO London in 1951 was brief. He had hoped to arrange a sitting with Winston Churchill but, so Churchill's private secretary told him by letter, "Owing to great pressure, he regrets that he does not wish to avail himself of your offer to make a colour portrait."[5] Nor, to Karsh's disappointment, was he invited to represent Canada at Queen Elizabeth's coronation in 1953; that honour went to the thirty-seven-year-old photographer Donald McKague. Nor was Karsh's attempt to photograph the new queen two years later any more successful. "Her Majesty does not at the present time require Mr. Karsh to take any special photograph," was the message that the ever-helpful Campbell Moodie sent to Karsh from Canada House.[6]

Though clearly disappointed at not being chosen to attend the coronation, Karsh had other prospects in the offing when he and Solange made preparations

for their second joint visit to continental Europe in 1954. Karsh had a commission from *Life* magazine to produce portraits for a photo essay dealing with leading intellectual, military, and political figures in France.[7] Camera Press's energetic manager, Tom Blau, had lined up an impressive list of writers, statesmen, musicians, and other people who, unlike the British royal family and Churchill, were willing to sit for Yousuf Karsh. Both prospects gave Karsh an opportunity to produce more photographs for the British and European press and to gather more photographs for another volume of portraits, this time one devoted to artists.

There was nothing new in such a proposal. In 1884, the British photographer J. P. Mayall had published *Artists at Home*. During the 1930s, the Hungarian-born photographer Brassaï began photographing artists in their studios. And, following the Second World War, Britain's Bill Brandt, among many others, made a point of photographing artists, writers, and musicians in their studios too. On his first trip to Britain, in 1943, Karsh had taken time to photograph artists. In 1946 he had told the violinist Yehudi Menuhin that he wanted to publish a book devoted to "Great Artists."[8] In 1951, he drew up a list of his favourite portraits of actors, with the intention of publishing them, along with Solange's commentaries, in a "Hollywood Album." Simon and Schuster rejected his manuscript later that year. This made Karsh change his tack; he would produce a volume of photographs focused on "the people that influence the peace."[9]

Like every major trip that Karsh now took, his 1954 visit to Europe was documented by Solange. Yet this assignment had an additional chronicler: the witty, independently-minded twenty-year-old American amateur photographer, sportsman, and university student Peter Miller. Over the course of the summer, Miller carried heavy bags, set up and dismantled photography equipment, changed light bulbs and film, and drove Karsh's unwieldy American car.

Miller, who was an enthusiastic member of the University of Toronto's camera club, was just finishing the last year of a degree in English literature when Solange offered him a chance to spend the summer in Europe with herself and Yousuf Karsh. During his interview, which took place at Toronto's Royal York Hotel, Solange told Miller that Karsh was gathering material for a new book.

She also warned him that "since Karsh was a genius he could be temperamental." Miller got along with Solange "like a house on fire" and, when he met Karsh a couple of weeks later with similar success, he was offered $75 a month plus all of his expenses to accompany them to Europe.[10]

The trio left New York on the *Liberté* in mid-May. Miller did not see Yousuf and Solange, who were on the first-class deck, until the ship docked at Le Havre. They must have been an amusing sight as they drove towards Paris in Karsh's ostentatious Chrysler. Yousuf, Solange, and Miller sat shoulder to shoulder in the front seat and their thirty-four pieces of luggage were piled on the roof rack, crammed into the back seat, and stuffed into the trunk of the car. With Miller at the wheel, the trio drove straight to Paris, installed themselves in the Hotel Astor, and then met for a scotch and a du Maurier cigarette. Karsh invariably made a little toast before the first drink of the evening. On this occasion he looked at his young assistant and said, "To your first visit to Paris."

When he accepted the job, Miller never envisioned that he would work so hard, go to bed without dinner, lose his illusions about the glamorous and the great, or learn so much about the technical side of photography. He did not expect, above all, that the most fascinating people he would meet during his two-and-a-half-month-long journey through France, England, Germany, Austria, and Italy would be Madame, as he called Solange, and Mr. Karsh.

It did not take Miller long to discover that Madame possessed a firecracker temper and a Gallic flair for fun, that she had a talent for showing a warm interest in everyone she met, and that her most coveted item during the trip was her "cat" Trudy, a wool knitting bag which she cradled in her arms like a child and never let out of her sight. As for Mr. Karsh, he was "completely the artist—impatient and absorbed when he was working" and, Miller added, "sulky, explosive or deadly polite when he was upset, and infectiously gay when he was off duty."[11] Moreover, "like most artists," Miller later recalled, "he had doubts about his abilities and his place in the world, and he could unleash a mercurial temper, which found me as a target each time I made some blunder during a sitting."[12]

Karsh revealed himself to Miller to be as vain as the subjects he was photographing. He was happy when Miller took his photograph with Albert Schweitzer and other dignitaries they met. On the other hand, he was annoyed when Picasso did not invite them into his villa but confined them to the pottery studio. Miller was amused that Karsh's most safely guarded piece of luggage—besides his lenses—was the scarlet leather-bound book of portraits that he showed to every subject before a sitting. The book, Karsh told Miller, was his "little diplomat" or "magic door-opener." This was no exaggeration. When the trio had difficulty crossing the Italian border, Karsh showed the guard his red leather book of portraits and the barrier was immediately raised.

Miller's education began during the first sitting, with Viscount Montgomery of Alamein, and ended in early August during the last, with the Earl and Countess of Harewood. Miller quickly discovered the extent to which the outcome of a photograph depended on the cooperation of the sitter as much as on the skill of the photographer. Pablo Casals and the art critic and archaeologist André Malraux were cooperative. The fashion designer Christian Dior and the composer Benjamin Britten, along with the richest man in France, Marcel Boussac, were not. Some subjects were generous with their time; Albert Schweitzer gave Karsh a whole day. Others, like Picasso, showed Karsh the door within an hour.

Pablo Picasso
with Jug, 1954

Miller also observed the way in which Solange used her flattering repartee to establish a warm and friendly atmosphere with every client before a sitting. He noted, during the sitting itself, how Karsh kept his subjects alert by asking them a stock set of questions ("Who is the greatest person of this century?" was his favourite). How Karsh went through the list of questions that Tom Blau had prepared for him in advance. And how Karsh would recall—usually at Miller's expense—the humorous situations in which the photographers had found themselves during the course of their travels. Miller also observed how, through "conversation and careful listening," Karsh extracted a subject's character so that it was not only expressed by words "but also by the features of the face, where light and shadow, a gesture, an expression, a certain glimmer in the eye," came perfectly together.[13]

Miller quickly came to respect Karsh's need for quietude before and even after every sitting. "He works a bit like one of his strobe lights," was how Miller chose to describe his boss, "a flare of intense concentration followed by a period

of recharging." Miller continued, "While he's waiting for his vitality to drain back into him, he hates anyone to talk to him and I learned just to hand him cigarettes, which he would take wordlessly."

There were some occasions, however, when Karsh did talk to Miller. He told the young man that he was not interested in politics but in humanity and that it was his aim to reveal the kindness that he felt was inherent in almost every face. And, when this was not possible—on one occasion a photograph of a well-known individual revealed that he possessed a strong sadistic cruelty—how he would neither exhibit nor publish the portrait.

Karsh was equally generous with his technical knowledge. Miller learned how he modelled a face by using two banks of diffused photofloods, a photo-flood backlight, and three 500-watt spotlights. "The spots and floods had barn doors to control the light," Miller later recalled. Karsh used these lights to highlight either side of the face and the hands, which "he lit as carefully as the face."[14] Miller also noted how Karsh minimized the bald head of the French million-aire industrialist Marcel Boussac by pulling back the lights, and how he reduced the size of André Malraux's large nose and Augustus John's bulging eyes by using a softer light.

Miller also learned that Solange and Yousuf's day did not end with the last sitting. During the evening Madame changed into a sea-green negligee, got out her portable typewriter, and transcribed the notes that she had jotted down during that day's sittings. Transforming his bathroom into a darkroom in order to develop that day's film, Mr. Karsh employed his skills as a developer. "He was amazing, he used photograph paper, rich in silver gelatin, triax D23 was his developer," Miller recalled, "and he produced very thin negatives—none of the highlights were burned out."[15]

Although they all worked hard—"When we work, we work," Madame told Miller—they did make time for fun—"when we play we really let our hair down." In Paris, Yousuf and Solange took Peter Miller to the top of the Eiffel Tower. They took him to the Louvre, where the only object that Karsh looked at was the Venus de Milo. They introduced Miller to champagne and got him eating baby octopus, truffles, and snails. They took him to an Armenian restaurant just off the Champs Elysées where, following several glasses of raki, Solange got up and danced. "She was in a fawn wool suit and low-heeled shoes," Miller recalled, "but she dipped and pivoted and twirled around to the music all the same." She "got a big hand" from her fellow diners when she sat down. In Venice, Yousuf and Solange took Miller for a ride in a gondola and to their favourite shops. "In one hat shop Karsh had a wonderful time trying on berets and women's big floppy beach hats."[16] Finally, on the French Riviera, in Cannes, the trio spent the day on the beach. "Nice flesh tones, eh?" was Karsh's only comment about the bikini-clad women.

The trip, during which Karsh photographed some thirty dignitaries on the continent and a little over half that number in England, was, Solange reported to an acquaintance, "a most interesting and fruitful tour," which resulted in "a most imposing gallery of portraits of great creative artists and other world personalities."[17] Solange was hardly exaggerating. In France, Karsh had photographed the leaders of the newly established NATO, writers of the stature of John Steinbeck and Albert Camus, and prominent architects, actors, and musicians. The most significant subjects from Karsh's point of view, however, were Pablo Casals and Albert Schweitzer.

According to Miller, Albert Schweitzer was Karsh's idol. This was why Karsh was nervous before the sitting, and why, during it, "his face shining with excitement and awe," he tiptoed reverently around his subject. Schweitzer, who had recently been awarded the Nobel Peace Prize for his work among lepers at Lambaréné in Gabon, was unequally impressed with Karsh. The strong-minded humanitarian and accomplished organist insisted on setting the poses himself. And he refused to be photographed wearing his glasses. "At one point Karsh tried pretending he had to adjust the camera and," Miller recalled, "just for an instant Schweitzer's eyes closed and his shoulders slumped." It was at this moment that Karsh clicked the shutter and got the photograph he wanted.

Pablo Casals was far more cooperative than his friend Albert Schweitzer. Casals's living quarters at the Villa Colette in the dusty French town of Prades were much too cramped for the sitting, so the entourage went to another location, the nearby abandoned abbey of St. Michel de Cuxa. Karsh began by

photographing Casals from the shoulders up. Then he asked Casals to move into a small alcove of the abbey and instructed Miller to focus the lights on the subject's back. Casals had brought his cello to the sitting. "Soon the old abbey was throbbing with the music…of an almost unearthly quality," Karsh later recalled. "I hardly dared to move or talk," he continued, "for fear of breaking the spell."[18] But Karsh must have moved, for it was at this point that he depressed the bulb which clicked the shutter.

Photographing his subject from behind made the diminutive figure of Casals look larger. It allowed Karsh to avoid capturing the rather unsightly wart on the cellist's face. Above all, as Peter Miller recalled, it enabled Karsh to capture the strength, power, and the tautness evident in Casals's shoulders. Placing his subject under a high, small window not only gave Karsh a point of comparison, it also made the setting resemble a prison cell. The setting and the pose reinforced the point that in 1940 Casals had opted for exile to France rather than life under Franco's fascist regime. At the same time the pose enabled the viewer almost to hear the musician playing the suites Pablo Casals, 1954 of Bach, which Casals had retrieved from virtual oblivion a few years earlier.

Compared to the continent, England was bleak. It rained too much, the food was terrible, and Solange was ill. While Madame remained at the Savoy Hotel, Karsh and Miller set to work on the list of sittings that Tom Blau had prepared for them in advance. They photographed the artist Augustus John, the composer Benjamin Britten, the conductor Sir Malcolm Sargent, the actors Sir Laurence Olivier and Dame Edith Evans, and the author of *The Winslow Boy*, Terence Rattigan. Karsh and Miller also added a number of businessmen, politicians, and aristocrats. But nothing in England compared to the experience of photographing Picasso at the Madoura pottery studio in Vallauris, in Provence, or to spending a day with Schweitzer and Casals, or to meeting many of France's leading intellectuals, playwrights, and politicians. Moreover, when Karsh arrived in England, he had run out of steam. Peter Miller had worked so hard that he lost fifteen pounds. And Solange, for whom visiting her native Brittany had been a highlight, was ready to go home.

Because Madame was still ill during the return voyage to New York, Miller spent half of his time in the first-class section of the *Ile de France*. He and Karsh drank Pernod and watched movies. They played deck tennis. Karsh was proud of his tennis but Miller was more impressed with Karsh's casual dress—he had exchanged his dark suit for print shorts and clear plastic sandals. Mr. Karsh "was quite a sight with his spindly legs and the hair on his chest," Miller recalled.

When they arrived in New York, Karsh deposited his colour transparencies at the Kodak plant for processing, and then he and Solange had one last drink with Peter. As they raised their glasses of scotch, Karsh said, "To a good trip."[19]

FOLLOWING THE SECOND WORLD WAR, Karsh, like Canada's post-war government and business sectors, became more focused on the United States than on Great Britain. In 1951, when he and Solange hosted a cocktail party in New York, the guest list, which included the Canadian consul general, advertising executives, newspaper and magazine editors, book publishers, other business executives, and a number of celebrities—and, according to Solange, a "few DAMN good looking girls"—reflected the extent to which most of Karsh's business was now on the other side of the border.[20]

The Canadian consul general may have looked out of place at Yousuf and Solange's cocktail party, but officials at the Department of External Affairs continued to support Karsh because, in their view, he was the country's best cultural export. External Affairs was willing to give Karsh "the normal courtesies and assistance" through its embassies when he was in Europe in 1949 and 1954.[21] And, in recognition of the "very considerable prestige value" of Karsh's portraits of Americans, they were "anxious" to see him established in Canada House in New York.[22] Officials at Canada House did not have to make room for Yousuf and Solange in their new building, however, because by 1956 the couple had acquired a brownstone apartment in downtown Manhattan, just down the street from the Canadian Consul. It was from this location, at 18 East 62nd Street, that Karsh launched a third company.

Karsh of Ottawa, though it sounded too much like a peerage to one British journalist, had been Yousuf's byline since the late 1940s.[23] In July 1955, however, it became the name of the new American company. Like Little Wings, Karsh of Ottawa was essentially a marketing company dependent, to a large extent, on the production of the Karsh Studio. Forming the new company gave both Solange and Yousuf another salary, and it allowed their rented Manhattan apartment to be claimed as a business expense. Karsh of Ottawa delegated the day-to-day financial arrangements to Karsh's New York agent, Leon Daniel of Pix Incorporated, who had been handling Karsh's stock photographs since 1949.

There was another important reason for setting up the American-based company. Karsh could thereby avoid paying Canadian tax on the profits from the photographs that he took in Europe and the United States, since these amounts were now taxed at the lower American rates. Moreover, providing that he and Solange spent less than 180 days a year in the United States, they could claim a nonresident tax credit of 15 percent on whatever they earned.[24]

At the beginning of 1956 Solange had complained to Joyce Large that "for all Yousuf's tremendously hard work it does not seem as if we would ever have a decent bank balance to take care of expenses."[25] By the end of the year, however, Karsh of Ottawa had a turnover of $36,000. And, because this amount was offset by $15,000 in costs and $20,000 in expenses, the company only had to pay tax to the American government on $279.00.

Karsh of Ottawa did well from the start. In 1956 Karsh had never been so busy and during the course of the next four years the pace did not change. There were more commissions from advertising companies as well as from religious leaders and celebrities. There were more trips to Europe: two in 1955 and 1958 and one in 1959. There was another trip to Hollywood, in 1956—"Yousuf Karsh does want to do a few really glamour pusses," Solange told Joyce Large.[26] After photographing film stars and film producers and attending the Academy Awards ceremony, Karsh, Solange, and Monty Everett drove to New Mexico and photographed the artist Georgia O'Keeffe. After that, they flew to Cuba and captured the expatriate writer Ernest Hemingway.

In addition to all of these trips, there were frequent visits to Washington, D.C., where Karsh photographed the charismatic young senator John Kennedy and his captivating wife, Jackie, as well as President Eisenhower and virtually every other important politician in the capital. There were more sittings and meetings with advertisers, publicity agents, publishers, and magazine editors in New York. And, finally, there was the possibility of an assignment in Mardin, Turkey.

It was Kadri Kayabal of the Turkish Haberler Ajansi Institute in Istanbul who approached Karsh's London agent, Tom Blau, in 1959. Kayabal wanted portraits of high-ranking Turkish officials and a photo essay on the city of Karsh's birth in southeastern Turkey. Blau predicted a negative response when he approached Karsh: "So as not to hurt his personal feelings I did not mention that you may hate the notion of ever going back to Turkey."[27] But Karsh did not say no. He told Blau that he would consider undertaking the assignment pro-

John F. and Jacque-
line Kennedy, 1957

viding it was "financially profitable."[28] In the end, Karsh's busy schedule and, more significantly, Kayabal's inability to meet Karsh's high fees quashed the project. If Kayabal had come up with the funds, Karsh might very well have returned to Mardin, because he was already in the midst of planning a trip to the Middle East, his first since immigrating to Canada in 1923.

It was on one of his sojourns to New York in 1952 that Karsh photographed the handsome, charismatic writer and broadcaster who was responsible for his trip to the Middle East in 1959. In preparation for his first sitting with Bishop Fulton Sheen, Karsh had read the bishop's book on the life of Christ. Karsh had also tuned in to Sheen's popular radio program. When the two men eventually met, they got on well. And, a few years later, when Sheen was looking for someone to photograph him for the American edition of the highly successful book *This Is the Mass*, published in 1958, he turned to Karsh.

It is not surprising that Karsh would go on to produce three more books with Bishop Fulton Sheen.[29] Like Sheen, Karsh was a Roman Catholic. Had it not been for the Armenian genocide, Karsh might very well have fulfilled his mother's wishes by becoming a priest himself. He had always been awed by religious leaders, from Pope John XXIII to Cardinal Agagianian, Cardinal Spellman, and

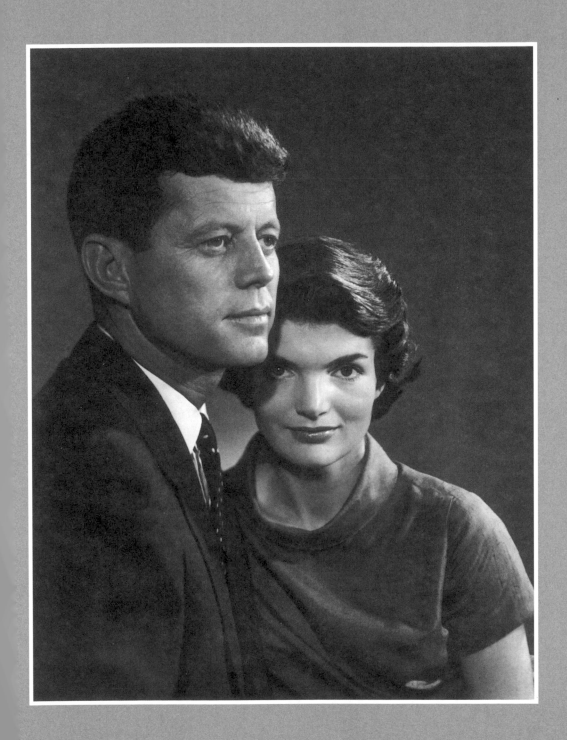

Cardinal Léger—all of whom he photographed. Though he was a lapsed Catholic when he met Sheen in 1952, this did not prevent Karsh from feeling that his work was "a form of thanks and worship of God."[30] Or from adhering to the Augustinian belief that public life somehow transcended the ethics of the marketplace as a self-interested struggle for power, thereby giving world leaders a spiritual quality. It was Karsh's belief that great people were inherently good, a fact which prevented him from photographing some famous people. This was a subjective judgement, of course, as when his fellow Catholic François Mauriac warned him that the leader of the European existentialist movement, Jean-Paul Sartre, was "an apostle of negation" who possessed "a very bad and dangerous state of mind."[31] Consequently, Sartre never sat for Karsh.

Bishop Sheen was as fiercely critical of the shortcomings of Western civilization as was Sartre. However, for Sheen world poverty and communism took precedence over these other concerns, especially in the mid-1950s, when he began a popular weekly television program, *Life Is Worth Living*. On his travels through the Middle East with Karsh and with the British writer H. V. Morton, Sheen adapted stories from the Bible to contemporary life. This impressed Karsh. It made up for his disappointment in discovering while in Israel "the mutual hatred" that existed between the Israelis and the Arabs and "the lack of harmony among Christians."[32]

In 1959, Bishop Sheen—and, to a lesser extent, his two great-nephews who accompanied him, Yousuf, Solange, and Morton to the Holy Land—was the subject of almost every photograph that Karsh took there with his 35-mm camera: Sheen breaking bread on the edge of the Sea of Galilee; Sheen emerging from the tomb of Lazarus; and Sheen visiting other sacred spots—the Mount of Temptation near Jericho, Mount Sion, the Mount of Olives, and the Grotto of the Annunciation in Nazareth. On a few occasions Karsh did focus his lens on yet another place sacred to Christians or on the dry, rocky landscape. But the angelic boys and the handsome bishop, all of whom appeared more saccharine than sacred, were usually the subjects of Karsh's photographs.

With Catholicism riding a wave of popularity during the 1950s and early 1960s, the books, which brought Karsh's photographs of Sheen together with H. V. Morton's travelogue prose, sold well. But Karsh had not joined the project to make money or to gather photographs for a future book. For him the enterprise had been an act of devotion: to Bishop Fulton Sheen and to the Catholic faith.

It would be tempting to link Karsh's assignment with the work he did for the Montreal arms manufacturer Canadair. After all, both Sheen and Canadair were critical of communism and proselytizers of the American way of life. While the first engendered support through prayer and devotion to the Catholic Church, the second won the public's support through anti-Communist rhetoric and the production of armaments. But it is doubtful whether Karsh himself made such a connection. Whereas his work with Sheen served in part to compensate for his own shortcomings as a lapsed Roman Catholic, his assignment with Canadair chiefly represented good—and profitable—business.

WHEN SOLANGE AND YOUSUF returned to Ottawa from Europe in 1954, Solange began drafting short essays to accompany a number of the new photographs. The following year, Karsh submitted the text and photographs to the British publisher E. P. S. Lewin and Porteous and to the American-based Simon & Schuster. Both publishers rejected the manuscript. Seemingly undaunted, Karsh submitted the manuscript to Alfred Knopf in New York. The four people who read the manuscript for Knopf found Karsh's writing stiff and amateurish and the material uninteresting. Leaving the door open for a further submission, they suggested that Karsh hire "a big name writer" to produce a new text.[33]

It was with this view in mind that Karsh asked the award-winning writer and editor of the *Victoria Times*, Bruce Hutchison, for assistance. Hutchison agreed to rework Solange's essays, and Karsh agreed to pay Hutchison the enormous sum of $5,000 to do so. Although other people became involved in the revisions—for example, Karsh's old friend Hugh Keenleyside rewrote the essay on Dag Hammarskjöld—it was Hutchison who rewrote most of the ninety-six profiles. "I am trying to put some life into every item and that is not always easy with the material available," he wrote Karsh from his weekend cottage on Vancouver Island.[34] "I have had to invent my own impressions in every case," he told Karsh in a later missive; "you must make changes where, through lack of information, I may have got off track."[35]

It is unlikely that Karsh made any alterations to Hutchison's reworked essays. "I found them excellent," Karsh told him in July 1957.[36] With the revised manuscript in hand, Karsh sought a final opinion from Tom Blau. His British agent's response was anything but positive: "Far too many of these articles merely dilly-dally about the surface." The essay on Marion Anderson, he continued, "reads as if you were dealing with a saint not a singer." And to call Winston Churchill "a gigantic passage in human history" was "a very unfortunate image" to choose for the former British prime minister.[37]

Ignoring Blau's criticism, Karsh submitted the new manuscript, provisionally entitled "The Great and the Famous," to the University of Toronto Press. Unlike everyone else, the press's director, Marsh Jeanneret, and the production editor, Paul Arthur, saw potential. After its editorial team, headed by Francess Halpenny, subjected the text to yet another revision and retitled the book *Portraits of Greatness*, it was published in Canada in time for the Christmas market in 1959. Thomas Nelson and Sons brought the book out in the United States and in Great Britain the following year.

Karsh was convinced that *Portraits of Greatness* was "unlikely to be a 'best seller.'"[38] He could not, however, have been more wrong. Anticipating the book's success, Marsh Jeanneret had ordered an impressive print run of 14,500 copies.

"Yousuf Karsh launched his second book last night, in a manner grand, promotional and relaxed," a writer for the Ottawa *Journal* announced on November 27, 1959, one day before the official publication. It was a stylish occasion, with a lot of hand and cheek kissing. Many of the portraits from the book were displayed on the walls of the reception hall. The only thing missing were the books themselves: all 14,500 copies had already been sold. This meant that the diplomats, the artists and photographers, and the librarians and archivists who attended the Ottawa book launch had to wait until the press produced a second print run of 16,000 in order to get their copies.

The University of Toronto Press was right to boast in a laid-in sheet that *Portraits of Greatness* represented "a unique achievement in the history of printing."[39] Unlike Karsh's first book, *Faces of Destiny*, the reproduction values in this second volume were stunning. The prestigious European printer Enschedé of Haarlem had done Karsh proud by using the sheet-fed gravure process for the photographs. The printer had developed special soft inks—not commercially available—that enabled it to make near-perfect facsimiles of the original photographs. And, in order to avoid the unsightly threads of sewn signatures and to facilitate the removal of the portraits for display, the press had chosen a thermoplastic rather than a sewn binding. Unlike the murky reproductions in Karsh's first book, there was nothing here to suggest that he had used a soft-focus lens. The Héliomat paper and the type—Spectrum and Dubbele Augustijn Open Kapitalen, designed by the firm's Jan van Krimpen—were far superior to those used in the earlier publication too.

Needless to say, Karsh had overseen the whole process. Putting aside his usual charming manner, he rejected prints when they did not capture the tonal contrasts and crispness of the original photographs, when the blacks did not resemble the velvety blacks of the originals, and when details had been either lost or exaggerated. But the superb production values in the resulting publication were due not only to the skill and patience of the European printing house and to the persistence of Karsh. Enschedé had been given good material to start with.

During his 1954 trip to Europe, Karsh had boasted to Peter Miller that he was "probably the best photograph printer in the world."[40] While Karsh may have been right to claim that he could "do in two days what it takes a technician two weeks to do," the images that found their way into *Portraits of Greatness* owed much to the technical abilities of Ignas Gabalis and Hella Grabar, who had joined the Karsh Studio in 1952 and 1953 respectively.

When Ignas Gabalis first came to Canada in 1949, he had worked for Malak Karsh. However, when Malak experienced a recurrent bout of tuberculosis in 1951, Barbara Karsh, who continued to run the studio in her husband's absence, had to reduce the staff. It was at this point that the Lithuanian-born photographer, who was Yousuf's junior by eight years, joined the Karsh Studio. Although Gabalis had run a portrait studio in Denmark before immigrating to Canada, his forte was in developing and printing. According to Joyce Large, "he was wonderful at what he did."[41] And Hella Grabar called him "top in the whole world."[42]

Karsh and Gabalis were both perfectionists. Where Gabalis was slow and methodical, however, Karsh was fast and sometimes sloppy. "Karsh would complain that Dad was the slowest printer ever," Gabalis's daughter, Sonja Mortimer, recalled. But he nevertheless relied on Gabalis "to pull prints when Karsh himself would botch a print job." While Mortimer remembered that "Mr. Karsh...could be a bit of a work-room tyrant," her father's boss did express his gratitude every Christmas.[43] According to Karsh, Gabalis was "the only one on whom I can always count," and "the perfectionist who is becoming more and more perfect every year." A few years before Gabalis retired in 1992, Karsh told him that he was "grateful not only for your superb artistry, but for your good friendship and wonderful loyalty."[44] Karsh also gave Gabalis tangible evidence of his appreciation by raising his salary annually.

An equally significant addition to the technical department of the Karsh Studio was Hella Grabar. Like Gabalis, Grabar had been trained as a photographer in Europe, though she insisted that "I am not a photographer, but I can see things."[45]

She arrived in Canada from Cologne with her husband and son in 1953. Almost immediately she applied for a job in the Karsh Studio. During the interview Karsh "was tough, I didn't take to him at all." But she had heard about his portraits in Germany and wanted the job. When she got it, Grabar washed, spotted, gold-toned, and touched up Karsh's prints. She helped him select images for his books. And she laminated the enlarged portraits for display.

Like her colleague Gabalis, Grabar received annual raises. And, a few years before she left the Karsh Studio in 1975, Karsh expressed his gratitude: "You take all projects concerned with me...and smooth my path in many ways and make it possible for me to concentrate on my work."[46] But for most of her time at the studio, Karsh had been stinting in praise. "Gabalis and I slaved for him, we did," Grabar remembers, "and do you think he would ever say Gabalis and Hella?" While Karsh was "always trying to get more and more," it was Solange, according to Grabar, who was always ready to acknowledge how hard she and Gabalis worked.[47]

Karsh gave little public credit to Grabar or Gabalis. Yet the difference their contributions made to the quality of his finished portraits was there for everyone to see. For example, in *Portraits of Greatness* Karsh had included a number of old chestnuts: the double portrait of Richard Rogers and Oscar Hammerstein,

and the photographs of Sibelius, Shaw, and Low. But it was his most recent portraits, of Georgia O'Keeffe (1956), Ernest Hemingway (1957), and Tennessee Williams (1956)—all printed by Grabar and Gabalis—that elevated Karsh's work to a new level of artistic achievement. These, in the judgement of the prestigious journal *Popular Photography*, were the portraits that, like his photograph of Churchill in 1941, helped earn Karsh a place in 1958 among the ten greatest photographers in the world.[48]

BY THE 1950S, KARSH HAD become as much of a celebrity as many of his subjects. He was also as financially successful and as well known as any other photographer in North America or Europe. Yet, more work, more money, and more praise for his portraits did not necessarily give him a greater sense of fulfillment, of financial security, or of artistic success. This was why he took on more portrait commissions and more advertising jobs than ever before. And this was equally why, by the end of the decade, his erratic pace   Georgia O'Keeffe, 1956 had become detrimental to the efficiency of the studio, to his relationship with Solange, and to his own health.

One of the problems was that Karsh was running the studio in the same autocratic manner as he had in the early days. This might have been all right in the 1930s when the demands on Karsh and his staff were limited, but things had changed since then. The volume of work had increased. The staff had grown. He and Solange were out of the country almost as much as they were in it. And all of this led to delays. Although some clients did not mind waiting for their finished portraits, others did—like one advertising executive from McClure and Wilder in New York. "For two weeks you are here, there, everywhere," Robert Kenyon scolded Karsh in 1957, "yet once you get into Canada you completely disappear... One would think the border between the States and the Provinces was of the Iron Curtain variety."[49]

Things might have been better if Yousuf and Solange had executed a plan that they had devised in the early 1950s. "After much study and planning," went Solange's draft to the local newspaper, "Karshmont portraits are being introduced in Ottawa in answer to the demands of so many deserving a service from the distinguished studios at a moderate cost."[50] The idea was to have Karsh's former assistant Monty Everett share some of the workload in the camera room. But the plan to bring Everett into the studio as a fellow portrait photographer never came to fruition. While Everett continued to accompany Karsh on many of his travels abroad, he maintained his independence by operating his own studio farther down Bank Street.

Although commissions were plentiful during the 1950s, this did not mean that Karsh necessarily got every sitting he wanted. He still desperately wanted another royal sitting, for example. By the late 1950s, however, even Cecil Beaton was having trouble photographing the queen, because a new rival, Antony Armstrong-Jones — who would marry Princess Margaret in 1960 — had become the palace's favourite photographer.

Karsh had also been unsuccessful in persuading Winston Churchill to pose for him again. Hoping to work his way into the former prime minister's household, Karsh photographed Churchill's physician, Lord Moran, and Winston's son, Randolph Churchill. Though this did not result in the much-sought-after private sitting, Karsh did, in fact, get to photograph the eighty-year-old Churchill at the Draper's Hall in London when the former prime minister received the Colonial Williamsburg Award in December 1955. After encountering a group of press photographers, Churchill and the other trustees were led into the Drapers Hall, where the ceremony was to take place. It was here that Karsh, suitably dressed in black tie for the occasion, photographed Churchill for a second time.

A writer for the *Financial Post* was convinced that the resulting photograph of Churchill would become a "historic picture."[51] Karsh, who found Churchill's face "lined with wisdom and knowledge," was equally hopeful that the sitting would produce a masterpiece.[52] The results, however, were far from satisfactory. This was partly because Karsh had no opportunity to engage in the kind of chit-chat that usually put his subject at ease. It was also because he had to use a small flash rather than his usual set of bank and floodlights. Consequently, as a writer for the *Los Angeles Times* exclaimed a few years later, the resulting portrait made the elderly Churchill look like a "sort of bull dog."[53]

Never one to accept defeat, Karsh asked Churchill's son-in-law Duncan Sandys, whom he had met during the ceremony, to help him arrange a private sitting so that he could do justice to Churchill. Sandys approached his father-in-law but Churchill was not interested. There was talk that he was still perturbed that Karsh had had the impertinence to remove the cigar from his mouth during the sitting back in 1941. But this was not all. Karsh had sensationalized the cigar story by repeatedly telling it to the press. Moreover, Churchill felt that the Canadian photographer had benefited financially from the sale of the photograph.

In his reply to the rejection, Karsh did not remind Sandys that his father-in-law had used the portrait for the cover of his war speeches, *The Unrelenting Struggle*. Nor did Karsh suggest that Churchill's anger might have come from the feeling that he had somehow been upstaged. After all, the portrait had become indelibly associated with the anecdote about the removal of the cigar. Sensing this, Karsh instead attempted to justify his actions. "It was an instinctive artistic impulse, and in no sense a premeditated move," he told Sandys. "Ever since I have felt anxious and unhappy about the disproportionate publicity given to that incident in the gossip columns of the press, but how can one ever stop that sort of thing?"[54]

Karsh was hurt. He had been rejected by his most famous subject—and scuppered by his most famous anecdote. Convinced that Churchill would pose for a further portrait, he had prepared the questions to ask during the sitting. "Of our human virtues what do you consider the greatest?" and "Have you any thoughts on space travel?" were two of the questions on Karsh's list.[55]

Karsh had also told his agents in London and New York that a new photograph of Churchill was imminent. During the sitting he had planned to take not just one photograph but "an informal and somewhat daring photographic study of Churchill in detail—his face in repose or even in anger, the formation of his ears, the shape of his chin, the close-up of his hands as he slept," all of which would appear in a book devoted to Churchill.[56] However, the opportunity to make such a detailed study of the former British prime minister, which, as Karsh told Sandys, would represent "the culmination of my life's work," was dashed.[57]

IF THINGS WERE TROUBLING on the business front, they were even worse in the Karsh household. In 1958 Karsh's much-loved mother died. The following year, not only was he himself at death's door but Solange was diagnosed with a malignant tumour.

Solange had been suffering from recurrent headaches and gout since 1954. She knew that she smoked and drank too much, that too much air travel led to sinus attacks, and that her efforts to recuperate in Florida or in Bermuda had little effect. She also knew that her infirmities and her absences from the studio were becoming a serious problem. Her inability to hold up her end at work, to manage the household staff at Little Wings, and to be the wife that Yousuf wanted her to be brought matters to a head in the late autumn of 1958.

Yousuf was away when Solange wrote him a missive entitled "TO BE TAKEN IN YOUR STRIDE AND READ IN SMALL INSTALLMENTS IF NECESSARY." The pretext for the letter was to inform Yousuf that their housekeeper, Louisa, and their grounds-man, Eric, had quit their jobs. It seems that Solange had scolded the young couple for not "playing the game." In retaliation, they had left Little Wings.

But the incident with the recently arrived couple from Estonia was not all that was bothering Solange. She was unhappy with her inability "to stay the person you married because you knew I had something to offer." She was displeased with "always thinking about other people and not enough of you and I." And there was more. During a recent drive to Kingsville, Yousuf had accused her of "daydreaming" and of not taking sufficient interest in the Karsh Studio. Solange did not deny having lost interest in the studio and in Little Wings. She admitted that she was "getting somewhat neurotic," losing not only her sense of proportion and humour but also "far too much weight in too short a time." Above all, she was fed up with returning from a day's work at the studio and having to prepare dinner "from A to Z."

Solange made no apologies for "blowing up" in her letter to Yousuf. Rather, she hoped that by understanding her problems he would be able to take "still greater portraits."[58] Yet there is no indication as to how Karsh responded to Solange's letter or indeed if he ever read it.

Certainly no one who saw Yousuf and Solange when they appeared on Edward R. Murrow's *Person to Person* television show a few months later would have known that there was anything amiss. According to Joyce Large, "they 'came across' with a great deal of poise, dignity and a human message."[59] In fact there was an obvious sexual tension lying under their formality. And, far from appearing to be the dominant member of the pair, it was Yousuf who, throughout the program, looked to Solange for assurance. All of this was less in keeping with Solange's letter than with her earlier observation that Karsh was "like a child and I look after him."[60]

Karsh soon needed such attention. During his book launch in November 1959, he had uncharacteristically remained seated. Why was this so? Was he travel weary? Was he worried about Solange, whose trips to Florida and Bermuda were failing to restore her energy? Was he still mourning the death of his much-loved mother the previous year? Or had the preparation of the book, in addition to all of the other projects that dominated his professional life, been too much? Physical exhaustion was nothing new to Karsh, and a trip to the Caribbean had usually restored his energy, but there was something else going on here. Karsh was not a well man. A few months earlier, on July 8, while photographing Hubert Humphrey for *Parade* magazine in Washington, D.C., Karsh had had a coronary thrombosis.

The press was quick to report his illness and the Karsh Studio and the Washington Hospital Center were flooded with good wishes for his recovery. Irving Penn, Philippe Halsman, and Ansel Adams—three of the other photographers whom *Popular Photography* had selected as among the ten best in the world—expressed their concern. John Kennedy, whom Karsh was scheduled to photograph the following day, sent mums and gladioli, Tom Blau sent white carnations and shaggy asters, and Malak and Barbara Karsh sent Yousuf a bowl of mauve flowers. Even Pope John XXIII promised to remember Karsh in his prayers.

Most of Karsh's friends had seen his heart attack coming; at least, that is what they said in the letters, telegrams, and notes that were delivered to the Washington Hospital Center. "We had anxiously watched signs of fatigue becoming more apparent in your looks and attitude," Ted Bullock wrote from New York.[61] Though "shocked to hear" of Karsh's attack, another friend was "frankly, not too surprised although we had come to think of you as superman."[62]

Members of the Karsh family were full of advice. Reminding him of his own coronary attack ten years earlier, George Nakash hoped "that this warning will make you realize the situation and be kinder to yourself."[63] Jamil Karsh, who had just been made a fellow of the American College of Surgeons, advised his brother to "be a good boy and don't forget to do the 'impossible.'"[64]

Less than two weeks after the heart attack, Karsh told Hella Grabar, "I miss my work, and I am eager to get back to it."[65] He nevertheless took advantage of the enforced rest. Indeed, after he had been released from hospital, he told his old friends Jean and Floyd Chalmers that "I have been going at such a hectic pace for so many years, that it was time to stop and reflect."[66]

During his five weeks in hospital, Karsh did a lot of reading: everything from Colette's *My Mother's House* and Art Buchwald's *Paris* to Duff Cooper's *Old Men Forget*. Karsh listened to music—mostly classical. He telephoned Joyce Large daily in order to keep abreast of what was happening at the studio. He gave up smoking, but probably not drinking scotch and brandy. And he became more inward looking: "I must be resolute and optimistic and triumph over my difficulties"; and, he told himself, "when ready to start working, work gradually."[67]

But what did getting back to work mean? Would Karsh really make "every effort in the world" to guard his health when he returned to Ottawa, as he promised Hella Grabar?[68] Solange, who had rushed to his bedside from Ottawa when she heard the news of his attack, was not as optimistic about the future. Indeed, she asked Yousuf's doctor to refrain from suggesting that her husband could expect to resume his "so-called 'normal' way of life." Because, she continued, "his idea of a 'normal' life was such that not even the youngest and wiriest of his traveling assistants could keep up with him."[69]

The day before Karsh had collapsed in Hubert Humphrey's office, Solange learned that she was suffering from a possible malignancy in her breast. "A rather shattering piece of news which obviously I could not transmit to Yousuf," she told her old friend B. K. Sandwell. Her response to her bad news was characteristic: "So immediately after returning from Yousuf's bedside at the end of the first few critical days, I started my treatments at the Civic Hospital for deep radiation and cobalt bomb."[70]

The cancer treatments that followed sapped Solange's strength but they did not dampen her spirits. Before Karsh returned to Ottawa from his sickbed in Washington, she had followed his instructions to write to all of his friends and acquaintances who had expressed concern for his health. And when Yousuf was safely home, Solange nursed him back to health. She watched his diet by counting the calories and weighing every portion of food that he ate. She also saw to it that he did not exert himself. Indeed, Solange's efforts to restore Yousuf's health would prove more effective than the attention she gave to her own condition.

PART THREE

THE
LIVING
LEGEND

An End and a Beginning

It was Solange who now faced a fatal illness. She refused to have an operation: "I will not be mutilated," she told Yousuf.[1] Just before Christmas 1959, however, she did agree to undergo a cobalt implant. The doctors were hopeful that the treatment would eradicate the cancer cells. Alas, it did not. Over the course of the following year her condition deteriorated. Even so, Solange was adamant that her increasingly poor health would not interfere with Yousuf's work.[2] He took this injunction seriously—it was the ethic by which they had always lived—and therefore he continued to be as professionally active as ever.

There were ongoing portrait commissions in the United States as well as in Canada. There was an assignment from *Chatelaine* magazine: it wanted Karsh to photograph eight Canadian churches representing different denominations.[3] There was another trip to the Middle East with Bishop Fulton Sheen and H. V. Morton. Karsh's former assistant, Monty Everett, took Solange's place. Hawthorn Books brought out *This Is the Holy Land* in 1960.

Farther afield, Karsh went to South Africa to open the touring exhibition From Our World, which introduced his photographs from the 1959 publication *Portraits of Greatness*, admittedly to an exclusively white public. It was on this trip that the normally apolitical Karsh had an opportunity to show that he was willing to engage in politics if a political issue came between him and his camera. Prohibited by the apartheid government from photographing the leader of the African resistance and recent winner of the Nobel Prize for Peace, Albert Luthuli, Karsh, to his credit, cancelled his sitting with the South African prime minister, Hendrik F. Verwoerd.

After South Africa, there was Karsh's solo exhibition Portraits of Greatness at the National Gallery of Canada. This, according to Karsh, represented "the greatest honor a photographer can be paid and the culmination of my efforts."[4]

The country's premier gallery had been committed to treating photographs as works of art since the 1930s. It had taken Edward Steichen's Family of Man exhibition during its tour of North American galleries two decades later. The National Gallery had also given a solo exhibition, The Decisive Moment, to the famous French photographer Henri Cartier-Bresson. And, long before this, the gallery had played host to a number of national and international photographic societies. The only thing that the National Gallery had not done for the art of photography was to give a solo exhibition to Canada's leading photographer.

Portraits of Greatness opened on September 22, 1960. Just like Karsh's touring show in South Africa, the exhibition included photographs that had all appeared in Karsh's 1959 publication of the same name. Speaking at the opening, the newly appointed director of the National Gallery, Charles Comfort, said that Karsh's portraits represented "the indisputable framework of identity… that sets each study apart as an individual discovery." Comfort also told the large gathering that the work surrounding them left no doubt in his mind that Yousuf Karsh was an artist.[5]

Karsh was, of course, already a household name across Canada. Most people had seen his work illustrated in newspapers or in magazines like Saturday Night. Almost every adult knew that Yousuf Karsh was the man who had taken the cigar out of Winston Churchill's mouth. (In order to reinforce the significance of the resulting portrait, a larger-than-life-sized reproduction of Karsh's defiant image of the British statesman greeted visitors as they entered the exhibition in 1960.) But few people had had an opportunity to view large professional prints of Karsh's portraits in a gallery setting and thereby consider them as works of art. Or to appreciate the extent to which Karsh could reveal, as one commentator noted, "the mind and the soul of the subject."[6] Or, as one critic noted, to see how Karsh's more recent portraits showed "a tendency to get away from his low key effects of softly lighted faces and figures and dark backgrounds" and included "backgrounds and surroundings" which indicated the profession of the subjects.[7] Or, finally, to read so many critical assessments of his work.

The National Gallery's decision to send the exhibition on tour throughout Central and Eastern Canada changed all of this. Suddenly, a larger number of Canadians were exposed to Karsh's portraits than ever before. Everywhere the exhibition went, from small communities like Brantford and Shawinigan to larger centres like Halifax, the portraits of predominantly famous European, Canadian, and American personalities drew record crowds and critical attention from the press. Writing from Ottawa, Carl Weiselberger noted how the seventy-five portraits on display gave "the essence…of human faces" and offered a welcome counterpart to the less accessible and less popular paintings of the Abstract Expressionist school of art. Weiselberger also felt that Karsh's portraits brought a wealth of human goodness and genius, thereby providing "an optimistic note to the judgment of our time: its critics, who like to see it predominantly in the sinister light of unspiritual mechanization, regimentation, mass thinking, [and] cheap materialistic pleasure-hunt."[8] Unconfined by the trappings of non-representational art, Karsh's portraits of famous men and women were accessible to everyone who viewed them and, as Weiselberger made clear, could be an uplifting experience.

IT SEEMS THAT SOLANGE was well enough to attend the opening of Portraits of Greatness at the National Gallery. After all, she had recently driven with Joyce Large to Stratford, Ontario, where the two women had had "a wonderful week" attending the theatre. But the next few months, Large later recalled, were "tragic."[9] The disease, which Solange had been dodging since the spring of 1959, began to spread from her breast to her bones. In preparation for her death she drew up her will. In it she asked that her "dear husband" provide for her mother, Héloise Gauthier, and her father-in-law, Amsih Karsh, following her death.

Yousuf wrote a new will too. This fulfilled Solange's wishes. He also willed $10,000 to his brother Salim, $5,000 "to my devoted employee, Joyce Large," money from insurance policies to his nieces and nephews, and "all other money to the assistance of arts and the artists."[10]

During the last year of her life, Solange had insisted on helping Yousuf research and write the first draft of a memoir. The manuscript was a compilation of anecdotes, as recorded by Solange in the camera room, of recollections, focusing on Yousuf's early years in Canada, and of reflections, mostly on the art of photography. Bruce Hutchison read, and criticized, early versions of the manuscript. Then the assistant director of the University of Toronto Press, Eleanor Harman, worked the manuscript into a publishable form.

Adhering to an autobiographical format, *In Search of Greatness: Reflections of Yousuf Karsh* focused on the high points of the first fifty years of Karsh's life: leaving the Middle East and immigrating to Canada as a boy of thirteen, studying with John Garo in Boston, meeting Solange Gauthier at the Little Theatre in Ottawa, winning the patronage of Prime Minister Mackenzie King, photographing Winston Churchill, travelling to wartime and post-war London, and photographing film stars, musicians, statesmen, and other notables.

There was, however, much that Karsh left out. He did not explain how his business, which began with borrowed money and orange crates for furniture, had added two further companies, Little Wings and Karsh of Ottawa, to its empire within fifteen years. He gave little attention to George Nakash, who had taught him the art of photography. (While Karsh would express his gratitude to his uncle in a letter or at the opening of an exhibition, he rarely did so in print.[11]) Karsh gave a back seat to the technical assistants and secretarial staff who ran the Karsh Studio. It was no different with Malak Karsh. Yousuf made light of his brother's contribution to the Karsh Studio in the years before he set up his own business. There was almost nothing of the accomplished landscape photographs that had made Malak's name known throughout the country or the industrial photographs that had influenced Yousuf's own work.

If Karsh's readers had expected a more reflective story, they would have been disappointed. True, Karsh had always maintained a formal distance between himself and the rest of the world. "He didn't analyze himself," a close friend would observe years later.[12] Indeed, there was only one point, towards the end of the book, at which he admitted to sometimes being self-centred and selfish.[13]

What accounts for these, and other, lacunae? Did Karsh feel that his own achievements might have been diminished if he had given the people who had helped shape his career a more prominent place in his memoir? Or did the omissions have more to do with others who had had a hand in producing the book, most notably Solange? After all, the Karsh myth was as much her creation as Yousuf's.

Certainly, Solange's ambition to present Karsh as a self-made man, a successful immigrant, a brilliant photographer, and, above all, a sophisticated man of the world was fully achieved. The book delights in giving detailed accounts of memorable meals and in providing the names of the famous chefs who had prepared them. If Yousuf prided himself on his ability to make a reluctant client—John D. Rockefeller was one—enjoy a sitting, this owed much to Solange's preparatory groundwork. And she undoubtedly shared his satisfaction in demonstrating in print that he was not only the photographer of many of the world's most illustrious citizens but also their friend and even their confidant. After all, had Glenn Gould not told Karsh, four years before anyone else knew that at the age of thirty he was planning to quit the concert platform and devote himself to composition and recording?[14] Completed during her fatal illness, *In Search of Greatness* represented Solange's final gift to Yousuf: her ultimate contribution in projecting and marketing her husband's public image.

Joyce Large, Hella Grabar, and Barbara Karsh were the most frequent visitors to Solange's bedside at Little Wings. And the nurse, Mrs. W. Ross Fraser, gave "her charming patient" comfort and loving care too.[15] During her last months, Solange displayed "a courage that was superb."[16] Preparing for Yousuf's future life without her, she asked Grabar "to watch that Yousuf does not go away from his artistic side and too much money."[17] During the Christmas festivities in 1960, Solange told Malak and Barbara Karsh that she was going to die and that she was leaving Yousuf in their hands.[18]

Still heeding Solange's wish that he should carry on with his work, Yousuf completed portrait commissions in Denver, Los Angeles, San Francisco, and New York, among other cities. By mid-January, however, he realized that he should be back in Ottawa. There he found Solange in an oxygen text, with Hella Grabar at her bedside. Grabar, who spent the last two nights with Solange before her death, recalled, "She just wanted Hella."[19] Within ten days of Yousuf's return, the woman who many people recognized as "the vital element" to Karsh's success died, on January 21, 1961.[20]

A High Mass was sung for Solange at Ottawa's Church of Saint Vincent de Paul. Karsh established a drama award in her honour. Warm tributes from friends and clients — Pope John XXIII was one — arrived at the Karsh Studio. These were of little consolation to the grieving Yousuf. Though Solange's death had been expected, it was nevertheless "a shattering experience" for him, as those around him could see.[21]

Karsh had not only lost his wife of more than twenty years; he had lost his business manager, a superb hostess, and his best friend. During the early months of 1961, he found it difficult to be on his own. When he returned from a trip, someone from the studio would meet him at the airport, and after he had been driven to Little Wings, fearful of entering an empty house, Yousuf would just sit on the patio.

Upon moving to Ottawa almost three decades earlier, work had been Karsh's antidote to the loneliness and loss that he had experienced as a young immigrant. Now, after he followed his doctor's orders to take ten days of complete rest in a climate warmer than that of Eastern Canada, work became even more of a necessity for his survival.

WHEN *IN SEARCH OF GREATNESS* appeared in 1962, Solange had been dead for a year and a half. Only one person who reviewed the book in Canada seemed unhappy with the memoir and that was Karsh's old English teacher, Dr. G. Ellery Read. Not only did Karsh's writing put "him on a par with publicity-seeking screen stars," Read wrote in the *Sherbrooke Record*, his former pupil had "become too enamored of the immigrant-boy-to-fame-and-riches image."[22] Almost everyone else who had access to the Canadian media professed themselves delighted with the book. "We don't have too many world-famous men in the Capital City," a reporter from Ottawa observed.[23] Others were proud that a Canadian had, as

Karsh himself put it, "the privilege of mingling with some of the great of this world."[24] And, finally, many journalists took a vicarious interest in having an "insider" view of their heroes and heroines, even though Karsh insisted in the preface of the book that he would be "the last person to take unfair advantage of the personalities I met in my work."[25]

The critics who reviewed *In Search of Greatness* in the foreign press took a less indulgent view of the book than did their Canadian counterparts. The art critic for the *Sunday Times* found Karsh's much-repeated anecdotes "definitely disappointing."[26] On the other hand, that critic liked the fifth chapter, "Photographic Reflections," where Karsh was "sharpest on the skills, tricks, and disciplines of photography."[27] It was here that Karsh reiterated his belief that he was capable of exposing the soul, the inner thoughts and "the inward power" of the people he photographed.[28] It was here, too, that Karsh admitted to being influenced "by the public image, by the legend that surrounds the great person or by the living legend that he has created."[29] As he told his readers, he did not get the same satisfaction from photographing people who had made no special contribution to the world.

By 1962 Karsh's views on photography were certainly out of date. What, one wonders, would the black South African photographers who were contributing images of illegal speakeasies, or shebeens, and migrant workers and other disfranchised blacks to the *Drum* magazine have thought of Karsh's 1961 exhibition if they had been granted entry to it? How would the hard-edged American photographer Diane Arbus, with her "snap-shot aesthetic" and "freak show" photographs of dwarfs, prostitutes, and transvestites, approach Yousuf Karsh's portraits? What would Andy Warhol have thought of them? Warhol's unrefined, larger-than-life multiple silk-screen images of Marilyn Monroe, Elizabeth Taylor, and Jacqueline Kennedy had, unlike Karsh's work, given these mid-century female icons a back seat by making the process rather than the image itself the subject of the work.

Technically, too, Karsh was no longer at the cutting edge. This was apparent when he told his readers why he preferred taking his photographs in black and white rather than in colour. For Karsh, working in colour meant that he had to become the servant rather than the master of the camera and that his heroes would look like the man or woman next door. Working with black-and-white film was different. There was more scope for and more control over the subtle graduation of illumination from light to dark. He could manipulate the middle tones of the black-and-white print in order to create a sense of the third dimension. And, above all, he could imbue the most unpromising subject with gravitas. All of these things, in Karsh's view, gave the black-and-white photographer "true artistic satisfaction." This did not mean that he never encountered problems: "I cannot always avoid some duplication." But if he did duplicate a pose or a composition, Karsh insisted that he did so with full awareness.[30]

And what about Karsh himself? How did his immaculate conservative attire and his deliberately courteous manner compare with the photographer in the early 1960s film *Blow Up*, who not only worked rapidly and frantically with his subjects but also persuaded them to take off their clothes? Would Karsh's younger colleagues have concurred with Margaret Bourke-White's view that his photographs led the way in portraiture?[31] Or would they have been more inclined to agree with the critic for Toronto's *National Home Monthly* who in 1946 had labelled Karsh a "court photographer" whose "capacity for hero worship was working overtime?"[32] Or, twenty years later, with Barry Callaghan's devastating observation in the *Toronto Telegram* that there was "a sameness about all Karsh's work, a dreadful odor of piety and respectability," which came as a result of "pursuing greatness as though it were a commodity ready to be picked from the faces of those who are great."[33]

By the late 1950s Karsh was fully aware that the next generation of photographers would take their portraits in a different way. In 1955 he had asked, in reference to modern art, music, and technology, "are we not more preoccupied with the ways of saying things than with the things we say?"[34] (This was several years before Marshall McLuhan, whom Karsh would photograph in 1974, coined his influential mantra "the medium is the message.") Karsh knew full well that his younger contemporaries were obsessed with process, manifested by blurring, zooming, fogging, and eccentric cropping. This is why he was so concerned about the reception of *Portraits of Greatness* in 1959. "All I can hope for," he told Bruce Hutchison, "is that it will be an artistic success."[35]

Karsh desperately wanted the critics' approval of his work because during the 1950s he had received several negative reviews. The *Manchester Guardian* had noted how some critics felt that Karsh was "too much taken up with carefully arranged highlights and shadows and with lines and wrinkles dramatically emphasized."[36] During his London exhibition in 1953 Karsh's portraits were criticized by the same newspaper for their "over elaboration of detail."[37] Following the publication of *Portraits of Greatness*, his hopes for unanimous approval were dashed when a writer for the prestigious *British Journal of Photography* noted how the narrow angle of his spotlights gave "an exaggerated skin texture resulting...in what one might call brutality."[38] Other British reviewers joined Stuart Black in questioning Karsh's emphasis on detail, as did critics in the United States. A writer for the *New York Times*, for example, expressed concern about the high burnished sheen on the faces of Karsh's subjects, which gave "the sitters a look as if they had been lacquered in bronze." "But then," the critic churlishly added, "perhaps bronze is the proper medium of greatness."[39]

Critics in Britain also opened up a new topic for discussion: why did Yousuf Karsh include so few portraits of women in his book? Noting that men outnumbered women by six to one, a reviewer for the *Daily Express* asked, "Can it be that he is chary of taking them?" The critic continued, "Perhaps the unmistakable technique that Karsh has evolved of dazzling highlight, deep etched shadow and brilliant texture is inappropriate to a woman's world."[40] Feeling that the writer was taking "a controversial approach" to his work, Karsh struck back. "It is not true that I am chary of taking them," he replied, before going on to cite his recent portraits of Susan Strasberg and Anita Ekberg. "Nor," he continued, "do I treat them harshly as you say." He concluded by referring to himself in the third person: "But let me assure you, Karsh is not unkind to women."[41]

The reviewer for the *Daily Express* was right in claiming that women had played "an unaccustomed secondary role" in *Portraits of Greatness*. He was wrong, however, in suggesting that Karsh dealt only with "power and rugged emphasis." While on tour with him in Europe in 1954, Peter Miller had observed how Karsh had used harsher lighting for men because he felt they could afford to show the lines on their faces and reveal their characters. When it came to photographing women, Karsh had pulled back the floodlights and aimed the spotlights at the hair and shoulders in order to soften the faces of his female subjects.[42]

If Karsh had included his portrait of Anita Ekberg in *Portraits of Greatness*, the critic for the *Daily Express* might have seen a more balanced view of his work. Taken a few years before the Swedish actress took her famous plunge in Rome's Fontana di Trevi in Frederico Fellini's *La Dolce Vita*, the portrait is so sexually charged that Karsh might have been accused of producing a pin-up. But the portrait of Ekberg — and that of Brigitte Bardot — found no place in a book that was devoted to celebrating people who, as Karsh wrote in the preface, "have left their mark upon our time."[43]

Karsh's first two books of portraits made it clear what he was after: greatness, not sex; dignity, not glamour; authority, not sensation. As he told an interviewer a few years later, "I know it would be more sensational if I photographed a famous person taking a bath."[44] But unlike his contemporary, Philippe Halsman, Karsh would never have asked the physicist Robert Oppenheimer, or the Duke of Windsor and Mrs. Simpson, to jump into the air as he clicked the shutter. Or, like Ben Ross, have portrayed the young actress Audrey Hepburn looking tired and a little depressed. Or, like Flip Schulke, have donned a wet suit and bought an underwater camera so that he could photograph Cassius Clay shadowboxing on the bottom of a swimming pool. Or, finally, like Robert Frank, have brought out a book — *The Americans* — whose photographs would be pronounced "sinister, perverse, anti-American."[45]

Anita Ekberg, 1956

What Karsh may not have anticipated, however, was the extent to which magazine editors would impose new demands on their photographers. By the 1960s they wanted photographs of a new generation of people who were just on the verge of making names for themselves. It was a mood caught by the young British photographer Terry O'Neill, who was not awed by any of his famous subjects and felt comfortable photographing the Rolling Stones, the Beatles, and other youthful pop-culture celebrities. Likewise Lord Snowdon, who from his cozy vantage point — he had married Princess Margaret in 1960 — was proclaiming that photographers weren't artists but just "snappers" and was making his clients, from the queen to the American jazz singer Sammy Davis Junior, enter his studio by the back door.[46]

Karsh should not have been surprised, therefore, when Tom Blau told him in 1961 that he no longer wanted "normal Karshing." Or when his London agent encouraged him to be "a little more gimmicky" by suggesting that he photograph politicians dictating mail or memoranda into a tape recorder. Or, finally, when Blau suggested that Karsh "try and get them with their wives, that [show], as it were, the Power behind the Throne."[47]

Karsh took up some of Blau's suggestions, but he never wavered from his fundamental style or from his purpose: to bring out what was good, honest, and noble in his subjects.[48] He knew that his reputation rested on the fact that he could be counted on to present his subjects literally in the best light. He knew, as he wrote in his memoir, "that no purpose would be served if I were consciously to seek to convert what could be a portrait of greatness into a moment of weakness." Such moments, he added, were "not worthy of recording."[49]

Karsh was surely right. Long after he had become unfashionable, a portrait by Karsh—just like a Jaguar car or a Burberry raincoat—was still

Karsh in Morocco, very much in demand. Moreover, the saying "You hadn't arrived
by Marc Riboud, 1961 until you'd been 'Karshed'" was still valid. This was why, however much scrutiny Karsh's work was subjected to during the 1950s and 1960s, critics like Stuart Black would continue to proclaim that "without any doubt whatever Karsh is the greatest living photographer portraitist."[50] And this was why, whenever a new Karsh print arrived at Camera Press in London, "It was never just another portrait; it was always *the* portrait, *the* one that mysteriously defined the subject."[51]

BEFORE SHE DIED, Solange told Joyce Large that since Yousuf was completely incapable of living alone, he must remarry.[52] During the year following her death, Yousuf's busy schedule often kept him away from Ottawa and this also meant away from any tangible memory of Solange.

There were new ventures, like producing stills for Embassy Pictures' film *The Last Days of Sodom and Gomorrah*. The assignment took Karsh to Quazazate in Morocco in May 1961. During his month-long visit to North Africa, he went

on a deer hunt with the Moroccan prince, who chose to do his hunting from a helicopter. Karsh rode a camel in temperatures of 100 degrees Fahrenheit. He attended a folk-dance festival and an Oriental feast. And he took pictures.[53]

There were old ventures, too, during his year of mourning. Another collaboration with Bishop Sheen and H. V. Morton took Karsh to Rome in the autumn of 1961. The resulting book, *These Are the Sacraments*, was published in 1962. The same year, Karsh took on another assignment in Washington, D.C. This time he photographed the personalities around President Kennedy. Following Tom Blau's advice, Karsh made a note to portray the president with his brother, and to capture subjects outside of their buildings or while dictating memoranda into a tape recorder.[54]

Karsh never found it difficult to find assistants to accompany him on his travels or to have a friend read, then heavily revise, the text of a speech or any essay. Joyce Large did a marvellous job of keeping the correspondence and the phone calls moving in the right direction, and Hella Grabar and Ignas Gabalis managed things splendidly from their end. But there was no one to oversee the business, to do research prior to a sitting, or to take notes of the conversation during it. Above all, Karsh had no one with whom he could share a relaxing meal at his favourite Chinese restaurant, and no one to host the tennis and dinner parties at Little Wings that helped him solidify old connections and build on new ones.

Solange's absence from the camera room and on location sometimes put Yousuf in embarrassing situations. While photographing Bruce Hutchison in the early 1960s at the writer's Shawnigan Lake retreat on Vancouver Island, Karsh made one of his greatest faux pas. In preparation for the outdoor sitting he asked a handyman to stand in for Hutchison so that he could adjust the focus. He then ordered the man to hose down an arbutus tree in order to make it glisten and to do other jobs in preparation for the portrait. When the sitting was over Hutchison revealed, to Karsh's astonishment, that the handyman who had willingly followed his instructions was none other than the chief justice of British Columbia, J. O. Wilson. "Yousuf, a gentleman of sensitive manners could think of nothing to say and," Hutchison recalled, "drowned his confusion by plunging, fully clothed, into the lake."[55]

As his appointment book shows, Karsh first met Estrellita—also known as Estelle—Nachbar in Chicago on March 21, 1961.[56] He was in the city on assignment. His client, Dr. Walter C. Alvarez, was a man who had done for medicine what Bishop Fulton Sheen had done for religion. Dr. Alvarez's syndicated newspaper columns, his articles in *Geriatrics* and *Modern Medicine*, along with his many books, had made him the best-known physician in the United States. Helping him write his popular columns, his learned articles, and his books was a young and attractive medical researcher and writer.

Estrellita Marie Nachbar had been born to Philip Nachbar and Rachel Levi on June 19, 1930, in Newark, New Jersey. The young woman had specialized in English literature at Ohio Antioch College. Her literary skills stood her in good stead as assistant to Dr. Alvarez, whose photograph Karsh was taking for the cover of *Modern Medicine* magazine. Although she jokingly told a journalist that when she met Karsh, "something else clicked besides the shutter," Estrellita was absent from the sitting because she had the flu. It was not until the evening following the sitting, that Dr. Alvarez invited his young assistant to join him and the Canadian photographer for dinner.[57] Asked whether Karsh impressed her during their meeting in the Pump Room of Chicago's Ambassador East Hotel, Estrellita replied that "the first thought that came to me were his yearning eyes, something yearning about him."

Their courtship had an unpromising beginning. A few weeks after they had met, Joyce Large called Estrellita to ask whether she would like to accompany Yousuf to a performance of the Chicago Symphony Orchestra. "Thank you," Estrellita replied, "but I already have season tickets." Large tried again a few weeks later: "Mr. Karsh would like to know if there is anything you haven't seen?" There was, and the next time Karsh was in Chicago he took Estrellita to the theatre; shortly after that he took her to the Stratford Theatre in southern Ontario.[58]

For Karsh, "the team of a writer and photographer … held greater fascination than each of us operating independently, and I succeeded in convincing Estrellita (Spanish and Austrian origin) of the wisdom of this merging."[59] Estrellita, who later recalled being "past the panic side of twenty-five," never thought of getting married. "I was happy, I was fine, I was reading a hundred journals a month in the forefront of medicine." Even so, she soon discovered that she and Yousuf— whom she would sometimes affectionately refer to as Puppy Face, "were very comfortable together; it was as if we had known each other all our lives."[60]

Yousuf made several trips to Chicago after meeting Estrellita. Sometimes the visits were linked to a portrait sitting but more often they were made simply to court Estrellita. She in turn travelled to Ottawa. In May 1962, for example, Hella Grabar put Estrellita up for a week. By April 1962 the couple must have come to some sort of understanding. That month they met with Bishop Fulton J. Sheen in New York. It was on this occasion that he welcomed Estrellita into the Roman Catholic faith.[61]

Wedding, August 28, 1962: Estrellita Karsh, Bishop Fulton Sheen, Yousuf Karsh, by William Lovelace

Like everything that Karsh did, his marriage to Estrellita Nachbar on August 28, 1962, was big news. In fact the photograph that William Lovelace took of Karsh and his young bride was the first image to be sent from New York to the *Daily Express*'s headquarters in London by the satellite Telstar. In Lovelace's photograph Estrellita looked, as one journalist observed, "quite like the Mona Lisa."[62] Petite, animated, and exquisitely dressed and coiffed, Mrs. Estrellita Karsh was a match for any of Karsh's previous female subjects.

Hella Grabar and Joyce Large made the journey down to New York for the wedding. They saw Walter Alvarez walk the bride down the isle at St Patrick's Cathedral and Bishop Sheen perform the marriage ceremony in the intimate Lady Chapel. Malak Karsh, along with the rest of the Karsh family, was absent. Prior to the wedding, "Yousuf came to the studio and I thought he was going to tell me something," Barbara Karsh recalled, but "then he changed his mind." The news that Yousuf had remarried thus came as a shock to Karsh's ailing father and to his siblings. "I didn't know anything about it," Barbara recalled; "then I got a call from the *Citizen* asking me about Yousuf."[63]

It is an understatement to say that it must have been difficult for Estrellita to fill the shoes of Solange or that the move from Chicago to Ottawa was not easy. Estrellita was much younger and less well travelled than Solange. Estrellita was a stranger to Yousuf's family and friends. Above all, she professed little interest in photography. But the young woman possessed a sharp mind,

a formidable memory, and accomplished social skills, which she soon put to use in the studio.[64]

The fact that Estrellita was better educated than her husband became a joke between them. "Only this morning," Yousuf once recalled, "she told me that I was unburdened with professional education."[65] "You almost feel," Yousuf's niece Vivian Saykaly observed, "that she is a doctor herself."[66] Estrellita possessed a forceful personality, which she used to protect her husband. In order to make sure that Yousuf had no worries, she often played the bad cop to his good cop in dealing with other people.[67] Nor was Estrellita afraid of acting as Karsh's spokesperson in front of prying journalists. During a luncheon interview with a reporter for the *Toronto Telegram*, for example, it was Estrellita and not Yousuf who held forth. "Karsh let his very scintillating Estrellita do a lot of the talking while he, listening with a gentle smile, ate his seafood cocktail, rare beef, and cantaloupe."[68]

Alfried Krupp, 1964

A formidable editor and researcher, Estrellita helped Karsh formulate his thoughts just as she had helped Dr. Alvarez.[69] Well organized, she used this skill to help run the Karsh Studio and to plan her many trips with Yousuf. Photogenic, Estrellita was a good subject for her husband's camera. "I feel I have captured a beautiful woman of great photographic variety," Karsh told a British reporter after making a stunning portrait of his wife in 1963.[70]

Estrellita brought her passion for Greek and Roman archaeology and for medical and biblical history into the Karsh household. This helped to shape and develop Karsh's own interest in these things. It also made him take time off during an assignment. In Athens to photograph Constantine, the young king of Greece, Yousuf was walked off his feet by Estrellita's insistence that they visit the National Archaeological Museum, the Acropolis, *and* the Comita Epidaurus at Mycenae. "Karsh is becoming an archaeology nut," she reported to Joyce Large back in Ottawa.[71]

Karsh was, of course, anxious to please his young wife. This was why he agreed to take a break from his assignment in Germany to photograph the industrialist Alfried Krupp and the politicians Willy Brandt, Ludwig Erhard, and Konrad Adenauer for *Stern* magazine, in order to journey down the Rhine

and view the historic castles and to spend a day visiting both sides of the divided German city of Berlin. Karsh had seldom let pleasure interfere with his work before he met Estrellita. On the other hand, he had never had such an energetic, curious partner who was eager to discover Europe and eager to build on her knowledge of archaeology and medical history.

DURING HIS FIRST TRIP to Europe with Estrellita in September 1962, Karsh was interviewed on the steps of London's National Gallery. When the reporter asked whom he was going to photograph next, Karsh replied, "I don't know… Who is there left? I seem to have done them all."[72] This was not, of course, true. During the remainder of the decade, he and Estrellita made frequent trips to the United States and several trips to Europe. They also travelled to more exotic places like the Middle East, South Africa, and the Soviet Union in search of greatness.

Not everyone, however, wanted to pose for Karsh of Ottawa. President Charles de Gaulle and the king of Belgium declined an invitation in spite of the best efforts of the Canadian Embassy's staff in Paris and Brussels. The leaders of communist China and North Vietnam did not want to sit for Karsh either. Moreover, Karsh's hope for a private sitting with Winston Churchill was dashed in 1962 when Karsh found that the old man was too ill to be photographed. "Karsh did not want to intrude," Estrellita recalled.[73]

Two years later, Churchill rallied for his grandson's marriage to Minnie d'Erlanger. Randolph asked Karsh to take "exclusive official photographs" at his wedding reception, which was being held in his parents' Hyde Park Gate home in July 1964.[74] When Karsh arrived for the sitting he discovered that he did not have exclusive access to the wedding party. Randolph had hired a second photographer, Anthea Sieveking. The confusion of having two photographers on the job became apparent when *Time* magazine printed a photograph of Churchill at the reception holding a cat. The photograph was attributed to Karsh but he had not been close enough to the wedding party to take it.[75] The photograph had been taken by Sieveking.

The *Sunday Telegraph* got things right four months later when they published one of the photographs that Karsh had taken of Churchill at the reception. The photograph was used to mark the former prime minister's ninetieth birthday.[76] Cigar in hand, glass of his favourite champagne at his side, Churchill looks disgruntled and unamused as he peers into the lens of Karsh's camera. The photograph that Karsh produced was not how the British public and the rest of the world wanted to remember the great wartime leader. For Karsh the moment had clearly passed. His classic portrait, taken more than twenty years earlier, would have to stand. That it did so was shown by the fact that this was the photograph that newspaper editors chose to use to announce Churchill's death in the winter of 1965.

There were, of course, many important figures that Karsh did photograph during the 1960s. In 1963 he gained access to the new pontiff, Pope John XXIII. The same year Karsh returned to South Africa. At Rorke's Drift, where King Cetewayo had led a band of 4,000 Zulus against 250 British soldiers in 1879, Karsh produced stills for the film *Zulu*. In 1966 he was invited to make a portrait of Queen Elizabeth and the Duke of Edinburgh for Canada's centennial celebrations the following year. French president Georges Pompidou — unlike Charles de Gaulle — was also happy to have his portrait taken by Karsh. The next year Karsh was back on a film set, providing stills for the science fiction film *Planet of the Apes*. This time he did not get any further than Hollywood. But he did get to photograph Charlton Heston, to stay in his favourite hotel in Beverly Hills, and to earn the handsome fee of $4,000 for three days' work. Also in 1967, Karsh got the largest attendance at any exhibition to date when his Men Who Make Our World opened at Expo 67 in Montreal; and his prediction that the world's fair would give Canada "a new sense of its own validity" was realized.[77]

Throughout the 1960s there was an ongoing flood of commissions. High-profile companies like Mutual Life and Pepsi-Cola required portraits of their executives for their annual reports. And Karsh needed more portraits of outstanding personalities for his future publications. In 1965, Joan Miró, Man Ray, Max Ernst, Alberto Giacometti, and Jean-Paul Riopelle, among other artists, agreed to sit for Karsh. The same year, Laurence Olivier, whom Estrellita found to be as good-looking and as charming onstage as off, posed for Karsh, and so did Leslie Caron. Karsh also took on more exotic assignments and made the time for more archaeological excursions. In 1966, for example, Karsh took a break from photographing President Gamal Abdel Nasser to sail on the Nile with Estrellita to the Valley of the Kings. As usual, there were more assignments to be completed for *Life* magazine.

In 1964 Karsh photographed the new president of the United States, Lyndon B. Johnson, for *Life*. Repeating the reverential hand-clasped pose used in earlier portraits of Albert Einstein and President Kennedy, the resulting portrait was as uncharacteristic of the hard-hitting and frequently vulgar Lyndon Johnson as it had been for the womanizing John F. Kennedy. Karsh completed other assignments for *Life* during the 1960s but none was as exciting as what he called his "Mission to Moscow."

KARSH HAD WANTED to photograph Joseph Stalin since the closing days of the Second World War. Solange, Karsh wrote in 1949, had "the fantastic idea that perhaps the men of the Kremlin would want to claim me as one of their Nationals, considering I am Armenian, and she, having faith in me, thinks they would dearly love to have me portray them as they would want to be portrayed to the world."[78] By the spring of 1963, when he arrived in Russia, however, Stalin was long dead — and now, so too was Solange. A new regime, headed by Nikita Khrushchev, who had denounced Stalin's reign of terror in 1956, was carrying on its own Cold War. The campaign against the West had reached a tense moment in the autumn of 1962 when the Soviet Union had a standoff with the United States over Soviet plans to establish a missile base in Cuba. The missile crisis was resolved only when the Soviet Union's ships carrying the weapons agreed to turn back on the condition that the United States dismantle its missile bases in Turkey.

It may have seemed unlikely that a Canadian photographer would be welcomed into the Soviet Union in the spring of 1963. Yet, since 1956 Canada had been supplying wheat to the eastern regions of the Soviet Union and in 1963, the year that Karsh visited Moscow, Canada would sell a spectacular six million tons. During the same period, Soviet officials had been consulting private companies and government departments in Canada over everything from cement, road construction, natural gas, and irrigation to atomic energy. Works by Canadian writers, from former general secretary of the Canadian Communist Party Tim Buck to the travel writer William Irvine, the poet Wilson MacDonald and short-story writers Charles G. D. Roberts and Ernest Thompson Seton had been translated into Russian. Moreover, Glenn Gould and actors from Canada's Stratford Theatre Company had recently toured the Soviet Union.[79]

Karsh was invited to visit the country in 1962 by the Soviet-Canadian Friendship Society. In February 1963 he applied for, and later received, a visa to make "photographic portraits of some of the men and women of achievement in the USSR."[80] Karsh also hoped to mount an exhibition in the Soviet capital but according to Canada's ambassador in Moscow, Arnold Smith, the Russians were too heavily booked to organize it.[81]

Karsh, and his young assistant Peter Mitchell—Estrellita was to follow later—arrived at the Moscow airport in the middle of April 1963. Their first evening at the Bolshoi Ballet marked the beginning of a tightly organized itinerary. Arnold Smith, who had helped Karsh compile a list of personalities, arranged the appointments with the politicians, composers, astronauts, dancers, poets, and actors with the help of Soviet officials. Tom Blau of Camera Press in London helped Karsh too, giving him a series of questions to pose. Karsh thus asked the composer—and fellow Armenian—Aram Khachaturian what he thought about experimental music. Karsh asked the traditional painter Rave Korin to name the painters in the West whose work he admired and to list his favourite Old Masters. When Karsh ran out of questions relating directly to his subject's profession, he asked a number of general questions. What were the effects of the cold weather on the Russian temperament? Were Russians handy with tools and paint brushes like North Americans? How did Russians deal with alcoholism? And what were their views on the link between smoking and lung cancer?

Karsh did not get to photograph such controversial poets as Yevgeny Yevtushenko or Andrei Voznesensky or any of the avant-garde artists from Eli

Beliutin's Moscow studio, whose exhibition, held a month before Karsh arrived, had angered the Soviet premier. Karsh did, however, photograph most of the personalities on the list that Arnold Smith had compiled for him. Politicians were among Karsh's most enthusiastic subjects. A room had been set aside in Lenin's former apartment in the Kremlin, and when Karsh arrived he found a dozen or more politicians lined up outside the door. The only politician Karsh got to photograph in more congenial surroundings was the premier of the USSR and first secretary of the Soviet Communist Party, Nikita Khrushchev.

When Yousuf, Estrellita, and Peter Mitchell drove twenty-five miles west of Moscow to Khrushchev's dacha in Usovo, they found the Soviet leader looking tanned. Khrushchev had just returned from his summer residence on the Black Sea and, in Karsh's view, looked "like a man without a worry in the world."[82] This was, of course, hardly the case. There was a power struggle fermenting within the Soviet Communist Party. Before his dismissal in the autumn of 1964, Khrushchev would be accused of creating a personality cult, of introducing erratic administrative practices, and of making errors in foreign policy. On that warm spring day when Yousuf and Estrellita found Khrushchev surrounded by his wife, Nina, his daughters, and his grandchildren, he possessed an air of confidence. His wife, Nina, according to Estrellita, was "the most liberated, sensitive woman."[83]

Nikita Khrushchev, 1963

Khrushchev proved to be "an easy and obliging subject" for Karsh.[84] He allowed the Canadian photographer to photograph the palms of his hands. The resulting photograph was analyzed by a palmist, who pronounced the Soviet leader sensitive, possessing high aspirations, great ambition, pride, and a sense of personal dignity.[85] Khrushchev also posed with his arm high in the air, as if saluting the troops. And, following Karsh's instructions once again, he donned a heavy fur coat and knitted hat. "Be quick it's very warm," Khrushchev exclaimed, "and this is a ferocious animal. It is likely to eat me up."[86]

Karsh was not, of course, the first Western photographer to portray Khrushchev in such a relaxed manner.[87] Yet he was probably one of the few Western photographers who could be relied upon to produce a positive image of the Soviet leader. This was important, because the image that most people in the West had of Khrushchev was of a man who exuded a peasant shrewdness, was mistrustful, and possessed a fiery temperament that had caused him to bang his shoe on a table at the United Nations in 1959. Karsh had himself shared this view of the Soviet premier. Less than a year before meeting Khrushchev, he had told a reporter that the Soviet leader had "a dull, uninteresting face—like a meatball."[88] When Karsh met Khrushchev six months later, however, he found the Soviet leader jovial and Estrellita found him charming. And this was how Karsh portrayed him.

KARSH'S CONTACT AT the Soviet Canadian Friendship Society was concerned when he learned that Karsh's photographs were to appear in the conservative publication *Life*. Respecting that concern—and the wishes of the Canadian ambassador, who hoped that the magazine would "be appropriately dignified and non-controversial"—Karsh secured the editor's promise that his portraits would be accompanied by "objective" captions.[89]

Karsh's colour portrait of the Soviet leader wearing his snow leopard fur coat appeared in *Life*'s special issue on the Soviet Union on September 13, 1963. For the magazine's staff writer, this photograph represented "one of the proudest trophies of the famous Canadian portraitist's long career of photographing the shakers and movers of the world."[90] The text accompanying the portraits of Nina Khrushchev and other dignitaries was not, as Karsh feared they might be, heavy handed. Moreover, the magazine's Moscow correspondent went out of his way to point out that the inconsistencies within the Soviet Union held promise and "that the contending winds of the Cold War can blow warmer than any realist, East or West, expected not so very long ago."[91]

Karsh was pleased that the main objective of his "Mission to Moscow" had been achieved, namely, making his portraits serve "as messengers of good will."[92] According to the *Daily Express*, which published his Russian portraits before *Life*, Karsh had given "Communism a Face." Khrushchev and his colleagues did not look like politicians, or tyrants, or "men who came up in the days of Stalin when a badly timed smile could earn a bullet in the neck." President Leonid

Brezhnev looked no different from a hard-bargaining sales director. Even Karsh's portrait of the tough-minded party secretary, L. F. Ilyichev, resembled, in the journalist's view, a well-heeled middle-class American businessman in the process of giving a tip on the stock market.[93] And this is precisely how Karsh saw everyone he photographed in the Soviet Union too: "I have come to the conclusion that the Russians I photographed had much in common with portrait subjects everywhere."[94]

Not everyone was happy with Karsh's visit to the Soviet Union. Karsh had told Khrushchev that the Canadian Embassy would forward him copies of his portraits soon after the sitting. But since the Soviet Union did not subscribe to the World Copyright Convention, the Canadian ambassador was reluctant to do this: "if the Soviet leaders get advance copies, the portraits might be published here first."[95] It was not, therefore, until January 1964 that the Canadian Embassy in Moscow duly presented Khrushchev with Karsh's Russian photographs. The Soviet officials were happy with the results when they eventually received them. Indeed, the American branch of the Soviet Friendship Society was so pleased that one of its members, Mandel Terman, wanted to recommend Karsh for the Lenin Peace Prize.[96] Karsh asked the Canadian minister of External Affairs, Paul Martin, whether he should accept the prize should it be offered to him. Because the award was notoriously given to someone who had served the Soviet cause, Martin suggested that Karsh might save himself—and no doubt the Liberal government too—from possible embarrassment by suggesting that the recommendation be quashed.[97]

Karsh nevertheless received more tangible rewards from his "Mission to Moscow." Germany's *Stern* and London's *Daily Express* and *Illustrated London News* paid handsomely for the rights to the black-and-white photographs Karsh took in Moscow.[98] *Life*, which had secured the rights to Karsh's colour work, along with other newspapers and magazines in North America that produced his photographs in black and white, paid him well too.

But this was not the only reason Karsh's earnings began to soar. On November 22, 1963, President John F. Kennedy was assassinated. Due to the marketing skills of Alacaret Reproductions, Karsh's portrait of John and Jackie Kennedy became the fastest-selling lithograph in North America. At the same time Karsh decided to employ Rapho-Guillumette Pictures, rather than Pix Incorporated, to handle the American sales of his photographs. Little wonder that 1964 was a bumper year for Karsh of Ottawa.[99] Little wonder also that earnings from portrait sittings, for which Karsh now charged $1,000, took second place to the sale of his prints.

Unfashionable Karsh may have been by the late 1960s but he was certainly richer than ever before. Requests for reproductions of his photographs and for sittings had never been more plentiful. Over sixty by the end of the decade, Karsh had also learned to take some time off. This did not mean that he now chose to rest on his laurels or that he planned to ease himself into retirement. Karsh remained a man of enormous energy. He defined himself through his work, through his accumulation of personalities—both as subjects and, often, as friends. Moreover, he had an energetic young wife who was eager to take his work in new directions and to new audiences. One chapter of his career had closed; another was opening.

Yousuf Karsh and
Estrellita Karsh, by
Malak Karsh, National
Arts Centre, 1969

Apotheosis

Speaking at the Château Laurier Hotel's seventy-fifth birthday celebration in 1987, Karsh told his audience, "To work in the Chateau is to be a citizen of a city within a city."[1] The famous hotel had not only made Karsh an honorary member but had helped make him become a citizen of the world. The Château had been the venue of his first significant commission, when, under the direction of his boss, John Powis, he had photographed the British prime minister Neville Chamberlain at the Imperial Economic Conference in 1932. The Château had exhibited his work—more than once. During the early years of his career, the Château's winding staircase, its alcoves, and intimate corners had provided settings for his portraits. And, in the recent past, the Château's ballroom had shown his portraits of the popular rock group Rush and the classical violinist Jascha Heifetz. It was not surprising, therefore, that a collection of rooms in the hotel became Karsh's Ottawa studio in 1972.

Hella Grabar had always found the Sparks Street studio too large.[2] The new studio, located on the sixth floor of the hotel, had one-third the floor space of the former studio. There was a camera room—much smaller than before—as well as a tiny finishing room, a room for Ignas Gabalis, and a reception room—now manned by the capable Mary Alderman, who had recently replaced Joyce

Large. Over the course of the next twenty years it was in this studio that, with the help of Mary Alderman and his assistants, Karsh would photograph the jubilant Canadian Nobel laureate Gerhard Herzberg, the brilliant Inuit artist Kenojuak Ashevak, the weary and determined Bishop Desmond Tutu, along with many other personalities.

According to the former manager of the Château Laurier, Franco J. Anglesio, "the Château benefited from him [Karsh] being there, so he was able to get an arrangement." And Anglesio was not surprised to find that Karsh soon became "an institution."[3] On cold winter days Karsh avoided the black ice on Ottawa's slippery sidewalks by taking his exercise in the hotel's long corridors. Often at his heels was the black poodle Clicquot, to whom the hotel turned a blind eye. Most of the time, however, Karsh was in room 658, working.

A few years earlier, Estrellita had given Karsh's domestic environment a facelift. With the help of the interior decorator Claude Vermette, the walls of the Little Wings music room were adorned with beige-gold Japanese wallpaper. A ceiling-high ceramic fireplace, flanked by a gold-flecked panel, was installed in the living room. Bookcases were built in the library to house Estrellita's prized collection of nineteenth-century children's books. A buzzer was concealed under the dining room table so that the cook could be discreetly summoned from the kitchen. Yousuf's bathroom was refurbished in black marble with gold plumbing fixtures. And every electrical outlet in the house was hidden: "I can't tell you how many times I would take a picture and there was a light switch there," Karsh told the young student Pamela Belyea.

A friend of Malak and Barbara Karsh's teenage son Laurie, Pamela Belyea got a summer job at Little Wings around the time that Karsh moved his studio into the Château Laurier. Yousuf and Estrellita's long-time chauffeur-gardener and maid-cook had just been dismissed and Pamela and Laurie were a temporary solution to the loss of professional staff.

It was a daunting summer job for the seventeen-year-old high school student. Among Belyea's daily chores were preparing poached eggs at breakfast, changing the bed linen and towels, washing down the flagstones, polishing the floor-to-ceiling glass windows, feeding the dog—Clicquot ate from a silver dish—and dealing with the laundry. When the Karshes were out of town, Pamela followed

Estrellita's list of things to do. "The house was scary on my own," Belyea recalled, "because you would keep seeing your reflection in three or four panes of glass."

Although Belyea later claimed to have worked twelve to fourteen hours a day and lost ten pounds, she felt that she could never fulfill what was required. "They soon discovered how imperfect I was," said Belyea, who parted company with the Karshes at the end of the summer. Yet for the young student, who would go on to become the director of the Seattle Academy of Fine Art, Little Wings was in retrospect an exciting place to be. There was a Venetian glass chandelier and a sarcophagus collected on one of the Karshes' many trips to Europe. There were works by Chagall, Moore, Lipschitz, Epstein, and Picasso — all gifts from artists whom Karsh had photographed. As Belyea recalls, "the whole home was a showcase."[4]

Little Wings had to be a showcase because it was here that Yousuf and Estrellita entertained prospective clients. In the winter of 1979, for

Estrellita Twirling (in
the Château Laurier
apartment), 1983

example, Joan Baez, the architect Arthur Erickson, the designer Francisco Kripacz, the former Canadian ambassador to Egypt and to Russia, Arnold Smith, along with Alberta premier Peter Lougheed and his wife, Jeanne, were among Estrellita and Yousuf's guests for dinner. Not surprisingly, most of them were to find their way to his studio and most of them would frequently return to Little Wings as friends.

When a suite of rooms on the third floor of the Château Laurier became Yousuf and Estrellita's permanent home in 1982, the couple made sure that they were still "surrounded by things they loved."[5] Refurbished in the art deco style by the interior designer Lary Aune, the apartment not only had a convenient location, it also solved Yousuf and Estrellita's domestic employment problems. It put Yousuf closer to his studio. And it made entertaining more convenient: guests no longer had to drive to the outskirts of the city on a snowy evening, and dinner could be ordered from the Château's kitchen. At the Karshes' first dinner party in their new home in February 1982, for example, were the former cabinet secretary Gordon Robertson and his wife, the ambassador of Austria, August Aarter, Lady Moran, the wife of the British high commissioner, and Ambassador and Madame Nourreddine Hasnoui of Morocco.

Most of the people whom Yousuf and Estrellita entertained would not only be photographed, they would become friends. The Karshes' circle of friends was wide ranging. It included not only their clients, lawyers, doctors, and accountants but also the hotel staff at the Château Laurier. All of these people were treated in the same gracious manner.

Karsh had always entertained his clients at home with a view to drumming up business. And during the 1970s and 1980s it was no less important for him to do so. This was partly because the global economic downturn that began in the early 1970s had caused magazines like *Life* and *Collier's Weekly* to be suspended or closed down altogether. Karsh, who had contributed to both magazines, was not surprisingly "disheartened" by this turn of events, calling it a "tragedy for creative photography."[6]

The increasing prominence of other portrait photographers—some of whom were better connected than Karsh to the younger generation of celebrities and others who put the candid shot above the dignity of the person they were photographing—was another concern for Karsh. Getting to the younger members of Britain's royal family, for example, was particularly difficult, because Lords Lichfield and Snowdon had priority since they were related by blood or marriage.

Pierre Elliott
Trudeau, 1968

Though Karsh photographed the queen, the duke, and their grandchildren in 1984 and again in 1987, his repeated attempts to make portraits of the Duke and Duchess of York and, above all, of Prince Charles and Diana, Princess of Wales came to naught, even though Prime Minister Pierre Elliott Trudeau had introduced Karsh to the Prince of Wales and his consort at a barbecue in 1983. "They had been photographed by Snowdon and Lichfield," a disappointed Tom Blau reported to Karsh from London, "and a thousand times by a band of paparazzi who live off them as maggots live off apples."[7]

Karsh could, to be sure, still rest content that American presidents and British prime ministers continued to summon him to the White House and to Number Ten Downing Street. But many other high-profile personalities—from Frank Sinatra and Marlon Brando to Margaret Trudeau, British playwright Harold Pinter, and statesmen like the German Chancellor Helmut Schmidt and China's Mao Zedong—were simply not interested in being Karshed. And even many of the people who did eventually agreed to sit for Karsh had initially been reluctant to accept. Sophia Loren would not cooperate if the portrait was destined "for *Playboy* etc." It was only when she was assured that the Canadian photographer intended to use the photograph in one of his books that she professed herself "happy to meet with Yousuf Karsh."[8]

In a further effort to drum up business, Karsh drew on his old tactics. He made a point of keeping in touch with important clients. In 1980 he gave Prime Minister Trudeau his "warmest congratulations on your recent triumph and your return to guiding the destiny of our nation," adding, at the end of his letter, that the time had come "when I should make a more up to date portrait of you, not only for a forthcoming book but also for the world press."[9] Following a sitting with Fidel Castro, he told the Cuban leader, "I am pleased to have, at long last, the opportunity of photographing you—a man who has made an impact on history of the twentieth century."[10]

Gérard Depardieu, 1985

Karsh also saw to it that any potential client received a copy of his most recent publication. "To President Elect Ronald Reagan and the First Lady, Nancy Reagan who carry on their shoulders the hope and dreams of the United States of America" was how Karsh inscribed a volume of photographs in 1981.[11] Casting the net more widely, he took out an advertisement in the *New Yorker* for portrait sittings.

Karsh also accepted assistance from friends and acquaintances like the Calgary businessman Ted Riback. It was Riback who, in the mid-1970s, introduced Karsh to potential clients in Calgary and at his Rancho Mirage in Palm Springs, California. Riback even drove Karsh and his assistant Joseph Zedar to their appointments and, on several occasions, waited while Karsh took a two-hour nap after lunch, before driving him to the next appointment.[12] Above all, Karsh rarely refused an invitation to a dinner party where he might meet potential clients. At Mr. Liu's Chinese restaurant in Hollywood in 1972, for example, he met Ann-Margret, Jean-Louis Trintignant, and Julie Andrews, all of whom would be photographed.

Karsh also continued to rely on Tom Blau at Camera Press in London to sell his photographs in Europe and to arrange further assignments. Karsh's two big commissions with *Paris Match* magazine, in 1981 and 1985, came as a result of Tom Blau's efforts. This was how Karsh came to photograph the actors Gérard

Depardieu, Sophia Loren, and Jean-Paul Belmondo, and the French politicians Valéry Giscard d'Estaing, François Mitterrand, and Jacques Chirac. These commissions not only kept Karsh's name before the European public, they were also lucrative. When one of Karsh's portraits was used on the cover of *Paris Match*, he got a handsome $12,000. If the image appeared inside the magazine, the fee went down to $3,500.[13]

In the days before frequent-flyer air points, Karsh used his charm to reduce his travel expenses. "My visit to Rome," he told an airline executive in 1979, "was made all the more leisurable [*sic*] the moment I stepped on the Pan American plane and met with your efficiency and ability to smooth my way through customs and immigration."[14] Pan American Airlines had not only helped Karsh through customs, they had also given free passage to his heavy photographic equipment. And the airline did this more than once.

By the late 1960s, Karsh knew that publishing lavish books of photographs and attracting important clients went hand in hand. Calling on the writing skills of Estrellita, the organizational know-how of Hella Grabar, the printing ability of Ignas Gabalis, and the support of editors at the University of Toronto Press, Karsh brought out *Karsh Portfolio* in 1967, *Faces of Our Time* in 1971, *Karsh Portraits* in 1976, *Karsh Canadians* in 1978, and in 1983 the handsome volume *Karsh: A Fifty-Year Retrospective*. Karsh's fans could purchase a special edition of the last book — enclosed in a case lined with white silk and accompanied by a portrait of Winston Churchill, Ernest Hemingway, Pablo Casals, or Georgia O'Keeffe — for $1,000.

In 1992 Karsh changed publishers. That year Boston's Bulfinch Press brought out his first book of colour photographs, *Karsh: American Legends*, and, four years later, a revised edition of *Karsh: A Fifty-Year Retrospective* titled *Karsh: A Sixty-Year Retrospective*. Once again the staff at the Karsh Studio, along with Karsh's assistant Jerry Fielder and Estrellita, who took time out from her lecturing and writing assignments in the medical world, helped Karsh prepare this book for publication.

As important as it was to put his portraits between covers, equally so was to show them on the walls of art galleries. From the late 1960s Karsh got maximum exposure from every exhibition that was mounted of his work. For example, the portraits brought together for a major exhibition at Expo 67, entitled Men

Who Make Our World, not only toured galleries in North America, Australia, and Japan over the course of twenty years but were published in the book *Karsh Portfolio*. The same procedure was followed with the 1983 exhibition Karsh: A Fifty-Year Retrospective. Eastman Kodak, which sponsored the exhibition at the International Center of Photography in New York, sent the show on tour throughout North America and Europe, while the University of Toronto Press ensured that the photographs on display were brought together in a book bearing the same name as the exhibition.

Art galleries were happy to show Karsh's work and to sell his books. They were also eager to acquire his portraits. Some — like the Metropolitan Museum of Art and the Museum of Modern Art in New York and the Bibliothèque nationale de France in Paris, to name just three — already had some of Karsh's work in their permanent collections. But other galleries had no examples of his work at all. Karsh changed this by making entire exhibitions available for purchase. He also made his exhibitions attractive by frequently including portraits that related to the town or country where the exhibition was being held. In Japan, where he had served as photographic advisor to EXPO '70, for example, he saw to it that portraits of the literary Nobel laureate Yasunari Kawabata, along with other Japanese "living human treasures," were featured when his work was shown at a later date. He did the same in other museums and galleries where his work appeared. If Karsh had been a painter or sculptor, museums would not have been in a position to purchase an entire exhibition. Photographs, however, were easily reproduced, giving the owner the "original" copy. Photographs were easy to transport. And, above all, they were inexpensive compared to paintings and sculptures.[15] This is why the Glenbow Art Gallery in Alberta and other museums and galleries around the world were able to acquire extensive collections of Karsh's work.

WHILE THE EXHIBITION, publication, and acquisition of Karsh's photographs by public institutions during the 1970s and 1980s made him known to a larger number of people than ever before, his fame came at a price. Why, critics started to ask, was Karsh publishing and exhibiting his portraits of personalities

from the 1940s and 1950s—Sibelius, Shaw, Einstein, Hemingway, and, of course, Churchill—again and again?"[16]

Recounting the same stories during Karsh's many interviews with the press and public lectures was a related cause for complaint. "The anecdotes are many and polished, but in the spaces between them his conversation is halting and guarded," wrote the journalist Douglas Fetherling after interviewing Karsh in 1976; and it was now that he perceptively called Karsh an unknown quantity who "would likely remain so even if he gave two interviews twice daily."[17] Yet many people who knew Karsh personally would talk about his sense of fun. Here was a man who had spent an hour trying on women's hats in an Italian shop and who had jumped into a lake after he had mistaken a high-ranking official for the local handyman. Karsh never exposed this side of his personality to anyone who interviewed him. Instead he went into work mode and that meant talking about his encounters with famous people and keeping the interviewers at a distance by hiding behind his old-world charm. As a result, he could appear shallow and repetitive, and this was increas-   Yasunari Kawabata, 1969
ingly how journalists represented him in the press.

There were other criticisms of Karsh too, potentially more damaging to his reputation than comments on his own personality. Writing in the prestigious *Popular Photography* magazine, A. D. Coleman went further than most when he observed that "Karsh's work has evidenced no growth or change in several decades, and that his much-vaunted style appears to be a trap from which he is incapable of escaping even momentarily." Admittedly, Coleman's attack met with a barrage of responses from Karsh supporters. One of them claimed, in a letter to the editor of the journal, that Coleman was unworthy to kiss the ground on which Karsh walked, while another suggested that the critic was simply jealous.[18]

For all that, such observations possessed an undeniable element of truth. Karsh did repeat stories relating to his portrait sittings, telling Jerry Fielder that he did not want "to keep telling the same stories but people wanted to hear them."[19] He did publish the same photographs—mostly from the 1940s and 1950s—in successive books. And, even though he added a lengthy biographical

W. H. Auden, 1972

Tom Wolfe, 1990

chapter to *Karsh: A Fifty-Year Retrospective*, there was little of a personal nature that had not already appeared in his 1962 memoir, *In Search of Greatness*.

On the other hand, some of the criticism that was directed toward Karsh was unwarranted. He was in fact open to experiment. In the early 1970s he began to lighten the background in his portraits, a device that he had always reserved for royalty. He depicted more of his subjects in full and three-quarter-length poses. Karsh brought these stylistic innovations together in the stunning portrait of the French actor Gérard Depardieu. Karsh also began to take more of his portraits out of doors. The portrait of W. H. Auden taken at dusk in the London garden of fellow poet Stephen Spender shows what Karsh could do with a 35-mm camera and minimal light when he abandoned his spots and flood-lights, his large-format 8-by-10-inch Rolleiflex camera, and his 14-inch lens. Finally, there was an immediacy in portraits like that of Depardieu and Tom Wolfe which avoided what Barry Callaghan had called the "white vinyl qual-ity" that sometimes made the skin and hair of Karsh's earlier subjects appear inhuman.[20]

KARSH ALWAYS INSISTED that he and Estrellita blended their worlds, "each adding a new dimension to the other."[21] This was never more apparent than in the 1970s and 1980s. While Estrellita became a force in the studio following her marriage to Yousuf in 1962, she had maintained her medical interests. She spoke at numerous conferences devoted to the history of medicine, contributed articles to medical journals as well as to the *Encyclopaedia Britannica*, and curated exhibitions relating to medicine. Yousuf encouraged Estrellita in these endeavours: in 1976 he inscribed a catalogue accompanying an exhibition, The Physician as Artist, that Estrellita had curated in Boston: "I am very proud of you, darling."[22] And he benefited from her knowledge and her connections in the medical world. Thanks to Estrellita, Yousuf watched Dr. Michael E. DeBakey perform open-heart surgery. In 1975 Karsh mounted an exhibition of portraits including Carl Jung and Albert Schweitzer, under the rubric Healers of Our Age, at Boston's Frances Countway Library of Medicine. And from the

middle of the 1960s he took the annual photograph of a selected child for the Muscular Dystrophy Association.

Karsh threw himself into this last project. He visited the muscular dystrophy clinic in New York and kept in touch with many of the children who had appeared on the annual posters. When he learned in 1978 that two of the poster children had died, "he went to pieces."[23] Karsh even appeared with the former comedian Jerry Lewis in fundraising telethons for the Muscular Dystrophy Association. On television in June 1973, Karsh was shown standing in front of four easels. Displayed on three of them were his portraits of Sir Alexander Fleming, who discovered penicillin, Dr. Jonas Salk, who developed the vaccination against polio, and Dr. Charles Best, who developed insulin. The fourth easel remained vacant because, Karsh told his television audience, "I am still eager to photograph the man or woman who will help bring muscular dystrophy under control."[24]

Sophia Loren with Her
Son Eduardo, 1981

There were other signs that Karsh was widening his repertoire. In 1978 he devoted an entire volume of photographs, *Karsh Canadians*, as "a loving tribute to the human side of our nation."[25]

Booksellers were apparently relieved that there would be "some new faces among all those tired old heroes."[26] He also made an effort to exhibit and to publish photographs that he had produced in the 1950s for his Canadian cities and industrial assignments. His attempts to do so were met with a reprimand from one publisher, who felt that photographs of landscapes, cities, and factories would not be expected and would complicate the format of a publication devoted largely to Karsh's portraits.[27]

Karsh also made his definition of greatness more inclusive. In his portrait session with Sophia Loren in 1981 he included her son Eduardo. Karsh had begun to photograph younger subjects because, in his view, they exhibited "a deep sense of responsibility and concern and response to the world which no longer fits the old stereotype of youthfulness."[28] He felt that artists, writers, and musicians were important subjects too, because their influence appeared to be even greater and more enduring than that of politicians.

Although Karsh still said, defiantly, that he was a hero-worshipper and preferred photographing men, by the 1970s he was less restrictive about whom he

photographed—as long as they were famous, of course. His book *Faces of Our Time* included the Indian sitar player Ravi Shankar; *Karsh Portraits* included the boxer Muhammad Ali; and in *American Legends* there was not one political figure to be found among the chefs, actors, sportsmen and sportswomen, and jazz musicians.

In 1970 Karsh agreed to photograph the creator of *Playboy* magazine, Hugh Hefner. During the sitting, the two men got along well. Following his visit to the Playboy Mansion, Karsh was inspired to purchase a rabbit's head from Steuben Glass Works. He also made an unprecedented decision to allow Hefner to keep the colour transparencies from the sitting and exert the copyright on them.

In almost every other case, however, Karsh retained copyright over the images he produced. This enabled him to have a say in where and how his work was published and exhibited. For example, in the late 1980s Karsh presented a print of his iconic portrait of Churchill to the curator of the Cabinet War Rooms in London, with the hope that hanging the portrait in the entrance foyer would provide "a splendid introduction to the War Rooms and to Churchill."[29] When Karsh discovered that the portrait had been installed in the newly opened Conference Room instead, he rebelled. In 1987 Karsh exercised more control over where another copy of the same portrait would hang in the Speaker's Office of the Canadian Houses of Parliament. Following Karsh's instructions, it was hung on the wall in front of where Winston Churchill had stood for his portrait.

Less reverently, in 1970 a hairdressing salon in Miami called Churchill's used a version of "The Roaring Lion" in a newspaper advertisement. It was not the salon's satirical adaptation of Churchill's phrases—"We shall never surrender to a bad haircut"—that gave Karsh cause for concern, but rather the way in which his portrait had been altered: an imaginative artist had given Churchill a bouffant hairstyle.[30] On the other hand, Karsh himself was ready enough to cash in on the Churchill link. During preparation of the television documentary *The Young Winston*, Karsh willingly agreed to photograph the actor Simon Ward in the Speaker's Chamber. The copycat pose was published on the cover of *Life* in 1972.

Karsh was less particular about where and how his other photographs appeared during the 1970s and 1980s. For example, in 1983 he allowed the mass-circulation *People* magazine to print his portraits of O'Keeffe, Nureyev, Khrushchev, Lorre, and Casals in their December issue. And even though he always considered his work in black and white to be his best, he began to include colour photographs in his books. Commenting on the twelve colour plates that appeared in *Karsh: A Fifty-Year Retrospective*, Paul Russell felt that Karsh had not achieved "the sense of monumental portraition that always distinguished his monochromes." This was a telling point. Karsh had only moved to colour because, as one of his assistants recalled, "all the clients expected it."[31] But Karsh had to pay a high price for pleasing his clients. As Russell rightly noted, colour could "transform a hero into the man next door," while black and white kept "the hero at a distance which is where, and how, heroes remain heroic in the public mind."[32]

KARSH HAD GIVEN many well-received public talks at art galleries and to photographic societies since the days when he and Solange had performed their skits. Such talks sometimes led to more formal lectures and to teaching. In 1951 he had given a short course in press photography at the William Taylor School of Journalism at Kent State in Ohio. In 1966 he had done the same at the famous school of photography in Westport, Connecticut. Due to the expansion, from the late 1960s, of departments of fine art and the addition of photography to their curricula, Karsh found himself attached to the college of fine arts to Ohio State University in 1967 and to Emerson College in Boston.[33] He welcomed these brief but intensive sessions with students, reporting, towards the end of his career, that he had been "buoyed by the contact with fresh viewpoints and youthful experimentation, in a humanistic setting" at both institutions.[34]

From the 1970s on, there were many other opportunities for Karsh to lecture. Photographers like Ansel Adams and Richard Avedon, who were just as eager to pass on their skills to the next generation of students, offered summer school courses and workshops. In 1977 Karsh joined a week-long workshop run by

Ansel Adams in Yosemite, California. There, Karsh successfully instilled in his students the values of humility, honesty, diplomacy, and striving for perfection.[35] "Judging from the letters and comments," Adams told him after the conclusion of the workshop, "you have inspired many of the students and impressed them greatly, both as an artist and as a 'humanist.'"[36] Karsh was to return to Yosemite in 1988.

Dressed in suits designed by Angelo Litrico from Men's High Fashion in Rome and in stylish shirts with their unique collars made by Ottawa's equally fashionable tailor Levonian, Karsh would stand before his students and tell them about his escape from Mardin, Turkey, about studying with John Garo in Boston, and about establishing his own studio in Ottawa. He stressed the importance of being well read and well versed in music and art; photographers were more than just good technicians. He urged his class to study the work of the masters—Julia Margaret Cameron, Edward Steichen, and Alfred Stieglitz—and of the younger generation of photographers like Irving Penn and Richard Avedon. Karsh advised his students to pay attention to all aspects of their subjects before clicking the shutter. This entailed noting everything from what their subjects thought to how their voices sounded and realizing that "a portrait sitting must develop between the two on both sides of the camera." It was only by doing these things that the student-photographers would be able to capture the "fire" that Karsh insisted all great men had "burning away" inside them.[37]

Karsh did not jump on to the more lucrative lecture podiums until 1973. That year he joined speakers including Canadian filmmaker Norman Jewison and writer Arthur Hailey on the Odyssey of Knowledge cruise, which took him and Estrellita to ports around the Mediterranean on the luxury liner QE2. A decade later, Karsh participated in IBM's Pride of Performance lecture series, which saw the likes of the British ballerina Margot Fonteyn telling executives and their spouses how she became the person she was. Paying $8,500 a talk plus first-class travel expenses, this lecture series took Yousuf and Estrellita to engagements in San Diego, Zurich, San Francisco, and Vancouver, among other places. Besides being lucrative and good publicity, it was "a lot of fun." Participating in lecture tours like this, Estrellita recalls, "was one of the perks of being famous."[38]

IBM obviously hoped to inspire their executives by bringing them face to face with people like Fonteyn and Karsh. A number of duly appreciative comments from IBM's employees suggest that the company had achieved its goal. "Your entire presentation was so incredible," one employee gushed to Karsh after hearing him speak in Vancouver, "I felt so fortunate, at twenty-five years of age, to be in the presence of such a great human being as yourself who has met so many history makers and wonderful entertainers."[39] Another wrote, feelingly, that Karsh's rags-to-riches story and his account of photographing famous people had helped reveal "the hope in John F. Kennedy's portrait, the infinite wisdom and understanding in Hemingway's eyes, and the absolute strength of Churchill's character."[40]

Such comments do not simply represent approbation of a good lecture; they are a homage to the lecturer. By this stage of his career, here was a uniquely famous photographer. "Yes, Karsh, the man who takes pictures of greats, has become one of the greats himself," was how one journalist put it.[41] This was indeed flattering. But the point is not so much whether Karsh fulfilled his own conception of "greatness" but that, like many of the people he was photographing, he was now a celebrity too. He attracted the sort of attention that celebrities attract; and he cultivated it, not least by doing a number of things that celebrities do.

Known as a connoisseur of the human form, Karsh became a judge during the late 1960s and early 1970s of the Miss Universe, Miss U.S.A., and Miss Dominion of Canada beauty pageants. As in everything he did, Karsh took the job seriously. He followed the ethnically restrictive judging instructions to make sure that the torso was well formed, that the back lines of the shoulder were almost flat, and that no hard edges separated the face from the hair. He also compiled a series of questions to ask the candidates: "How important is a woman's beauty to your goal in life and to your happiness?" And "Which of your personality traits do you like best about yourself and which least?"[42]

Karsh had long taken on advertising commissions. On assignment for Ontario's Department of Tourism and Information in 1970, he travelled on the Algoma Central Railway to Northern Ontario in order to photograph Northerners both as individuals and as symbols of the rugged Northern Ontario landscape.

In Sault Ste. Marie he demonstrated his wit and charm when a female reporter met him at the train station. "I'd like to arrange an interview with you, perhaps in your hotel room," she told Karsh. "Alone, I hope," was Karsh's cheeky reply.[43]

Like other celebrities, Karsh was paid to endorse products. In the mid-1970s he became "a roving ambassador" for the newly developed Polaroid camera. In writing to an executive of the company in 1975, Karsh showed that he fully appreciated what this bargain entailed. "In accepting this position, I will give it my reputation, my pride, and every presentation I do will be done with dedication and integrity," he affirmed, and the fact that his reputation was at stake was naturally reflected in the terms he demanded: "It must be assumed that I am on a retainer fee for Polaroid."[44] The company agreed and Karsh received an annual fee — one year it reached $12,000 — to endorse the new camera. According to a writer for Toronto's *Globe and Mail* who observed Karsh counting off the seconds after taking a portrait with a Polaroid camera of the conductor of the Boston Pops, Arthur Fiedler, "Karsh came up with a finished portrait that will stand with anything else he has done."[45]

There was a further twist to the sort of celebrity endorsements in which Karsh became involved. In 1988, for example, he photographed Wayne Gretzky "not as a hockey player, but as a high-profile North American businessman… who worked hard to achieve success and believes that a caring, and hard-working bank has a role to play in achieving future goals."[46] Thus the Canadian branch of Lloyds Bank was paying the celebrity photographer to photograph the celebrity hockey player, whom they were also paying, in order to link all their names together to mutual advantage.

EVER SINCE PUBLISHING his portrait of Churchill in 1942, Karsh had been besieged with requests from young photographers to join his studio. He had graciously answered every request but rarely took anyone on as an apprentice.[47] One reason was that he travelled too much. Another was that he preferred to choose his assistants by advertising in the local press.

Things changed, however, after Karsh visited the prestigious Brooks Institute of Photography in Santa Barbara, California. During the course of receiving an honorary degree and giving a lecture there, Karsh had been impressed by the students. He had good reason to be. Brooks was ranked among the ten best photography schools in the world. During a four-year course that led to a bachelor of science degree, the students not only learned every aspect of portraiture and other areas of photography, they also learned how to photograph a shooting bullet and the heat rising from a hand. This level of education would make the sort of assistant that Karsh was looking for. When he started to import his assistants from the Brooks Institute, calling them Karsh Fellows, he was getting the cream of the crop among photography students in North America.

Or was he? According to Charles Britt, who became a Karsh Fellow in 1986, "If you were a great photographer, he wouldn't have chosen you; and if you had too big of an ego, he wouldn't have been interested." Indeed, Britt felt that his interview for the fellowship, which took place in the Beverly Hills Hotel, in Los Angeles, was more about manners than about photography. Even so, Britt came to the conclusion that becoming Karsh's assistant "would be a good step towards becoming a commercial photographer."

The terms of Britt's employment were strict: he had to live within walking distance of the studio and he was not allowed to ski or to own a car. And, Britt further recalled, he "received low pay — I did not make enough to pay off my student loan." But the job, which entailed not only lifting equipment, changing film, and adjusting lights but also driving Karsh's car down to Montreal in order to buy his stuffed vine leaves, was, Britt maintained, "relatively easy because he would tell you exactly what he was going to do."

During the course of Britt's five years at the Karsh Studio, he and Karsh "never bonded; we never connected." Karsh took little interest in Britt's work: "there was no give and take, it was me giving and him taking." This lack of empathy was a professional, not a personal, matter. When Britt developed a serious problem with his ear, Yousuf and Estrellita's parental attitude towards their employees immediately kicked in. Britt was put on a flight to Boston, where over the course of the next two weeks he had surgery and a long recovery period, all at the expense of the Karsh Studio.

Karsh's lack of concern about Britt's own work is not to suggest, however, that Britt learned nothing during his years in the Karsh Studio. He readily acknowledged that Karsh "knew the whole box—he could do everything in that box," but Britt was surprised to discover that the master's techniques and skills were fifty years out of date. Nevertheless, Karsh showed Britt the importance of carefully observing clients before they were photographed and of making them feel relaxed: "Mr. Karsh would sit in the sitting room in the studio and talk to see what positions were comfortable." He also made Britt realize that, during a sitting, "the limits are yours."[48]

Preparing the client for a sitting and keeping him or her happy during it was really the job of Karsh's other assistant, Jerry Fielder. As Britt put it, the tall and handsome Fielder, who had joined the studio in the late 1970s, was "a smoother-over; if Mr. Karsh was meeting a lot of people, Jerry would be there." As Fielder himself put it, his role was not primarily in the camera room: "I would try and disappear as much as possible during a sitting."

Following a degree at the University of California in Los Angeles, Jerry Fielder became manager of the promotions department at NBC. Then he enrolled at the Brooks Institute of Photography. During the course of his third year, in 1979, his life changed when Karsh came to the Brooks Institute in search of a new assistant. Fielder was not initially enthusiastic about becoming a Karsh Fellow and agreed to attend the interview only in order to please his dean. During the interview Fielder showed himself to be personable and well rounded. He also let it be known that he was interested in the curatorial side of photography. No wonder he was "stunned" at the end of the day when Karsh told him, "I'll see you in Ottawa in two months' time." Fielder duly showed up in Ottawa two months later with the purpose of telling Karsh that he did not want the job. As he wryly recalled, he left the capital twenty-three years later.[49]

Fielder accompanied Karsh on his *Paris Match* assignments in France, he helped Karsh photograph the queen at Buckingham Palace in London in 1988, and he even took a month-long French course with Karsh at the Institut d'Études Française de Touraine in July 1982. While most of the students lived in modest accommodation, Jerry and Yousuf put up at the luxurious Château d'Artigny. During their travels, Fielder formed a close relationship with Karsh. He called him Papa. When Fielder wrote to him from California, he addressed

Karsh as *Cher Papa* in his letters. And when Karsh closed his studio in the Château Laurier, Fielder was kept on as his assistant and—more important—as his archivist.

Like Charles Britt, Jerry Fielder developed a great respect for Karsh's perfectionism in the camera room: "sometimes he would ask the sitter to leave the studio while he spent half an hour readjusting the lights."[50] Fielder marvelled at the fact that, unlike most photographers, Karsh knew how to take *and* how to develop his photographs. Fielder was equally amazed by the way in which Karsh "treated everyone the same—the same courtesy and time—gave everyone the same attention and care." Britt puts it slightly differently, observing how Karsh turned off his famous gracious manner as soon as his client left the camera room. Both assistants, however, were well placed to see that, unlike Henri Cartier-Bresson, Karsh did not wait for the magic moment or take several exposures with the hope that one might turn out to be satisfactory. He was the sort of photographer who "made things happen." And when things did not happen exactly according to plan he was upset.[51]

This was brought home to Britt when he and Fielder accompanied Karsh to the White House in 1993 to take the portrait of the newly elected American president, Bill Clinton, and his wife, Hillary. It was "the best sitting Jerry and I ever had; it just worked," Britt recalled. "We were all on the same wavelength," he continued, "and it was a long day and at the end of it I put everything away and Jerry and I were glowing from the whole thing."[52] The president, who had hung "The Roaring Lion" on the wall when he moved into the White House, was well disposed to Karsh. Following the sitting Hillary Rodham Clinton wrote to Karsh, "I feel I have a new and special friend."[53] Indeed, everyone was glowing—except Karsh. "I am going to have to tell Mrs. Karsh that I failed," he confided to an astonished Charles Britt during their trip back to Ottawa, before falling into a deep silence.[54]

What had happened to make Karsh think that the portraits of Bill and Hillary would be a failure? Britt suggested that Karsh had come to this conclusion even before the sitting had begun. Clinton had been uncertain about which tie he should wear for the portrait. When he consulted Karsh, the president's

manner was "very abrupt." This was apparently enough to put Karsh off, because establishing a good relationship with his subject "was all that mattered to Mr. Karsh."[55]

Perhaps allowances should be made for age in trying to understand this apparent lack of robustness and even failure of confidence. After all, Karsh was now eighty-four. He had recently closed his own studio and was relying on Britt to provide the technical facilities in Ottawa. The three men had set out for Washington surely realizing that this was the last president who would probably be Karshed.

When they returned to Ottawa, the prints were processed in Britt's studio and the proofs inspected. "They were so good," Britt remembered, "that Mr. Karsh hardly touched them up."[56] Even though Karsh had clearly been shaken by the president's brusque manner, the sitting had proved a success. The Clinton photograph can stand with any in Karsh's oeuvre and, though not literally the last photograph he took, shows that Karsh's professional career concluded on a triumphant note.

Bill and Hillary
Rodham Clinton, 1993

CHAPTER SIXTEEN

The Legacy

When Karsh was sixty-nine he told a reporter that he did not believe in retirement.[1] Five years later, in 1983, he reinforced this view by insisting that "They will have to carry me out with my boots on."[2] Even so, less than a decade later he had closed his studio at the Château Laurier. "It was an emotional wrench to say good-bye to my studio family and to the camaraderie of working together," Karsh later recalled.[3]

This did not mean that Yousuf Karsh stopped taking photographs when he closed his studio in 1992. A year later the Clintons sat for Karsh and a couple of years after that the American ambassador to Canada, James Blanchard, who along with his wife Janet had become "family" to Yousuf and Estrellita, was Karshed too.[4] Charles Britt, to whom Karsh had given some of his developing equipment in order to help him set up his own business, remembers how his former boss "kept coming over to the house — I'd process the film for nothing."[5] Nor did retirement mean that Karsh's agent, Roger Eldridge, Tom Blau's successor, who was about to secure sole rights to Karsh's work, would stop supplying his photographs to magazines and newspapers around the world. Karsh of Ottawa, however, was no more after June 1992. Neither Roger Eldridge's Camera Press nor his California-based Weston Gallery, which had handled the sale of Karsh's photographs to the public since 1975, could expect to receive any new portraits from the studio of Yousuf Karsh.

Karsh was, after all, eighty-three years old when he retired. This trumped his equally energetic uncle George Nakash, who had closed his Montreal photography studio in 1972 at the age of eighty-two. Moreover, by 1992 Karsh had deposited the bulk of his visual archive in the National Archives of Canada.[6] "Yousuf's negatives could have burst into flame," Estrellita recalled. "He had a whole lifetime of work there; it was very important that it should be preserved."[7] Karsh eventually deposited his camera, and other equipment that he had not already given to Britt, in Ottawa's Science and Technology Museum.

The National Gallery of Canada and the National Archives of Canada celebrated the acquisition of 355,000 negatives, prints, and transparencies by mounting Karsh: The Art of the Portrait.[8] In the catalogue accompanying the 1989 exhibition, Lilly Koltun described the breadth of the new acquisition. It began with a photograph that Karsh had taken of a country lane outside of Sherbrooke in 1926 and ended with the work that Karsh had completed up to March 31, 1987, the date that the collection was deposited in the National Archives. This meant that virtually every photograph that Karsh had taken to this date—from the Dominion Drama Festival photographs and early experimental works, the portraits of Hollywood stars and Canada's cities and factories, to the seminal portraits of Churchill and other leading statesmen and women of the twentieth century—was now safely in the public domain. Here, Koltun wrote, was a "documentary density" that carved "a fifty-five-year slice from the social stratum at both the national and international levels." It offered scholars "a rich resource for sociological, historical and statistical interpretation," and enabled them to make a "comparative analysis: between one photograph and another, between recent works and those of the past," and between the negative and the finished print.[9]

Depositing his work in the National Archives of Canada was not the only thing that Karsh did with an eye to posterity during the last years of his life. In 1989 London's National Portrait Gallery celebrated the one hundred and fiftieth anniversary of the invention of photography with an exhibition that included everything from Robert Howlett's 1857 portrait of Brunel to the work of Julia Margaret Cameron, Cecil Beaton, Bill Brandt, Richard Avedon, and, among others, Yousuf Karsh. Impressed that the gallery's curators had been adding photographs to their permanent collection since 1965, Karsh presented them with ninety portraits. The donation, according to one official, "transformed the National Portrait Gallery's photography coverage of the formative years of the twentieth century."[10] Grateful for the generous gift, the gallery celebrated Karsh's work in September 1991 with the exhibition British Personalities — A Tribute Exhibition.

As with his previous exhibitions in Britain, Karsh found himself at the mercy of the British press. Charles Darwent resurrected several previous complaints when he questioned Karsh's obsession with greatness and his claim that he was merely portraying his subjects "as their generation imagines them." "In an era of Kitty Kelley," Darwent further observed, "this reverential ideal of portraiture may seem reassuring or reactionary depending on your point of view."[11] Another critic, Paula Weidejer, was less charitable. "There is something initially off-putting about someone setting out to make his life's work photographing 'important' people," she wrote after visiting the exhibition near Trafalgar Square.[12]

The notion that Karsh's oeuvre consisted solely of portraits of famous people had been dispelled in 1989 when the National Gallery of Canada and the National Archives of Canada had included photographs of factories, landscapes, and other "insignificant" subjects in their exhibition, Karsh: The Art of the Portrait. The impressive range of Karsh's work was also there for everyone to see eleven years later when the Deutsches Historisches Museum mounted the groundbreaking exhibition Yousuf Karsh: Heroes of Light and Shadow in Berlin and published a handsome book to go with it.[13]

But photographs of steel and automobile plants and Canadian cities were not the images that the public saw in the magazine articles, the books, and the touring exhibitions featuring Karsh's work. Or what the art historians wrote about when they discussed Karsh's work in their histories of photography.[14] Or the basis on which the Montreal photographer Sam Tata claimed in *Maclean's* magazine that Karsh's work was "an exercise in flattery and retouching."[15]

Was Karsh concerned that art historians and critics viewed him primarily as a photographer of the famous? Responding to Sam Tata's comments, he told

Maclean's, "I take no notice because it is uninformed."[16] Answering one British critic's charge that he only portrayed the Establishment, Karsh replied, "I also photograph people...you might call them the salt of the earth."[17] This was, of course, a weak response using patronizing language. Yet Karsh insisted that he was drawn to "the world's most remarkable cross-section of people" because it was "the minority who make the world go round not the majority."[18]

Any serious consideration of Karsh's oeuvre must, of course, take into account his commercial photographs and the photographs he took of the not-so-famous, where he showed himself to be innovative, even adventurous, and ready to experiment in any genre. But Karsh knew that it was the proliferation of his portraits of great men—and occasionally of great women—that had allowed him to dominate the field of portraiture for over fifty years. He had long realized that "if the truth were told...many of us would very much like to be all the great photographers rolled into one," as he had told the Photographers' Association of America over forty years earlier, adding, "Because we are all individuals, little by little, each of us become conscious of a more or less specialized field of endeavour."[19]

Specialization had its price. Had Karsh taken on more commercial work, or had he spent more time in the studio than on the road, he would never have accumulated so many photographs of famous people for his books, his exhibitions, and illustration in newspapers and magazines. He would, in short, have been a jack of all trades rather than the world's leading portraitist. And he would have taken all of his pictures in his Ottawa studio rather than in the Vatican, the Kremlin, Buckingham Palace, and the White House, to name a few of the places where Karsh set up his equipment.

If Karsh made a tactical error during the last three decades of his career, it was in repeatedly exhibiting and publishing the same images—primarily from the 1940s and 1950s—and so often telling the same stories to accompany these images. Even Karsh's loyal supporter Jerry Fielder felt in retrospect that "Papa did himself a disservice by producing so many large-format books which left out so many good photographs of the not-so-famous and repeated the icons again and again thereby giving people a narrow view of his work."[20]

Even so, by the time Karsh closed his studio in 1992 he had few regrets. Admittedly, he would have liked to photograph Adolf Hitler and Joseph Stalin;

of course he regretted that he had never made that trip to China to photograph Mao; and for a man who was convinced that his best photograph was yet to be taken, he was naturally disappointed that Winston Churchill had persistently refused to give him another sitting. But none of this weighed heavily on Karsh's mind. By the time he retired he had accumulated at least twenty-five honorary degrees, the first of which was given to him by Ottawa's Carleton University in 1960. During the latter part of that decade he received the Order of Canada and was awarded the Canada Council Medal. The Directors' Club of Chicago and the Art Directors' Club of Montreal had already recognized his contribution to commercial photography in 1950 and 1955, respectively. In 1989 he was given the Creative Edge Award and in 1991 the Gold Medal of Merit, among many other American awards and honours. On top of all of this, Edward Steichen, whom Karsh had always considered to be "the master of us all," proclaimed photographs that Karsh had taken on a visit to him in 1970 to be "all jim dandies!"[21]

If every immigrant's wish, as Canadian writer Peter C. Newman has observed, is to move from the periphery of society to the centre and to "ingratiate themselves into the core of their adopted country," then Karsh had certainly done this by 1992.[22] This was why he and Estrellita now felt free to choose to spend the winter months at the Ritz Carlton in Florida or travel farther afield to the Hawaiian Islands. It was why Karsh had more time for his friends and former clients. Why he saw his brothers and their families more frequently. And finally, why, despite the common observation that self-made people never stop, this is precisely what Karsh did. Leisure was his reward for six decades of hard work and Karsh accepted his retirement as graciously as he had welcomed the next client into the camera room.

FIVE YEARS AFTER closing the studio in Ottawa, Yousuf and Estrellita began making plans to move to Boston. "We knew a lot of people," Estrellita recalled, so "it was a normal progression."[23] Indeed, it was surprising that Karsh had not moved to the United States earlier. His most important clients were there. The world's leading agents and advertisers were there. He had a comfortable brownstone apartment in a fashionable part of New York. And, given the international scope of his activities, any major city on the East Coast of the United States would have been a more convenient base than relatively inaccessible Ottawa. On the other hand, Canada had given Karsh a home as a young refugee from Mardin, Turkey. Little Wings had been a haven, too, until his move to the Château Laurier in 1982. As long as Karsh was in business, he was "Karsh of Ottawa."

In any case, Karsh had long claimed that Boston was his second home. It was here that he had apprenticed with John Garo in the late 1920s. Here, in the early 1970s, that he had taken up a visiting professorship at Emerson College. Here that he had given the Bromsen Lecture at the Boston Public Library, an institution that, along with the city's Museum of Fine Arts, had been his "university" during his early years. Here that the Museum of Fine Arts had kicked off his 1968 touring exhibition, Men Who Make Our World. And, finally, here that the museum had mounted a retrospective exhibition of its own, Karsh Portraits: The Searching Eye, in 1996 and helped publish *Karsh: A Sixty-Year Retrospective* the same year.[24]

There were other things that made the move south attractive. Boston offered a milder climate than Ottawa, it had the best doctors in North America, and, for Estrellita, who had spent more than thirty-five years in Ottawa, Boston would mean a return to the country of her birth.

Yousuf and Estrellita moved into an apartment above Boston's Ritz Carlton Hotel in December 1997. From this point on, Karsh became "an essentially private person."[25] After rising in the morning, he looked down to the Boston Public Garden and saluted the statue of George Washington. He and Estrellita opened the day's mail and read the newspaper before Yousuf went for a stroll in the Public Garden, where "he enjoyed chatting with people, meeting and being greeted."[26] Following lunch, Estrellita recalled that there was always "some little project." This might have entailed entertaining friends for a meal in the Ritz Carlton's restaurant or visiting officials at the Museum of Fine Arts or at the Brigham and Women's Hospital.

According to the director of the Museum of Fine Arts, Malcolm Rogers, Karsh was "an active presence in the museum" to the very end of his life. He and Estrellita not only attended every exhibition but also took their place among the museum's major benefactors. Yousuf and Estrellita gave the museum works from their private collection. This included sculptures by Emilio Greco and Ossip Zadkine, paintings by Josef Albers and Adolph Gottlieb, and an Egyptian lintel dating from the New Kingdom, among other works. Yousuf and Estrellita publicly acknowledged the museum's long commitment to photography by donating 199 of Karsh's portraits to the permanent collection.[27] (This made the Museum the largest repository of Karsh's work in the United States.) They endowed an annual Karsh Lectureship in Photography. They encouraged a new generation of photographers, often working in highly experimental styles, by offering an annual Karsh Prize in Photography to the best student from the museum school. Finally, Yousuf and Estrellita made it financially possible for the museum to employ a full-time curator to oversee its important collection of photographs.

The Boston Museum of Fine Arts was not the only institution to receive financial and moral support from Estrellita and Yousuf Karsh after the couple moved to Boston. Working through their doctor, the renowned clinician Dr. Marshall Wolf, the Karshes saw to it that twenty portraits of medical and scientific luminaries were installed in the Nesson Pike corridor of the Brigham and Women's Hospital. They donated a further twelve portraits and oversaw their installation in the Robert and Ronnie Bretholtz Center for Patients and Families in the same hospital. These gifts were appreciated by visitors and staff alike. This was because, as the surgeon Anthony Whittermore observed, Karsh's photographs "converted antiseptic spaces into extraordinary and inspiring places."[28]

WHAT ESTRELLITA REFERRED to as their "very nice, serene existence" was disrupted in 1997. In February of that year, Karsh underwent a triple bypass operation on his heart.[29] The recovery period following the two back-to-back surgical procedures was, not surprisingly, slow for a man approaching his ninetieth year. Jerry Fielder, now living in California, from where he carried out his duties as Karsh's archivist, flew to Boston for the operation. What he thought would be a short visit lasted nine months. With Jerry's assistance, Estrellita encouraged, supported, and strengthened Yousuf in nursing him back to health. She never allowed any question of whether or not Yousuf would recover. As Karsh's surgeon wryly recalled, "Those of you who know Estrellita know that he had little choice in the matter: he was going to get better."[30]

During the next four and a half years—the last of Yousuf's life—Estrellita kept him not only "fit and alert" but, as an old friend put it, "I suppose one has to say focused."[31] While these were "sick years," Estrellita later affirmed, "they were not unhappy years." Yousuf "was at peace; a great sense of peace." Even in the hospital bed, where he proudly wore his Order of Canada pin on his pajamas, Yousuf had "a presence," Estrellita recalled; "the nurses loved him."[32] Although he had told Hella Grabar, during his visit to Canada in 1998 to receive the key to the city of Ottawa, "I miss everything so much," Estrellita insisted after his death that "he had no regrets."[33] Indeed, it seemed to Karsh's physician, Marshall Wolf, that, unlike many of his elderly patients, Yousuf became even "nicer as he aged; what came out was joy and kindness."[34] And when Roger Eldridge of Camera Press visited Karsh in 2001, Karsh "seemed a contented man enjoying his retirement and happy to recall telling moments in his fruitful life."[35]

THE KARSHES WERE a long-lived family. Yousuf's father, Amsih, who died in 1962, had reached almost ninety. On July 13, 2002, his son Yousuf died from internal bleeding following surgery at the Brigham and Women's Hospital. He was ninety-three. Yousuf's brother Jamil had died a week earlier, aged eighty-one. And Malak Karsh, now in his eighty-sixth year, would be dead within a few months.

Most of the tributes to Yousuf Karsh appeared in the obituary columns of newspapers around the world before the funeral service took place in Ottawa. All of the obituarists agreed that during most of the twentieth century Karsh had been the unchallenged master of the formally posed portrait.[36] They also agreed, as Peter Pollack had already observed in his *Picture History of Photography*, that Karsh had transformed the human face into a legend. "That Karsh and Rembrandt could be mentioned in the same breath," wrote a journalist for *The Economist*, was not surprising to most commentators.[37] That Karsh had escaped the atrocities in Turkish Armenia, arrived penniless in North America, and become a celebrity long before the end of his career, fitted the story of many successful immigrants to the New World. That Karsh was not unlike the court painter of an earlier era in giving his clients the heroic image they wanted was widely acknowledged. Finally, none of the obituarists disagreed about the status of Karsh's seminal portrait of Winston Churchill: that it owed as much to chance and to the vagaries of the Second World War as it did to Karsh's audacity; and that it appositely matched the expression on Churchill's face with, as one writer put it, "the widespread feeling about the British leader, pugnaciously leading a brave nation against an all-conquering foe."[38]

Estrellita hoped that the funeral would be a private affair for just the family and a few friends but many people seemed to know that a funeral service for Yousuf Karsh was to be held in Ottawa's Notre Dame Cathedral. When the cortège passed by a group of construction workers on Sussex Drive, they removed their hats out of respect. And when the cortège arrived at the Neo-Gothic cathedral across from the National Gallery of Canada, the procession was greeted by a row of Mounted Police, who stood "in full regalia with their hats over their hearts."[39]

Shortly before he died, Karsh told his sister-in-law Barbara that he wanted a big choir and the Archbishop, Marcel Gervais, to conduct the service.[40] And this is what happened. "The choir was exquisite," Estrellita recalled, "and the service was classic and beautiful."[41] Decorated with ornate wooden carvings of saints, prophets, and apostles, the recently renovated cathedral, whose foundations dated from the 1840s, was a fitting place for Yousuf Karsh's funeral.

JUST DAYS AFTER SOLANGE'S death in January 1961, Karsh had purchased plot 46, lying next to her grave, in Notre Dame's cemetery, a short distance from the cathedral. Karsh had never been happy with the location, however, so he had persuaded the bishop to move Solange's coffin to a different part of the cemetery. Solange's remains thus came to rest in a plot lying next to those of the former Canadian prime minister Sir Wilfrid Laurier. Wanting to be buried near his wife, Karsh purchased the plot lying next to Solange's. This proved to be satisfactory until Karsh married Estrellita Nachbar in August 1962. Then he faced a problem. Should he still be buried next to Solange, in Ottawa's oldest and most prestigious cemetery?

The deterioration of Karsh's health in the late 1990s prompted him to seek advice from his relatives on this matter. "He said to me, I have a dilemma—which wife should I be buried beside?" a favourite niece, Vivian Saykaly, recalled. "I said, 'I can't answer that.'"[42] Karsh then asked his brother Salim and his sister-in-law Barbara to help him decide. His queries to them met with no more success.[43] In the end Estrellita graciously made the decision for Yousuf. She saw to it that he was buried beside Solange—and within close proximity of one of the country's most distinguished prime ministers. Then, with the help of Jerry Fielder, Estrellita organized two memorial services.

The first memorial service at Notre Dame Cathedral was held a month following Karsh's death. It was a grand affair. Penny Johnson, who was at the Julliard School of Music on a scholarship, played Bach during the service. The Governor General, Adrienne Clarkson, whose father, William Poy, had posed for Karsh many years earlier, was there. The former American ambassador to Canada, James Blanchard, who spoke to a packed congregation, had come up from the state of Michigan. The presence of these and other dignitaries prompted Karsh's niece Vivian Saykaly to recall that "I don't think that any of us in the family ever realized how famous he was…he was never shown to us as famous."[44]

The second memorial service, in late October, was a more secular affair. Held in Boston's Museum of Fine Arts, it celebrated the life of Yousuf Karsh, albeit from an American perspective. The museum's director, Malcolm Rogers, set the tone by claiming that he often thought how fortunate Karsh had been to gain access to virtually every great figure of the twentieth century. "And then I think," he added, "how fortunate they and we were to have our lives touched by this very remarkable man and artist."

During the course of the celebration it became clear how Karsh had not only touched but also shaped the lives of many people. Roger Eldridge, who had represented Camera Press since Tom Blau's death in 1984, told how Karsh remained "the undisputed star" of the firm's photographers, among whom were Lord Snowdon, Baron, and Cecil Beaton. Then Eldridge recalled what it was like when Karsh's photographs arrived in London. "I will never forget the buzz in the office when a new series of photos arrived from Ottawa…and how Tom Blau dropped whatever he was doing, donned his brown trilby hat, and set off to do the round of Fleet Street editors who always competed to publish the latest Karsh portrait."

Two of Karsh's former assistants also paid tribute to their old boss. Herman Leonard, who had apprenticed with Karsh during the late 1940s, recalled how "my optic changed, my direction changed." Karsh had taught him not only "how to print, how to see, what to look for" but, most important of all, how to "tell the truth in terms of beauty." Peter Miller, who had accompanied Karsh and Solange to Europe in 1954, also mounted the podium. He spoke of Karsh's generosity. In the late 1950s Karsh had helped him get a job at *Life* magazine. Thirty years later, when Miller's book of photographs featuring the people of Vermont was published, Karsh reconnected with his former assistant in order to tell him that his book was "wonderful." Miller also remembered the "great sense of compassion" that Karsh had for his subjects and, above all, the way in which he let a subject's personality come through during a session in the studio.

Jerry Fielder, who had worked with Karsh for a longer period of time than had either Leonard or Miller—and who continued to be the archivist of Karsh's work—recalled what it had been like to work for a man who thrived on work. "He was a hard man to keep up with...we used to say at the studio that it was the profession that kept him young *and* made all of us old." Even so, Fielder continued, Karsh had been "a great friend, warm, bright, quick, and funny...He had a way of making everyone feel at ease...you felt that you could trust him and you could, and he found the best in his fellow human." Fielder added, "When he met someone, he looked for what was good and noble, honest and true." And these, Fielder concluded, were the qualities that Karsh sought to reveal in everyone he photographed.

During the course of the tributes it became clear that everyone who had come within Karsh's ambit, from gallery directors and curators, lawyers and physicians, to the recipients of the annual Karsh prize in photography, had had their lives enriched in one way or another. This was a marvellous tribute to a man who had not cultivated intimacy, who had often hidden behind old-world manners and endless stories, and who had moved heaven and earth to get his own way whether he had been taking a portrait or negotiating the sale of his work. The abiding impression that emerged from the service—and which explained why Karsh had been able to do what he did—was best expressed by gallery owner Maggie Weston: "In his presence he made everyone feel special; he was always courtly and complimentary; he was always interested in you, how were you [and] how were you feeling."[45]

There was one thing missing that would have made the celebration of Karsh's life complete: a Canadian point of view. It is true that a memorial service had been held in Ottawa the previous month. And that the voice of Canadian contralto Maureen Forrester was heard at the end of the memorial in Boston singing Leonard Bernstein's "There's a Place for Us." However, there was nobody that day to focus on what Karsh had done for Canada; nobody to point out how the international reputation that followed set standards for several generations of portrait photographers in Canada as well as in the rest of the world; nobody to dwell on how he had put the country on the cultural map with his 1941 portrait of Churchill; nobody, in short, to speak about him as Karsh of Ottawa.

THE CELEBRATION OF Karsh's life at the Boston Museum of Fine Arts did not represent a closure in the usual sense. "I never walk past that group of photos without seeing people looking at them," Marshall Wolf said of the photographs hanging in the Pike corridor at the Brigham and Women's Hospital.[46] Moreover, thanks to continuing endowments from Estrellita Karsh, hospitals in Ottawa and Boston have not only found themselves with new medical facilities and with innovative research programs, they have also had their premises enriched by the portraits of Yousuf Karsh.[47]

Karsh's work continues to be exhibited around the world, published in books, and donated to institutions—thanks again to the generosity of Estrellita Karsh and the organizational skills of Jerry Fielder.[48] And, though Peter Miller may be right to suggest that Karsh has a reputation among some modern photographers for producing "fuddy-duddy stuff," Miller is surely likewise right to insist of Karsh's work that "if his pictures were blown up, his critics would say, 'Holy Shit.'"[49]

Yousuf Karsh created his finest portraits not through some technical miracle but, as he himself said in trying to explain the "Karsh secret," by finding "in the short space of a sitting, a common denominator with the sitter, whereby the subject assumes just that one attitude, expression and mood, which makes the beholder of the portrait say: 'That is a wonderful portrait — it is the man.'"[50] Whether or not this allowed him to reveal the soul of his subject, as he often claimed, is more debatable.

If there was a "Karsh secret" then it lay in recognizing, and then in showing, that a good portrait was the result of a collaboration between the subject and the photographer. Karsh knew that it was up to him to set the mood and the tone of the sitting so that the necessary collaboration could take place. One only has to look at one of the many films recording Karsh's portrait sittings to see how he could sometimes make his sitter as malleable as putty, through a mixture of old-world charm, gentle bullying, and by demonstrating a profound respect for and knowledge of the person he was photographing.

It is no accident that so many of Karsh's images remain indelible in our minds. He embraced grandeur but his work also dignified the mundane. Thus, he has left us a powerful image of Churchill to match his noblest wartime rhetoric; but Karsh also made us, whether we like it or not, associate Hemingway and Einstein with scruffy but comfortable sweaters. Through the publication of his many books, his exhibitions, and his exposure in so many other ways, Karsh brought a private act — the collaboration of photographer and subject within the confines of a small space — into the public arena. By doing so, he gave a face to people who touch all of our lives.

Karsh frequently compared himself to an historian and this, ultimately, is what he was. He recorded faces and gestures for posterity as much as for publication in the press. As the gatekeeper of his own images, Karsh, along with his agents, his publishers, his gallery dealer, and his archivist, determined where, when, and in which form we see the work itself. Karsh knew that the work would live and continue to win recognition after his death — recognition as among the greatest photographs of the twentieth century.

Acknowledgements

Books don't write themselves. But while biographers must take responsibility for every word that appears under their names, they could not write the books they do without the cooperation of many people. And this is why biographers accumulate such enormous debts by the time they write the last sentence of their books.

In 1998, following the National Archives of Canada's acquisition of Yousuf Karsh's papers the previous year, I approached Karsh. My offer to write his life story met with resistance. Approaching his ninetieth birthday, wanting to live a private life after being in the limelight for so many years, and convinced that he had already told his story in his many autobiographical writings, Yousuf Karsh graciously—very graciously—saw me out the door. After his death I approached his widow, Estrellita Karsh. By this time the Karsh papers, which occupied over fifty metres of shelf space in the National Archives of Canada, had been catalogued. Most of the manuscripts were open to anyone who wished to view them but some of them could be consulted only with the permission of Mrs. Karsh. A writer and historian herself, Estrellita Karsh knew that a comprehensive biography of her husband could not be written unless the author was given full access to the Karsh papers. When she granted me access to them,

I chalked up my first debt. And when she and the long-time archivist of the Karsh estate, Jerry Fielder, agreed to share their memories of Yousuf and to help me get the best possible reproductions of Karsh's work by providing most of the images for me, my debts mounted.

During the four years that I have spent writing this book, my list of creditors kept on growing. Karsh's only living brother, Salim; his favourite niece, Vivian Saykaly; his cousin Raymond C. Setlakwe; and Malak Karsh's widow, Barbara Karsh, were among the many relatives who spoke with me—some more than once. Karsh's assistants—Charles Britt and Peter Miller in particular—told me what went on in the camera room. Joyce Large, who was Karsh's longest-serving secretary, told me what happened in the reception room. Margaret Mitchell (née Bradley) and her sister Moira Bolton told me what Karsh was like as a boy fresh off the boat from Syria. Ted M. Riback, J. Franco Anglesio, and Governor James J. Blanchard were among the people who shared their recollections of the adult Yousuf Karsh. His physician, Dr. Marshall A. Wolf of Boston's Brigham and Women's Hospital, told me about his friendship with Karsh and about his former patient's medical condition. The New York–based dancer Betty Low shared her memories of her friendship with Yousuf and Solange in the 1930s and 1940s. Khaled El Rouayheb translated the letters that were written to Yousuf in Arabic. Two other Arabic scholars, Professor Geoffrey Khan and Ghazzal Zouhair, along with the Ottawa-based diplomat Haig Safarian, helped me understand life in early-twentieth-century Turkish Armenia, Syria, and Lebanon. Dr. Peter Goddard showed me Albert Einstein's office at the Institute for Advanced Studies, of which Dr. Goddard is the director, in Princeton. Pamela Belyea gave me a young woman's impression of what it was like to spend a summer working for Estrellita and Yousuf at Little Wings. Richard S. Rosenzweig sent me the colour portrait that Karsh had taken of Hugh Hefner at the Playboy Mansion. Anne Goddard, who will be sorely missed by all scholars of Canada's cultural history following her recent retirement from the National Archives of Canada, along with other staff members including Jill Delaney, gave me much-needed assistance during my visits to Ottawa. Libraries and archives at the University of Victoria, the Public Archives of Nova Scotia, Cambridge University, the University of Washington, the Boston Public Library, and the

Vancouver Public Library along with other institutions including Boston's Museum of Fine Arts, New York's Museum of Modern Art, London's Imperial War Museum, and Churchill College and Trinity Hall where Ginny Swepson and David Thomas, who provided the author photograph, should be thanked too. William Young, Allen Packwood, Sonja Karsh, Josée Audette, Jennifer A. Street, and Sonja Mortimer dug out manuscripts relating to Karsh or simply answered my questions. Finally, Mary Soames told me what her family really thought about Karsh's portrait of her father, Winston Churchill.

During the last twelve years of Karsh's life, two very remarkable exhibitions were mounted of his work: the first, Karsh: The Art of the Portrait, by the National Gallery of Canada; and the second, Yousuf Karsh: Heroes of Light and Shadow, by the Deutsches Historisches Museum in Berlin, Germany. I am grateful for the insights given to me by the curators who organized these exhibitions. Most especially helpful were the essays written by James Borcoman, Janet Yates, Lilly Koltun, and Rosemary Donegan.

Financial assistance and encouragement came at intervals from the Canada Council, the BC Arts Council, the Banff Centre, and Cambridge University, most especially Churchill College. Thank you!

Just as a biographer needs manuscripts, interviewees, libraries, archives, and museums, she or he also need friends. Dennis Avery, Tom Berger, Ann Cowan, Isabel Nanton, Floyd St. Clair, Anne Wood, Jan Bavelas, Carole Sabiston, David Watmough, Dan Curtis, James Osborne, Paul Delany, and Peter Buitenhuis, who sadly died before publication, all helped me in various ways.

Lilly Koltun, the director of the National Portrait Gallery of Canada, and Joan Schwartz of Queen's University agreed to read two chapters of the manuscript. Vivian and Dianne Nelles and Fay Bendall, to whom this book is dedicated, read every word. Peter Clarke not only read but also listened to my manuscript on the deck of our home on South Pender Island. Joining me on a research trip to Ottawa, he also consulted the financial records relating to Karsh's various businesses, all while completing his own book on the last thousand days of the British Empire. After that, the manuscript was put in the hands of my energetic agent, Sally Harding, and then given to House of Anansi Press. A warm thank you to everyone at Anansi for helping me tell the story of a very remarkable Canadian.

Selected Publications by Yousuf Karsh

Faces of Destiny: Portraits by Karsh
1946, Ziff-Davis (Chicago and New York), and 1947, George G. Harrap (London)

This Is the Mass
with Bishop Fulton J. Sheen and Henri Daniel-Rops
1958, Hawthorn Books (New York), and 1959, World's Work (Kingswood, England)

Portraits of Greatness
1959, University of Toronto Press (Toronto), and 1960, Thomas Nelson and Sons (New York and London)

This Is Rome: A Pilgrimage in Words and Pictures
with Bishop Fulton J. Sheen and H. V. Morton
1959, 1960, Hawthorn Books (New York), and 1961, Image Books (New York)

This Is the Holy Land: A Pilgrimage in Words and Pictures
with Bishop Fulton J. Sheen and H. V. Morton
1960, Hawthorn Books (New York), and 1960, World's Work (Kingswood,
England)

Yousuf Karsh & John Fisher See Canada
with John Fisher
1960, Thomas Allen (Toronto)

In Search of Greatness: Reflections of Yousuf Karsh
1962, University of Toronto Press (Toronto) and Alfred A. Knopf (New York)

These Are the Sacraments: As Described by Bishop Fulton J. Sheen
and Photographed by Yousuf Karsh
with Bishop Fulton J. Sheen
1962, Hawthorn Books (New York)

Karsh Portfolio
1967, University of Toronto Press (Toronto) and Thomas Nelson
and Sons (New York)

Faces of Our Time
1971, University of Toronto Press (Toronto)

Karsh Portraits
1976, University of Toronto Press (Toronto) and New York Graphic
Society (Boston)

Karsh Canadians
1978, University of Toronto Press (Toronto)

Karsh: A Fifty-Year Retrospective
1983, University of Toronto Press (Toronto) and Secker & Warburg (London)

Karsh: American Legends
1992, Bulfinch Press (Boston) and Little, Brown Canada (Toronto)

Karsh: A Sixty-Year Retrospective
1996, Bulfinch Press (Boston) and Little, Brown Canada (Toronto)

Notes

PREFACE

1. Douglas Fetherling, "The Mythology of Yousuf Karsh," *Ottawa Citizen*, October 30, 1976. See Chapter 15 for context.
2. Yousuf Karsh quoted in the *Vancouver Sun*, February 24, 1978.
3. Yousuf Karsh, *Karsh: A Sixty-Year Retrospective* (Boston: Little, Brown and Company, 1996), 23.

CHAPTER ONE: BEGINNINGS IN ARMENIA

1. Raymond Setlakwe, interview with the author, September 25, 2005.
2. James S. Woodsworth, cited in Valarie Knowles, *Strangers Within Our Gates* (Toronto: Dundurn Press, 1972).
3. Salim Karsh, interview with the author, November 1, 2003.
4. There is no written evidence to corroborate this date. Family members are divided as to whether the Karsh family left Mardin in 1921 or 1922.
5. Yousuf Karsh, *In Search of Greatness* (Toronto: University of Toronto Press, 1962), 14.
6. National Archives of Canada (henceforth NAC), Yousuf Karsh Fonds (henceforth KF), 317–29, Yousuf Karsh to Eleanor Harmon, "Notes for Yousef Karsh's Autobiography," December 7, 1961.
7. Madge Macbeth, "Yousuf Karsh," *Saturday Night*, 1938.
8. NAC, RG 76, T-15085, "Declaration of Passengers to Canada," Immigration Branch, December 31, 1923.
9. NAC, KF, 3, Yousuf Karsh to Malak Karsh, August 2, 1937.
10. Zouhair Ghazzal, correspondence with the author following his contact with Faud Karsh and Issa Touma in Syria, February 10, April 8, and May 5, 10, 20, 2004.
11. Yousuf Karsh, *In Search of Greatness* (Toronto: University of Toronto Press, 1962), 10–11.

CHAPTER TWO: WELCOME TO CANADA

1. Vivian Saykaly, interview with the author, November 30, 2003.
2. Betty Guernsey, *Nakash* (Montreal: La Corporation des éditions Fides, 1981), 31.

3. NAC, Audio Visual, Aziz Nakash interviewed by A. Birrell, July 6, 1972.
4. NAC, RG 76, T-15085, Immigration Branch, Form 30A, "Declaration of Passenger," January 1, 1924.
5. Yousuf Karsh, *In Search of Greatness* (Toronto: University of Toronto Press, 1962), 5.
6. NAC, KF, 32, Yousuf Karsh's talk upon the donation of the "Nakash Papers and Photographs" to the National Archives of Canada and to the McCord Museum, December 1, 1981.
7. Yousuf Karsh, *In Search of Greatness* (Toronto: University of Toronto Press, 1962), 17.
8. J. T. M. Anderson, *The Education of the New-Canadian* (Toronto: J. M. Dent, 1918).
9. Eastern Townships school board records of Joseph Karsh, grade 1 and grade 2, January to June 1924.
10. NAC, KF, 311, Yousuf Karsh's handwritten notes, August 1985.
11. NAC, KF, 311, Yousuf Karsh, "First Draft, Speech to Canadian Citizenship Council at Château Laurier," May 29, 1953.
12. Margaret Mitchell (née Bradley) and Fredericka Boulton (née Bradley), interview with the author, March 24, 2004 and March 5, 2004, respectively.
13. NAC, KF, Box 14, Yousuf Karsh, "Speech to University of Miami" (typescript), April 24, 1968.
14. n.a., "The Man Behind Karsh, Nakash of Montreal," *Canadian Photography*, December 1970.
15. Raymond Setlakwe, interview with the author, September 25, 2005.
16. NAC, KF, 131, Beverley Mitchell, "The Man with the Photographic Memory — a Personal Profile," *Montreal Star*, November 21, 1972.
17. NAC, Audio Visual, Aziz Nakash interviewed by A. Birrell, July 6, 1972.
18. n.a., "The Man Behind Karsh, Nakash of Montreal," *Canadian Photography*, December 1970.
19. McCord Museum Archives, George Nakash Papers, P667, Correspondence 1971–1972, "Aziz Nakash's Speech to the Rotary Club of Montreal," (circa 1970).
20. Vivian Saykaly, interview with author, November 30, 2003.
21. M. J. Rosenau, "Garo, Master of Many Arts, Gives His Opinion of the Art of True Living," *Boston Herald*, June 13, 1937.
22. See, for example, n.a., "Special Garo Number," *Camera*, April 1915.
23. NAC, KF, 1, John Garo, "Talk at Cleveland Convention, 1926."
24. Ibid.
25. NAC, KF, 52, Franklin Jordan, "John H. Garo," (typescript), May 2, 1951.
26. M. J. Rosenau, "Garo, Master of Many Arts, Gives His Opinion of the Art of True Living," *Boston Herald*, June 13, 1937.

CHAPTER THREE: **THE APPRENTICE**
1. Yousuf Karsh, *In Search of Greatness* (Toronto: University of Toronto Press, 1962), 30.
2. Virginia Woolf and Roger Fry, eds., *Victorian Photographs of Famous Men and Fair Women, by Julia Margaret Cameron* (London: Hogarth Press, 1926).
3. Otto Walter Beck, *Art Principles in Portrait Photography* (New York: Baker & Taylor Company, 1907), 15.
4. n.a., "Lessons from the Masters," *The British Journal of Photography*, vol. LXXIV, no. 3526, (December 2, 1927), 713.
5. M. J. Rosenau, "Garo, Master of Many Arts, Gives His Opinion of the Art of True Living," *Boston Herald*, June 13, 1937.
6. NAC, KF, 1, John Garo, "Talk at Cleveland Convention, 1926."
7. NAC, KF, 30, Yousuf Karsh, "Proposed for the *Faces of Destiny*" (typescript), n.p.
8. NAC, KF, 38, Yousuf Karsh, "Notes for Kent State Talk," 1951.
9. NAC, KF, 43, Yousuf Karsh, "Ladies and Gentlemen," speech to the Photographers Association of America, New York, July 6, 1951.
10. NAC, KF, 30, "Proposal for the *Faces of Destiny*" (typescript), n.p.
11. NAC, KF, 61, Francis J. Eresian to Yousuf Karsh, February 6, 1947.
12. NAC, Audio Visual, Yousuf Karsh "National School Telecast," 1962.

13. NAC, KF, 311, Yousuf Karsh, "Notes" (handwritten), August 1985.
14. NAC, KF, 14, Yousuf Karsh, "Speech to University of Miami" (typescript), April 24, 1968.
15. NAC, KF, 43, Yousuf Karsh, "Speech to the Photographer's Association of America" (typescript), July 6, 1951.
16. n.a., "Karsh of Ottawa," *The Image*, 1973, 34–43.
17. NAC, KF, 3, Franklin Jordan to Yousuf Karsh, February 19, 1930.
18. Ibid.
19. Yousuf Karsh, *In Search of Greatness* (Toronto: University of Toronto Press, 1962), 27.
20. Ibid., 37.
21. Ibid., 28.
22. NAC, KF, 3, John Garo to Yousuf Karsh, March 19, 1930.
23. NAC, KF, 47, *The Catalogue*, The Layton School of Art and the North West Mutual Life Insurance Company, 1952.
24. NAC, KF, 3, John Garo to Yousuf Karsh, April 12, 1930.
25. n.a., "Portrait of a Boy," *The Mitre*, October 1932.
26. Vivian Saykaly, interview with the author, November 30, 2003.
27. Bruce Downes, "Karsh, His Work" *Popular Photography*, May 1945, 58; Nakash Studio advertisement, *Sherbrooke Daily Record*, October 9, 1924, 4; McCord Museum Archives, George Nakash Papers, P667, Correspondence 1971–1972, "Aziz Nakash's Speech to the Rotary Club of Montreal," (circa 1970).
28. NAC, KF, 5, Yousuf Karsh to Uncle (George Nakash), January 20, 1942.
29. NAC, KF, 5, Yousuf Karsh to J. Helders, June 2, 1942.

CHAPTER FOUR: **JOE GOES TO OTTAWA**

1. A. H. D. Ross, *Ottawa Past and Present* (Toronto: Musson Book Company, 1927), 201.
2. NAC, KF, 63, *Women's Wear Daily*, September 10, 1971.
3. NAC, KF, 309, Yousuf Karsh, "The University of Miami, Communications Conference, Coral Gables, Florida," April 24, 1968.
4. NAC, KF, 63, *Women's Wear* Daily, September 10, 1971.
5. *Maclean's*, September 1, 1942, 19–20.
6. NAC, KF, 3, Yousuf Karsh to John Garo, September 24, 1935.
7. NAC, KF, 3, Yousuf Karsh to Malak Karsh, August 2, 1937.
8. NAC, KF, 3, Yousuf Karsh to John Garo, 1937.
9. *Maclean's*, September 1, 1942, 19–20.
10. "Yousuf in Wonderland," *National Home Monthly*, May 1946, 19.
11. Yousuf Karsh, *In Search of Greatness* (Toronto: University of Toronto Press, 1962), p. 40.
12. Martha A. Sandweiss, ed., *Photography in Nineteenth-century America* (New York: A. N. Abrams, 1991).
13. NAC, KF, 311, "Article for Gevaert," April 10, 1940.
14. NAC, KF, 311, Yousuf Karsh, "Self Portrait, Chapter One" (1944).
15. NAC, KF, 311, Yousuf Karsh, "In Search of Greatness," *Michigan Business Review*, vol. XVII, no. 4, July 1966.
16. Dennis Breo, "Photographer Karsh Honors Medicine with 'Healers of Our Age,'" *American Medical News*, February 16, 1976.
17. Susan Sontag, *On Photography* (New York: Anchor Press, 1990), 24.
18. David Pressman, "The Drama Festival," *New Frontier*, vol. II, no. 2, June 1937, 26.
19. NAC, MG28 130, Ottawa Drama League, vol. l, Rupert Caplan to D. C. Scott, May 27, 1930.
20. Yousuf Karsh, *In Search of Greatness* (Toronto: University of Toronto Press, 1962), 42.
21. n.a., "The Other Half of Karsh," *Canadian Home Journal*, May 1951.
22. Vivian Saykaly, interview with the author, November 30, 2003.
23. Peter Miller as told to Barbara Moon, "Stalking Celebrities with Karsh," I, *Mayfair*, December 1954.
24. Raymond Setlakwe, interview with the author, September 25, 2005.

25. n.a., "The Other Half of Karsh," *Canadian Home Journal*, May 1951.
26. NAC, KF, 3, Yousuf Karsh to Charles Aylett, May 2, 1935.
27. NAC, KF, 42, *The Catalogue*, The Layton School of Art and the North West Mutual Life Insurance Company, 1952.
28. Peter Miller as told to Barbara Moon, "Stalking Celebrities with Karsh," I, *Mayfair*, December 1954.
29. n.a., "The Other Half of Karsh," *Canadian Home Journal*, May 1951.
30. NAC, KF, 2, Solange Karsh, "Karsh, You've Monopolised Me" (typescript talk given by Solange just back from Bermuda).
31. NAC, KF, 2, Solange Karsh to Jamil Karsh, April 1, 1947.
32. NAC, KF, 2, Solange Karsh, "Karsh, You've Monopolised Me" (typescript talk given by Solange just back from Bermuda).
33. Bruce Downes, "Karsh, His Work," *Popular Photography*, May 1945, 24.
34. NAC, KF, 344, Yousuf Karsh, "Scrapbook," 1933.
35. Yousuf Karsh interviewed on February 11, 1994, by Lilly Koltun. Cited in Dieter Vorsteher and Janet Yates, eds., *Yousuf Karsh: Heroes of Light and Shadow* (Toronto: Stoddart, 2001), 126–37.
36. NAC, MG28 130, Speech given by Yousuf Karsh to the Montreal Women's Club, Salle Doree, March 29, 1943; NAC, KF, 309, Yousuf Karsh, "The University of Miami, Communications Conference, Coral Gables, Florida," April 24, 1968.
37. NAC, KF, 344, see Karsh's Scrapbook for the work he submitted to *Mayfair Magazine* in May 1933. See also Karsh's Studio Register, NAC, KF, 150, citing his commission for *Mayfair* and *Saturday Night*.
38. *Saturday Night*, May 6, 1933.
39. NAC, KF, 4, B. K. Sandwell to Yousuf Karsh, "Telegram," December 28, 1933.
40. *Saturday Night*, January 6, 1934.
41. NAC, KF, 4, Yousuf Karsh to John Garo, January 3, 1934.
42. "Viscount Duncannon's 'Romeo to Juliet by a Police Chief's Daughter,'" *The Sketch*, January 24, 1934, 142.
43. "Camera Study by Karsh, Ottawa" *Saturday Night*, May 12, 1934.
44. Robert R. Miller, "Capturing Shadows in Stageland," *The American Annual of Photography*, 1932, 193–99; Hunton D. Sellman and Lessley Merrill, *Essentials of Stage Lighting* (New Jersey: Prentice-Hall, 1982).
45. NAC, KF, 29, "Mr. Karsh's Interview," January 27, 1947.
46. NAC, KF, 43, Yousuf Karsh, "Speech to Photographers Association of America," July 6, 1951.
47. NAC, KF, 309, Yousuf Karsh, "The University of Miami, Communications Conference, Coral Gables, Florida," April 24, 1968.
48. Yousuf Karsh, *In Search of Greatness* (Toronto: University of Toronto Press, 1962), 48.
49. Lilly Koltun in Dieter Vorsteher and Janet Yates, eds., *Yousuf Karsh: Heroes of Light and Shadow* (Toronto: Stoddart, 2001), 125.
50. *Maclean's*, September 1, 1942, 19–20.
51. NAC, KF, 309, Yousuf Karsh, "The University of Miami, Communications Conference, Coral Gables, Florida," April 24, 1968.
52. Lilly Koltun in Dieter Vorsteher and Janet Yates, eds., *Yousuf Karsh: Heroes of Light and Shadow* (Toronto: Stoddart, 2001), 134.
53. Juliet MacBrien, *Saturday Night*, November 14, 1933.
54. *Maclean's*, September 1, 1942, 19–20.
55. NAC, KF, 3, Yousuf Karsh to John Garo, November 14, 1938.

CHAPTER FIVE: **COURT PHOTOGRAPHER**

1. Louis Paul Flory, "The Status of Professional Photography in America," *The American Annual of Photography*, 1927, 152–54.
2. NAC, KF, 3 Yousuf Karsh to John Garo, May 5, 1933.

3. Yousuf Karsh, *In Search of Greatness* (Toronto: University of Toronto Press, 1962), 45.

4. NAC, KF, 4, Yousuf Karsh to George Nakash, July 5, 1933.

5. Ibid., September 15, 1933.

6. NAC, KF, 344, Yousuf Karsh, "Scrapbook," 1933.

7. Arthur G. Willis, *Photography as a Business* (London: Pitman and Sons, 1928), 31.

8. NAC, KF, 244, "Modern Photography by Karsh" (unattributed), May 27, 1933.

9. NAC, KF, 344, Yousuf Karsh, "Scrapbook" (undated clipping), 1934.

10. NAC, KF, 3, Yousuf Karsh to Comtesse de Dampierre, January 11, 1937.

11. NAC, KF, 3, Yousuf Karsh to Major M. F. Gregg VC, April 5, 1936.

12. NAC, KF, 3, Yousuf Karsh to C. A. Atwood, February 15, 1938.

13. NAC, KF, 322, Yousuf Karsh, "The Language of Light," *Sun Life*, October 1951.

14. Bruce Downes, "Karsh, His Work," *Popular Photography*, May 1945, 24.

15. NAC, KF, 4, Yousuf Karsh to George Nakash, November 13, 1933.

16. Ibid., April 15, 1935.

17. NAC, KF, 3, T. Eaton Company to Yousuf Karsh, May 5, 1936.

18. NAC, KF, 346, "Portrait Studies at the Little Theatre," (unattributed), April 10, 1935.

19. NAC, KF, 3, Yousuf Karsh to Mr. and Mrs. John Garo, April 21, 1937.

20. NAC, Yousuf Karsh, "Two Young Girls with Doll and Glass Ball," circa 1934.

21. Ronald J. Gedrim, ed., *Edward Steichen* (Oxford: Clio Press, 1996), 25.

22. Madge Macbeth, "Yousuf Karsh," *Saturday Night*, September 24, 1938.

23. "Brilliance Attends Opening of Parliament," *Saturday Night*, February 3, 1934.

24. Yousuf Karsh, *In Search of Greatness* (Toronto: University of Toronto Press, 1962), 50.

25. NAC, KF, 3, Yousuf Karsh to comptroller, March 27, 1934.

26. Yousuf Karsh, *In Search of Greatness* (Toronto: University of Toronto Press, 1962), 48.

27. *The Tatler*, April 3, 1935, 17.

28. NAC, KF, 3, comptroller to Yousuf Karsh, March 28, 1934; "I am desired by Their Excellences," the comptroller informed Karsh, "to inform you that you are authorized to use the words 'By Appointment of Their Excellences the Governor-General and Countess of Bessborough.'"; Ibid., comptroller to Yousuf Karsh, April 20, 1935. When Lord and Lady Tweedsmuir arrived in 1936, Karsh was granted the same privilege; NAC, KF, 303, comptroller to Yousuf Karsh, May 8, 1936.

29. NAC, KF, 3, Yousuf Karsh to Lt. Col. E. D. Mackenzie, July 4, 1936.

30. NAC, KF, 3, Yousuf Karsh to Lysle Courtenay, February 25, 1938.

31. NAC, KF, 4, Yousuf Karsh to Herbert Hodgins, May 4, 1933.

32. NAC, KF, 4, Yousuf Karsh to Florence Nakash, September 27, 1935.

33. It should be noted that the Grange Art Gallery (now the Art Gallery of Ontario) gave an exhibition to "Jay" Jaycocks in the print room in February 1934.

34. NAC, KF, 346, "Scrapbook, 1934–1939" (unattributed clipping, 1934).

35. NAC, KF, 311, Yousuf Karsh, "Photography — Your Side and My Side," May 1935.

36. n.a., *Maclean's*, September 1, 1942, 19–20.

37. NAC, KF, 311, Yousuf Karsh, "The Kindly Eye of the Modern Camera" skit for the Rotary Club of Ottawa, March 23, 1936.

38. n.a., "Photography Makes Progressive Art," *Ottawa Citizen*, March 24, 1936.

39. NAC, KF, 311, "Untitled Sketch: Karsh and Solange" (1938).

40. Louis Paul Flory, "The Status of Professional Photography in America," *The American Annual of Photography*, 1927, 152–54.

41. NAC, KF, 3, Yousuf Karsh to John Garo, March 11, 1935.

42. *New York Times*, May 31, 1936.

43. NAC, KF, 106, Yousuf Karsh, "Comments on Steichen Photography for *US Camera*" (typescript), May 1967.

44. NAC, KF, 3, Yousuf Karsh to John Garo, June 2, 1936.
45. NAC, KF, 10, Yousuf Karsh, "Comments on Steichen Photograph for *US Camera*" (typescript), May 6.
46. Ronald J. Gedrim, ed., *Edward Steichen* (Oxford: Clio Press, 1996), 23.
47. Patricia Johnson, "Romance, Class, Strategy, and Style: Edward Steichen's Photos for Jergens' Lotion," *Exposure*, vol. 26, no. 4 (Fall 1989), 4–22 3.
48. NAC, KF, 10, Yousuf Karsh, "Comments on Steichen Photograph for *US Camera*" (typescript), May 6.
49. NAC, KF, 150, Karsh Studio Register, November 27, 1936.
50. NAC, KF, 3, Yousuf Karsh to Lysle Courtenay, May 26, 1938.
51. Frank Crowninshield, "Foreword," *US Camera*, 1939, 10.
52. NAC, KF, 30, "City of Straws Photograph" (undated typescript).
53. Harvey V. Fondiller, *The Best of Popular Photography* (New York: Ziff-Davis, 1979), 271.
54. NAC, KF, 3, Yousuf Karsh to Edward Steichen, May 1, 1936.

CHAPTER SIX: **MARRIAGE**
1. NAC, KF, 3 John Garo to Yousuf Karsh, September 29, 1936.
2. Ibid., February 12, 1937.
3. MAC, KF, 3, Yousuf Karsh to John Garo, September 4, 1935.
4. Ibid., December 1936.
5. J. Vincent Lewis, "Facial Expression and Facial Analysis in Portraiture," *The American Annual of Photography*, vol. 51, 1927, 233.
6. NAC, KF, 311, Yousuf Karsh, "Article for Gavaret" (typescript), April 10, 1940.
7. NAC, KF, 3, Yousuf Karsh to S. Blumenfelt, November 26, 1936.
8. NAC, KF, 63, Armando Guzman, (translated from Spanish), date unknown.
9. NAC, KF, 4, Yousuf Karsh to George Nakash, March 15, 1936.
10. Barbara Karsh, interview with the author, October 29, 2003.
11. NAC, KF, 3, Yousuf Karsh to John Garo, September 4, 1935; March 11, 1935.
12. Salim Karsh, interview with the author, November 1, 2003.
13. NAC, KF, 3, Yousuf Karsh to John Garo, September 25, 1935.
14. NAC, KF, 3, Yousuf Karsh to Lysle Courtenay, October 7, 1937.
15. NAC, KF, 4, Malak Karsh to Yousuf Karsh, June 30, 1939.
16. Ibid., June 5, 1939.
17. Ibid., June 23, 1939.
18. NAC, KF, 4, Yousuf Karsh to John Garo, March 29, 1938.
19. NAC, KF, 4, Malak Karsh's statement to the White School; Malak Karsh, *Canada: The Land that Shapes Us* (Toronto: Key Porter, 1995), 29.
20. NAC, KF, 3, Yousuf Karsh to John Garo, October 14, 1937.
21. Yousuf Karsh, *In Search of Greatness* (Toronto: University of Toronto Press, 1961), 53.
22. Betty Low, interview with the author, December 14, 2003.
23. Solange Karsh, "The Other Half of Karsh," *Canadian Home Journal*, May 1951.
24. Betty Large, interview with the author, April 20, 2004.
25. NAC, KF, 3, Yousuf Karsh to John Garo, October 14, 1938.
26. *Maclean's*, September 1, 1942.
27. NAC, KF, 3, Yousuf Karsh to Lysle Courtenay, May 26, 1938.
28. Betty Low, interview with the author, December 14, 2003.
29. NAC, KF, 9, Yousuf Karsh to Solange Gauthier, January 5, 1939.
30. Yousuf Karsh, *In Search of Greatness* (Toronto: University of Toronto Press, 1962), 52.
31. Salim Karsh Archives, Jamil Karsh to Yousuf Karsh, June 3, 1939.
32. Peter Miller as told to Barbara Moon, "Stalking Celebrities with Karsh," I, *Mayfair*, December 1954.
33. Ibid.

34. Yousuf Karsh, *In Search of Greatness* (Toronto: University of Toronto Press, 1962), 55.

35. Peter Miller as told to Barbara Moon, "Stalking Celebrities with Karsh," I, *Mayfair*, December 1954.

36. "Yousuf in Wonderland," *National Home Monthly*, May 1946.

37. "The Other Half of Karsh," *Canadian Home Journal*, May 1951; "Artist's Wife, Her Interpretation," *Free Press* (London, Ontario), May 10, 1945.

38. NAC, KF, 2, Solange Karsh, "Karsh, You've Monopolised Me," (typescript talk given by Solange just back from Bermuda).

39. *Maclean's*, September 1, 1942.

40. NAC, KF, 4, Solange Karsh, September 25, 1940.

41. Yousuf Karsh, *Karsh Canadians* (Toronto: University of Toronto Press, 1978), 68–69.

42. NAC, KF, 3, Yousuf Karsh to Grey Owl, May 21, 1936.

43. Yousuf Karsh, *Karsh Canadians* (Toronto: University of Toronto Press, 1978), 68.

44. Bernice Caffey, "A Camera Can Be Tactful," *Saturday Night*, March 18, 1939.

45. NAC, KF, 3, Yousuf Karsh to John Garo, November 14, 1938.

CHAPTER SEVEN: **ANNUS MIRABILIS**

1. NAC, KF, 5, Yousuf Karsh to W. Dawson, January 20, 1942.

2. *Maclean's*, September 1, 1942.

3. NAC, KF, Yousuf Karsh to George Nakash, June 7, 1940.

4. Yousuf Karsh, *In Search of Greatness* (Toronto: University of Toronto Press, 1962), 103.

5. NAC, KF, 43, Yousuf Karsh, "Ladies and Gentlemen," speech to the Photographers Association of America, New York, July 6, 1951.

6. Ibid.

7. R. S. Lambert, "Art in Wartime," *Maritime Art*, vol. 3, no. 1, October/November 1942, 10.

8. Walter Abell, "Editorial Comments: Britain at War," *Maritime Art*, vol. 2, no. 2, December 1941, 35–36.

9. NAC, KF, 4, Tom Blau to Yousuf Karsh, November 26, 1940.

10. NAC, KF, 4, Yousuf Karsh to C. M. Graves, March 12, 1940.

11. NAC, KF, 5, Solange Karsh to Madge Macbeth, January 30, 1942.

12. Yousuf Karsh, *In Search of Greatness* (Toronto: University of Toronto Press, 1962), 64.

13. *Star Weekly*, October 19, 1940.

14. NAC, W. L. Mackenzie King Diaries, no. 152 (microfilm), August 21, 1940.

15. NAC, KF, 5, Yousuf Karsh to Mackenzie King, November 29, 1940.

16. NAC, W. L. Mackenzie King Diaries, no. 158 (microfilm), August 15, 1941.

17. Yousuf Karsh, *Karsh Canadians* (Toronto: University of Toronto Press, 1978), 90.

18. Yousuf Karsh, "Superlative Personalities," *American Annual of Photography*, 1946, 12.

19. NAC, KF, 114, W. L. Mackenzie King to Yousuf Karsh, January 10, 1948.

20. NAC, KF, 2, Yousuf Karsh to Alice Garo, August 12, 1941.

21. NAC, KF, 5, Solange Karsh to Yousuf Karsh, July 3, 1941.

22. NAC, KF, 4, Yousuf Karsh to George Nakash, April 15, 1940.

23. Richard Buckle, ed., *Self-Portrait with Friends: The Selected Diaries of Cecil Beaton 1926–1974* (London: Weidenfeld and Nicolson, 1979), 78.

24. Paul Addison, *Churchill, the Unexpected Hero* (Oxford: Oxford University Press, 2005), 182.

25. J. W. Pickersgill, *The Mackenzie King Record*, vol. 1, 1939–1944, (Chicago: University of Chicago Press, 1960), 325 (27 December 1941).

26. Lord Moran, *Winston Churchill: The Struggle for Survival* (London: Constable & Co., 1966), 18.

27. J. W. Pickersgill, *The Mackenzie King Record*, vol. 1, 1939–1944, (Chicago: University of Chicago Press, 1960), 325.

28. *Saturday Night*, January 3, 1942.

29. NAC, W. L. Mackenzie King Diaries, no. 1212, December 29, 1941.

30. Churchill College Archives (Cambridge), Winston S. Churchill Papers, CSCT 2/22, Winston Churchill to Clementine Churchill, August 15, 1929.

31. Lord Moran, *Winston Churchill: The Struggle for Survival* (London: Constable & Co., 1966), 18.

32. Winston S. Churchill, *The Unrelenting Struggle* (Toronto: McClelland and Stewart, 1942), 363.

33. NAC, KF, 5, Solange Karsh to Ronald P. Smith enclosing "Now It Can be Told about Churchill's Portrait," February 19, 1942.

34. Margaret Lawrence, "Greatness and Humility in Winston Churchill," *Saturday Night*, January 10, 1941.

35. Winston S. Churchill, "Preparation, Liberation, Assault," *The Unrelenting Struggle* (Toronto: McClelland and Stewart, 1942), 365, 367.

36. Yousuf Karsh, *In Search of Greatness* (Toronto: University of Toronto Press, 1962), 66. During the course of his speech, Churchill was either gripping his lapels or standing with his hands at his sides; he never took the pose that appeared in Karsh's "The Roaring Lion" photograph.

37. NAC, W. L. Mackenzie King Diaries (microfilm), December 30, 1941, 1223–24.

38. NAC, KF, 5, Yousuf Karsh dictating a letter to Solange Karsh addressed to B. K. Sandwell, December 31, 1941. There are many versions of how Karsh proceeded from this point. The most reliable, however, is what he told Solange after returning from the sitting. "Here are Yousuf's notes as given to me last night and I refuse to doctor them up," Solange told B. K. Sandwell, the editor of *Saturday Night*.

39. Ibid.

40. Martin Gilbert, *In Search of Churchill* (London: HarperCollins, 1994), 295.

41. NAC, KF, 5. Yousuf Karsh dictating a letter to Solange Karsh addressed to B. K. Sandwell, December 31, 1941.

42. NAC, KF, 42, "Interview with the *Milwaukee Journal*," October 20, 1952.

43. Alan Boyd, "The Vogue of Portraiture," *British Journal of Photography*, November 22, 1946, 421.

44. NAC, KF, 5, Solange Karsh to Ronald P. Smith enclosing "Now It Can Be Told about Churchill's Portrait," February 19, 1942.

45. Herman Leonard, "Karsh: Memorial Celebration," Boston Museum of Fine Arts, October 24, 2002.

46. NAC, KF, 5, Solange Karsh to Randolph Macdonald, February 19, 1942.

47. NAC, KF, 29, Solange Karsh (quoting Yousuf Karsh) to Lloyde Vorden, April 5, 1948.

48. Edward Steichen's photograph of J. P. Morgan was made under similar circumstances: the subject was unwilling to be photographed. Though Morgan is sitting in a chair, the pose, the luminous elements, and the generally dark "palette" are not dissimilar to Karsh's "The Roaring Lion" portrait of Churchill. See Graham Clarke, *The Portrait in Photography* (London: Reaktion Books, 1992), 116. Steichen's 1932 photograph of Churchill is even closer to Karsh's portrait. "Winston Churchill, 1932," George Eastman House Archives, New York.

49. Winston S. Churchill, "Preparation, Liberation, Assault," *The Unrelenting Struggle* (Toronto: McClelland and Stewart, 1942), 365.

50. Yousuf Karsh, *In Search of Greatness* (Toronto: University of Toronto Press, 1961), 68.

51. NAC, KF, 5, Solange Karsh to Ronald P. Smith enclosing "Now It Can Be Told about Churchill's Portrait," February 19, 1942.

52. NAC, KF, 5, Yousuf Karsh to W. Dawson, January 20, 1942.

53. NAC, KF, 5, Madge Macbeth to Arnold Bingrich (typescript for article in *Cornet*), February 3, 1942.

54. Ibid.

55. *Saturday Night*, October 2, 1943.

56. Mary Soames, interview with the author, June 5, 2004.

57. Both George W. Bush and Bill Clinton before him displayed Karsh's portrait of Winston Churchill in the Oval Office.

1. NAC, KF, 5, Solange Karsh to Ronald P. Smith, February 19, 1942.
2. NAC, KF, 5, Yousuf Karsh to Mrs. R. A. Daly, February 19, 1941.
3. NAC, KF, 5, Solange Karsh to Hamilton Miller, February 4, 1942.
4. NAC, KF, 5 Solange Karsh to W. Dawson, April 29, 1942.
5. NAC, KF, 5, Solange Karsh to Hamilton Miller, January 1942.
6. NAC, KF, 5, Solange Karsh to Arnold Gingrich, January 31, 1942.
7. Peter Clarke, *The Last Thousand Days of the British Empire* (London: Penguin Books, 2007). The "Big Three" were Churchill, Roosevelt, and Stalin.
8. NAC, KF, 6, Solange Karsh to "Dr. Bunny" (B. K. Sandwell), June 19, 1943.
9. NAC, KF, 6, Tom Blau to Yousuf Karsh, March 3, 1943.
10. *Maclean's*, September 1, 1942.
11. Yousuf Karsh, "Filming the Famous," *Journal of the Photographic Society of America*, vol. 10, no. 9, November 1944, 531.
12. NAC, KF, 2, Solange Karsh to Jamil and Salim Karsh, September 4, 1943.
13. NAC, KF, 6, Solange Karsh to T. L. Blau, August 26, 1943.
14. NAC, KF, 6, Solange Karsh to Yousuf Karsh, October 18, 1943.
15. NAC, KF, 6, "Yousuf Karsh, London, 1943" (typescript).
16. *Star* (London), September 16, 1943.
17. Roger Eldridge, "Karsh: Memorial Celebration," Boston Museum of Fine Arts, October 24, 2002.
18. Yousuf Karsh, *In Search of Greatness* (Toronto: University of Toronto Press, 1962), 77.
19. NAC, KF, 6, Yousuf Karsh to Solange Karsh, September 27, 1943.
20. Yousuf Karsh, *In Search of Greatness* (Toronto: University of Toronto Press, 1962), 76.
21. NAC, KF, 6, Yousuf Karsh to Solange Karsh, September 28, 1943.
22. NAC, KF, 6, Solange Karsh to Yousuf Karsh, September 13, 1943.
23. NAC, KF, 6, Yousuf Karsh, "Notes" Daily Prayer.
24. NAC, KF, 6, T. L. Blau to Solange Karsh, September 28, 1943.
25. NAC, KF, 6, T. L. Blau to Solange Karsh, October 23, 1943.
26. NAC, KF, 6, T. L. Blau to Solange Karsh, September 28, 1943.
27. NAC, KF, 6, "London Letter by Macdonald Hastings, North American Service, November 4, 1943" (typescript of broadcast).
28. Yousuf Karsh, *In Search of Greatness* (Toronto: University of Toronto Press, 1962), 73.
29. NAC, KF, RG 658, Yousuf Karsh, "Photograph of the Queen," October 28, 1943.
30. NAC, KF, 38, Yousuf Karsh (typescript of personalities).
31. Yousuf Karsh, "Superlative Personalities," *American Annual of Photography*, vol. 60 (Boston: 1945), 15.
32. "Leaders of Britain," *Life*, February 7, 1944.
33. NAC, KF, 6, Yousuf Karsh to Solange Karsh, September 27, 1943.
34. Trevor Burridge, *Clement Attlee: A Political Biography* (London: Jonathan Cape, 1985), 1.
35. Harold Dingman, "Photographer of Character," *Magazine Digest*, March 1945.
36. NAC, KF, 658, Yousuf Karsh, untitled (typescript), 1943.
37. NAC, KF, 6, "Yousuf Karsh, London, 1943" (typescript).
38. NAC, KF, 349, *The Current Times*, May 3, 1945.
39. "A Significant Exhibition of Photographic Portraits by Karsh," *Globe and Mail*, February 24, 1944.
40. NAC, KF, 311, Yousuf Karsh, "Speech to the Women's Canadian Club: Wartime Portraits of the Great," February 24, 1944.
41. *Sunday Times* (London), May 7, 1944.
42. NAC, KF, 7, Yousuf Karsh to Wilson Hicks, February 11, 1944.
43. Yousuf Karsh, *In Search of Greatness* (Toronto: University of Toronto Press, 1962), 73.

1. NAC, KF, 145, Financial ledgers and tax returns.
2. NAC, KF, 2, Jamil Karsh to Solange Karsh, June 8, 1942; Solange Karsh to Jamil Karsh, July 23, 1942.
3. NAC, KF, 63, Solange Karsh to J. Ross Tolmie, June 9, 1955.
4. Carol Squires, "Looking at *Life*," in *Illuminations: Women Writing on Photography from the 1850s to the Present*, Liz Heron and Val Williams, eds. (London: I. B. Tauris Publishers, 1996), 150.
5. NAC, KF, 11, Yousuf Karsh to J. E. Lewis, January 5, 1944.
6. NAC, KF, 8, Yousuf Karsh "Washington Trip File," 1944.
7. NAC, KF, 8, Malcolm Macdonald to Lord Halifax, March 9, 1944.
8. NAC, KF, 7, Yousuf Karsh to Wilson Hicks, February 11, 1944.
9. NAC, RG 24, vol. 3204, file 5312-40, Hugh Keenleyside to Lester Pearson, January 21, 1944; Anna K. Russell, "The Failure of Fringe Internationalism: Origins of Cultural Diplomacy in Canada 1945–1951," Master of Arts thesis, Carleton University, August 1994, 94.
10. Yousuf Karsh, *Faces of Destiny: Portraits by Karsh* (London: George G. Harrap Co. Ltd.; New York: Ziff-Davis Publishing Company, 1946), 130.
11. Ibid., 5.
12. NAC, KF, 2, Solange Karsh to Jamil Karsh, December 29, 1946.
13. NAC, KF, 8, Solange Karsh to Yousuf Karsh, March 14, 1944.
14. Yousuf Karsh, *Faces of Destiny: Portraits by Karsh* (London: George G. Harrap Co. Ltd.; New York: Ziff-Davis Publishing Company, 1946), 82.
15. NAC, KF, 21, Solange Karsh to Elizabeth Gordon, August 31, 1944.
16. *Life*, April 12, 1945.
17. Harold Dingman, "Photographer of Character," *Magazine Digest*, March 1945.
18. NAC, KF, 311, Yousuf Karsh, "Self Portrait, Chapter I," circa 1945.
19. Yousuf Karsh, *Faces of Destiny: Portraits by Karsh* (London: George G. Harrap Co. Ltd.; New York: Ziff-Davis Publishing Company, 1946), 126.
20. Yousuf Karsh, "Filming the Famous," *Journal of the Photographic Society of America*, vol. 10, no. 9, November 1944, 532.
21. Ruth Emily McMurry and Mina Lee, *The Cultural Approach* (London: Kennikat Press, 1947; revised edition: 1972), ix.
22. Charles Ritchie, *The Siren Years* (London: Macmillan, 1974), 188.
23. NAC, RG 613, vol. 9-43, Skippy Phillips, "My Experiences at the UN Conference on International Organization" (typescript, 1945).
24. NAC, KF, 10, Tom Blau to Yousuf Karsh, February 27, 1945.
25. NAC, RG 25, vol. 3204, A. D. Duton to H. L. Keenleyside (1943).
26. NAC, RG 25, vol. 3204, file 5312-40, secretary of state to Canadian ambassador, December 20, 1944. This was before the Canadian government discovered a few months later, in September 1945, that the Russians were operating a spy network in the embassy in Ottawa.
27. Yousuf Karsh, *Faces of Destiny: Portraits by Karsh* (London: George G. Harrap Co. Ltd.; New York: Ziff-Davis Publishing Company, 1946), 106.
28. "Karsh Just Back From the San Francisco Conference," *Province* (Vancouver), May 15, 1945.
29. NAC, RG 25, vol. 549, Solange Karsh talk to the Canadian Club, London, Ontario, May 10, 1945.
30. n.a., "Karsh of Ottawa," *Popular Photography*, November 1950, 64.
31. Bruce Downes, "Karsh, His Work," *Popular Photography*, May 1945, 21, 24.
32. Daniel Angeli and Jean-Paul Doussed, *Private Pictures* (London: Jonathan Cape, 1980). n.p.
33. "Karsh's Eight Hollywood Photographs," *Montreal Standard*, February 8, 1947.
34. NAC, KF, 311, Yousuf Karsh, "Karsh in Hollywood," *Photo Arts*, 1948.
35. "Karsh in Hollywood," *Ottawa Citizen*, weekly from November 23 to December 21, 1946.
36. NAC, KF, 12, Solange Karsh to Jean McJanet, January 31, 1946.

37. Yousuf Karsh, *In Search of Greatness* (Toronto: University of Toronto Press, 1962), 111.
38. NAC, KF, 12, Solange Karsh to Jean McJanet, February 19, 1946.
39. NAC, KF, 14, "Karsh's notes," n.d. (Hollywood, January–February 1946).
40. By the time Bette Davis's agent requested another sitting, Karsh was back in Ottawa.
41. NAC, KF, 151, Yousuf Karsh, "Selo Diary," 1944.
42. NAC, KF, 12, Solange Karsh to Jean McJanet, January 31, 1946.
43. Ibid.
44. Jeremy G. Butler, "The Star System and Hollywood" in John Hill and Pamela Church Gibson, *American Cinema and Hollywood, Critical Approaches* (Oxford: Oxford University Press, 2000), 117.
45. NAC, KF, 311, Yousuf Karsh, "Karsh in Hollywood," *Photo Arts*, 1948.
46. Ibid.
47. NAC, KF, 12, Solange Karsh to Jean McJanet, February 19, 1946.
48. "Karsh in Hollywood," *Ottawa Citizen*, weekly from November 23 to December 21, 1946.

CHAPTER TEN: **FACES OF DESTINY**

1. Thomas Mann, *Tagebucher 1946–1948* (Frankfurt: S. Fischer, 1989), 787.
2. NAC, KF, file 13, Thomas Mann to Yousuf Karsh, December 4, 1946; Ibid., March 19, 1948.
3. Carol Squires, "Looking at *Life*," in *Illuminations: Women Writing on Photography from the 1850s to the Present*, Liz Heron and Val Williams, eds. (London: I. B. Tauris Publishers, 1996), 150.
4. Yousuf Karsh, "Portraits of Famous Musicians," *The American Annual of Photography*, vol. 63, 1948, 69.
5. NAC, KF, 68, "They Greatest 'Eye' on Earth" (typescript), enclosed in Martin R. King to Yousuf Karsh, n.d.
6. Vance Packard, *The Pyramid Climbers* (London: Longmans, 1962), 4.
7. Bruce Downes, "Karsh, His Work," *Popular Photography*, May 1945, 25.
8. Charles M. Britt, interview with the author, April 6, 2004.
9. Joyce Large, interview with the author, March 20, 2004.
10. Yousuf Karsh, "Portraits of Famous Musicians," *The American Annual of Photography*, vol. 63, 1948, 66.
11. Yousuf Karsh, "When Musician Greats become Temperamental the Camera Artist Meets the Extra Challenge," *Saturday Night*, November 1, 1947.
12. NAC, KF, file 14, M. Seklemian to Yousuf Karsh, November 8, 1945.
13. NAC, KF, 152, see entries in Yousuf Karsh and Solange Karsh "Diary," November 7, 1945, to February 28, 1946.
14. Joyce Large, interview with the author, March 20, 2004.
15. Ibid.
16. NAC, KF, 114, W. L. Mackenzie King to Yousuf Karsh, January 10, 1948.
17. Clara Thomas and John Lennox *William Arthur Deacon, A Canadian Literary Life* (Toronto: University of Toronto Press, 1982) p. 227
18. "Yousuf in Wonderland," *National Home Monthly* (May 1946), p. 19
19. NAC, KF, 23, Yousuf Karsh to Solange Karsh, 29 November 1948
20. Janos Plesch and Peter H. Plesch, "Some Reminiscences of Albert Einstein," *Notes*, The Royal Society, no. 49 (2), 1995, 303–28.
21. Yousuf Karsh had made the recording at the request of the Canadian Broadcasting Corporation.
22. Jeremy Berstein, *Einstein* (London: Fontana, 1973), 13.
23. Ed Regis, *Who got Einstein's Office?* (London: Simon and Schuster, 1987), 36.
24. Alan J. Friedman and Carol C. Donley, *Einstein As Myth and Muse* (Cambridge: Cambridge University Press, 1985), 156.
25. Herman Leonard, "Karsh: Memorial Celebration," Boston Museum of Fine Arts, October 24, 2002.

26. NAC, KF, 122, "ZAP Productions" (typescript), n.d.

27. NAC, KF, 316, Yousuf Karsh, "Notes on Hemingway" (typescript).

28. NAC, KF, 24, Solange Karsh to Yousuf Karsh, February 2, 1948.

29. NAC, KF, 24, Solange Karsh to Franklin "Pop" Jordan, November 3, 1948.

30. NAC, KF, 13, George Harrap to Solange Karsh, August 21, 1945.

31. NAC, KF, 10, Solange Karsh to George Harrap, August 2, 1945.

32. NAC, KF, 20, Franklin "Pop" Jordan to Yousuf Karsh, April 13, 1945.

33. NAC, KF, 13, Tom Blau to Yousuf Karsh, October 27, 1945.

34. NAC, KF, 63, Yousuf Karsh to Paul Linwood Gitting, December 1, 1965.

35. Yousuf Karsh, *In Search of Greatness* (Toronto: University of Toronto Press, 1962), 115.

36. NAC, KF, 12, Solange Karsh to Yousuf Karsh, September 4–5, 1946.

37. Yousuf Karsh, *Faces of Destiny: Portraits by Karsh* (London: George G. Harrap Co. Ltd.; New York: Ziff-Davis Publishing Company, 1946).

38. NAC, KF, 313, L. W. Cotterill, publicity manager to Solange Karsh, July 25, 1947.

39. NAC, KF, 193, H. R. M. Clee to George Berner Ziff-David, October 10, 1947.

40. NAC, KF, 193, Solange Karsh to H. R. M. Clee, November 14, 1946.

41. Yousuf Karsh *In Search of Greatness* (Toronto: University of Toronto Press, 1962) p. 6.

42. "Faces of Destiny, Portraits by Karsh," *The British Journal of Photography*, June 27, 1947, 226.

43. NAC, KF, 313, Walter Harrap to Yousuf Karsh, June 17, 1947.

44. NAC, KF, 26, Franklin "Pop" Jordan to Yousuf Karsh, January 8, 1947.

45. NAC, KF, 12, W. L. Mackenzie King to Yousuf Karsh, December 31, 1946.

46. James G. Mandallon, "Faces of Destiny," *Hairenik Weekly*, June 5, 1947.

47. NAC, KF, 4, Yousuf Karsh to Edward J. Steichen, May 1, 1936.

48. Hugh MacLennan, "The Face of Power," *Maclean's*, May 1, 1947.

CHAPTER ELEVEN: **BACK TO EUROPE**

1. NAC, KF, 21, Solange Karsh to Elizabeth Gordon, September 14, 1944.

2. "Karsh to Photograph Noted Leaders of Post-War Europe," *Journal* (Ottawa), April 28, 1949.

3. Anna K. Russell, "The Failure of Fringe Internationalism: Origins of Cultural Diplomacy in Canada, 1945–1951," Master of Arts thesis, Carleton University, August 1994, 94.

4. NAC, KF, 17, Nicholas Haz to Yousuf Karsh, November 19, 1946.

5. NAC, KF, 311, Yousuf Karsh, "Talk," Art Association and Camera Club, Bermuda, May 19, 1948.

6. NAC, KF, 26, Yousuf Karsh to Franklin "Pop" Jordan, January 8, 1949.

7. NAC, KF, 27, "An Internal Memoir for Staff," *Newsweek* "Draft," February 21, 1949.

8. NAC, KF, 26, Franklin "Pop" Jordan to Yousuf Karsh, January 21, 1949.

9. NAC, KF, 193, Oscar Dystel to Yousuf Karsh, February 18, 1949.

10. NAC, KF, 195, Norton O'Meara to Yousuf Karsh, April 18, 1949.

11. NAC, KF, 3204, D. M. Cornett to Allan Anderson, Department of External Affairs, Ottawa, April 30, 1949.

12. NAC, KF, 49, Miss Patch, George Bernard Shaw's secretary, to Yousuf Karsh, May 5, 1949.

13. Ibid., July 1, 1949.

14. NAC, KF, 28, Solange Karsh to Betty Cookson and Joyce Large, June 10, 1949.

15. NAC, KF, 28, Yousuf Karsh to Betty Cookson and Joyce Large, June 8, 1949.

16. Yousuf Karsh, *Portraits of Greatness* (Toronto: University of Toronto Press, 1959), 130.

17. Baron, *Baron* (London: Frederick Muller Ltd., 1957), 205–206.

18. NAC, KF, 313, T. L. Blau to J. J. Gaute, August 18, 1949.

19. Lord Moran, *Winston Churchill: The Struggle for Survival 1940–1965* (London: Constable and Company, 1966, 1968), 294.

20. NAC, KF, 28, Solange Karsh to Betty Cookson and Joyce Large, June 10, 1949.
21. NAC, KF, 195, Yousuf Karsh to Charles Prilik, September 8, 1949.
22. In April 1950, Karsh flew to Rome carrying 15,000 copies. The remaining 35,000 were sent to Italy by post.
23. NAC, KF, 28, Betty Cookson to Solange Karsh, Yousuf Karsh, and Monty, June 17, 1949.
24. "Karsh to Photograph Noted Leaders of Post-War Europe," *Journal* (Ottawa), April 28, 1949.
25. NAC, KF, 26, Solange Karsh to Franklin "Pop" Jordan, August 30, 1949.
26. NAC, KF, 28, Solange Karsh to Betty Cookson and Joyce Large, June 10, 1949.
27. NAC, KF, 314, Yousuf Karsh to Solange Karsh, n d. (July 1949).
28. Ibid.
29. NAC, KF, 38, Yousuf Karsh, "Jean Sibelius" (typescript), n.d.
30. NAC, KF, 195, Yousuf Karsh to Charles Prilik, September 8, 1949.
31. NAC, KF, 316-4, Yousuf Karsh, "talk to the Canadian Club," November 1949.
32. NAC, KF, 314, Solange Karsh to "Yousuf, my dear" (on board the *Empress of Canada*, August 1949).
33. NAC, RG 613, 311-20 (Solange Karsh), "Questions and Answers" talk given to the Canadian Club, Ottawa, November 2, 1949.
34. NAC, KF, 316, Yousuf Karsh, "talk to the Canadian Club," November 1949.
35. NAC, KF, 30, "Speech to the Canadian Club, Ottawa 2 November 1949" (typescript).
36. NAC, KF, 314, Solange Karsh to "Yousuf, my dear" (on board the *Empress of Canada*, August 1949).
37. NAC, KF, 28, Solange Karsh to Betty Cookson and Joyce Large, June 10, 1949.
38. NAC, KF, 195, Yousuf Karsh to Charles Prilik, September 8, 1949.
39. Peter C. Newman, *Here Be Dragons: Telling Tales of People, Passion and Power* (Toronto: McClelland and Stewart, 2004), 129.
40. Baron, *Baron* (London: Frederick Muller Ltd., 1957), 205–206.
41. Dr. Anne Wood, Ross Tolmie's daughter, interview with the author, November 15, 2004.
42. NAC, KF, 7, Yervant Pasdermajian to Yousuf Karsh, February 7, 1944.
43. Charles Aznavour, *Yesterday When I Was Young* (London: W. H. Allen, 1979), 9.
44. NAC, KF, 4, Jamil Karsh to Malak Karsh, February 22, 1939.
45. Salim Karsh, interview with the author, November 1, 2003.
46. Yousuf Karsh, *Faces of Destiny: Portraits by Karsh* (London: George G. Harrap Co. Ltd.; New York: Ziff-Davis Publishing Company, 1946), 6.
47. NAC, KF, 2, Salim Karsh to Malak Karsh, September 14, 1943.
48. Salim Karsh, interview with the author, November 1, 2003.
49. NAC, KF, 2, Salim Karsh to Yousuf and Solange Karsh, June 8, 1942.
50. NAC, KF, 2, Yousuf Karsh to Jamil Karsh, December 29, 1946.
51. NAC, KF, 2, Bahiyah Karsh to Yousuf Karsh (translated from Arabic), October 24, 1947.
52. NAC, KF, 2, Yousuf Karsh to Jamil Karsh, December 29, 1946.
53. NAC, KF, 2, Jamil Karsh to Malak Karsh, November 5, 1947.
54. NAC, KF, 2, February 5, 1948.
55. NAC, KF, 2, Solange Karsh to Salim and Jamil Karsh, June 29, 1948.
56. Vivian Saykaly, interview with the author, November 30, 2003.
57. NAC, KF, 2, Jamil Karsh to Solange Karsh, January 7, 1948.
58. Salim Karsh, interview with the author, November 1, 2003.
59. NAC, Audio Visual Archives, 34888, Yousuf Karsh Radio Broadcast, 1967.
60. NAC, KF, 2, Yousuf Karsh to Salim Karsh, July 26, 1948.
61. NAC, KF, 3, Jamil Karsh to Yousuf Karsh, July 25, 1948.
62. NAC, KF, 376, "A New Portfolio by Karsh," *Popular Photography*, November 1950.

1. NAC, KF, 26, Franklin "Pop" Jordan to "Dear my kids" (Yousuf Karsh and Solange Karsh), October 18, 1949.
2. Yousuf Karsh, "The Secret Loves of Yousuf Karsh," *Maclean's*, July 1, 1951.
3. Yousuf Karsh, "The Face of Canada," *Maclean's*, November 15, 1952.
4. NAC, KF, 306, Solange Karsh to Ralph Allen, March 24, 1953.
5. NAC, KF, box 302, Solange Karsh to Joyce Large, August 18, 1952.
6. Yousuf Karsh, "The Face of Canada," *Maclean's*, November 15, 1952.
7. NAC, KF, 306, Solange Karsh to Ralph Allen, August 24, 1952.
8. NAC, KF, 306, Pierre Berton, "Notes on Vancouver for Yousuf Karsh," n.d.
9. NAC, KF, 306, Ian Sclanders to John Clare, June 14, (1952), (stamped 18 June 1952).
10. Martha Langford, "Introduction," *Contemporary Canadian Photography, From the Collection of the National Film Board* (Edmonton: Hurtig Publishers), 7.
11. *Leader Post* (Regina), March 24, 1952.
12. NAC, KF, 311, Yousuf Karsh, "Chapter One" (draft), n.d.
13. Mrs. F. Woodman, "Mail Bag," *Maclean's*, January 15, 1953.
14. R. M., "Mail Bag," *Maclean's*, January 1, 1953.
15. Edith A. Davis, "Mail Bag," *Maclean's*, March 1, 1953.
16. H. Hyslop, "Mail Bag," *Maclean's*, March 1, 1953.
17. Ola Stech, "Mail Bag," *Maclean's*, May 15, 1953.
18. Mrs. C. Cuthard, "Mail Bag," *Maclean's*, May 15, 1953.
19. Mrs. MacMillan, "Mail Bag," *Maclean's*, March 1, 1953.
20. NAC, KF, 306, Solange Karsh to George Fraser, November 27, 1952.
21. NAC, KF, 306, Solange Karsh, "Charlottetown Notebook."
22. "The City That's One Big Family," *Maclean's*, December 1, 1952.
23. *House of Commons Debates*, G. J. M. McIlraith, December 15, 1952, 670.
24. *House of Commons Debates*, W. Chester S. McLure, December 12, 1952, 600.
25. *House of Commons Debates*, G. J. M. McIlraith, December 15, 1952, 670.
26. *House of Commons Debates*, George A. Drew, December 16, 1952, 754.
27. L. E. G. Daviet, "Mail Bag," *Maclean's*, February 1, 1953; Ibid., Martha Banning Thomas.
28. Robertson Davies, *Peterborough Examiner*, December 31, 1952.
29. NAC, KF, 45, J. Arthur Clark to Yousuf Karsh, December 18, 1952.
30. NAC, KF, 306, Solange Karsh to Ian Sclanders, December 15, 1952.
31. NAC, KF, 28, Betty Cookson to Yousuf Karsh (1949).
32. NAC, KF, 307, "Solange's Notebook" (July 1953).
33. "Three Young Photographers," *New York Times*, December 21, 1947.
34. NAC, KF, 114, "Form Letter," n.d.
35. NAC, Audio Visual No 170683, Edward Steichen quoted on "CBC Tuesday Night," March 18, 1969.
36. *The Family of Man* (New York: Museum of Modern Art, 1955), 5.
37. Yousuf Karsh and John Fisher, *Yousuf Karsh & John Fisher See Canada*, (Toronto: Thomas Allen, 1960).
38. Yousuf Karsh, *In Search of Greatness* (Toronto: University of Toronto Press, 1962), 94. In Karsh's view, "Steichen was seeking something different" for the Family of Man exhibition. He was not after "a collection of portraits, but," Karsh concluded, a "record of interpretations of human emotions, human interests."
39. "Widening a Commercial Connection," *British Journal of Photography*, December 16, 1927, 742.
40. NAC, KF, 51, Solange Karsh to Yousuf Karsh, November 6, 1955.
41. NAC, KF, 31, Solange Karsh to John T. Elliott, April 11, 1950.

42. For example, when planning a feature on the American automobile industry, the editor of *Esquire* commissioned Karsh to produce a series of portraits of "the real leaders of industry" in order to "add human interest" and "to throw a bigger spotlight on American autos." NAC, KF, 193, David A. Smart to Yousuf Karsh, October 21, 1949.

43. NAC, KF, 195, Solange Karsh to Frederick W. Boulton, October 10, 1948.

44. NAC, KF, 304, Yousuf Karsh to Henry Boss (of F. H. Hayhurst Limited in Toronto), September 26, 1955.

45. NAC, KF, 303, David Cos (clipping fragment, 1955).

46. NAC, KF, 28, Fenton Powers to Yousuf Karsh, June 21, 1946.

47. Keith Davis, *Human Relations in Business* (New York: McGraw Hill, 1957), 6.

48. NAC, KF, 30-24, Solange Karsh's handwritten notes from the meeting with A. Earle Higgens, April 28, 1950.

49. NAC, KF, 51, Solange Karsh to Yousuf Karsh, November 6, 1955.

50. NAC, KF, 29, "Atlas Steels Company from Mr. Goulding's notes" (June 1950).

51. NAC, KF, 195, Yousuf Karsh to Thayer Jaccaci, November 14, 1950.

52. Yousuf Karsh quoted in "Karsh Focuses on the Workmen," *Province* (Vancouver), March 16, 1951.

53. NAC, KF, 29-24, "New Karsh Portraits Glorify Industrial Workers," A. Earle Higgens, director for release (typescript, 1950).

54. Rosemary Donegan, *Industrial Images/images Industrielles*, Art Gallery of Hamilton, 1988; see also her brilliant essay "Karsh's Working Man: Industrial Tensions and Cold War Anxieties" in Dieter Vorsteher and Janet Yates, eds., *Yousuf Karsh: Heroes of Light and Shadow* (Toronto: Stoddart, 2001), 153–61.

55. "How Atlas Developed Its 'Best' Promotional Idea," *Industrial Marketing*, January 1951, 50.

56. Compare Karsh's photograph of a worker on a compressor illustrated in "Busiest City in Canada," *Maclean's*, February 1, 1954, 19, with Malak Karsh, "Canadian Electric Plant in Peterborough," (1951), *Canada, the Land That Shapes Us* (Toronto: Key Porter Books, 1995), 44.

57. NAC, KF, 29, "New Karsh Portraits Glorify Industrial Workers," A. Earle Higgens, director for release (typescript, 1950).

58. Ibid.

59. NAC, KF, 32-4, Martin R. King to Yousuf Karsh, October 27, 1950.

60. NAC, KF, 30-24, Solange Karsh to Roy H. Davis, July 8, 1950.

61. For example, in 1953 Karsh set up his camera at the Westinghouse Plant and four years after that at Sharon Steel in Pennsylvania.

62. Rosemary Donegan, "Karsh's Working Man: Industrial Tensions and Cold War Anxieties," in Dieter Vorsteher and Janet Yates, eds., *Yousuf Karsh: Heroes of Light and Shadow* (Toronto: Stoddart, 2001), 153–61.

CHAPTER THIRTEEN: **CHASING SHADOWS**

1. Yousuf Karsh, *Portraits of Greatness* (Toronto: University of Toronto Press, 1959).

2. "How Karsh Portrayed the Royal Couple," *Atlas Steel News*, October 1951.

3. Tom Hopkinson, "Portraits by Yousuf Karsh," *Manchester Guardian*, January 16, 1953.

4. Cambridge University Library, newspaper clipping files, unidentified clipping, September 20, 1951.

5. NAC, KF, 47, Private Secretary of Winston Churchill to Yousuf Karsh, July 29, 1951.

6. NAC, KF, 303, Campbell Moodie to Yousuf Karsh, July 20, 1955.

7. "Portraitist in France," *Life*, October 1954.

8. NAC, KF, 13, Yousuf Karsh to Yehudi Menuhin, October 23, 1946.

9. Peter Miller as told to Barbara Moon, "Behind the Scenes with Karsh," II, *Mayfair*, January 1955.

10. All quotations are from Peter Miller as told to Barbara Moon, "Stalking Celebrities with Karsh," I, *Mayfair*, December 1954.

11. Ibid.

12. Peter Miller, *The First Time I Saw Paris* (New York: Random House, 1999), 2.

13. Ibid., 3.

14. Ibid.

15. Peter Miller, interview with the author, September 7, 2006.

16. Peter Miller as told to Barbara Moon, "Stalking Celebrities with Karsh," I, *Mayfair*, December 1954.

17. NAC, KF, 48, Solange Karsh to G. E. Jones, September 8, 1954.

18. NAC, Audio Visual Archives, 58061-2, interview with Yousuf Karsh, June 13, 1958.

19. Peter Miller, *The First Time I Saw Paris* (New York: Random House, 1999), 4.

20. NAC, KF, 31, "List for Proposed Cocktail Party," May 5, 1950.

21. NAC, RG25, 24031, A. J. Hicks to ambassadors in Italy, France, Belgium, and Switzerland, May 1958.

22. NAC, KF, 63, J. Ross Tolmie (Karsh's Canadian solicitor) to Philip Bastedo, a lawyer in New York (1955).

23. "Karsh of Ottawa," *Manchester Guardian*, June 4, 1959.

24. NAC, KF, 63, J. Ross Tolmie (Karsh's Canadian solicitor) to Philip Bastedo, Karsh's lawyer in New York (May 11, 1955).

25. NAC, KF, 53, Solange Karsh to Joyce Large, January 16, 1956.

26. NAC, KF, 55, Solange Karsh to Joyce Large, March 26, 1956.

27. NAC, KF, 58, Tom Blau to Yousuf Karsh, February 6, 1959.

28. NAC, KF, 58, Yousuf Karsh to Tom Blau, March 5, 1959.

29. *This Is Rome: A Pilgrimage in Words and Pictures* (1959), *This Is the Holy Land* (1960), and *These Are the Sacraments* (1962).

30. Hella Grabar Archive, Yousuf Karsh to Hella Grabar, July 28, 1959.

31. Yousuf Karsh, *Portraits of Greatness* (Toronto: University of Toronto Press, 1959), 130. For a discussion on Augustine's City of God, see Bertrand Russell, *The History of Western Philosophy* (London: George Allen and Unwin, 1946), 382.

32. Douglas J. Roche, "Photographer's Search for Greatness," *The Sign*, May 1961, 16.

33. NAC, KF, 313, Alfred A. Knopf to Yousuf Karsh, June 19, 1956.

34. NAC, KF, 313, Bruce Hutchison to Yousuf Karsh, 1957 (no date).

35. NAC, KF, 313, Bruce Hutchison to Yousuf Karsh, 1957 (no date).

36. NAC, KF, 313, Yousuf Karsh to Bruce Hutchison, July 19, 1957.

37. NAC, KF, 313, Tom Blau to Yousuf Karsh, December 24, 1957.

38. NAC, KF, 313, Yousuf Karsh to Bruce Hutchison, May 30, 1957.

39. Inserted flyer in Yousuf Karsh, *Portraits of Greatness* (Toronto: University of Toronto Press, 1959).

40. Peter Miller as told to Barbara Moon, "Stalking Celebrities with Karsh," I, *Mayfair*, December 1954.

41. Joyce Large, interview with the author, March 20, 2004.

42. Hella Grabar, interview with the author, October 3, 2005.

43. Sonja Mortimer to the author, September 23, 2004.

44. NAC, Audio Visual Archives, 2001 098 473, Yousuf Karsh to Ignas Gabalis, December 1967, 1978, and 1986.

45. Hella Grabar, interview with the author, October 3, 2005.

46. Hella Grabar Archive, Yousuf Karsh to Hella Grabar, 1971.

47. Hella Grabar, interview with the author, October 3, 2005.

48. "Who Are the World's 10 Greatest Photographers?" *Popular Photography*, May 1958.

49. NAC, KF, 5, Robert Kenyon to Yousuf Karsh, February 1, 1957.

50. NAC, KF, 31, n.a. (Solange Karsh), "'Karshmont' portraits—by Monty Everett."

51. *Financial Post*, April 21, 1956.

52. NAC, Audio Visual Archives, 14064, Yousuf Karsh, Edward R. Murrow, "Person to Person" (televised interview), January 1959.

53. *Los Angeles Times*, January 1, 1962.

54. NAC, KF, 114, Yousuf Karsh to Duncan Sandys, December 22, 1955.

55. NAC, KF, 114, Yousuf Karsh to Duncan Sandys, December 12, 1955.

56. Yousuf Karsh, *In Search of Greatness* (Toronto: University of Toronto Press, 1962), 161–62.

57. NAC, KF, 114, Yousuf Karsh to Duncan Sandys, December 22, 1955.

58. NAC, KF, 13, Solange Karsh to Yousuf Karsh, "TO BE TAKEN IN YOUR STRIDE AND READ IN SMALL INSTALLMENTS IF NECESSARY" (winter 1958–59).

59. NAC, KF, 303, Joyce Large to Mrs. Darrall, January 21, 1959.

60. Peter Miller as told to Barbara Moon, "Stalking Celebrities with Karsh," I, *Mayfair*, December 1954, 49.

61. NAC, KF, 59, Ted Bullock to Yousuf Karsh, July 18, 1959 (copy).

62. NAC, KF, 58, Dick and Hamilton Miller to Yousuf Karsh, July 18, 1959.

63. NAC, KF, 59, George Nakash to Yousuf Karsh, July 14, 1959.

64. NAC, KF, 59, Jamil Karsh to Yousuf Karsh, July 20, 1959.

65. Hella Grabar Archive, Yousuf Karsh to Hella Grabar, July 28, 1959.

66. NAC, KF, 59, Yousuf Karsh to Jean and Floyd Chalmers, September 9, 1959.

67. NAC, KF, 59, Yousuf Karsh, "Notes," July to August 1959.

68. Hella Grabar Archive, Yousuf Karsh to Hella Grabar, July 28, 1959.

69. NAC, KF, 59, Solange Karsh to Dr. Theodore Abernethy, August 5, 1959.

70. NAC, KF, 59, Solange Karsh to B. K. Sandwell, August 11, 1959.

CHAPTER FOURTEEN: **AN END AND A BEGINNING**

1. Yousuf Karsh, *In Search of Greatness* (Toronto: University of Toronto Press, 1962), 199.

2. Joyce Large, interview with the author, April 20, 2004.

3. *Chatelaine Magazine*, September 30, 1960.

4. "Exhibition: 'Culmination of All My Efforts,'" *Ottawa Citizen*, September 23, 1960.

5. Shirley L. Thomson, "Foreword," *Karsh: The Art of the Portrait* (Ottawa: National Gallery of Canada, 1989), 6.

6. *Queen's Journal* (Kingston, Ontario), October 3, 1961.

7. Arthur Gleason, "Karsh Exhibit at Art Museum Shows Contrasts in Technique," *London Free Press* (Ontario), April 9, 1960.

8. Carl Weiselberger, "Greatness by Karsh," *Ottawa Citizen*, September 23, 1960.

9. NAC, KF, 61, Joyce Large to H. M. Barbour, March 21, 1961.

10. NAC, KF, 180, "Yousuf Karsh's will," January 7, 1961. It should be noted that Karsh justified the exclusion of his other brothers from his will by stating that "I have in my lifetime made advances to my dear brothers Malak and Jamil Karsh." Following his marriage to Estrellita Nachbar in 1962, he drew up a new will. Ibid.

11. See, for example, Yousuf Karsh's remarks read at the opening of a joint exhibition of his and George Nakash's work organized by the Sherbrooke Museum of Fine Arts in May 2000. Vivian Saykaly Archives, Yousuf Karsh, (typescript), May 20, 2000.

12. Jerry Fielder, interview with the author, September 13, 2003.

13. Yousuf Karsh, *In Search of Greatness* (Toronto: University of Toronto Press, 1962), 203.

14. NAC, KF, 114, Glenn Gould to Yousuf Karsh, July 8, 1958. Gould ceased to perform on the concert platform in 1962.

15. NAC, KF, 221, Yousuf Karsh to Mrs. W. Ross Fraser, February 1, 1961.

16. NAC, KF, 61, Joyce Large to H. M. Barbour, March 21, 1961.

17. Hella Grabar, interview with the author, October 3, 2005.

18. Barbara Karsh, interview with the author, October 29, 2003.

19. Hella Grabar, interview with the author, October 3, 2005.

20. Herb Hansen, "Wife of Photographer Karsh Vital Element of Success," *Milwaukee Sentinel*, October 21, 1952.
21. NAC, Audio Visual Archives, 170683, Joyce Large, "Tuesday Night," March 18, 1969.
22. G. Ellery Read, *Sherbrooke Record*, October 10, 1962.
23. "Rembrandt of Camera Tells His Life Story," *Ottawa Citizen*, October 20, 1962.
24. Yousuf Karsh, *In Search of Greatness* (Toronto: University of Toronto Press, 1962), viii.
25. Ibid.
26. Derek Jewell, "Karsh by Karsh," *Sunday Times*, April 14, 1963.
27. Ibid.
28. Yousuf Karsh, *In Search of Greatness* (Toronto: University of Toronto Press, 1962), 96.
29. Ibid., 101.
30. Ibid., 114. The American photographer Nicholas Haz had warned Karsh of this pitfall as early as 1946, NAC, KF, 17, Nicholas Haz to Yousuf Karsh, November 29, 1946.
31. NAC, KF, 114, Margaret Bourke-White to Yousuf Karsh, October 22, 1963.
32. "Yousuf in Wonderland," *National Home Monthly*, May 1946, 19.
33. Barry Callaghan, "Pitfalls of Pursuing Greatness as Though It Were a Commodity," *Toronto Telegram*, September 30, 1967.
34. Yousuf Karsh in *Maclean's Fiftieth Anniversary*, October 3, 1955.
35. NAC, KF, Yousuf Karsh to Bruce Hutchison, May 30, 1957.
36. "Karsh of Ottawa," *Manchester Guardian*, July 4, 1959.
37. Tom Hopkinson, "Portraits by Yousuf Karsh, First London Exhibition," *Manchester Guardian*, January 16, 1953.
38. Stuart Black, "Portraits of Greatness," *British Journal of Photography*, February 19, 1960, 102.
39. *New York Times Magazine*, December 6, 1959, 54.
40. "Yousuf Karsh," *Daily Express*, October 27, 1959.
41. Yousuf Karsh, "Says Karsh, I Don't Really Think I'm Unkind to Women," *Daily Express*, October 31, 1959.
42. Ibid. See also Peter Miller as told to Barbara Moon, "Behind the Scenes with Karsh," II, *Mayfair*, January 1955.
43. Yousuf Karsh, *Portraits of Greatness* (Toronto: University of Toronto Press, 1959), 11. While Anita Ekberg was as much of an icon as the head of the British monarchy, Ekberg's portrait would not be included in any book by Karsh until *Karsh: A Fifty-Year Retrospective* (Toronto: University of Toronto Press, 1983).
44. NAC, KF, 73, "typescript of Karsh interview by Danziger," 1976.
45. Robert Frank, *Robert Frank* (London: Thames and Hudson, 1999), n.p.; Robert Frank, *The Americans*, 1958.
46. Simon Hatterston, "Snap Dragon," *Guardian*, May 30, 2005.
47. NAC, KF, 61, Tom Blau to Yousuf Karsh, December 4, 1961.
48. After 1960, whenever Karsh photographed an American president he made sure he photographed his wife too. Karsh also began using more environmental effects in his portraits of statesmen and businessmen.
49. Yousuf Karsh, *Portraits of Greatness* (Toronto: University of Toronto Press, 1959), 101.
50. Stuart Black, "Portraits of Greatness," *British Journal of Photography*, February 19, 1960, 102.
51. Roger Eldridge, "Karsh: Memorial Celebration," Boston Museum of Fine Arts, October 24, 2002.
52. NAC, Audio Visual Archives, 170683, Joyce Large, "Tuesday Night," March 18, 1969.
53. In 1962 Karsh was on another film set. This time he was in Bulgaria, producing the stills for *Lancelot and Guinevere*.
54. Among the people Karsh photographed were John Kennedy and his brother Robert, Arthur Goldberg, Pierre Salinger, John Kenneth Galbraith, and Walter Lippman.

55. Bruce Hutchison, *The Far Side of the Street* (1976), 84.
56. NAC, KF, 149, see Karsh Studio ledgers which refer to both "Estelle" and "Estrellita."
57. "Nearly Anything but Photographs by Mrs. Karsh," *Gazette* (Montreal), January 17, 1968.
58. Estrellita Karsh, interview with the author, September 8, 2006.
59. NAC, KF, 309, Yousuf Karsh, "Speech to the Canadian Women's Press Club Dinner," July 2, 1967.
60. Estrellita Karsh, interview with the author, September 7–8, 2006.
61. NAC, KF, 180, Estrellita Maria Nachbar, Certificate of Baptism, July 16, 1962.
62. "Karsh's Bride," *Daily Express*, August 30, 1962.
63. Barbara Karsh, interview with the author, October 29, 2003.
64. NAC, KF, 149, see Karsh Studio wage books from the early 1960s to the late 1980s.
65. NAC, Audio Visual Archives, 170683, Yousuf Karsh, "Tuesday Night," March 18, 1969.
66. Vivian Saykaly, interview with the author, November 30, 2003.
67. Franco J. Anglesio, interview with the author, April 16, 2004.
68. Elizabeth Dignam, *Toronto Telegram*, September 25, 1971.
69. "Karsh," *Ottawa Citizen*, July 18, 2002.
70. "Mrs. Karsh by Karsh," *Sun* (London), September 25, 1964.
71. NAC, KF, 122-14, Estrellita Karsh to Joyce Large, May 12, 1964.
72. "Greatness," *Daily Herald*, September 20, 1962.
73. Estrellita Karsh, interview with the author, July 11, 2004.
74. NAC, KF, 113, Randolph Churchill to Tom Blau, July 7, 1964.
75. *Time*, July 24, 1964, 37.
76. Emanuel Shinwell, "Churchill as the Voice of History," *Sunday Telegraph*, November 29, 1964. Karsh had asked Randolph Churchill in the autumn of 1964 if he could take a formal portrait of his father to mark his birthday. Randolph said no. NAC, KF, 113, Randolph Churchill to Yousuf Karsh, October 23, 1964.
77. NAC, KF, 309, Yousuf Karsh, CBC Radio (typescript), December 13, 1966.
78. NAC, KF, 57, Yousuf Karsh to James Finan, April 4, 1949.
79. J. L. Black, *Canada in the Soviet Mirror* (Ottawa: Carleton University Press, 1998), 240.
80. NAC, KF, 305, "Application for visa," February 19, 1963.
81. NAC, KF, 305, Arnold Smith to Yousuf Karsh, September 13, 1962.
82. *Gazette* (Montreal), April 23, 1963.
83. NAC, KF, 136, In conversation with Mrs. Karsh, Canadian Club, North Bay, April 1980.
84. Yousuf Karsh, "I Photographed the Krucheves [sic]," *Toronto Telegram*, November 9, 1963; *Daily Express*, May 20, 1963.
85. Yousuf Karsh, "I Photographed the Krucheves [sic]," *Toronto Telegram*, November 9, 1963.
86. NAC, KF, 15, "Karsh Memo," (April 1963).
87. Elliott Erwitt and Walter Corane had both photographed Khrushchev in 1959.
88. "Karsh's Bride," *Evening Standard*, August 30, 1962.
89. NAC, KF, 350, Arnold Smith to Yousuf Karsh, May 24, 1963; Richard Pollard to Yousuf Karsh, July 17, 1963.
90. "A Rare New View at the Top, Photographs by Yousuf Karsh," *Life*, September 13, 1963, 72–79.
91. Israel Shanker, "The Great Improviser," *Life*, September 13, 1963), 88.
92. NAC, KF, 350, Yousuf Karsh to Zabrodin, November 20, 1963.
93. "Gives Communism a Face," *Daily Express*, July 2, 1963.
94. NAC, KF, 62, Yousuf Karsh, (notes), n.d.
95. NAC, KF, 350, Arnold Smith to Yousuf Karsh, July 3, 1963.
96. NAC, KF, 350, Mandel Terman to Yousuf Karsh, December 31, 1963.
97. NAC, KF, 350, Paul Martin to Yousuf Karsh, January 11, 1964.
98. Karsh received advance sales from *Stern* for £1,500 and from the *Daily Express* for £2,000.

99. In 1964, Karsh of Ottawa increased its net profit by $15,000. See the tax returns for Karsh of Ottawa in NAC, KF, 145.

CHAPTER FIFTEEN: **APOTHEOSIS**

1. NAC, KF, 311, Yousuf Karsh (fragment), June 3, 1987.
2. Hella Graber, interview with the author, October 3, 2005.
3. Franco J. Anglesio, interview with the author, April 16, 2004.
4. Pamela Belyea, interview with the author, August 24, 2004.
5. Franco J. Anglesio, interview with the author, April 16, 2004; see also "Like Two Teenagers in Love," *Ottawa Citizen*, July 18, 2002.
6. Karsh quoted by Lesley Grancis, *Albertan* (Calgary), March 10, 1973.
7. NAC, KF, 100, Tom Blau to Yousuf Karsh, March 14, 1983.
8. NAC, KF, 137, Brian Melzack to Yousuf Karsh, (December 1976). Karsh would not photograph Loren until 1981, while on assignment for *Paris Match*.
9. NAC, KF, 101, Yousuf Karsh to Pierre Elliott Trudeau, February 21, 1980. Karsh photographed Trudeau for a second time.
10. NAC, KF, 130, Yousuf Karsh to Fidel Castro, August 6, 1971.
11. NAC, KF, 99, Yousuf Karsh to Ronald and Nancy Reagan, February 19, 1981.
12. Ted Riback Archive, "Journals," July 31, September 2, 3, 5, and 7, 1975; February 12 and 16, March 11 to 20, and November 11 to December 24, 1976.
13. Tom Blau, who arranged the commission, took 25 percent.
14. NAC, KF, 137, Yousuf Karsh to Nicoletta Morello, January 26, 1979.
15. With financial records relating to this period unavailable to the author, a full discussion of Karsh's finances is not possible.
16. *Karsh Portfolio* (1967): Only five out of the forty-seven works were from the 1960s. *Faces of Our Time* (1971) fared somewhat better, with fourteen out of the forty-nine works illustrated.
17. Douglas Fetherling, "The Mythology of Yousuf Karsh," *Ottawa Citizen*, October 30, 1976.
18. A. D. Coleman, *Light Readings: A Photography Critic's Writings, 1968–1978* (New York: Oxford University Press, 1979), 213.
19. Jerry Fielder and Estrellita Karsh, interview with the author, July 11, 2004.
20. Barry Callaghan, "Pitfalls of Pursuing Greatness as Though It Were a Commodity," *Toronto Telegram*, September 30, 1967.
21. Yousuf Karsh, *Karsh: A Sixty-Year Retrospective* (New York: Little, Brown and Company, 1996), 16.
22. This particular copy of *The Physician as Artist* is in the Estrellita Karsh Archive.
23. "The Legend Who Captures Legend," *Parade* (Pittsburgh), December 3, 1978.
24. NAC, KF, 132, "Sixty Second Spot for Muscular Dystrophy" (television), June 12, 1973.
25. Burt Howard, "Tribute to Canada," *Ottawa Citizen*, November 4, 1978.
26. Charlotte Gray, "Portrait of Karsh," *Globe and Mail*, October 21, 1978.
27. NAC, KF, 81, Tim Hill to Yousuf Karsh, March 1, 1977.
28. Jay Walz, "Karsh's Camera Aims at Person," *New York Times*, January 8, 1972.
29. NAC, KF, 85, Yousuf Karsh to Jon Wenzel, February 20, 1990.
30. *Miami Herald*, March 25, 1970.
31. Charles M. Britt, interview with the author, April 6, 2004.
32. Paul Russell, "Lights for the Human Soul," *Maclean's*, October 24, 1983.
33. Ohio State University also gave Estrellita Karsh an appointment.
34. Yousuf Karsh, *Karsh: A Sixty-Year Retrospective* (Boston: Little, Brown and Company, 1996), 15, 22.
35. NAC, KF, 82, undated clipping from the *Christian Science Monitor* enclosed in Andrea Turnage, Ansel Adams's secretary, to Yousuf Karsh, February 3, 1978.
36. NAC, KF, 134, Ansel Adams to Yousuf Karsh, July 15, 1977.

37. NAC, KF, 142, Yousuf Karsh, "Reedy Memorial Lecture," Rochester Institute of Technology, autumn 1987.
38. Estrellita Karsh, interview with author, September 8, 2006.
39. NAC, KF, 141, Iris W. Lever to Yousuf Karsh, June 11, 1986.
40. NAC, KF, 139, Kim O'Neill to Yousuf Karsh, July 26, 1986.
41. Barbara Hoover, "Karsh," *Detroit News*, April 30, 1979.
42. NAC, 129, handwritten notes by Yousuf Karsh for the Miss Universe Beauty Pageant, 1970, Miami, Florida.
43. *Star* (Sault Ste. Marie), August 31, 1970.
44. NAC, KF, 120, Yousuf Karsh to Eelco Wolf, November 26, 1975.
45. James Purdie, "Did Columbus Avoid a Traffic Jam?" *Globe and Mail*, February 28, 1978.
46. NAC, KF, 90, "Advertising Strategy," Lloyds Bank (October 6, 1988).
47. An exception was the young American photographer Herman Leonard, who spent a year in Ottawa in the late 1940s.
48. Charles M. Britt, interview with the author, April 6, 2004.
49. Jerry Fielder, interview with the author, September 13, 2003.
50. Ibid.
51. Charles M. Britt, interview with the author, April 6, 2004.
52. Ibid.
53. Estrellita Karsh Archive, Hillary Clinton to Yousuf Karsh, n.d.
54. Charles M. Britt, interview with the author, April 6, 2004.
55. Ibid.
56. Ibid.

CHAPTER SIXTEEN: **THE LEGACY**

1. *Vancouver Sun*, February 24, 1978.
2. Nancy Southam, "The Man Who Puts the Famous in Focus," *Vancouver Sun*, October 26, 1983.
3. Yousuf Karsh, *Karsh: A Sixty-Year Retrospective* (Boston: Little, Brown and Company, 1996), 23.
4. James J. Blanchard, *Behind the Embassy Door* (Chelsea: Sleeping Bear Press, 1998), 210.
5. Charles M. Britt, interview with the author, April 6, 2004. Note that Ignas Gabalis, Karsh's longest-serving employee, had retired in 1992.
6. Both Hella Grabar and, even more so, Jerry Fielder helped prepare the Karsh archive for deposition in the National Archives of Canada. The collection was acquired in 1987 and 1992 respectively.
7. Estrellita Karsh, interview with the author, September 9, 2006.
8. James Borcoman et al., *Karsh: The Art of the Portrait* (Ottawa: National Gallery of Canada, 1989).
9. Ibid., Lilly Koltun, "The Karsh Collection," 141. It should be noted that Karsh deposited his textual documents in the National Archives of Canada in 1997.
10. Malcolm Rogers, "Karsh: Memorial Celebration," Boston Museum of Fine Arts, October 24, 2002.
11. NAC, KF, 344, Charles Darwent, "Karsh Realities," n.d. (1991).
12. Paula Weidejer, "A Somebody Among Somebodies," *The Independent*, September 12, 1991.
13. Dieter Vorsteher and Janet Yates, eds., *Yousuf Karsh: Heroes of Light and Shadow* (Berlin: Deutsches Historisches Museum, 2000). Stoddart Publishing Co. Limited in Toronto produced an English version of the catalogue accompanying the exhibition in 2001.
14. See, for example, Helmut Gernsheim, *Creative Photography: Aesthetic Trends 1839–1960* (London: Faber and Faber, 1962); Beaumont Newhall, *The History of Photography* (London: Secker and Warburg, 1982); Graham Clarke, *The Photograph* (Oxford: Oxford University Press, 1997); Revel Golder, *Twentieth Century Photography* (London: Carlton, 1999); Robert Hirsch, *Seizing the Light: A History of Photography* (New York: McGraw Hill, 2000).

15. Ric Dolphin, "Karsh of Ottawa," *Maclean's*, April 24, 1989.
16. Ibid.
17. Paula Weidejer, "A Somebody Among Somebodies," *The Independent*, September 12, 1991.
18. "Karsh," *Guardian*, July 15, 2002.
19. NAC, KF, 43, Yousuf Karsh, "Ladies and Gentlemen," speech to the Photographers' Association of America, New York, July 6, 1951.
20. Jerry Fielder, interview with the author, September 13, 2003. Fielder redressed the perception of Karsh's work by producing *Karsh: A Biography in Images* (Boston: MFA Publications, 2003).
21. NAC, KF, 63, Yousuf Karsh, (typescript), 1965; Ibid., 114, Edward Steichen to Yousuf Karsh, July 7, 1970.
22. Peter C. Newman, *Here Be Dragons: Telling Tales of People, Passion and Power* (Toronto: McClelland and Stewart, 2004), 129.
23. Estrellita Karsh, interview with the author, September 9, 2006.
24. Yousuf Karsh, *Karsh: A Sixty-Year Retrospective* (Boston, Little, Brown and Company, 1996).
25. Jerry Fielder to the author, April 3, 1998.
26. Jerry Fielder, "Yousuf Karsh, 1908–2002," *Time*, July 29, 2002, 53.
27. The Boston Museum of Fine Arts had begun its photography collection in 1924 with a donation from the New York photographer Alfred Stieglitz.
28. Anthony Whittermore, "Karsh: Memorial Celebration," Boston Museum of Fine Arts, October 24, 2002.
29. Estrellita Karsh, interview with the author, September 9, 2006.
30. Anthony Whittermore, "Karsh: Memorial Celebration," Boston Museum of Fine Arts, October 24, 2002.
31. Roger Eldridge, "Karsh: Memorial Celebration," Boston Museum of Fine Arts, October 24, 2002.
32. Jerry Fielder, interview with the author, September 13, 2003; Estrellita Karsh, interview with the author, September 7, 2006.
33. Hella Grabar, interview with the author, October 3, 2005; Estrellita Karsh, interview with the author, September 7, 2006.
34. Marshall Wolf, interview with the author, September 8, 2006.
35. Roger Eldridge, "Karsh: Memorial Celebration," Boston Museum of Fine Arts, October 24, 2002.
36. "Yousuf Karsh," *The Independent*, December 28, 2003; "Yousuf Karsh," *New York Times*, July 15, 2002; "Karsh," *Ottawa Citizen*, July 18, 2002; *Guardian*, July 15, 2002.
37. "Yousuf Karsh," *The Economist*, July 20, 2002.
38. Ibid.
39. Estrellita Karsh, interview with the author, September 9, 2006.
40. Barbara Karsh, interview with the author, October 29, 2003.
41. Estrellita Karsh, interview with the author, September 9, 2006.
42. Vivian Saykaly, interview with the author, November 30, 2003.
43. Salim Karsh, interview with the author, November 1, 2003; Barbara Karsh, interview with the author, October 29, 2003.
44. Vivian Saykaly, interview with the author, November 30, 2003.
45. All quotations are from "Karsh: Memorial Celebration," Boston Museum of Fine Arts, October 24, 2002.
46. Marshall Wolf, interview with the author, September 8, 2006.
47. For example, in 2005 Estrellita Karsh endowed an emergency department and gave twenty portraits of Canadians to the Children's Hospital of Eastern Ontario. The following year, Estrellita gave the same hospital a molecular and genetics lab to train young scientists and established a program to enable researchers from the United States to come to Canada.

48. Among the recipients of Karsh's work have been the Rhode Island School of Design, the Supreme Court of the United States, the Boston Public Library, and the Perkins School for the Blind. Jerry Fielder has also supported the Art Institute of Chicago and the Boston Museum of Fine Arts in their plans to mount major retrospectives of Karsh's work in 2008, the centennial year of his birth.

49. Peter Miller, interview with the author, September 7, 2006.

50. Yousuf Karsh speaking at the Institute of Contemporary Art Awards in London, *Guardian*, July 15, 2002.

Index

Page numbers in italics refer to photographs. References to endnotes include note numbers.

Excess Profits Tax, 175, 211–12
Expo 67, 329, 346–47

face, idea that soul is reflected in, 44–45, 61–62
Face of Our Time (Sander), 50
face psychology, 44
Faces of Destiny (Karsh), 155, 218–24, 233, 243
Faces of Our Time (Karsh), 346, 356, 406*n*16
Faisal ibn Abdul Aziz, Prince, *188*, 189
The Family of Man (exhibition), 262–63, 400*n*38
fashion photography, 80, 96, 97–98
Fellig, Arthur. *See* Weegee
"Female Nude" (Karsh), 111
Fetherling, Douglas, 349
Fiedler, Arthur, 46, 208, 360
Fielder, Jerry, 346, 349, 362–63, 369, 372, 375, 376, 377, 407*n*6
Financial Post, 300
First Ladies, in Karsh portraits of presidents, 404*n*48
Fisher, John, 263
Fonteyn, Margot, 358–59
Ford, Henry, II, 204
Ford of Canada, 270–75
Forrester, Maureen, 377
Fortune, 177, 204
France
   occupation of Syria, 20
   post-war poverty, 229, 231–33
   troops leave Syria, 243
Frank, Robert, 318
Fraser, George, 258
Fraser, Mrs. W. Ross, 313
Frazer, Lord, 230
"The Fringe of Winter's Mantle" (Karsh), 99
From Our World (exhibition), 309–10

Gabalis, Ignas, 295–99, *297*, 322, 338, 346
Gable, Clark, 194, 215
Galbraith, John Kenneth, 404*n*54
Garbo, Greta, 193
Garland, Judy, 194
Garo, Aliée, 50–52
Garo, John, 34–38, 41–50, *51*, 60, 103, 123, 224, 371
   "Solange and Yousuf," *117*
Garson, Greer, 194
Gauthier, Héloise, 64, 112–14, 206, 311
Gauthier, Solange. *See* Karsh, Solange
General Electric, 204

George VI, King, 107, 120, 164, 168, *169*, 172–73
Germany, 326–28
   declares war on United States, 137–38
   post-war disarray, 229–30
Gervais, Archbishop Marcel, 374
Giacometti, Alberto, 329
Gianelli, Adéle, 68
Giscard d'Estaing, Valery, 346
Glenbow Art Gallery, 347
Gold Medal of Merit, 370
Goldberg, Arthur, 404*n*54
Goodrich Rubber Company, 263
Gordon, Elizabeth, 182–84
Gould, Glenn, 313, 331
Gouzenko, Igor, 226–27
Grabar, Hella, 295–99, *297*, 304, 313–14, 322, 324, 338, 346, 373, 407*n*6
Grabar (language), 16
Grange Art Gallery, 391*n*33
gravure process, 220, 294–95
Great Lakes Paper Company, 260, *261*
Greenstreet, Sydney, 193, 194, 196, 199
Gregg, Maj. M. F., 81
Grein, James T., 70
Gretzky, Wayne, 360
Grey Owl, 120–23, *122*
Gustafson, Ralph, 28

Hailey, Arthur, 358
Hairenik Weekly, 223
halftone process, 221
Halifax, Lord, 178, 180
Halifax (Nova Scotia), 25–26, 251, 252
Hallah, Jean, 25
Halpenny, Francess, 294
Halsman, Philippe, 193, 303, 318
Hamlet, 67
Hammerstein, Oscar, 298
hands, in Karsh portraits, 170, 184–85, 199, 203, 333
The Happy Gang (radio show), 105
Harewood, Earl and Countess of, 282
Harman, Eleanor, 312
Harrap, George G., 155, 220, 222
Harrap, Walter, 223
Harriman, Averell, 233, 240
Hart House Theatre, 76
Harvey, Rupert, 68
Hasnoui, Nourreddine, 340
Haz, Nicholas, 92, 96, 97, 99, 120, 227

DR. MARIA TIPPETT is one of Canada's most prominent cultural historians and the author of many books on art, culture, and history, including *Emily Carr*; *Stormy Weather: F. H. Varley, a Biography*; and *Bill Reid: The Making of an Indian*. She has lectured extensively on Canadian art and culture in North and South America, Japan, and Europe and has curated exhibitions in Canada and abroad. Her books have won numerous awards, including the Governor General's Literary Award for Non-Fiction and the Sir John A. Macdonald Prize for Canadian History. A Fellow of the Royal Society of Canada, she was for many years a Senior Research Fellow at Churchill College, Cambridge, and a member of the Faculty of History at Cambridge University. Maria Tippett lives with her husband, historian Peter Clarke, in British Columbia.